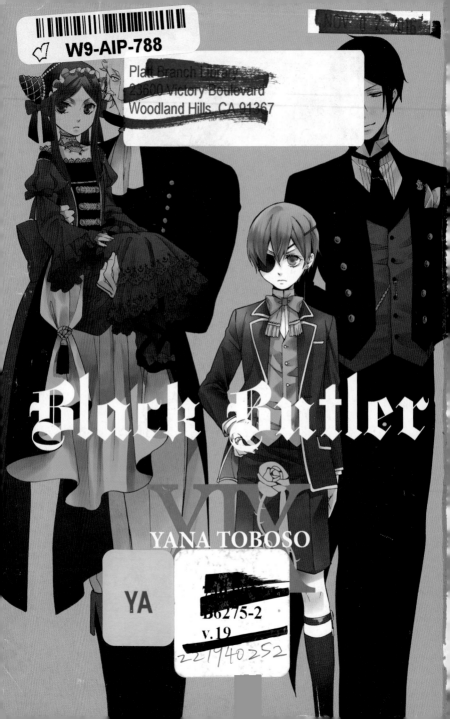

W9-AIP-788

Platt Branch Library
23600 Victory Boulevard
Woodland Hills, CA 91367

NOV 11 2015

YA

B6275-2
v.19
221940252

Black Butler

XIX

YANA TOBOSO

Contents

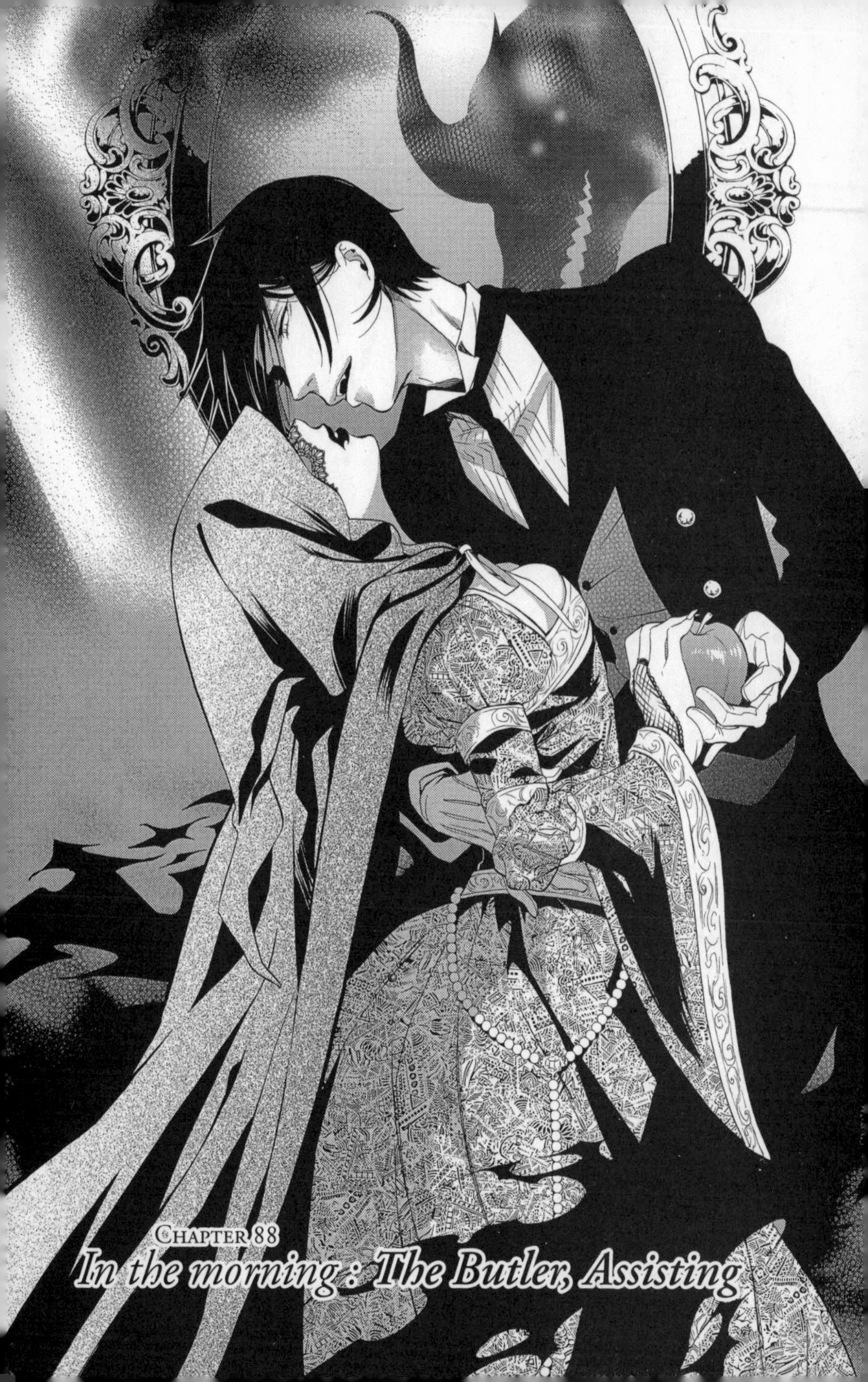
Chapter 88
In the morning : The Butler, Assisting

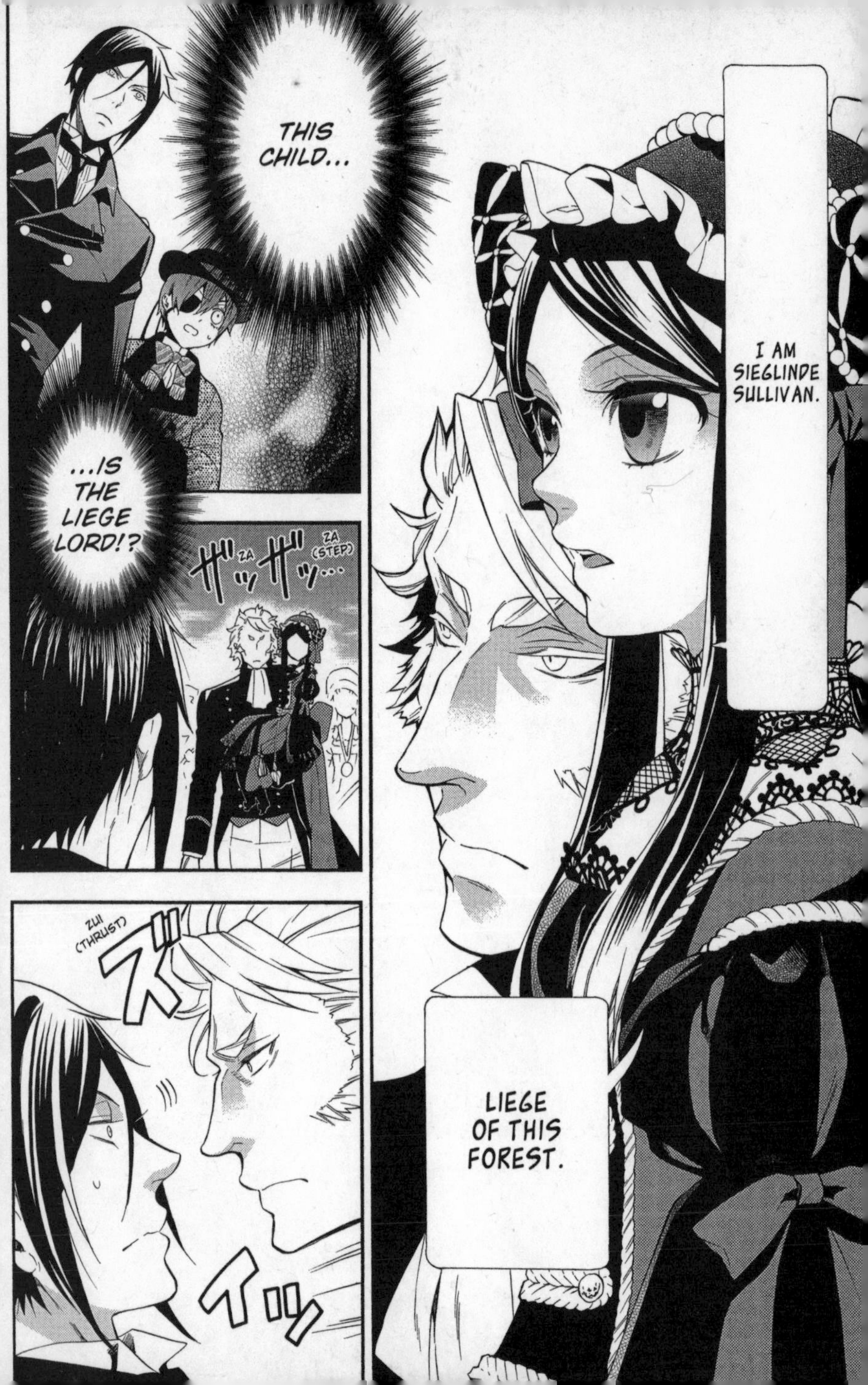
I AM SIEGLINDE SULLIVAN.
LIEGE OF THIS FOREST.
THIS CHILD...
...IS THE LIEGE LORD!?
ザッザッ...
ZA ZA (STEP)
ズイッ
ZUI (THRUST)

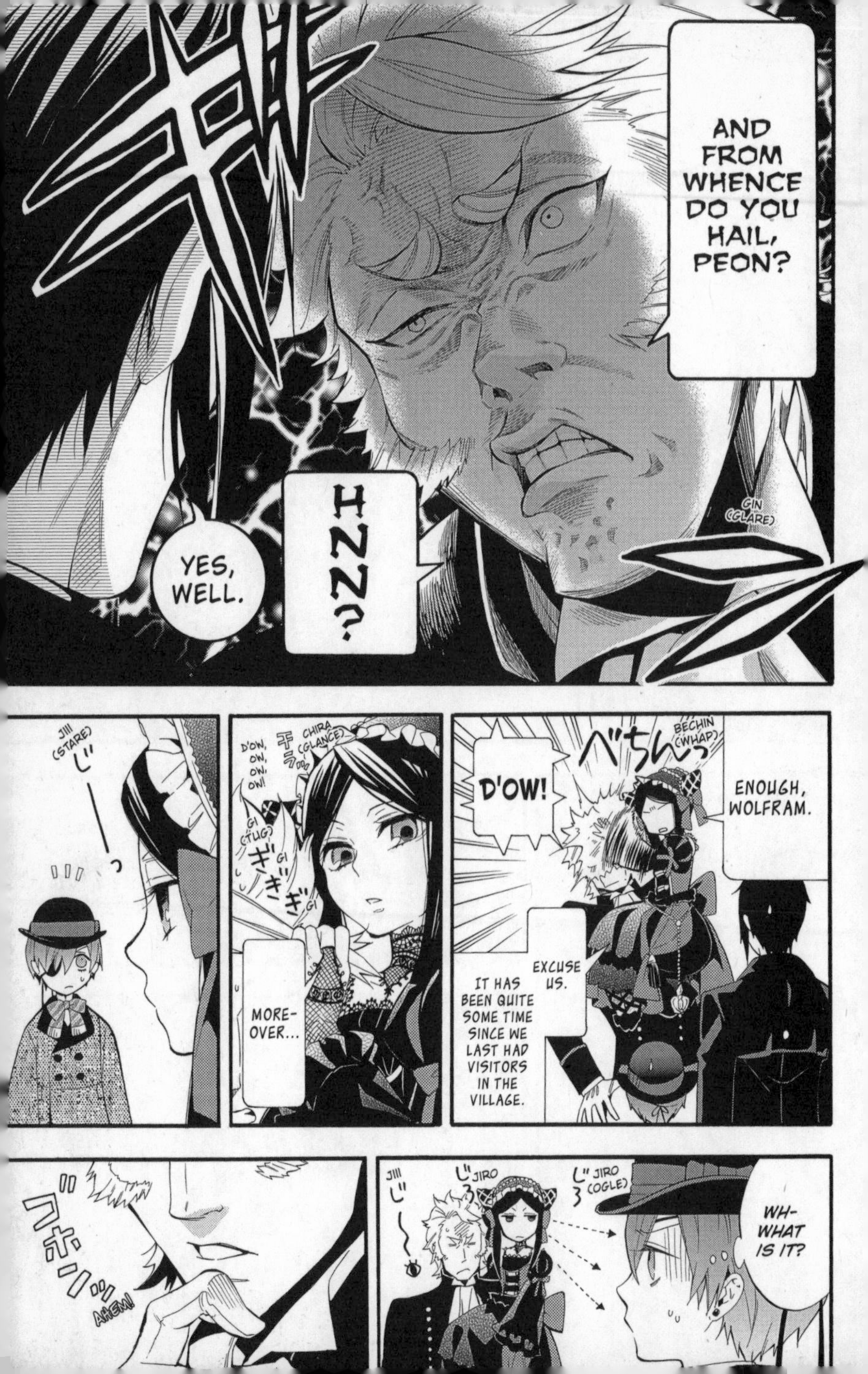
AND FROM WHENCE DO YOU HAIL, PEON?
GIN (GLARE)
HNN?
YES, WELL.
BECHIN (WHAP)
ENOUGH, WOLFRAM.
D'OW!
EXCUSE US.
IT HAS BEEN QUITE SOME TIME SINCE WE LAST HAD VISITORS IN THE VILLAGE.
CHIRA (GLANCE)
D'OW, OW, OW, OW!
GI (TUG)
GI
GI
MORE-OVER...
JIII (STARE)
WH-WHAT IS IT?
JIRO (OGLE)
JIRO
JIII
AHEM!

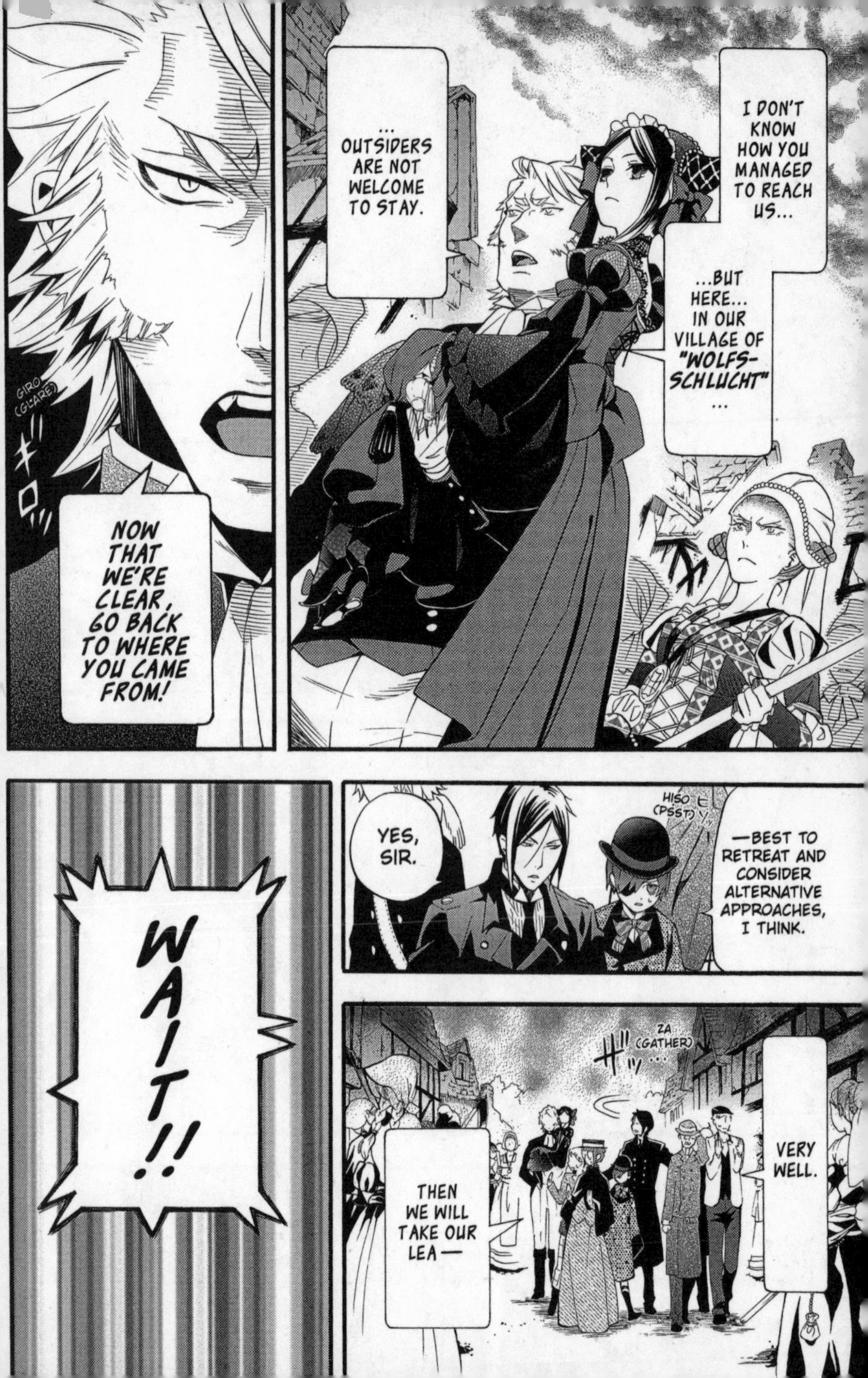
I DON'T KNOW HOW YOU MANAGED TO REACH US...
...BUT HERE... IN OUR VILLAGE OF "WOLFS-SCHLUCHT"...
...OUTSIDERS ARE NOT WELCOME TO STAY.
GIRO (GLARE)
NOW THAT WE'RE CLEAR, GO BACK TO WHERE YOU CAME FROM!
HISO (PSST)
—BEST TO RETREAT AND CONSIDER ALTERNATIVE APPROACHES, I THINK.
YES, SIR.
ZA (GATHER)...
VERY WELL.
THEN WE WILL TAKE OUR LEA—
WAIT!!

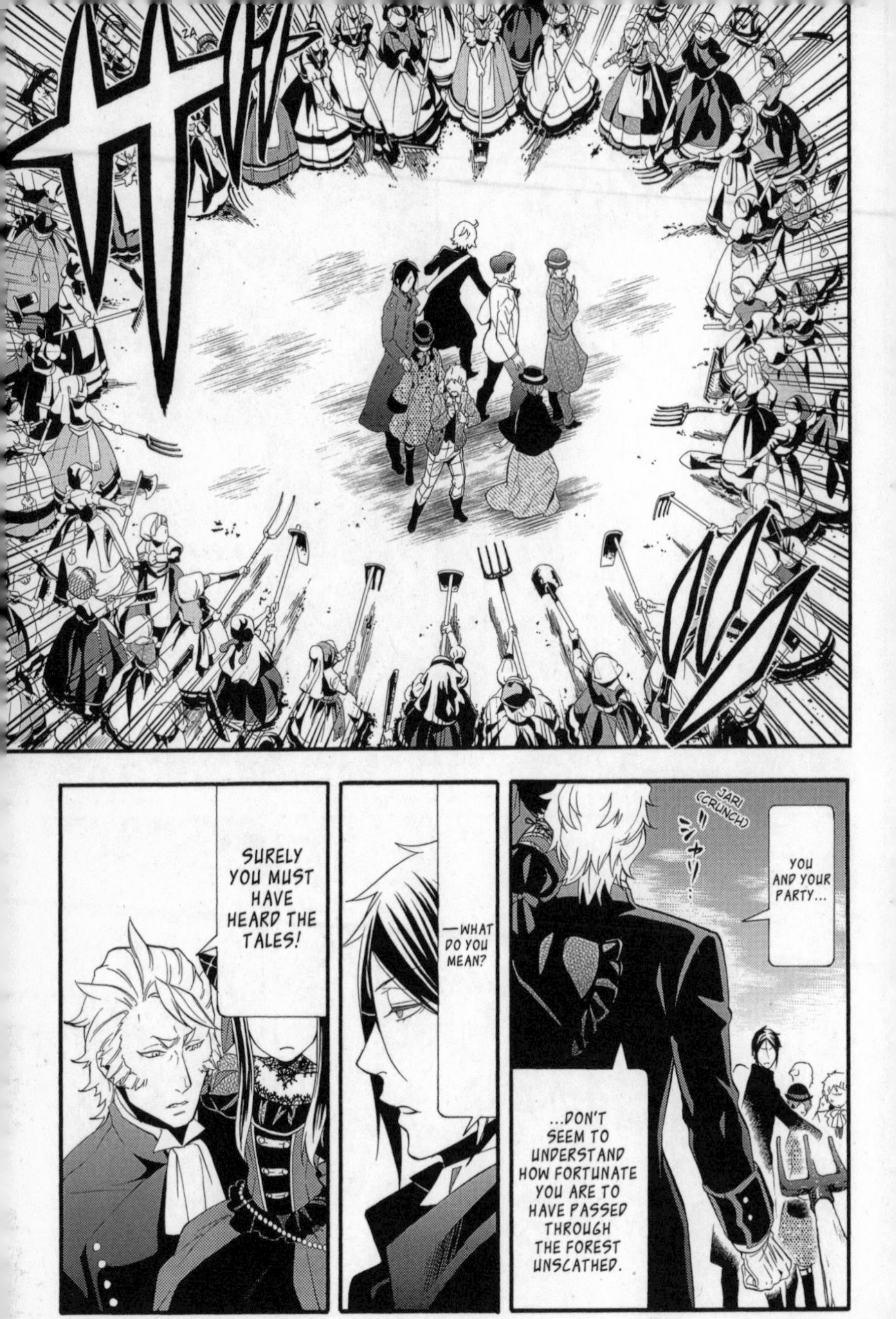
ZA
JARI (CRUNCH)
YOU AND YOUR PARTY...
...DON'T SEEM TO UNDERSTAND HOW FORTUNATE YOU ARE TO HAVE PASSED THROUGH THE FOREST UNSCATHED.
—WHAT DO YOU MEAN?
SURELY YOU MUST HAVE HEARD THE TALES!

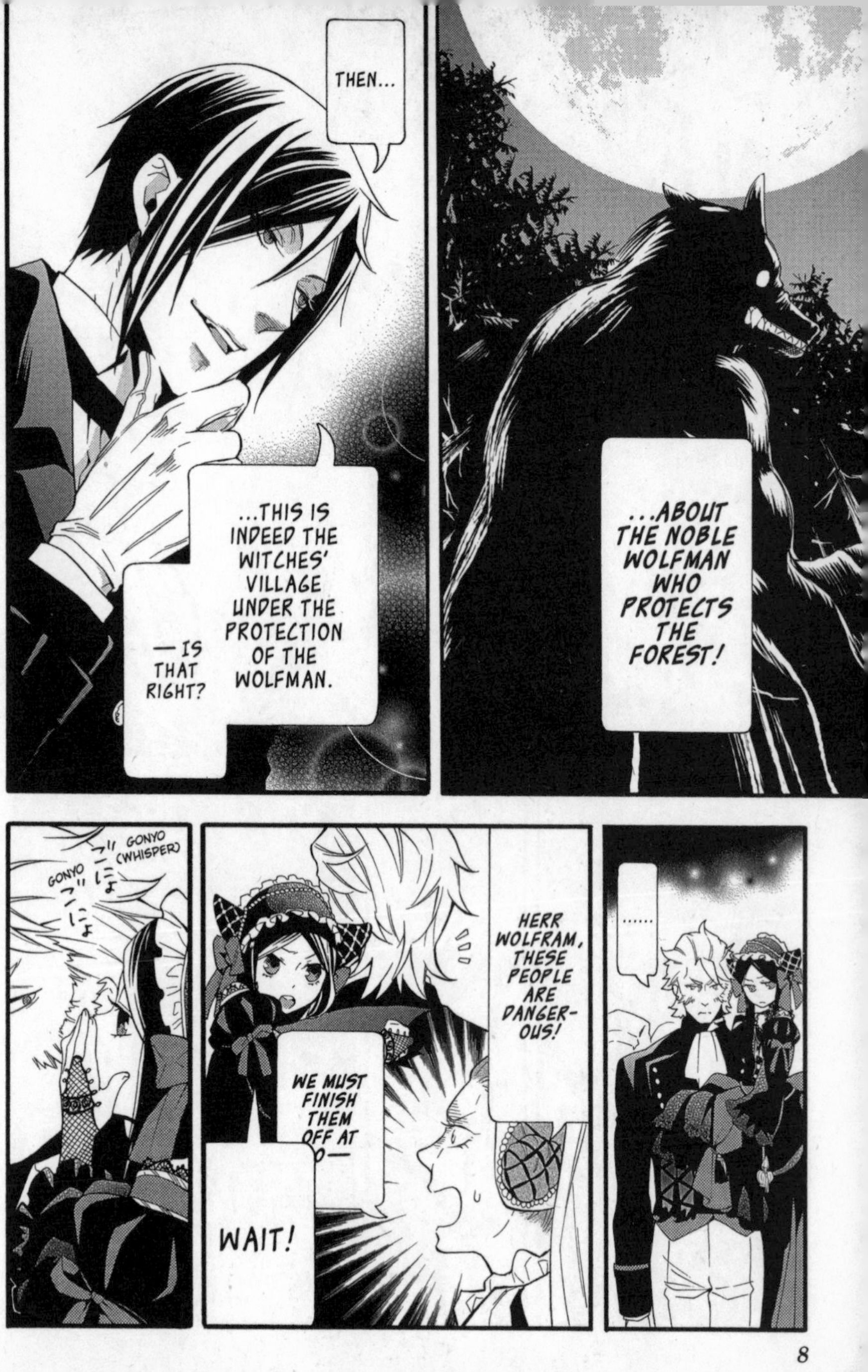
...ABOUT THE NOBLE WOLFMAN WHO PROTECTS THE FOREST!
THEN...
...THIS IS INDEED THE WITCHES' VILLAGE UNDER THE PROTECTION OF THE WOLFMAN.
—IS THAT RIGHT?
......
HERR WOLFRAM, THESE PEOPLE ARE DANGER-OUS!
WE MUST FINISH THEM OFF AT O—
WAIT!
ごにょ
GONYO (WHISPER)
ごにょ
GONYO

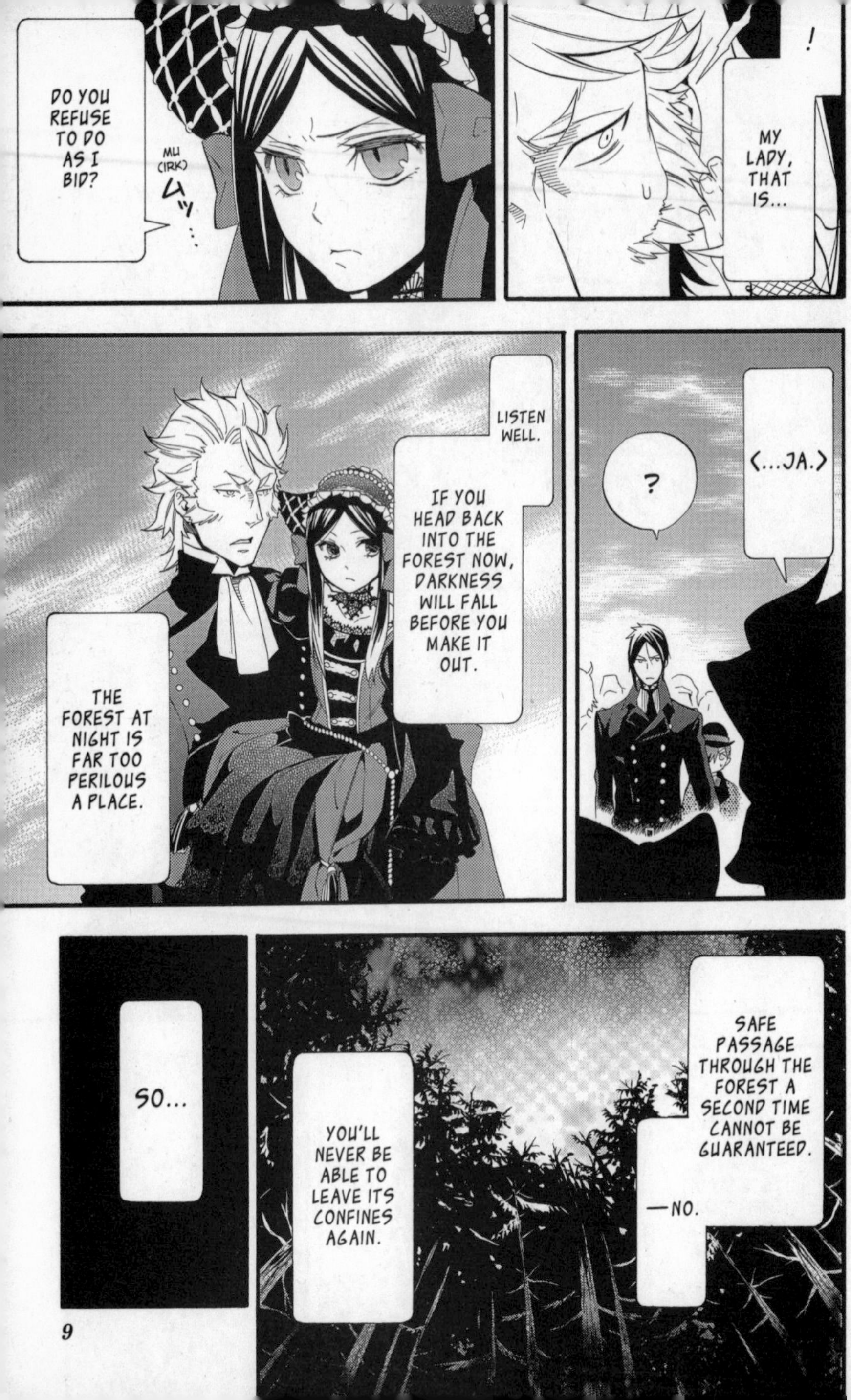
!
MY LADY, THAT IS...
DO YOU REFUSE TO DO AS I BID?
MU (IRK)
ムッ
⟨...JA.⟩
?
LISTEN WELL.
IF YOU HEAD BACK INTO THE FOREST NOW, DARKNESS WILL FALL BEFORE YOU MAKE IT OUT.
THE FOREST AT NIGHT IS FAR TOO PERILOUS A PLACE.
SAFE PASSAGE THROUGH THE FOREST A SECOND TIME CANNOT BE GUARANTEED.
—NO.
YOU'LL NEVER BE ABLE TO LEAVE ITS CONFINES AGAIN.
SO...

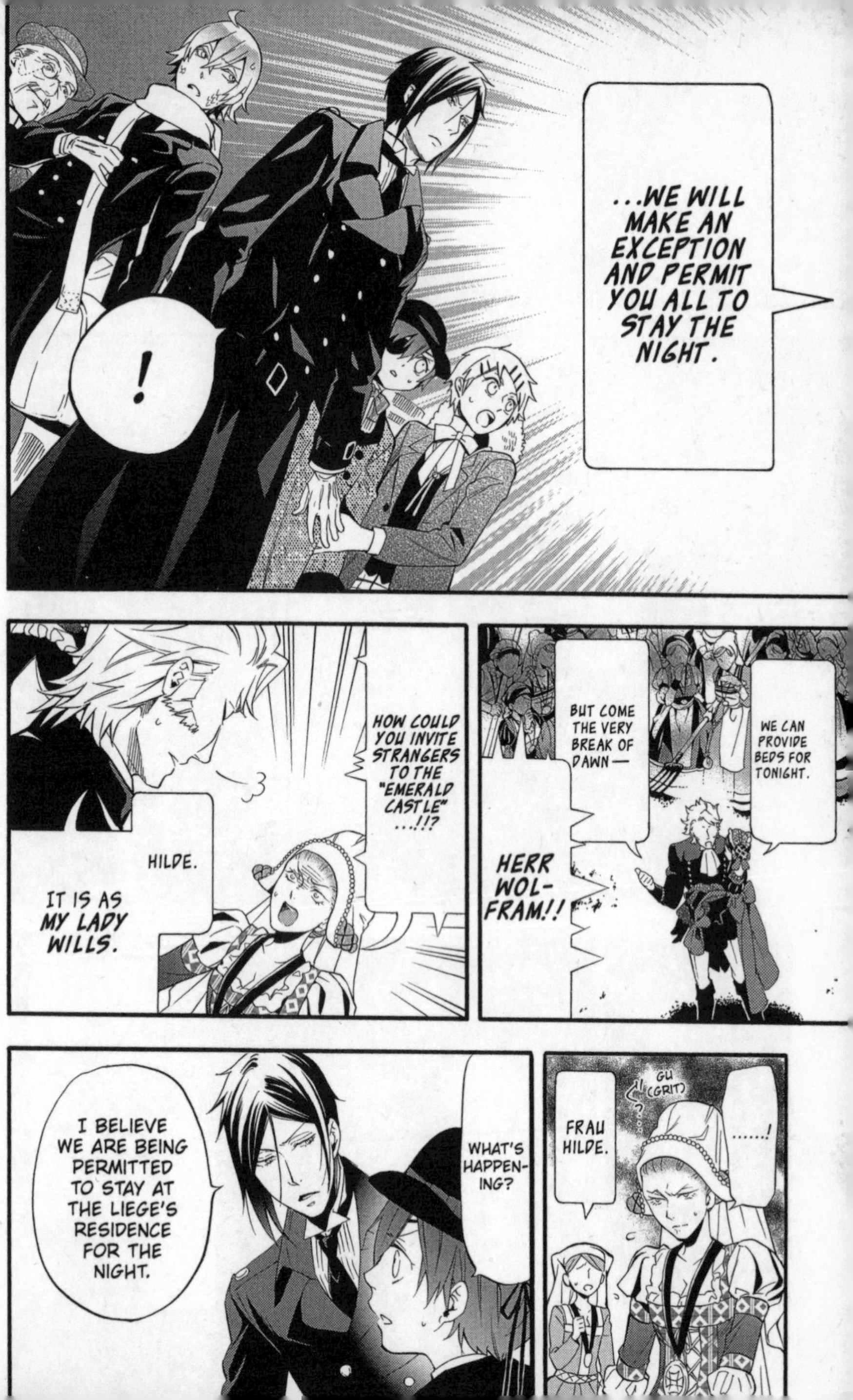
...WE WILL MAKE AN EXCEPTION AND PERMIT YOU ALL TO STAY THE NIGHT.
!
WE CAN PROVIDE BEDS FOR TONIGHT.
BUT COME THE VERY BREAK OF DAWN—
HERR WOL-FRAM!!
HOW COULD YOU INVITE STRANGERS TO THE "EMERALD CASTLE" ...!!?
HILDE.
IT IS AS MY LADY WILLS.
GU (GRIT)
......!
FRAU HILDE.
WHAT'S HAPPEN-ING?
I BELIEVE WE ARE BEING PERMITTED TO STAY AT THE LIEGE'S RESIDENCE FOR THE NIGHT.

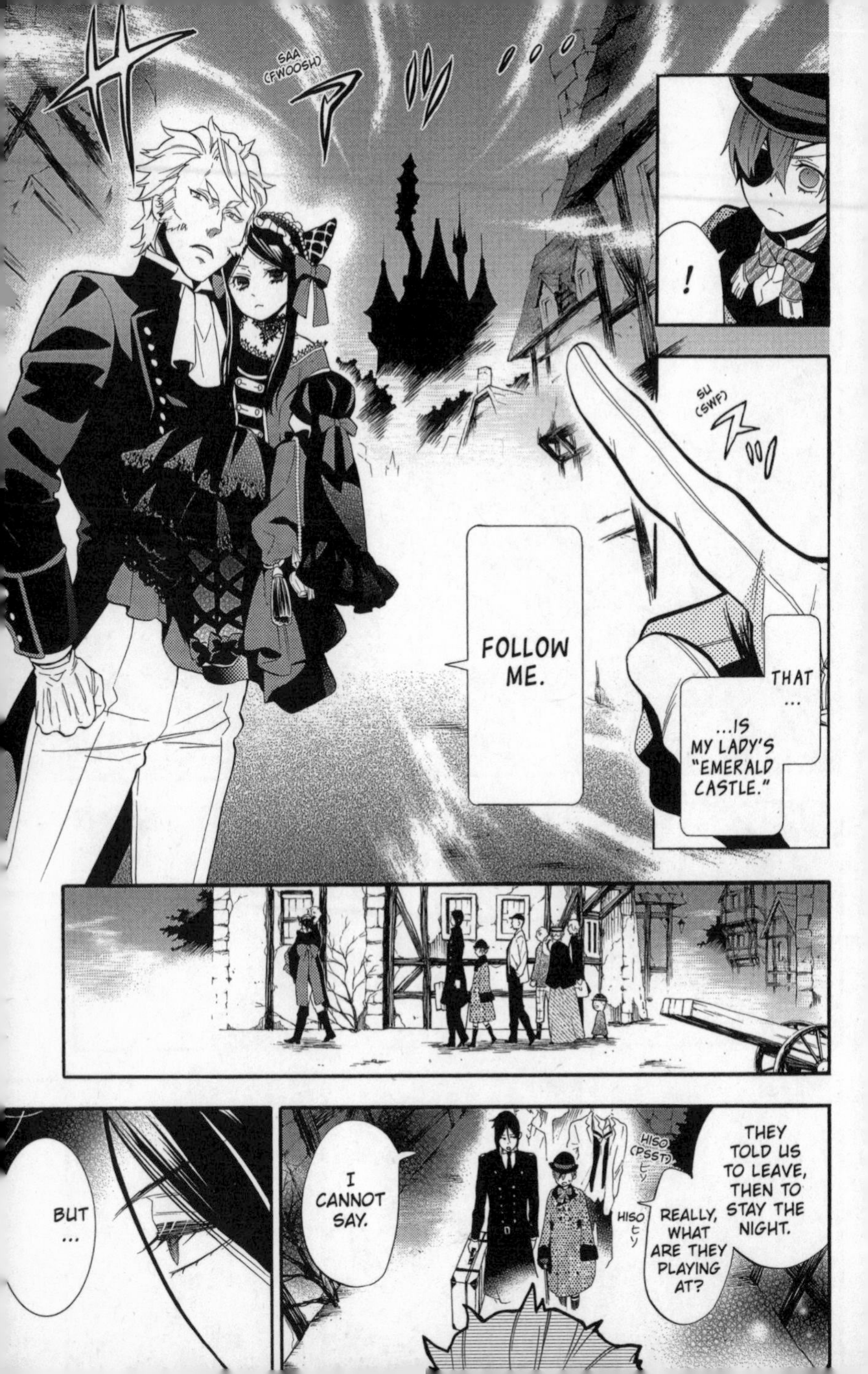
!
SU (SWF)
THAT...
...IS MY LADY'S "EMERALD CASTLE."
SAA (FWOOSH)
FOLLOW ME.
HISO (PSSST)
THEY TOLD US TO LEAVE, THEN TO STAY THE NIGHT.
HISO
REALLY, WHAT ARE THEY PLAYING AT?
I CANNOT SAY.
BUT...

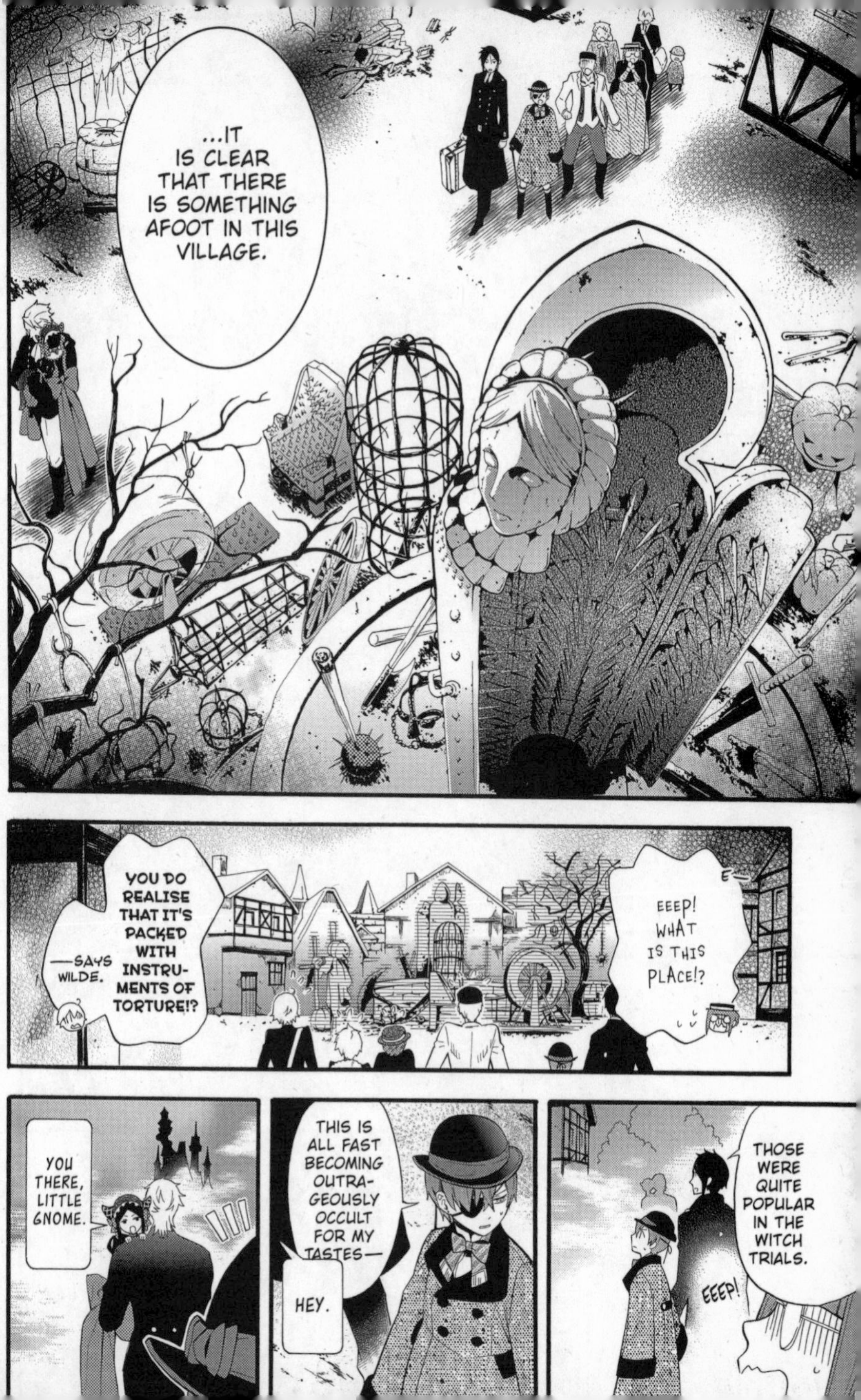
...IT IS CLEAR THAT THERE IS SOMETHING AFOOT IN THIS VILLAGE.
E—
EEEP! WHAT IS THIS PLACE!?
YOU DO REALISE THAT IT'S PACKED WITH INSTRUMENTS OF TORTURE!?
—SAYS WILDE.
THOSE WERE QUITE POPULAR IN THE WITCH TRIALS.
EEEP!
THIS IS ALL FAST BECOMING OUTRAGEOUSLY OCCULT FOR MY TASTES—
HEY.
YOU THERE, LITTLE GNOME.

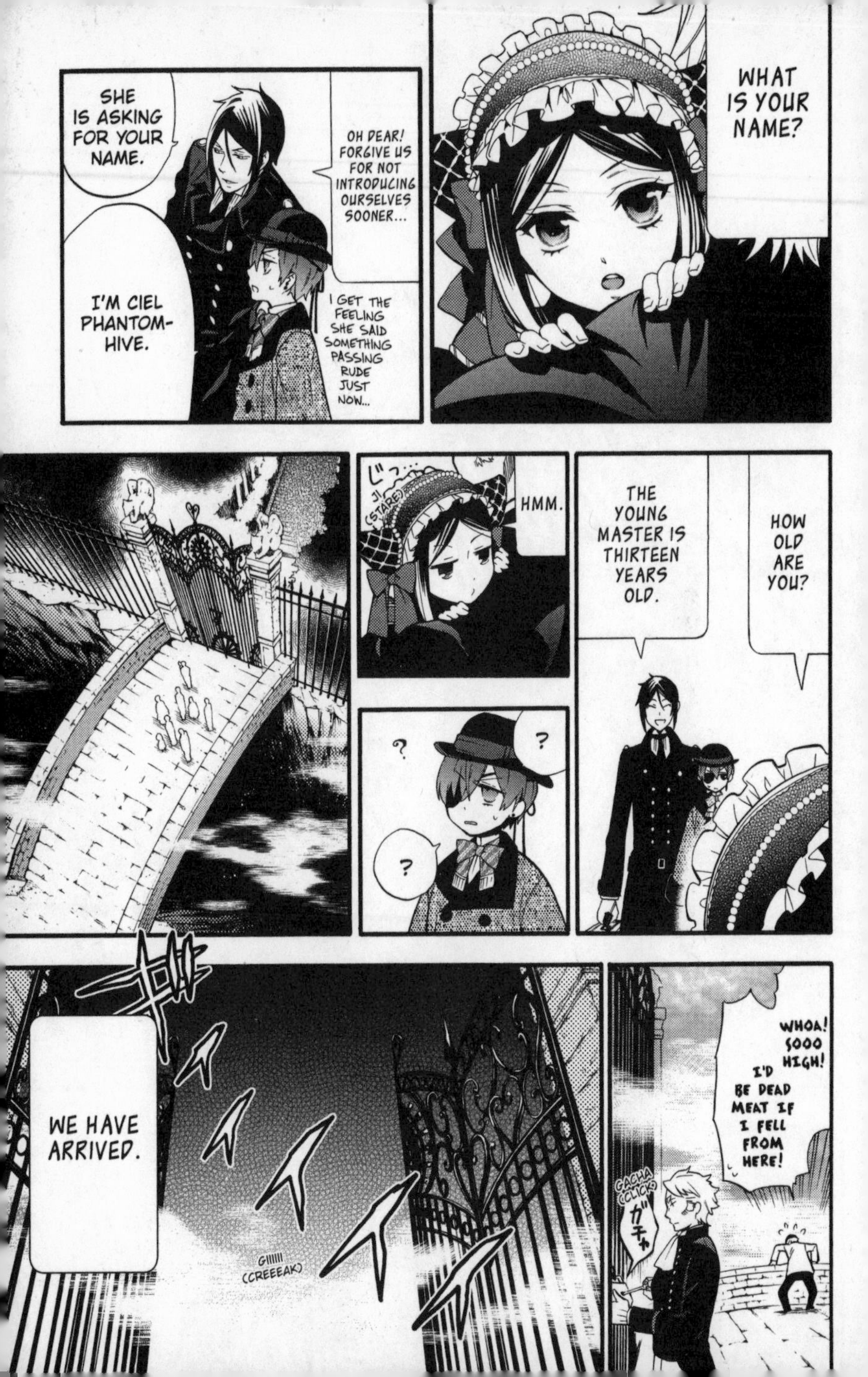
WHAT IS YOUR NAME?
OH DEAR! FORGIVE US FOR NOT INTRODUCING OURSELVES SOONER...
SHE IS ASKING FOR YOUR NAME.
I GET THE FEELING SHE SAID SOMETHING PASSING RUDE JUST NOW...
I'M CIEL PHANTOM-HIVE.
HOW OLD ARE YOU?
THE YOUNG MASTER IS THIRTEEN YEARS OLD.
じっ… JI (STARE)
HMM.
?
?
?
WHOA! SOOO HIGH!
I'D BE DEAD MEAT IF I FELL FROM HERE!
ガチャ GACHA (CLICK)
WE HAVE ARRIVED.
GIIIII (CREEEAK)

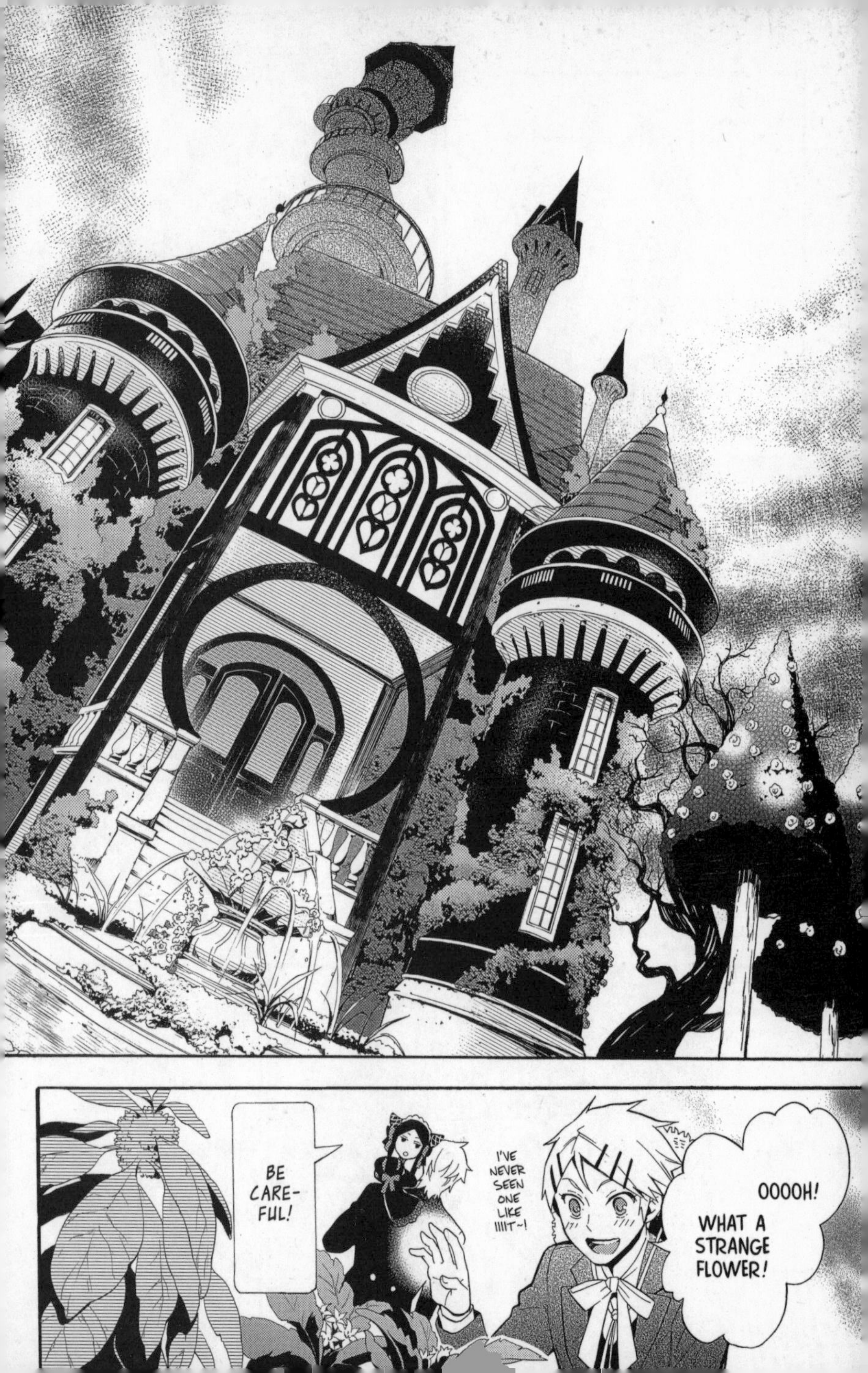
OOOOH! WHAT A STRANGE FLOWER!
I'VE NEVER SEEN ONE LIKE IIIIT~!
BE CARE-FUL!

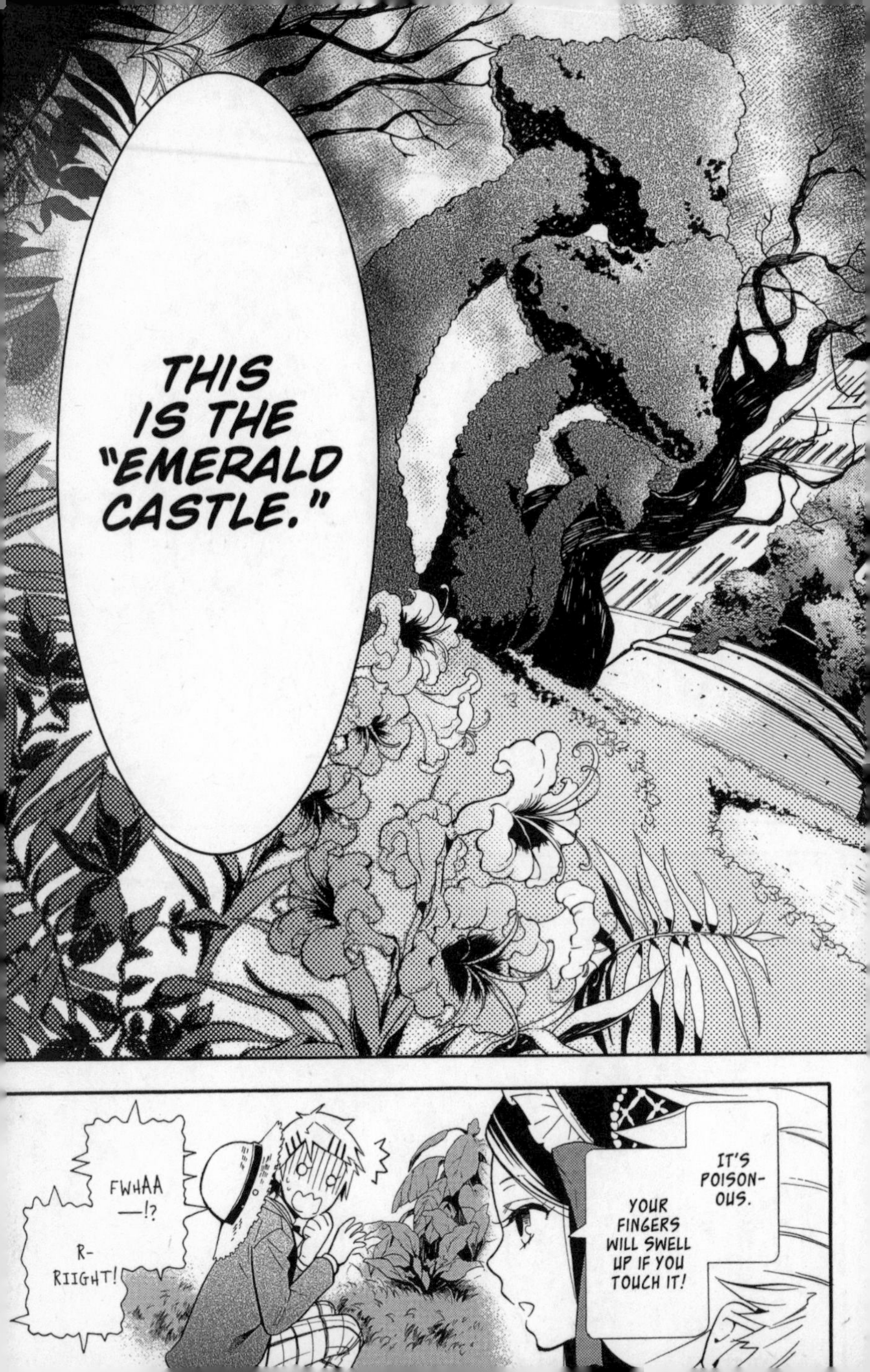
THIS IS THE "EMERALD CASTLE."
IT'S POISON-OUS.
YOUR FINGERS WILL SWELL UP IF YOU TOUCH IT!
FWHAA—!?
R-RIIGHT!

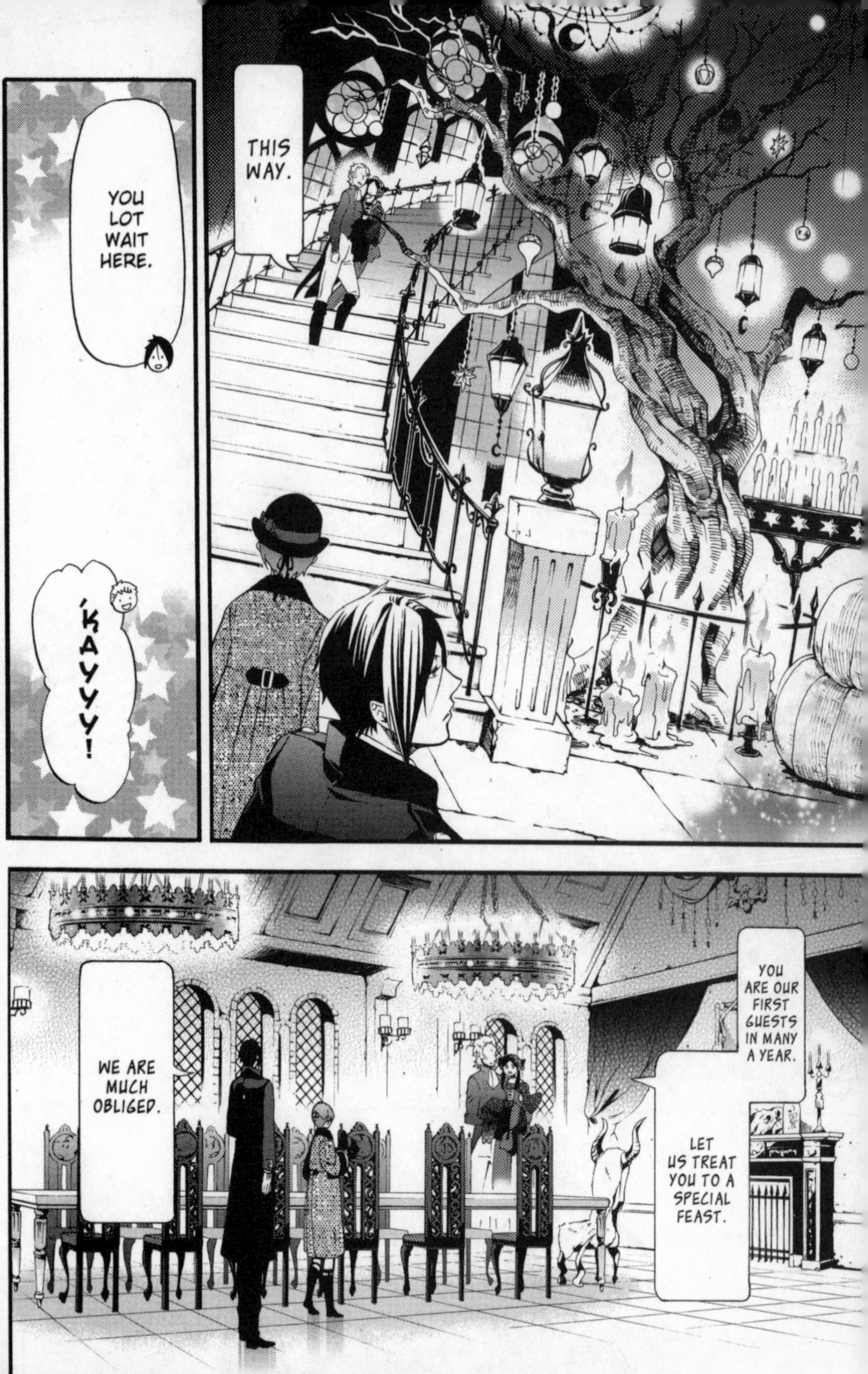
THIS WAY.
YOU LOT WAIT HERE.
'KAYYYY!
YOU ARE OUR FIRST GUESTS IN MANY A YEAR.
LET US TREAT YOU TO A SPECIAL FEAST.
WE ARE MUCH OBLIGED.

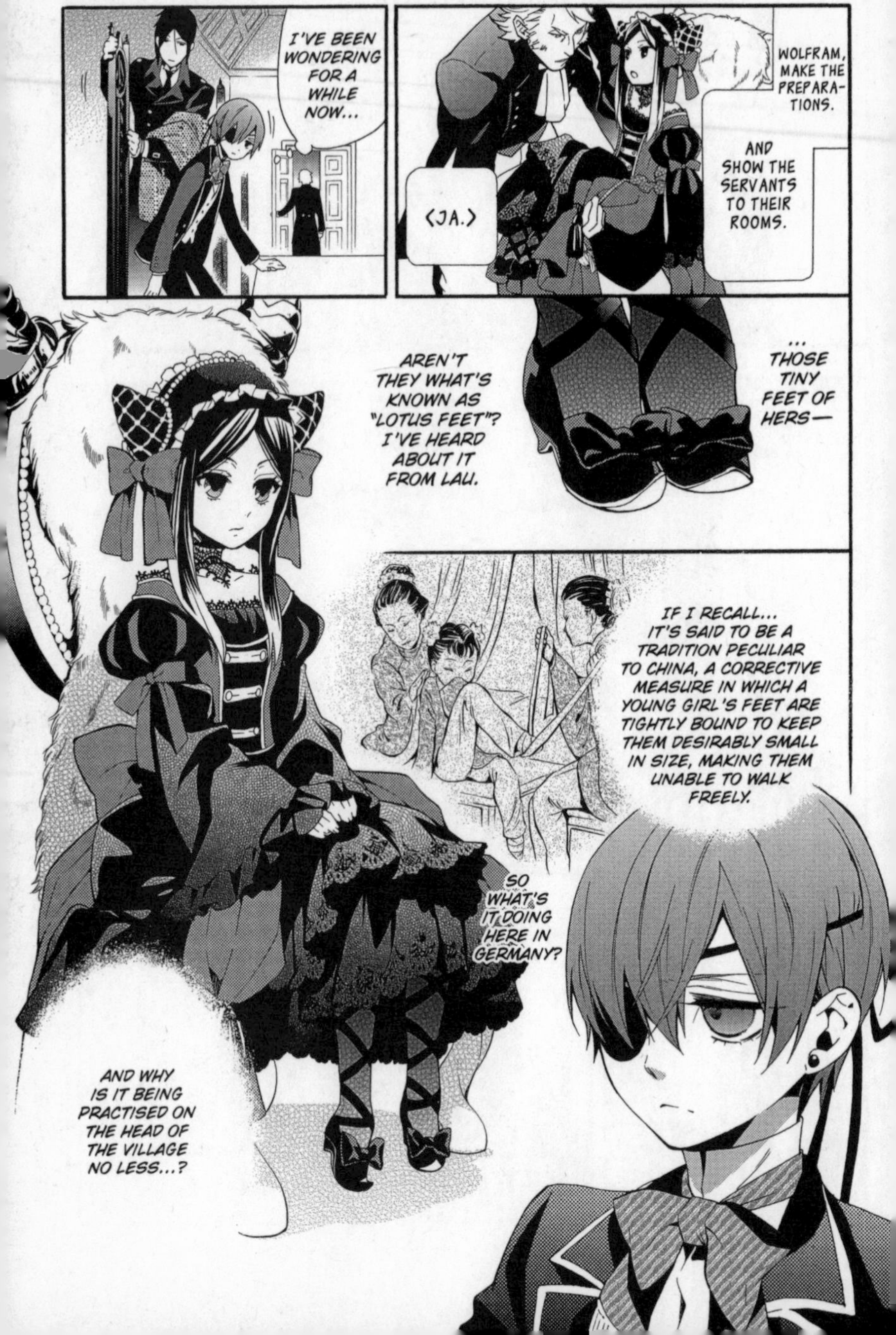
WOLFRAM, MAKE THE PREPARATIONS.
AND SHOW THE SERVANTS TO THEIR ROOMS.
<JA.>
I'VE BEEN WONDERING FOR A WHILE NOW...
... THOSE TINY FEET OF HERS—
AREN'T THEY WHAT'S KNOWN AS "LOTUS FEET"? I'VE HEARD ABOUT IT FROM LAU.
IF I RECALL... IT'S SAID TO BE A TRADITION PECULIAR TO CHINA, A CORRECTIVE MEASURE IN WHICH A YOUNG GIRL'S FEET ARE TIGHTLY BOUND TO KEEP THEM DESIRABLY SMALL IN SIZE, MAKING THEM UNABLE TO WALK FREELY.
SO WHAT'S IT DOING HERE IN GERMANY?
AND WHY IS IT BEING PRACTISED ON THE HEAD OF THE VILLAGE NO LESS...?

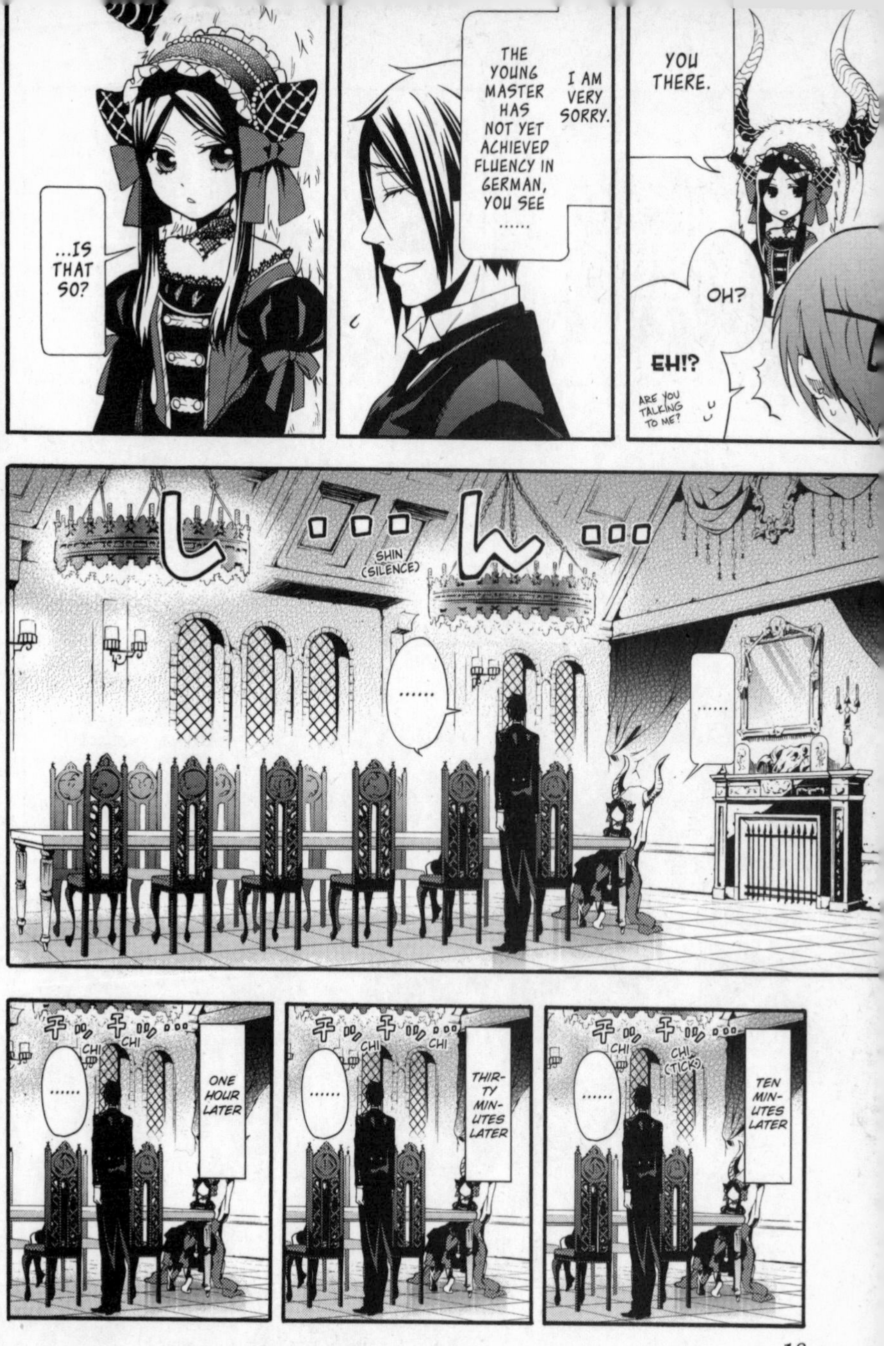
YOU THERE.
OH?
EH!?
ARE YOU TALKING TO ME?
I AM VERY SORRY.
THE YOUNG MASTER HAS NOT YET ACHIEVED FLUENCY IN GERMAN, YOU SEE ......
...IS THAT SO?
SHIN (SILENCE)
......
......
TEN MIN-UTES LATER
CHI CHI (TICK)
......
THIRTY MIN-UTES LATER
CHI CHI
......
ONE HOUR LATER
CHI CHI
......

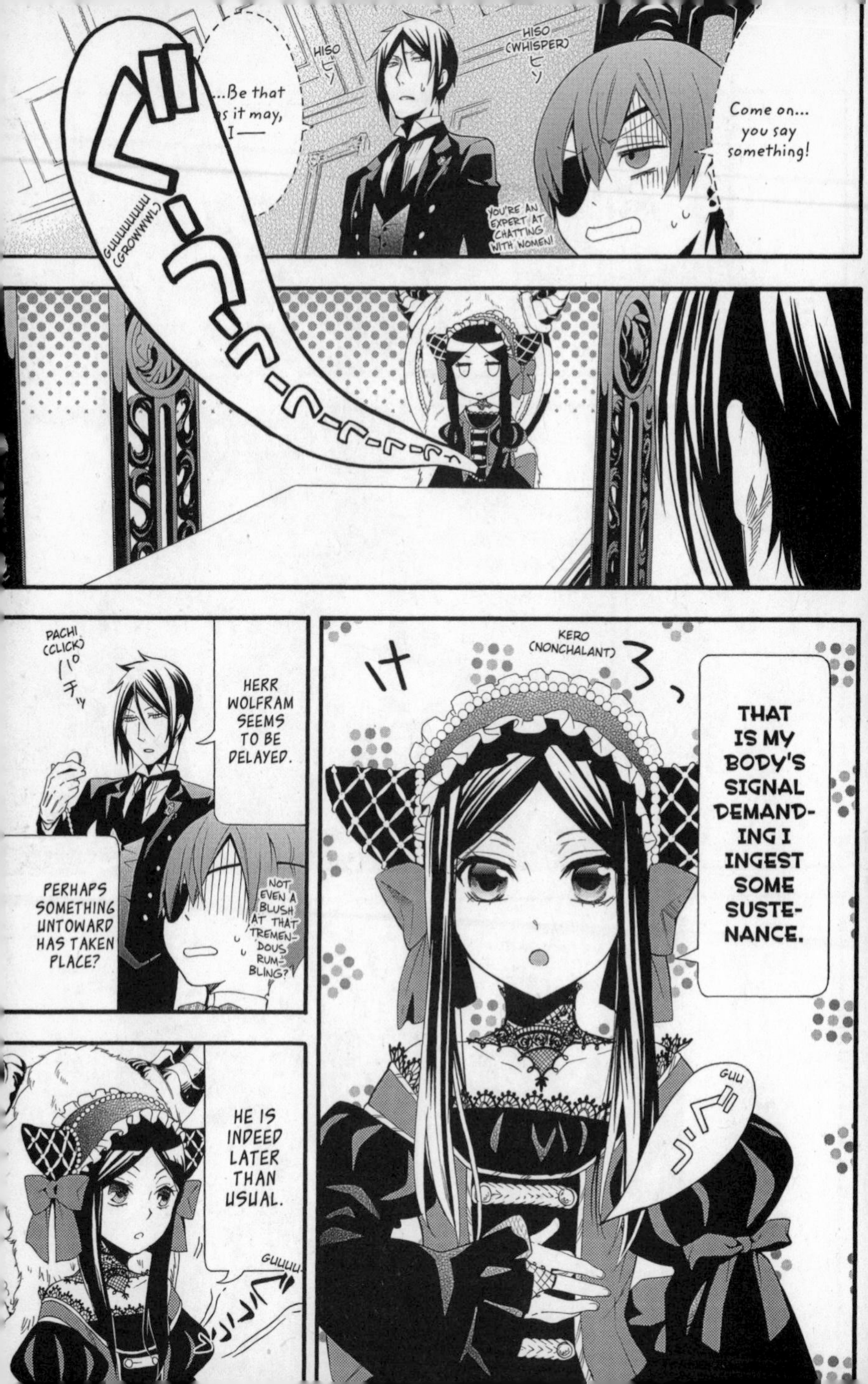

HISO (WHISPER)
Come on... you say something!
YOU'RE AN EXPERT AT CHATTING WITH WOMEN!
HISO
...Be that as it may, I—
GUUUUUUUNNNN (GROWWWL)
KERO (NONCHALANT)
THAT IS MY BODY'S SIGNAL DEMANDING I INGEST SOME SUSTENANCE.
GUU
PACHI (CLICK)
HERR WOLFRAM SEEMS TO BE DELAYED.
PERHAPS SOMETHING UNTOWARD HAS TAKEN PLACE?
NOT EVEN A BLUSH AT THAT TREMENDOUS RUMBLING?
HE IS INDEED LATER THAN USUAL.
GUUUU

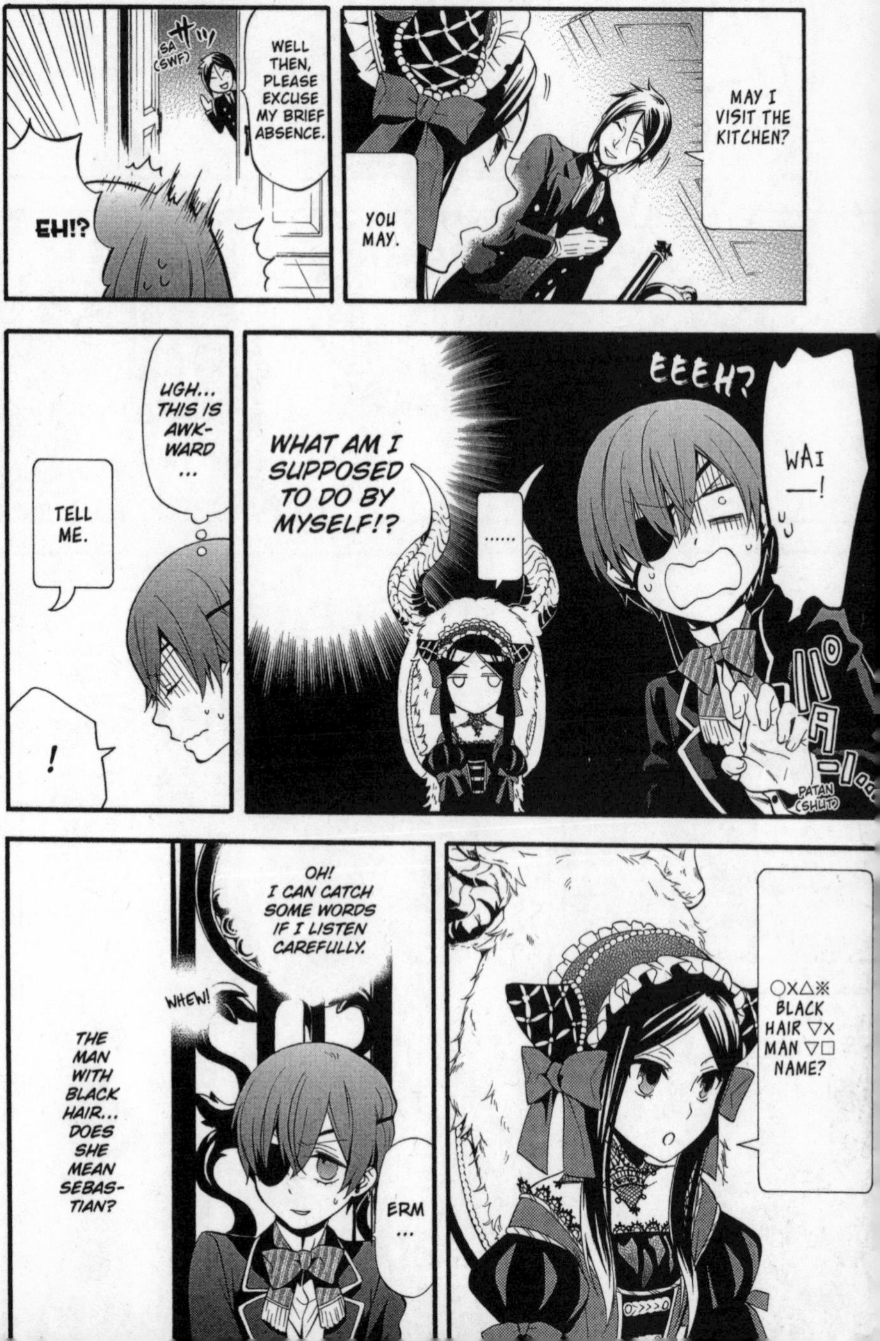

MAY I VISIT THE KITCHEN?
YOU MAY.
サッ SA (SWF)
WELL THEN, PLEASE EXCUSE MY BRIEF ABSENCE.
EH!?
EEEH?
WAI —!
PATAN (SHUT)
......
WHAT AM I SUPPOSED TO DO BY MYSELF!?
UGH... THIS IS AWK-WARD ...
TELL ME.
!
○×△※ BLACK HAIR ▽× MAN ▽□ NAME?
OH! I CAN CATCH SOME WORDS IF I LISTEN CAREFULLY.
WHEW!
THE MAN WITH BLACK HAIR... DOES SHE MEAN SEBAS-TIAN?
ERM ...

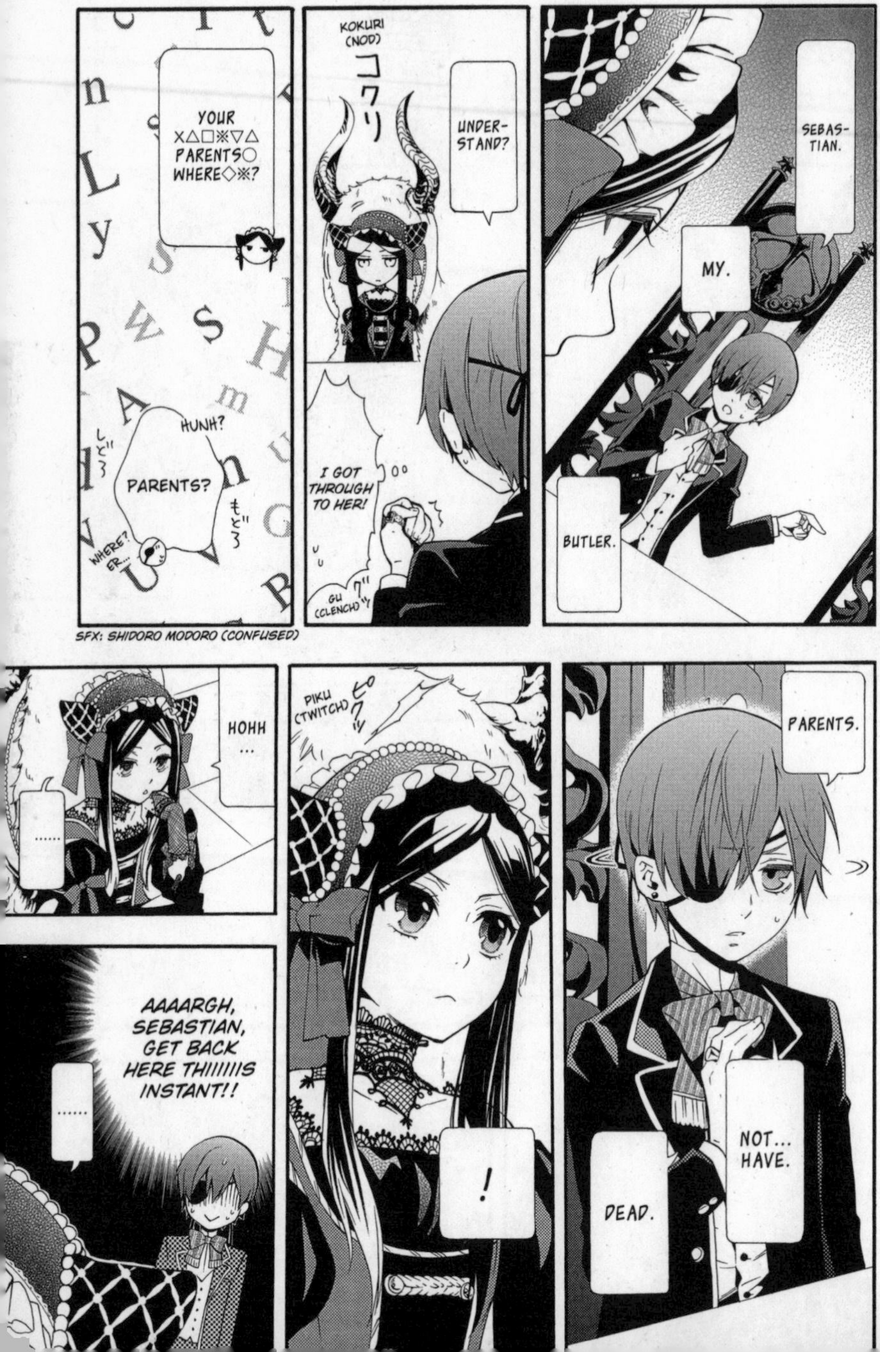
SEBASTIAN.
MY.
BUTLER.
KOKURI (NOD)
UNDERSTAND?
I GOT THROUGH TO HER!
GU (CLENCH)
YOUR ×△□※▽△ PARENTS○ WHERE◇※?
HUNH?
PARENTS?
WHERE? ER...
SFX: SHIDORO MODORO (CONFUSED)
PARENTS.
NOT... HAVE.
DEAD.
PIKU (TWITCH)
!
HOHH ...
......
AAAARGH, SEBASTIAN, GET BACK HERE THIIIIIIS INSTANT!!
......

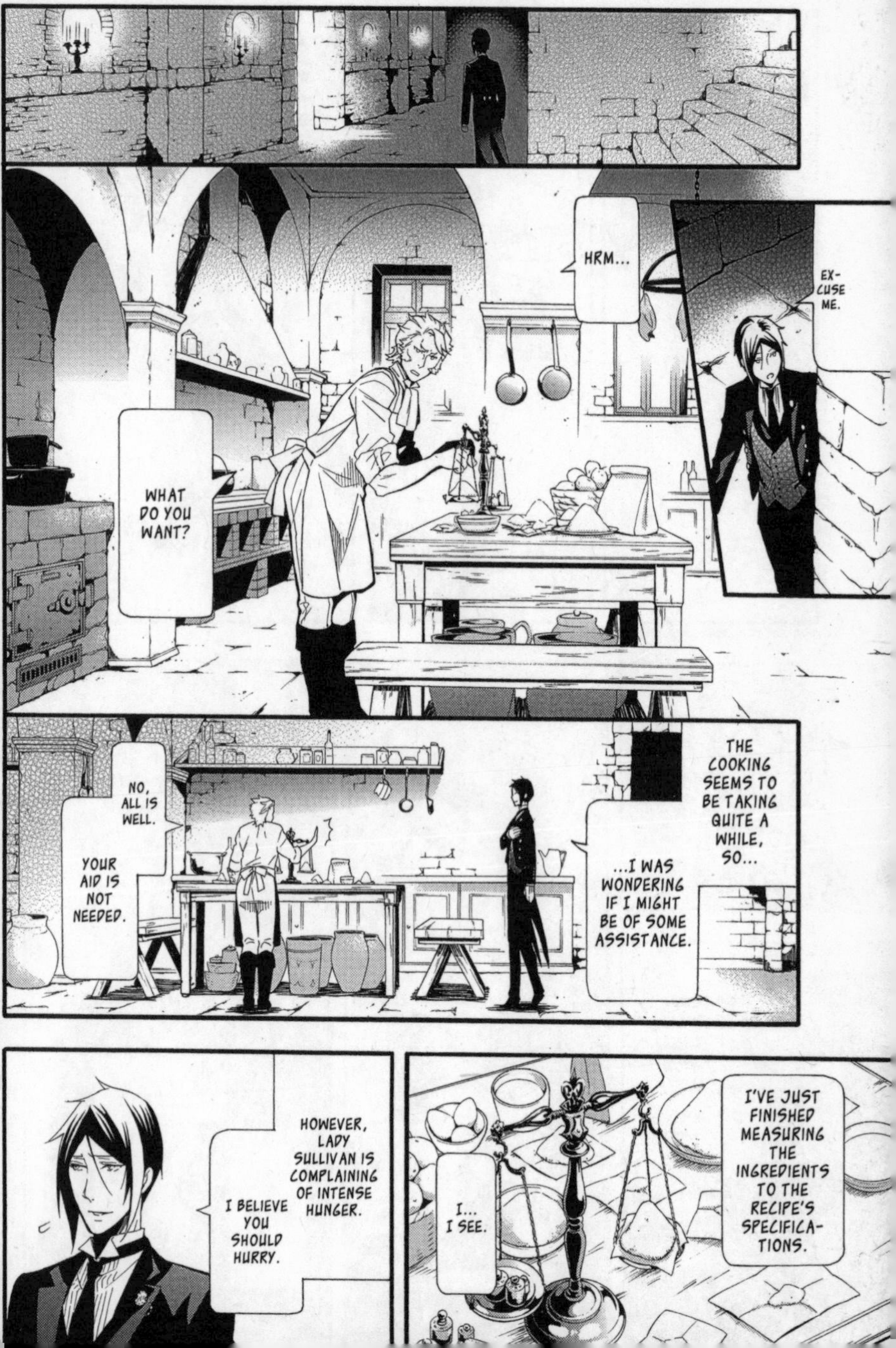
EX-CUSE ME.
HRM...
WHAT DO YOU WANT?
THE COOKING SEEMS TO BE TAKING QUITE A WHILE, SO...
...I WAS WONDERING IF I MIGHT BE OF SOME ASSISTANCE.
NO, ALL IS WELL.
YOUR AID IS NOT NEEDED.
I'VE JUST FINISHED MEASURING THE INGREDIENTS TO THE RECIPE'S SPECIFICATIONS.
I... I SEE.
HOWEVER, LADY SULLIVAN IS COMPLAINING OF INTENSE HUNGER.
I BELIEVE YOU SHOULD HURRY.

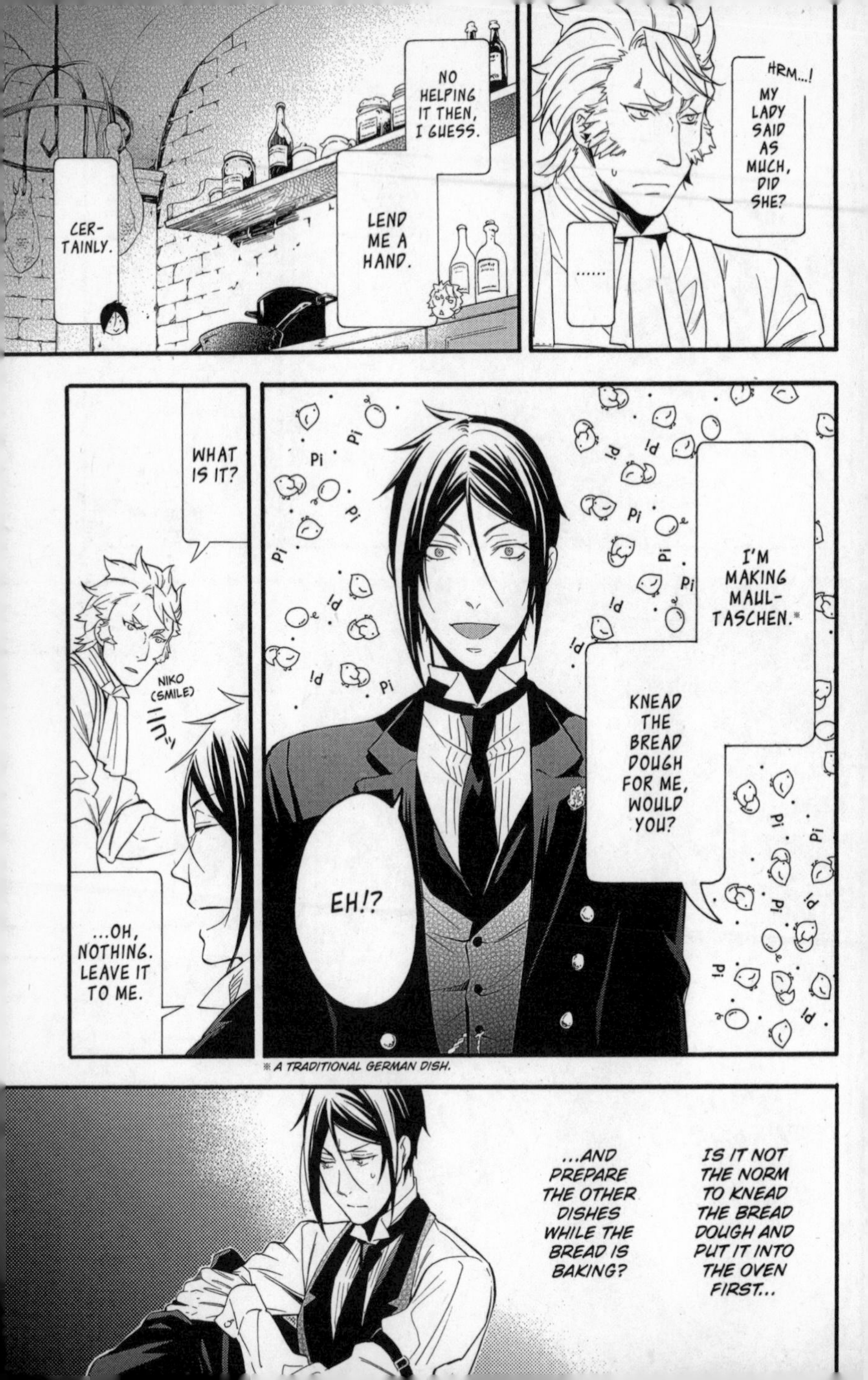
HRM...!
MY LADY SAID AS MUCH, DID SHE?
......
NO HELPING IT THEN, I GUESS.
LEND ME A HAND.
CER-TAINLY.
I'M MAKING MAUL-TASCHEN.※
KNEAD THE BREAD DOUGH FOR ME, WOULD YOU?
EH!?
Pi Pi Pi Pi Pi Pi Pi Pi Pi Pi Pi Pi Pi Pi Pi Pi Pi
WHAT IS IT?
NIKO (SMILE)
...OH, NOTHING. LEAVE IT TO ME.
IS IT NOT THE NORM TO KNEAD THE BREAD DOUGH AND PUT IT INTO THE OVEN FIRST...
...AND PREPARE THE OTHER DISHES WHILE THE BREAD IS BAKING?
※ A TRADITIONAL GERMAN DISH.

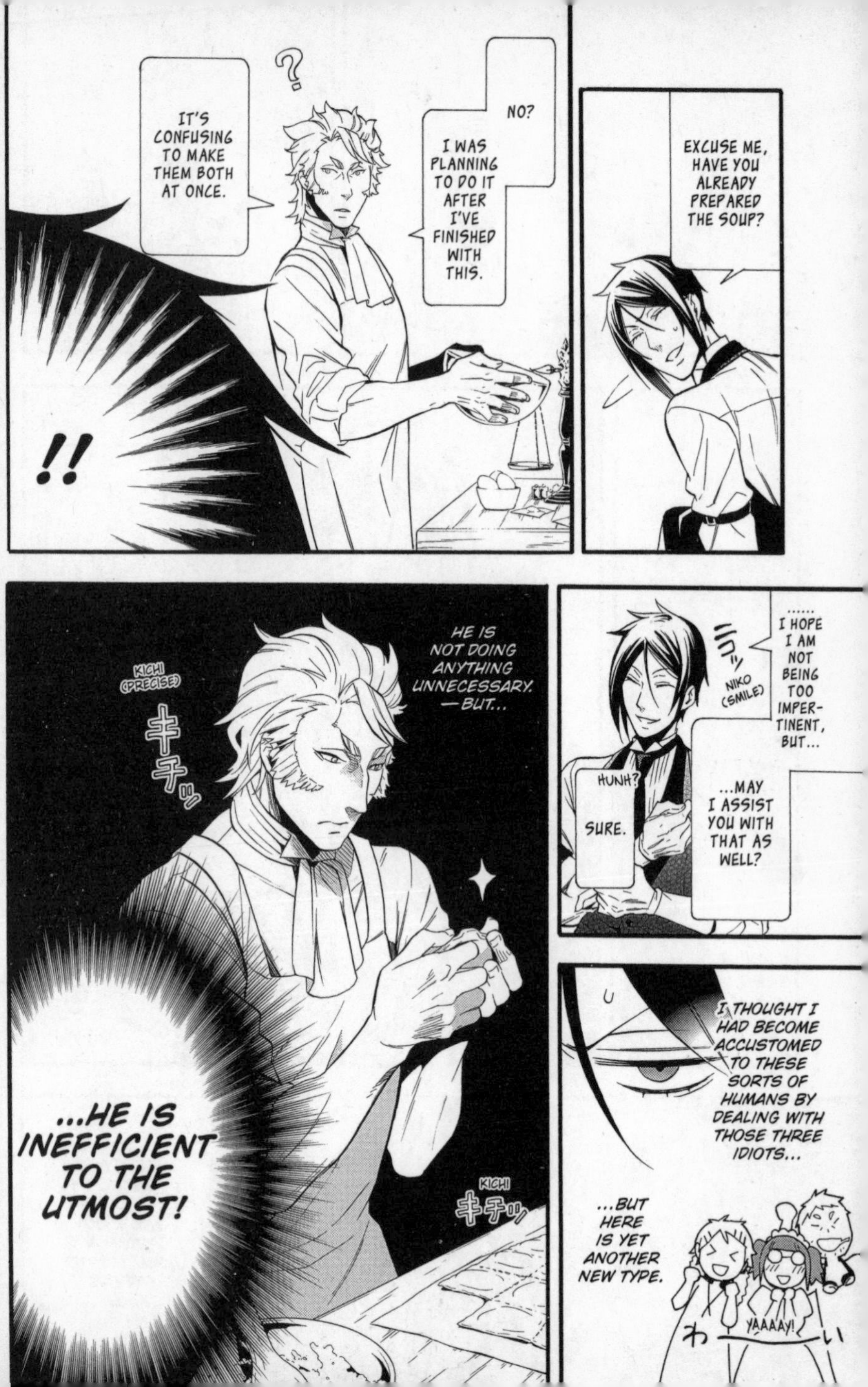
EXCUSE ME, HAVE YOU ALREADY PREPARED THE SOUP?
NO?
I WAS PLANNING TO DO IT AFTER I'VE FINISHED WITH THIS.
IT'S CONFUSING TO MAKE THEM BOTH AT ONCE.
!!
......I HOPE I AM NOT BEING TOO IMPERTINENT, BUT...
NIKO (SMILE)
...MAY I ASSIST YOU WITH THAT AS WELL?
HUNH?
SURE.
I THOUGHT I HAD BECOME ACCUSTOMED TO THESE SORTS OF HUMANS BY DEALING WITH THOSE THREE IDIOTS...
...BUT HERE IS YET ANOTHER NEW TYPE.
YAAAAY!
HE IS NOT DOING ANYTHING UNNECESSARY. —BUT...
KICHI (PRECISE)
KICHI
...HE IS INEFFICIENT TO THE UTMOST!

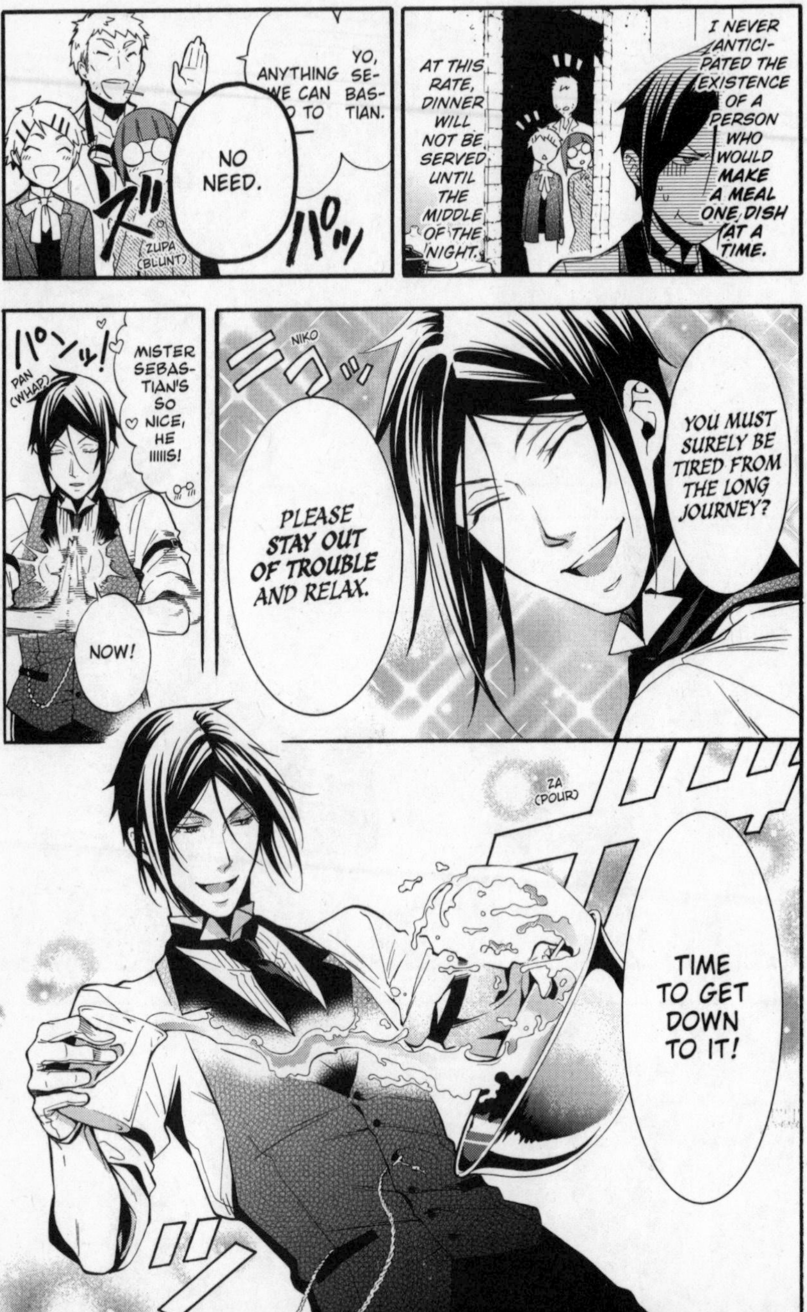
I NEVER ANTICIPATED THE EXISTENCE OF A PERSON WHO WOULD MAKE A MEAL ONE DISH AT A TIME.
AT THIS RATE, DINNER WILL NOT BE SERVED UNTIL THE MIDDLE OF THE NIGHT.
YO, SEBASTIAN.
ANYTHING WE CAN O TO
NO NEED.
ZUPA (BLUNT)
NIKO
YOU MUST SURELY BE TIRED FROM THE LONG JOURNEY?
PLEASE STAY OUT OF TROUBLE AND RELAX.
PAN (WHAP)
MISTER SEBASTIAN'S SO NICE, HE IIIIIS!
NOW!
ZA (POUR)
TIME TO GET DOWN TO IT!

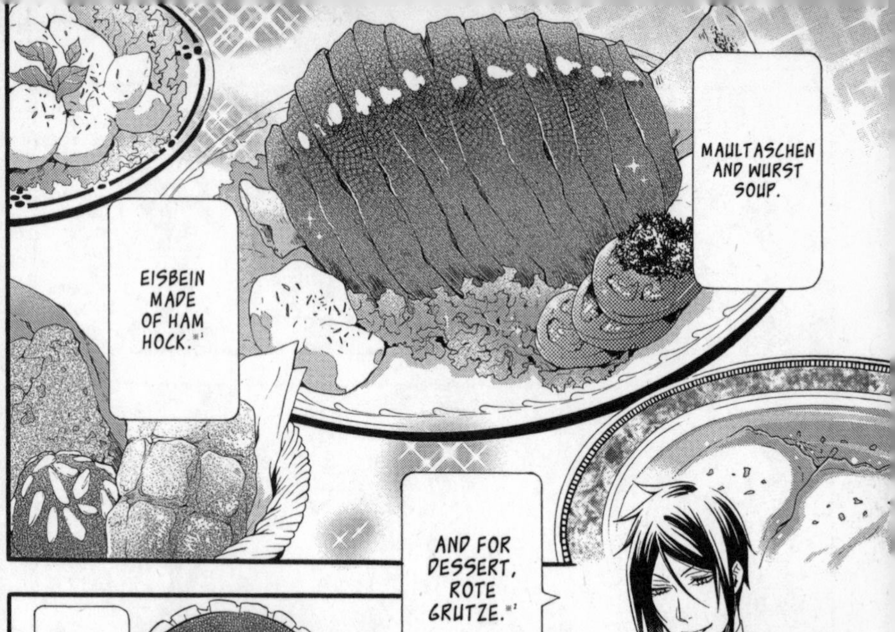
MAULTASCHEN AND WURST SOUP.
EISBEIN MADE OF HAM HOCK.※1
AND FOR DESSERT, ROTE GRUTZE.※2
HOHH... THIS IS QUITE...

※1 PORK STEWED FOR SEVERAL HOURS WITH HERBS AND SPICES. ※2 A DESSERT DISH WHERE SOUR BERRIES ARE BOILED AND THEN CHILLED TO JELLY, SERVED WITH CREAM.

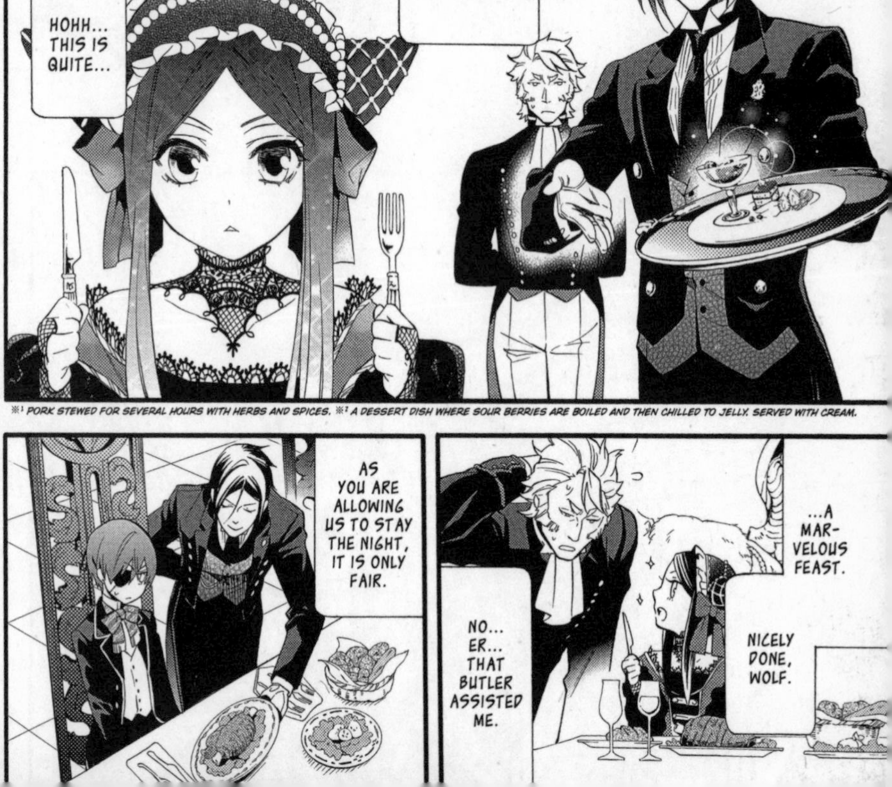
...A MAR-VELOUS FEAST.
NICELY DONE, WOLF.
NO... ER... THAT BUTLER ASSISTED ME.
AS YOU ARE ALLOWING US TO STAY THE NIGHT, IT IS ONLY FAIR.

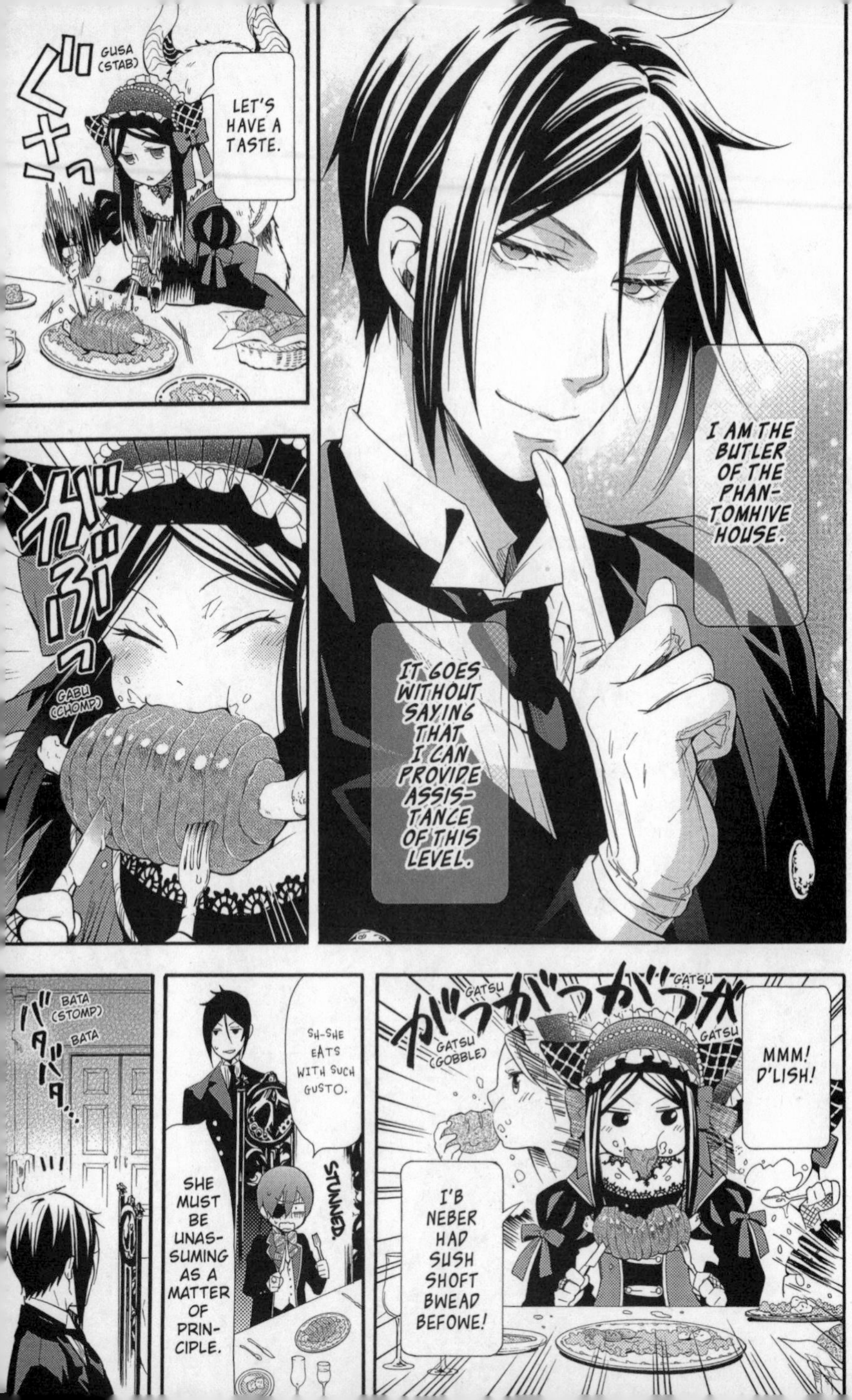
I AM THE BUTLER OF THE PHAN-TOMHIVE HOUSE.
IT GOES WITHOUT SAYING THAT I CAN PROVIDE ASSIS-TANCE OF THIS LEVEL.
GUSA (STAB)
LET'S HAVE A TASTE.
GABU (CHOMP)
GATSU GATSU GATSU GATSU (GOBBLE)
MMM! D'LISH!
I'B NEBER HAD SUSH SHOFT BWEAD BEFOWE!
SH-SHE EATS WITH SUCH GUSTO.
STUNNED.
SHE MUST BE UNAS-SUMING AS A MATTER OF PRIN-CIPLE.
BATA (STOMP)
BATA

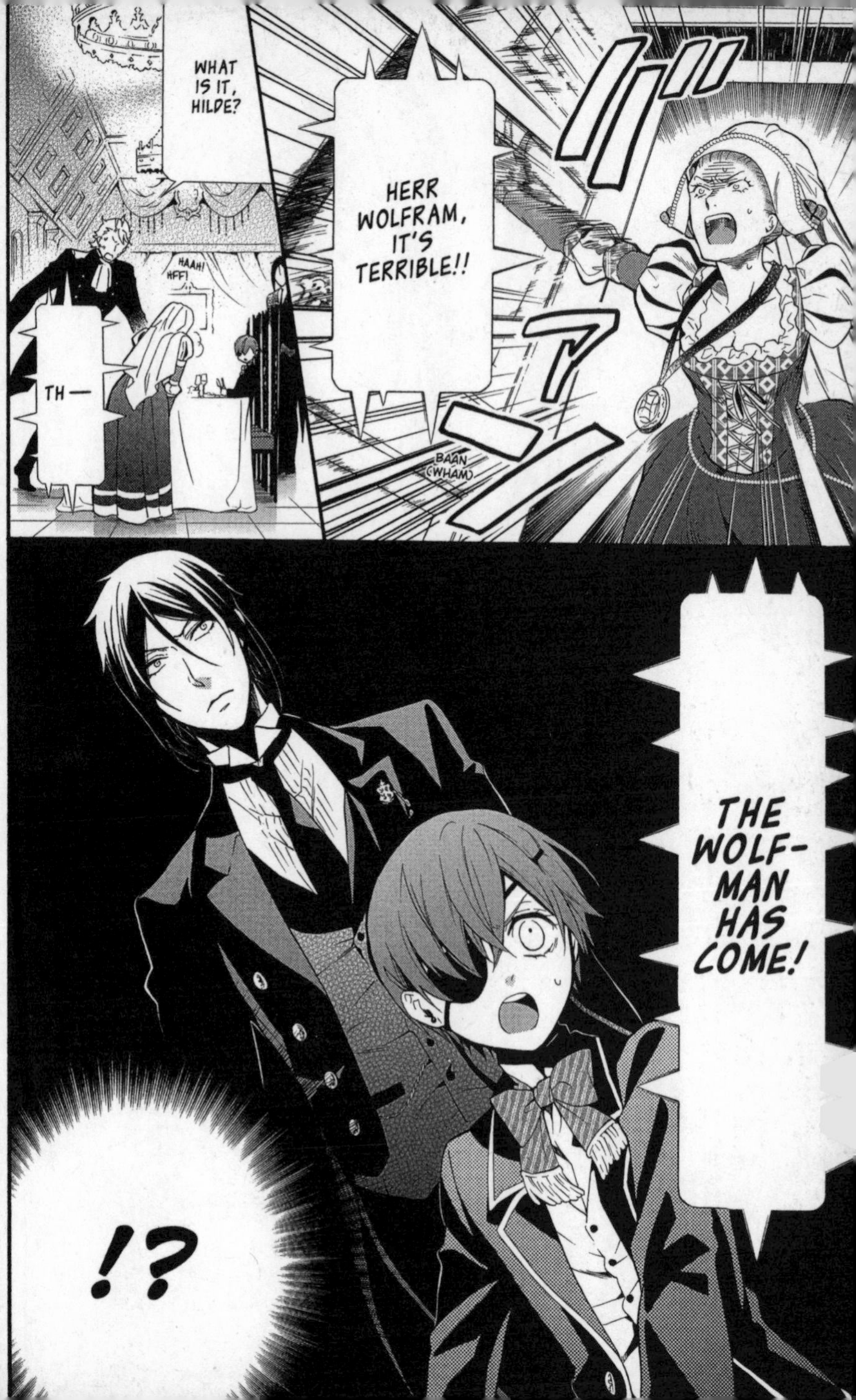
HERR WOLFRAM, IT'S TERRIBLE!!
BAAN (WHAM)
WHAT IS IT, HILDE?
HAAH! HFF!
TH—
THE WOLF-MAN HAS COME!
!?

Black Butler

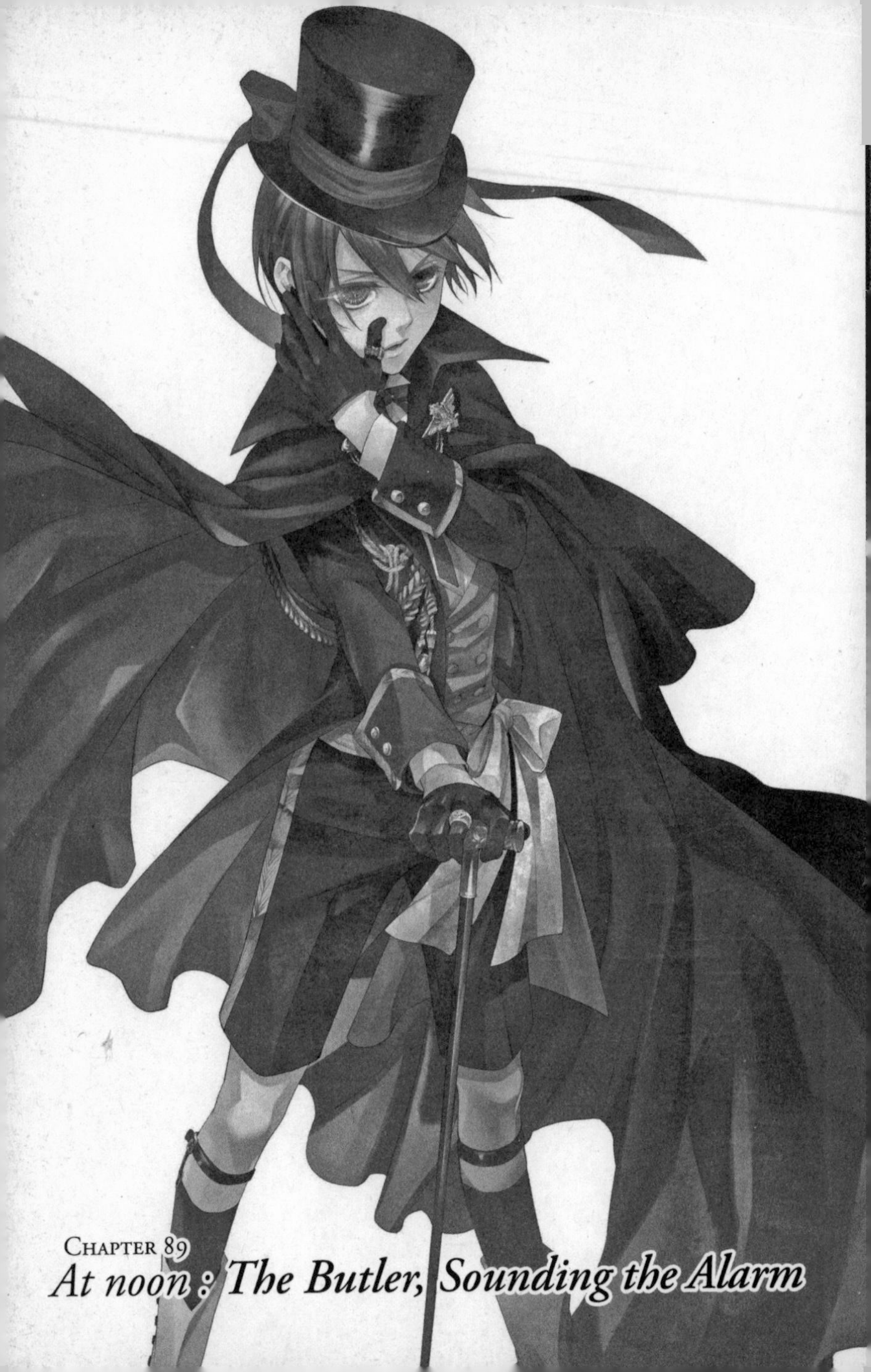

CHAPTER 89

At noon : The Butler, Sounding the Alarm

Black Butler

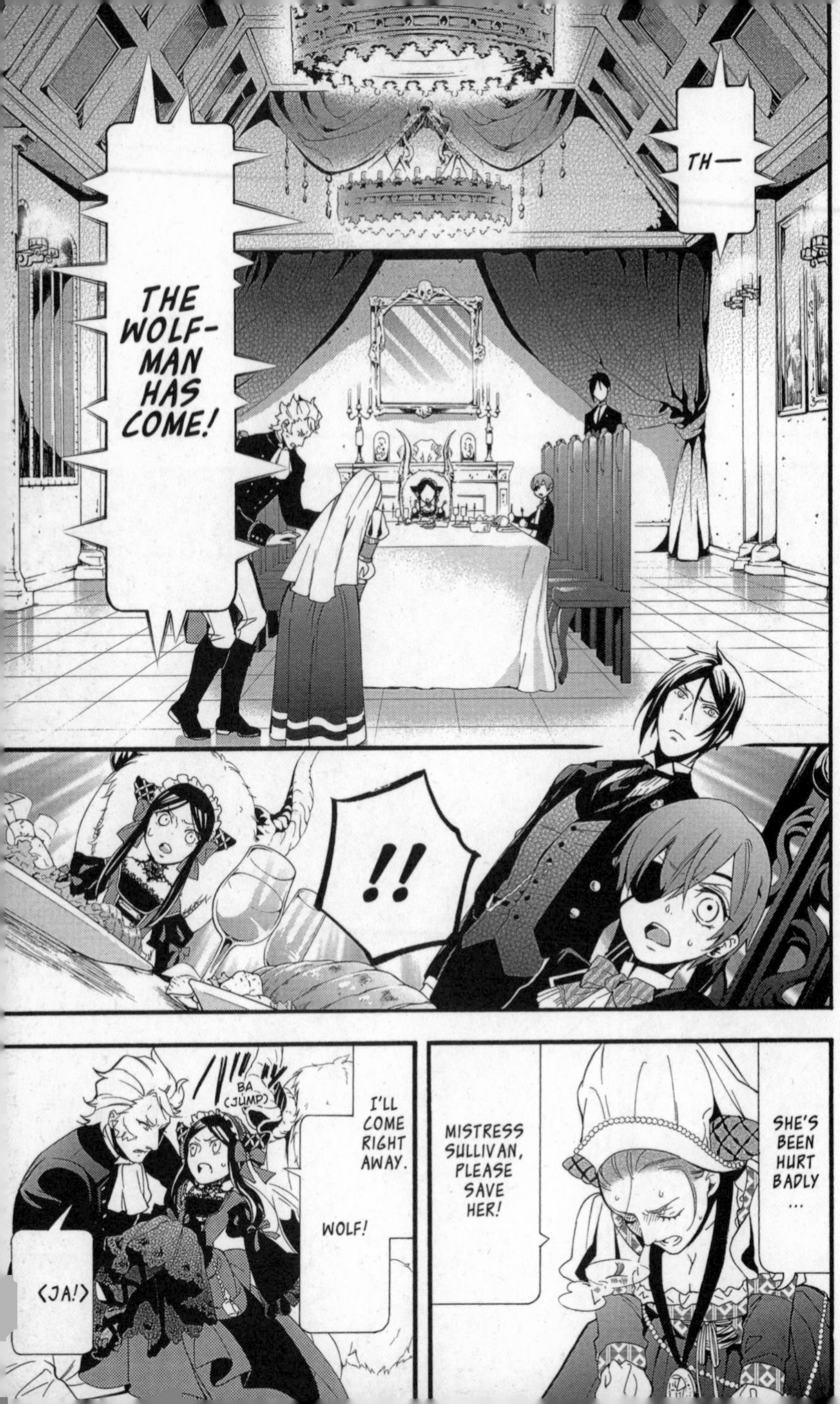

TH—
THE WOLF-MAN HAS COME!
!!
SHE'S BEEN HURT BADLY ...
MISTRESS SULLIVAN, PLEASE SAVE HER!
I'LL COME RIGHT AWAY.
BA (JUMP)
WOLF!
⟨JA!⟩

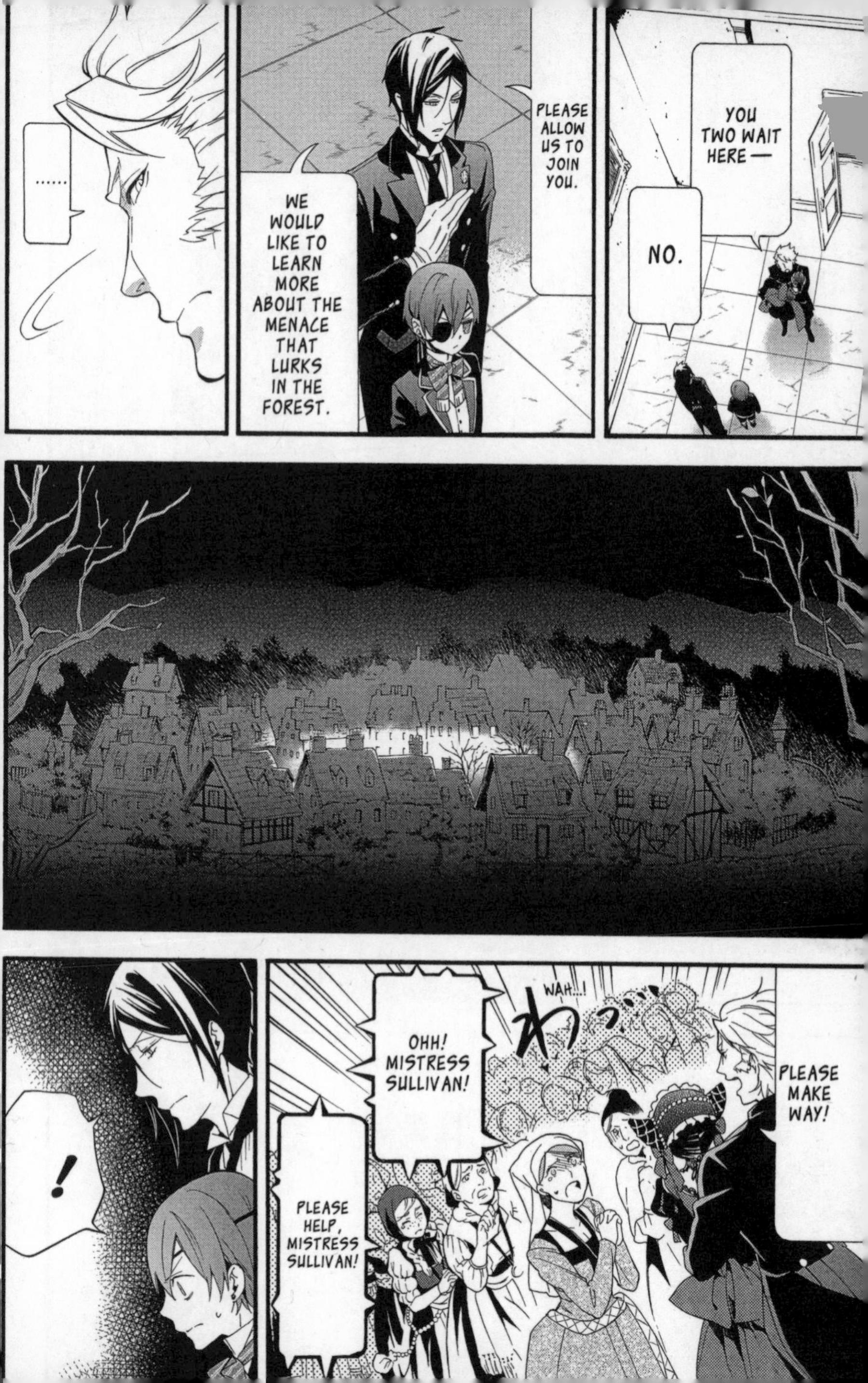
YOU TWO WAIT HERE—
NO.
PLEASE ALLOW US TO JOIN YOU.
WE WOULD LIKE TO LEARN MORE ABOUT THE MENACE THAT LURKS IN THE FOREST.
......
PLEASE MAKE WAY!
WAH...!
OHH! MISTRESS SULLIVAN!
PLEASE HELP, MISTRESS SULLIVAN!
!

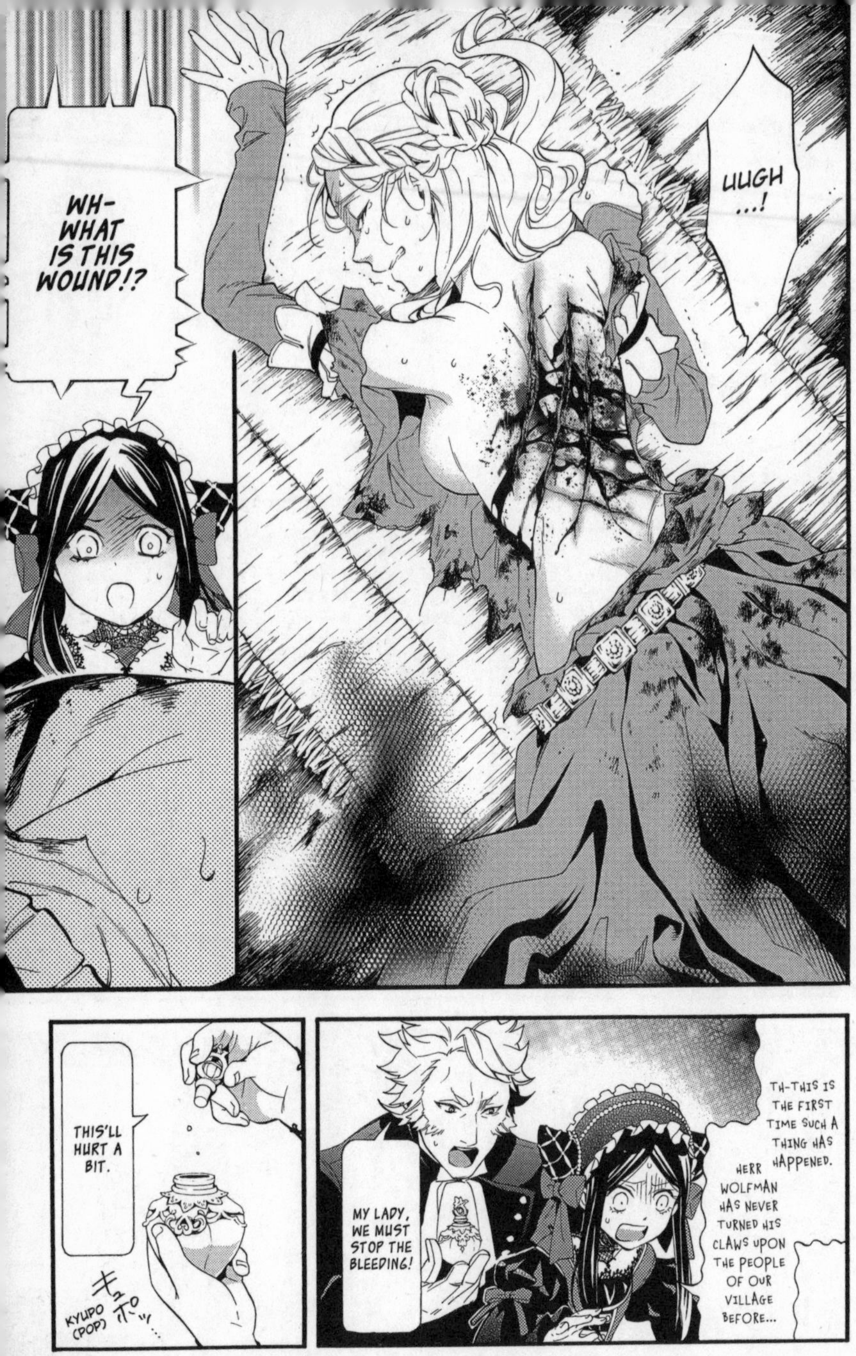
UUGH ...!
WH-WHAT IS THIS WOUND!?
TH-THIS IS THE FIRST TIME SUCH A THING HAS HAPPENED.
HERR WOLFMAN HAS NEVER TURNED HIS CLAWS UPON THE PEOPLE OF OUR VILLAGE BEFORE...
MY LADY, WE MUST STOP THE BLEEDING!
THIS'LL HURT A BIT.
KYUPO (POP)

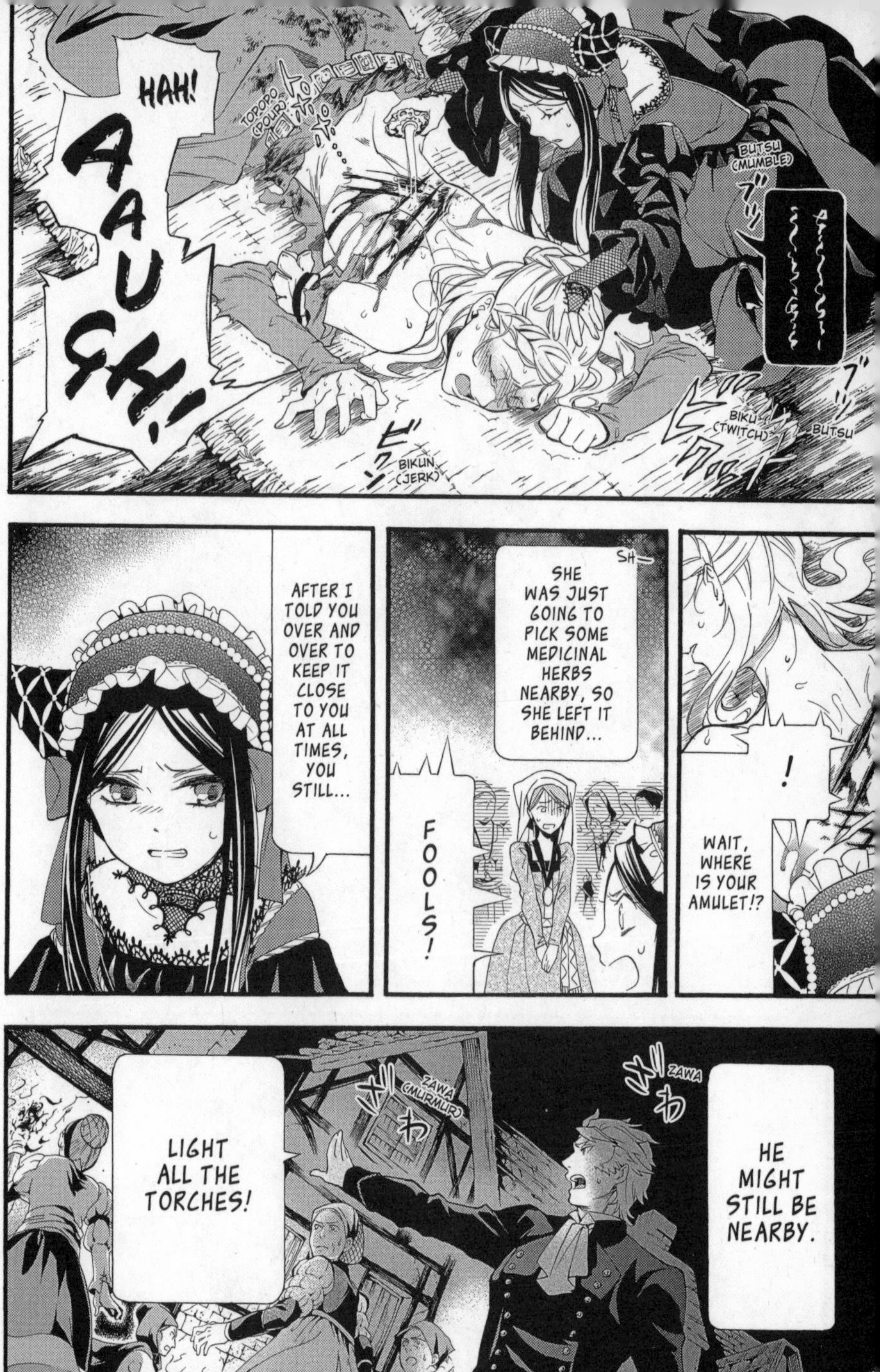
BUTSU (MUMBLE)
BIKU (TWITCH)
BUTSU
TOPOPO (POUR)
HAH!
AAUCHH!
BIKUN (JERK)
!
WAIT, WHERE IS YOUR AMULET!?
SH—
SHE WAS JUST GOING TO PICK SOME MEDICINAL HERBS NEARBY, SO SHE LEFT IT BEHIND...
FOOLS!
AFTER I TOLD YOU OVER AND OVER TO KEEP IT CLOSE TO YOU AT ALL TIMES, YOU STILL...
ZAWA
HE MIGHT STILL BE NEARBY.
ZAWA (MURMUR)
LIGHT ALL THE TORCHES!

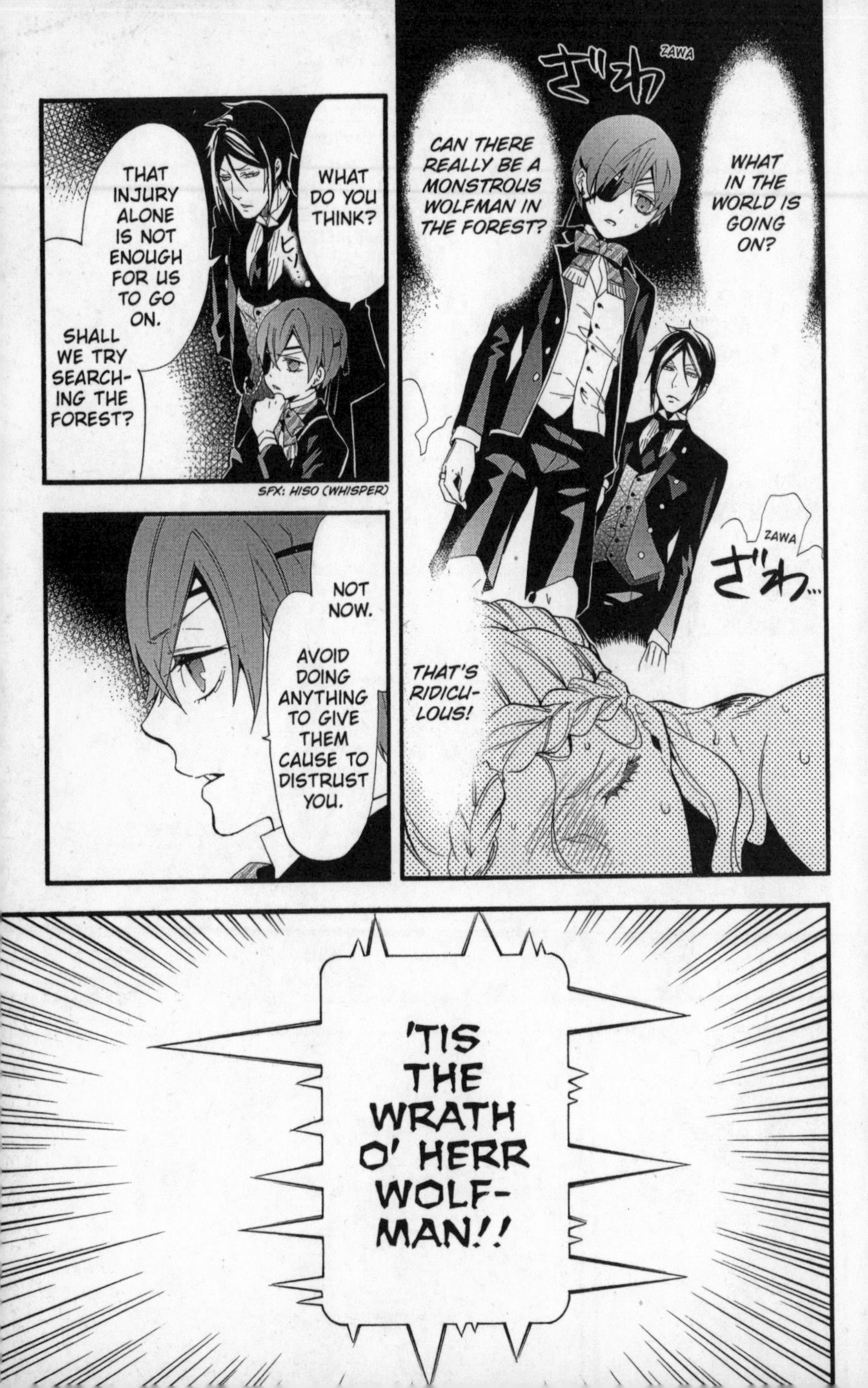
ざわ ZAWA
WHAT IN THE WORLD IS GOING ON?
CAN THERE REALLY BE A MONSTROUS WOLFMAN IN THE FOREST?
ZAWA ざわ…
THAT'S RIDICULOUS!
WHAT DO YOU THINK?
THAT INJURY ALONE IS NOT ENOUGH FOR US TO GO ON.
SHALL WE TRY SEARCHING THE FOREST?
SFX: HISO (WHISPER)
NOT NOW.
AVOID DOING ANYTHING TO GIVE THEM CAUSE TO DISTRUST YOU.
'TIS THE WRATH O' HERR WOLFMAN!!

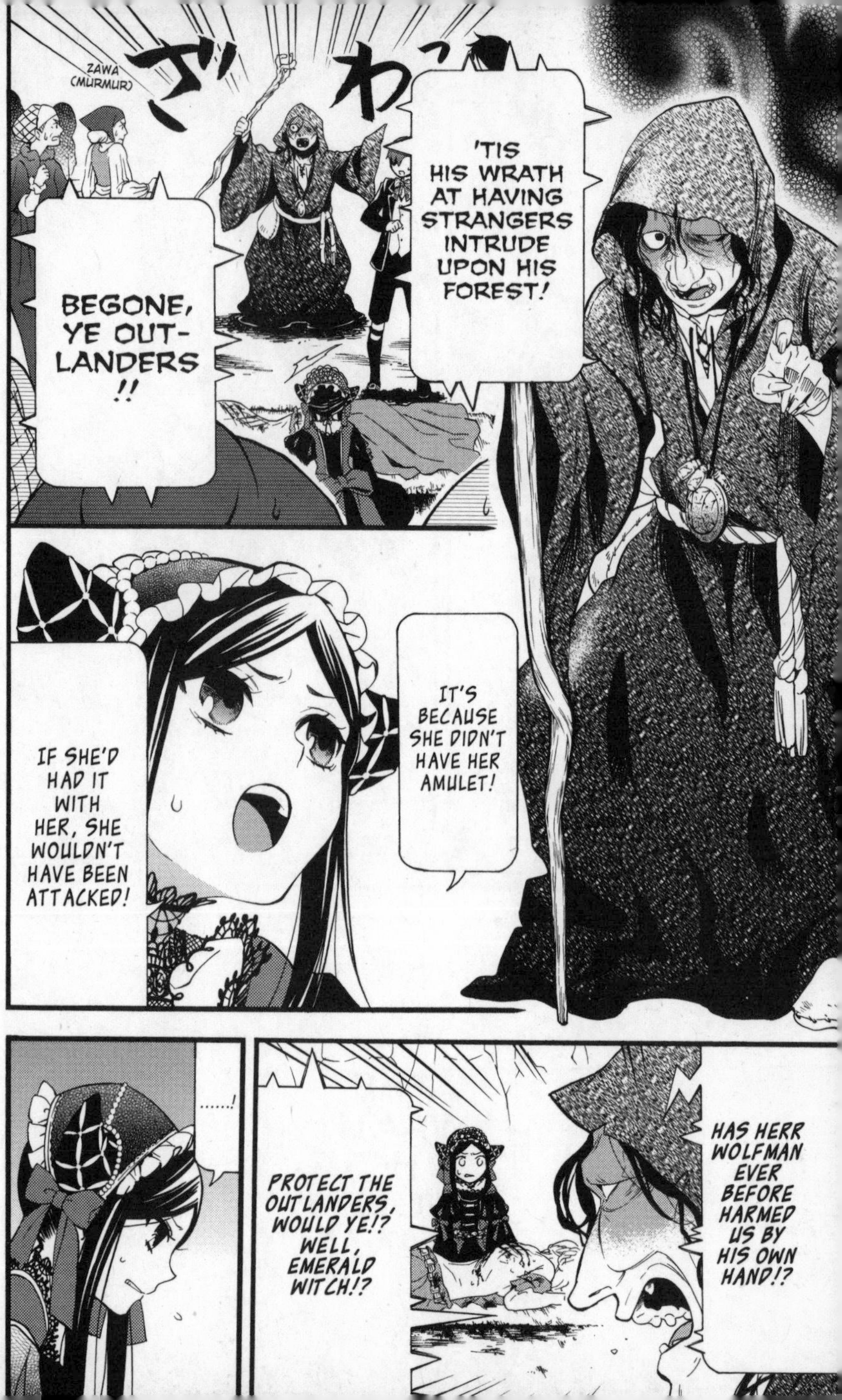
ざわっ
ZAWA (MURMUR)
BEGONE, YE OUT-LANDERS!!
'TIS HIS WRATH AT HAVING STRANGERS INTRUDE UPON HIS FOREST!
IT'S BECAUSE SHE DIDN'T HAVE HER AMULET!
IF SHE'D HAD IT WITH HER, SHE WOULDN'T HAVE BEEN ATTACKED!
HAS HERR WOLFMAN EVER BEFORE HARMED US BY HIS OWN HAND!?
PROTECT THE OUTLANDERS, WOULD YE!? WELL, EMERALD WITCH!?
......!

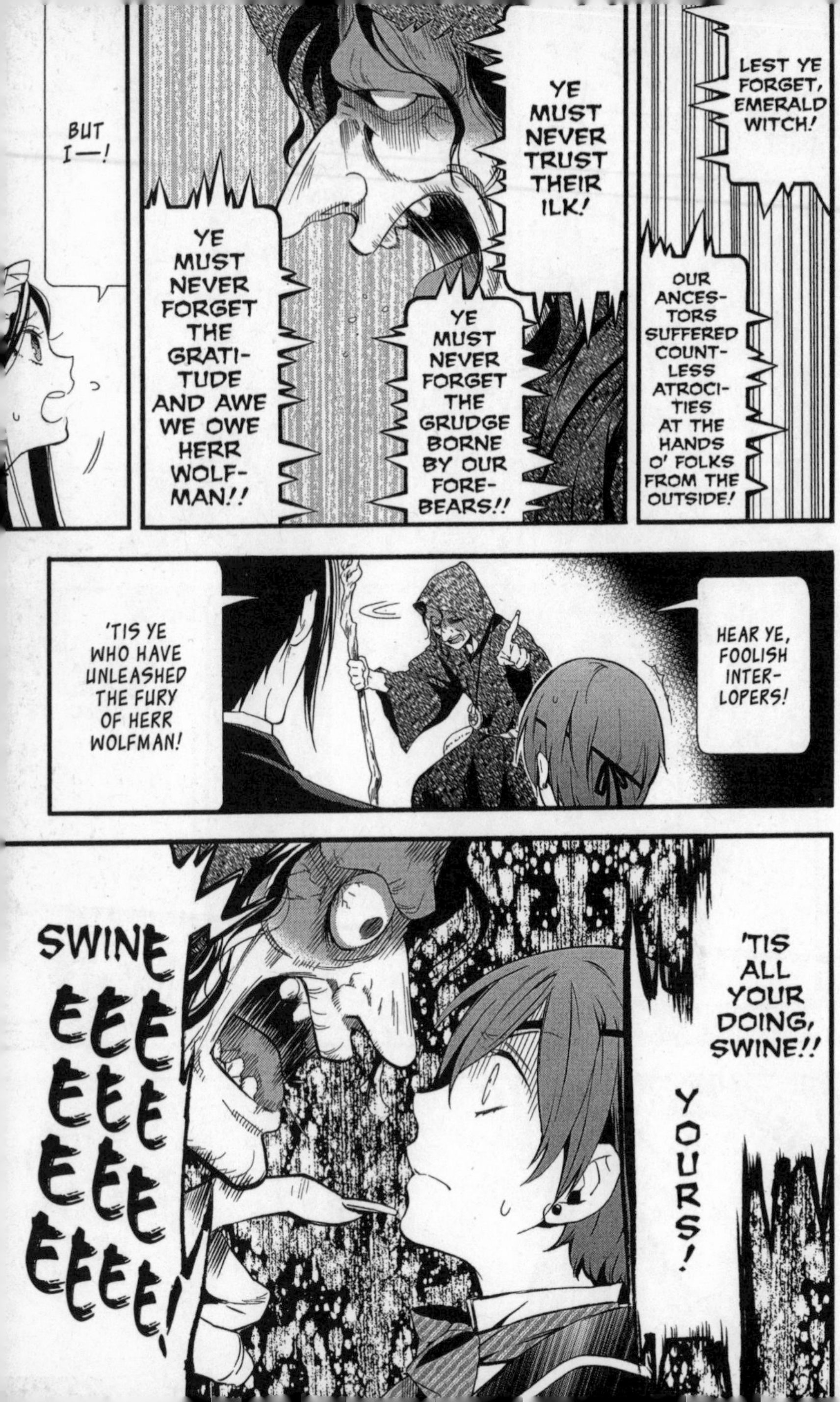

LEST YE FORGET, EMERALD WITCH!
OUR ANCESTORS SUFFERED COUNTLESS ATROCITIES AT THE HANDS O' FOLKS FROM THE OUTSIDE!
YE MUST NEVER TRUST THEIR ILK!
YE MUST NEVER FORGET THE GRUDGE BORNE BY OUR FOREBEARS!!
YE MUST NEVER FORGET THE GRATITUDE AND AWE WE OWE HERR WOLFMAN!!
BUT I—!
HEAR YE, FOOLISH INTERLOPERS!
'TIS YE WHO HAVE UNLEASHED THE FURY OF HERR WOLFMAN!
'TIS ALL YOUR DOING, SWINE!!
YOURS!
SWINEEEEEEEEEEEEEE!

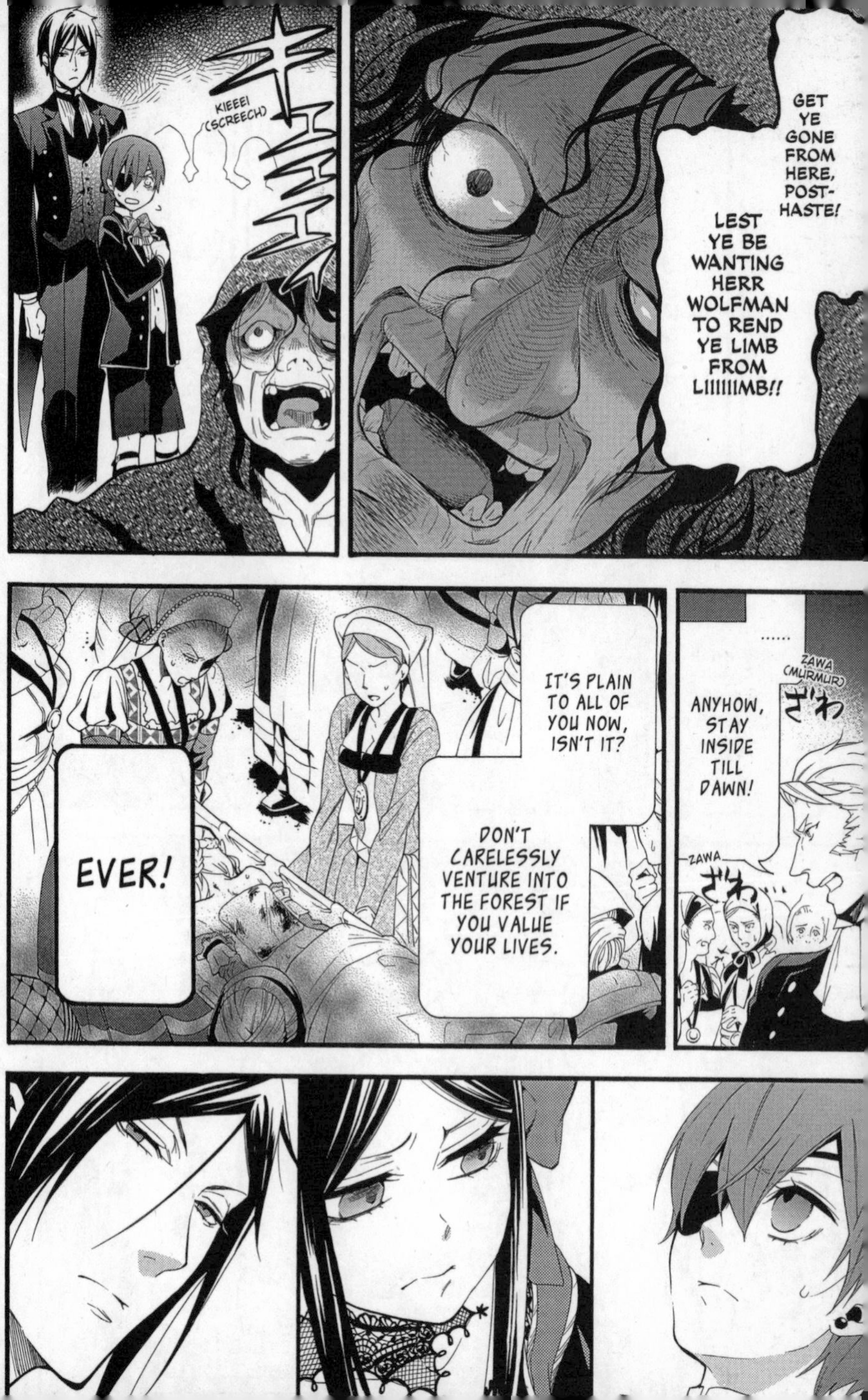
GET YE GONE FROM HERE, POST-HASTE!
LEST YE BE WANTING HERR WOLFMAN TO REND YE LIMB FROM LIIIIIIMB!!
KIEEEI (SCREECH)
......
ZAWA (MURMUR)
ざわ
ANYHOW, STAY INSIDE TILL DAWN!
ZAWA
ざわ…
IT'S PLAIN TO ALL OF YOU NOW, ISN'T IT?
DON'T CARELESSLY VENTURE INTO THE FOREST IF YOU VALUE YOUR LIVES.
EVER!

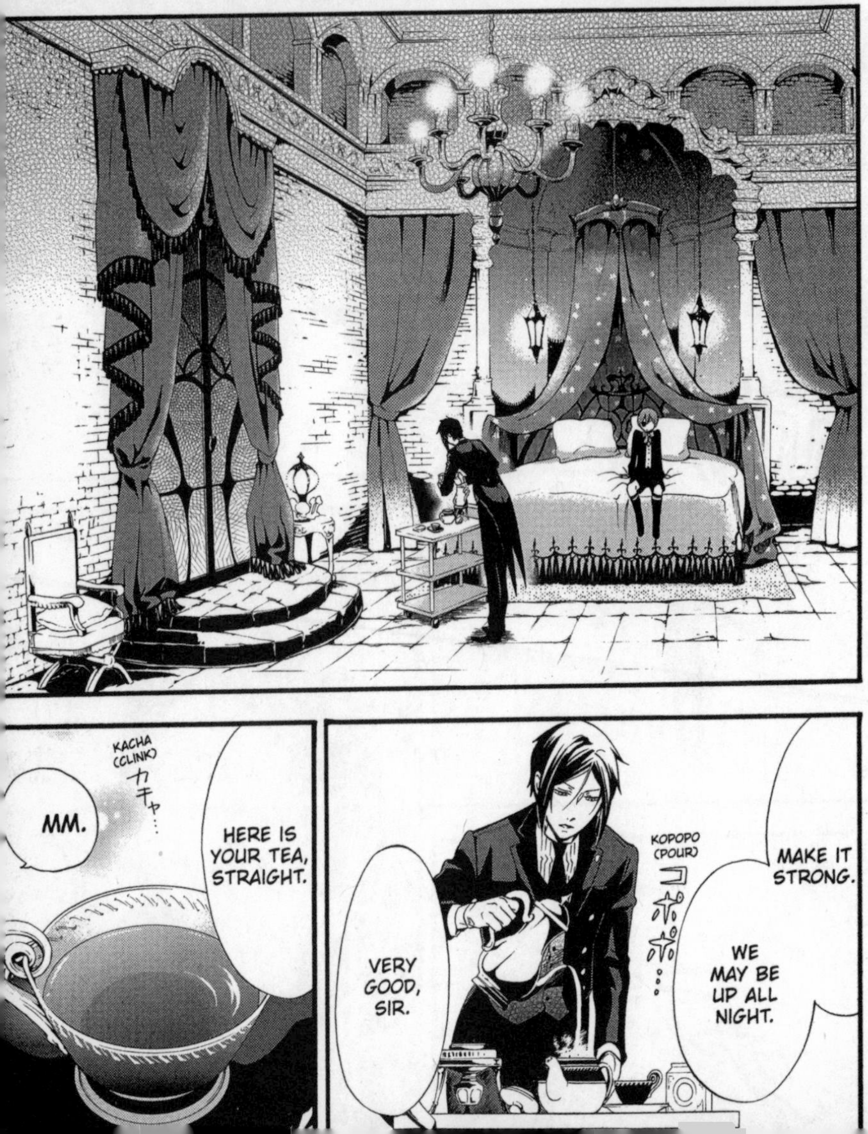
MAKE IT STRONG.
WE MAY BE UP ALL NIGHT.
KOPOPO (POUR)
コポポ…
VERY GOOD, SIR.
HERE IS YOUR TEA, STRAIGHT.
KACHA (CLINK)
カチャ…
MM.

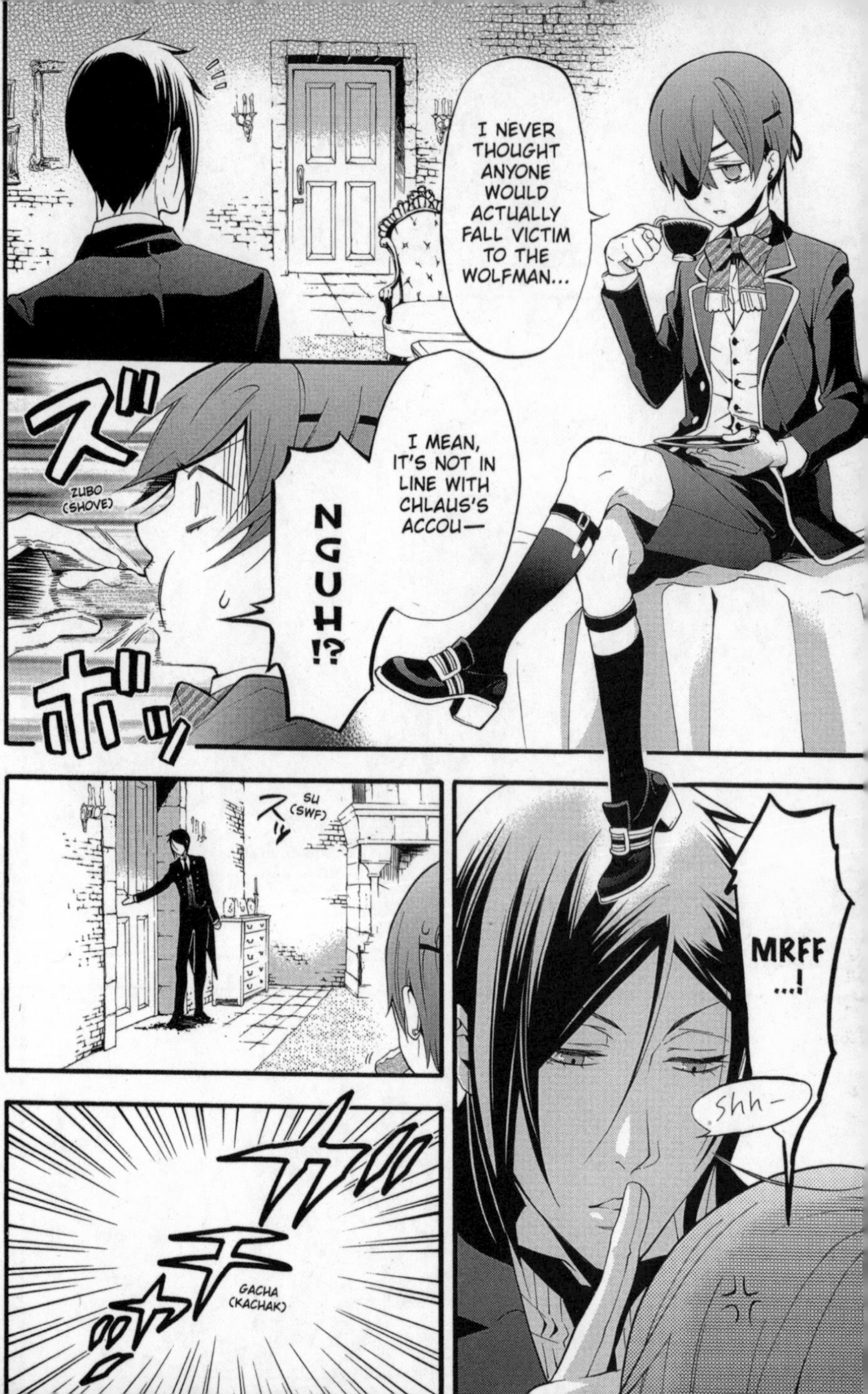
I NEVER THOUGHT ANYONE WOULD ACTUALLY FALL VICTIM TO THE WOLFMAN...
I MEAN, IT'S NOT IN LINE WITH CHLAUS'S ACCOU—
NGUH!?
ZUBO (SHOVE)
MRFF ...!
Shh-
SU (SWF)
GACHA (KACHAK)

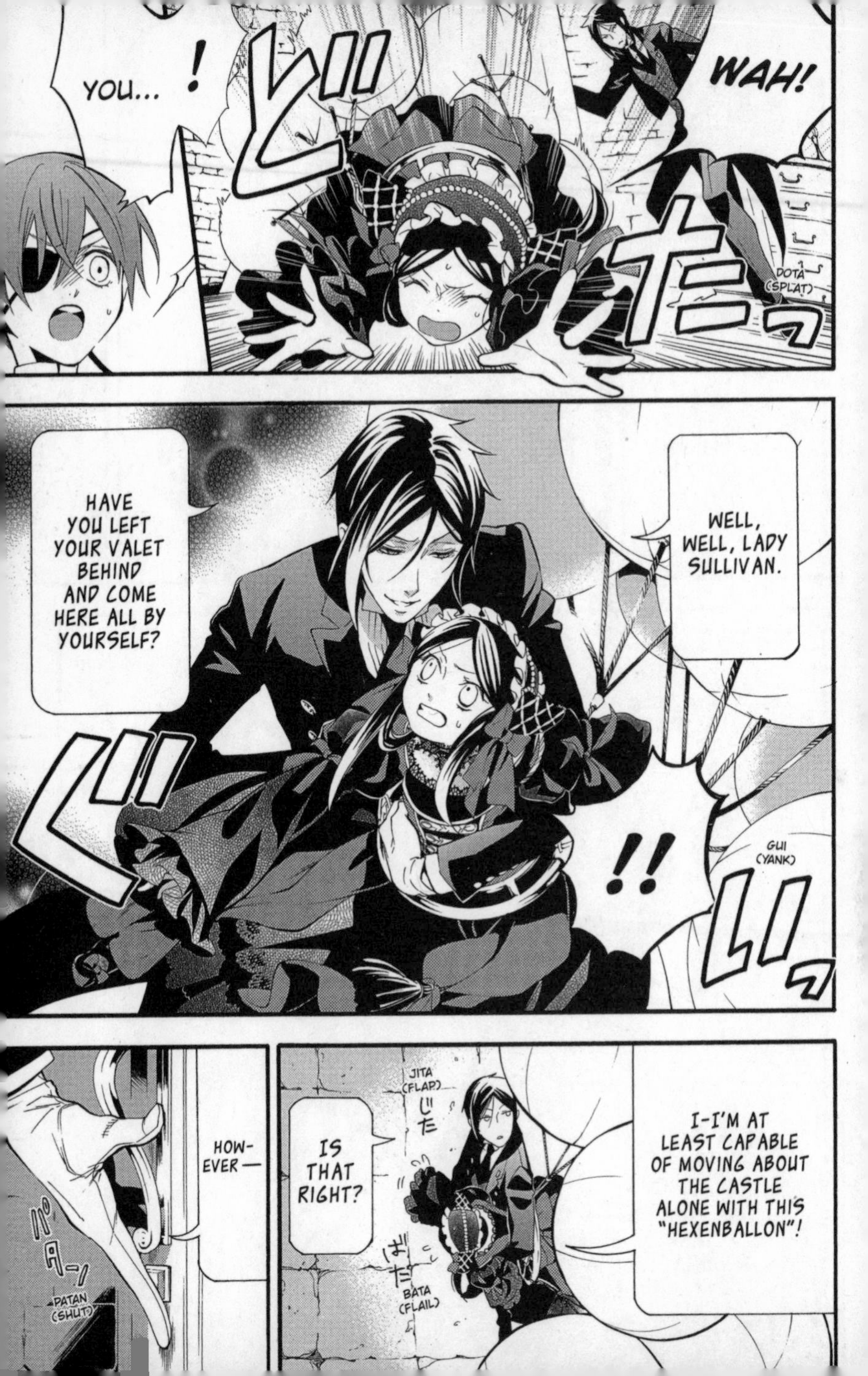
WAH!
DOTA (SPLAT)
YOU...
!
WELL, WELL, LADY SULLIVAN.
GUI (YANK)
!!
HAVE YOU LEFT YOUR VALET BEHIND AND COME HERE ALL BY YOURSELF?
I-I'M AT LEAST CAPABLE OF MOVING ABOUT THE CASTLE ALONE WITH THIS "HEXENBALLON"!
JITA (FLAP)
IS THAT RIGHT?
BATA (FLAIL)
HOW-EVER —
PATAN (SHUT)

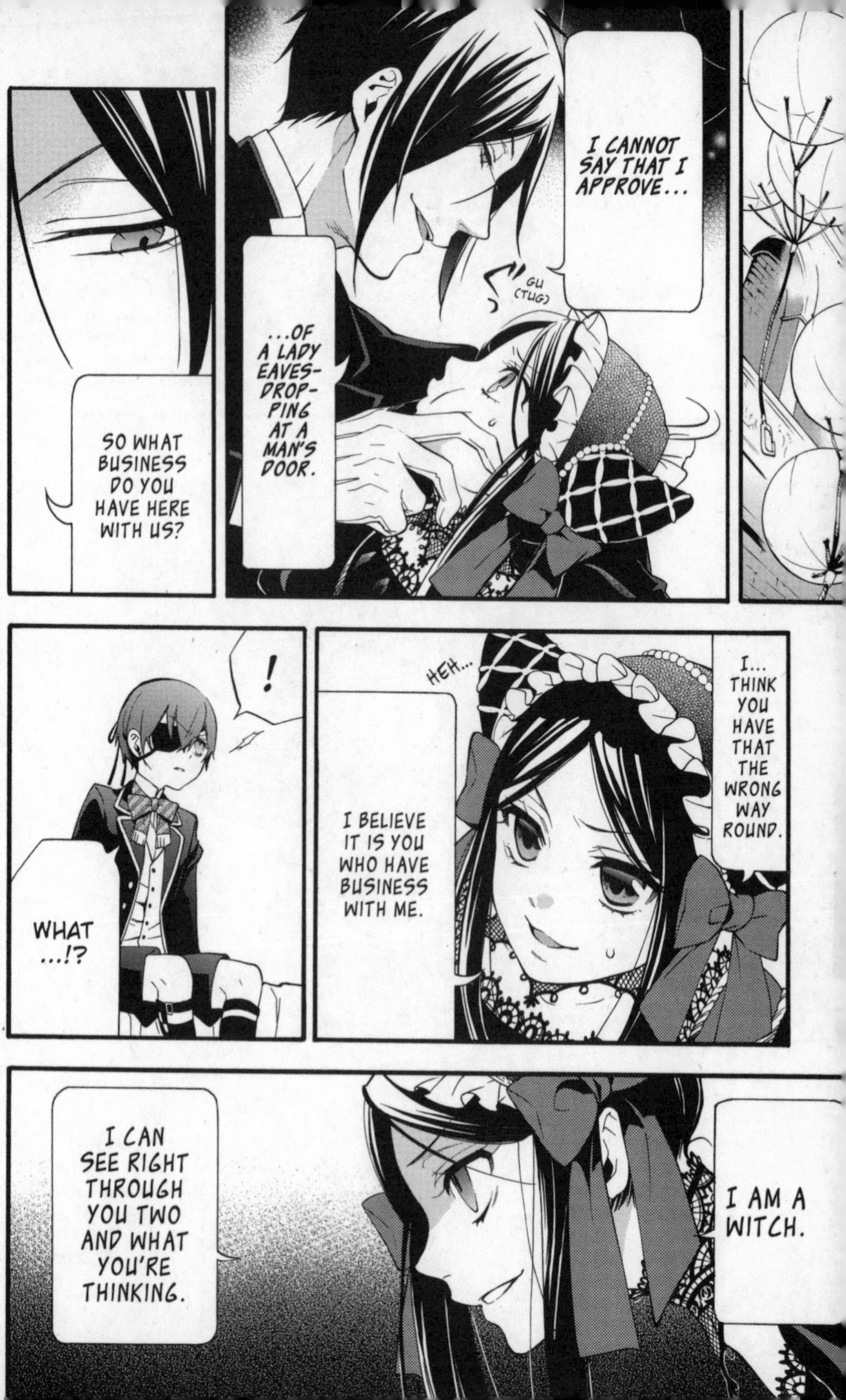
I CANNOT SAY THAT I APPROVE...
GU (TUG)
...OF A LADY EAVES-DROPPING AT A MAN'S DOOR.
SO WHAT BUSINESS DO YOU HAVE HERE WITH US?
I... THINK YOU HAVE THAT THE WRONG WAY ROUND.
HEH...
I BELIEVE IT IS YOU WHO HAVE BUSINESS WITH ME.
!
WHAT ...!?
I AM A WITCH.
I CAN SEE RIGHT THROUGH YOU TWO AND WHAT YOU'RE THINKING.

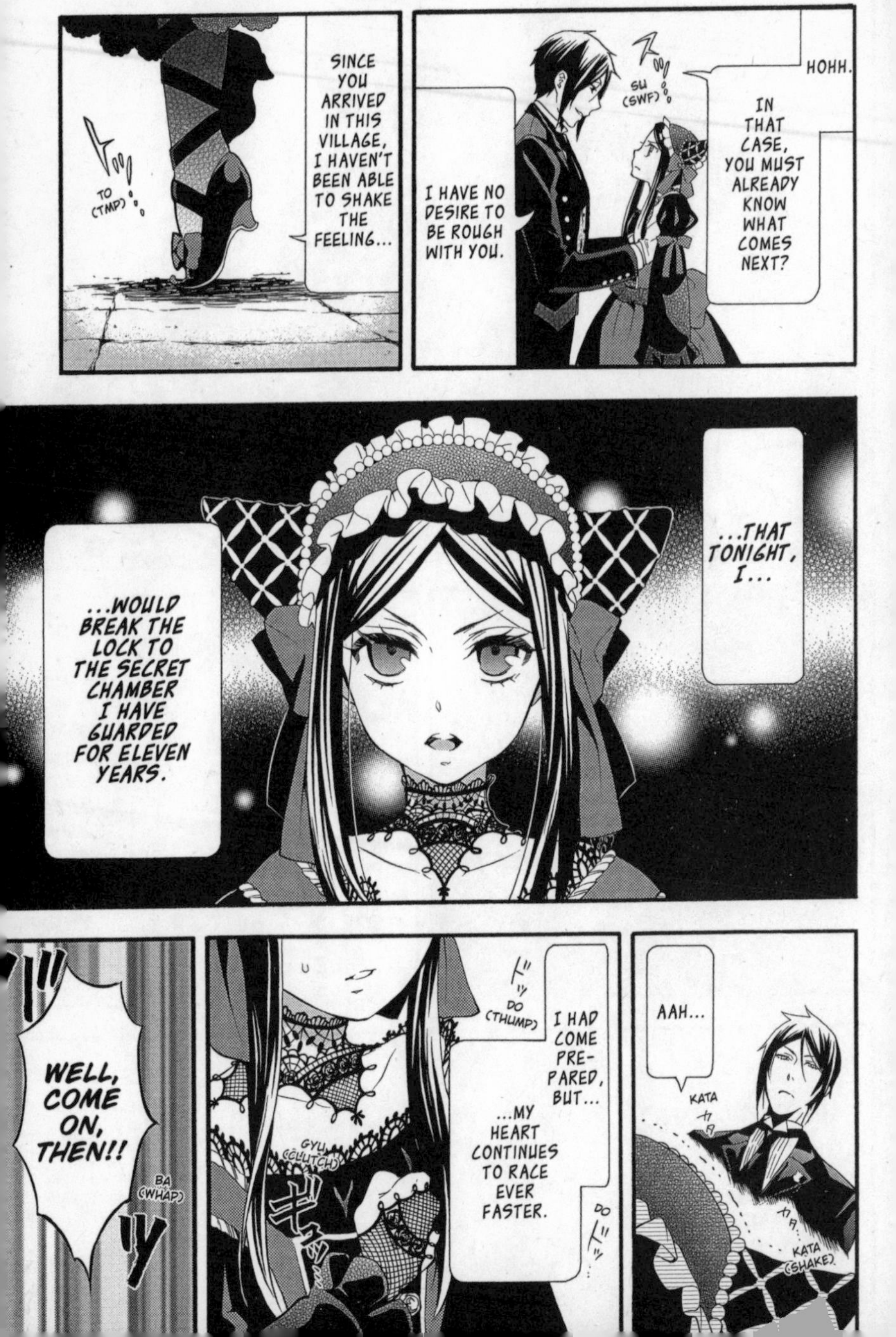
HOHH.
IN THAT CASE, YOU MUST ALREADY KNOW WHAT COMES NEXT?
SU (SWF)
I HAVE NO DESIRE TO BE ROUGH WITH YOU.
SINCE YOU ARRIVED IN THIS VILLAGE, I HAVEN'T BEEN ABLE TO SHAKE THE FEELING...
TO (TMP)
...THAT TONIGHT, I...
...WOULD BREAK THE LOCK TO THE SECRET CHAMBER I HAVE GUARDED FOR ELEVEN YEARS.
AAH...
KATA
KATA (SHAKE)
DO (THUMP)
I HAD COME PRE-PARED, BUT...
...MY HEART CONTINUES TO RACE EVER FASTER.
DO
GYU (CLUTCH)
WELL, COME ON, THEN!!
BA (WHAP)

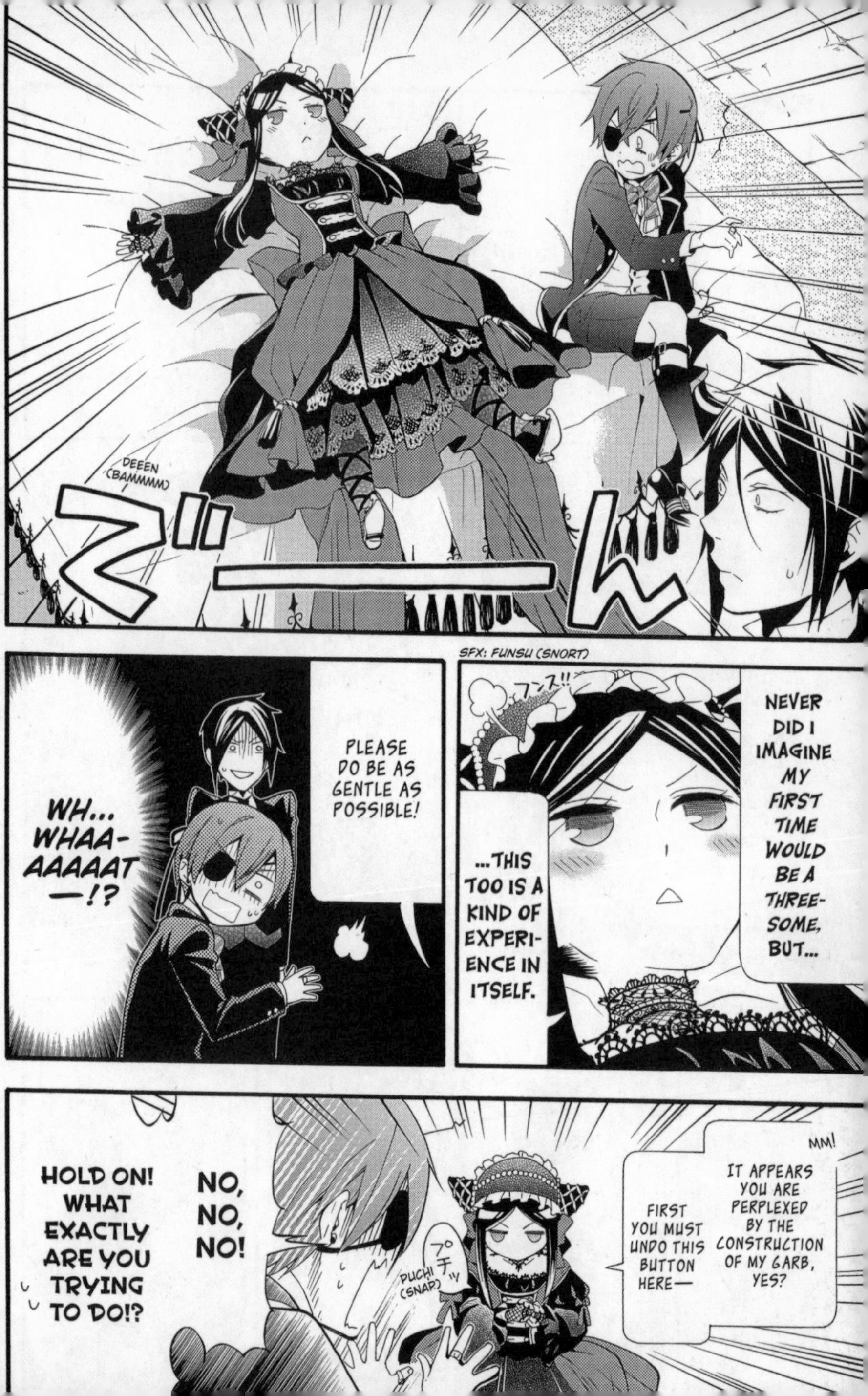
DEEEN (BAMMMMM)
ずーん
SFX: FUNSU (SNORT)
フンス!!
NEVER DID I IMAGINE MY FIRST TIME WOULD BE A THREESOME, BUT...
...THIS TOO IS A KIND OF EXPERIENCE IN ITSELF.
PLEASE DO BE AS GENTLE AS POSSIBLE!
WH... WHAA-AAAAAT—!?
MM!
IT APPEARS YOU ARE PERPLEXED BY THE CONSTRUCTION OF MY GARB, YES?
FIRST YOU MUST UNDO THIS BUTTON HERE—
プチッ
PUCHI (SNAP)
NO, NO, NO!
HOLD ON! WHAT EXACTLY ARE YOU TRYING TO DO!?

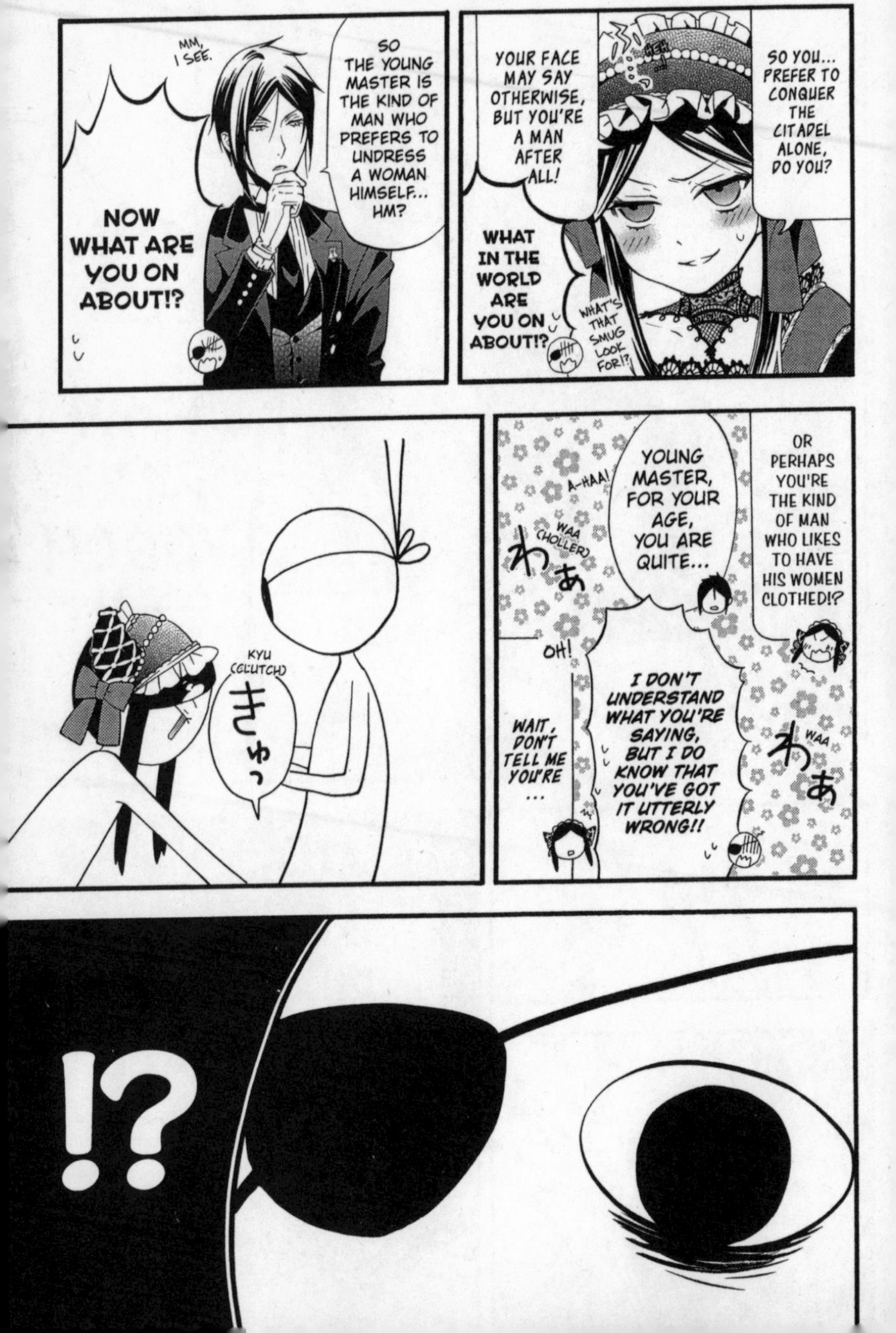
SO YOU... PREFER TO CONQUER THE CITADEL ALONE, DO YOU?
HEH...
YOUR FACE MAY SAY OTHERWISE, BUT YOU'RE A MAN AFTER ALL!
WHAT'S THAT SMUG LOOK FOR!?
WHAT IN THE WORLD ARE YOU ON ABOUT!?
SO THE YOUNG MASTER IS THE KIND OF MAN WHO PREFERS TO UNDRESS A WOMAN HIMSELF... HM?
MM, I SEE.
NOW WHAT ARE YOU ON ABOUT!?
OR PERHAPS YOU'RE THE KIND OF MAN WHO LIKES TO HAVE HIS WOMEN CLOTHED!?
わぁ WAA
YOUNG MASTER, FOR YOUR AGE, YOU ARE QUITE...
A-HAA!
わぁ WAA (HOLLER)
I DON'T UNDERSTAND WHAT YOU'RE SAYING, BUT I DO KNOW THAT YOU'VE GOT IT UTTERLY WRONG!!
OH!
WAIT, DON'T TELL ME YOU'RE ...
きゅっ KYU (CLUTCH)
!?

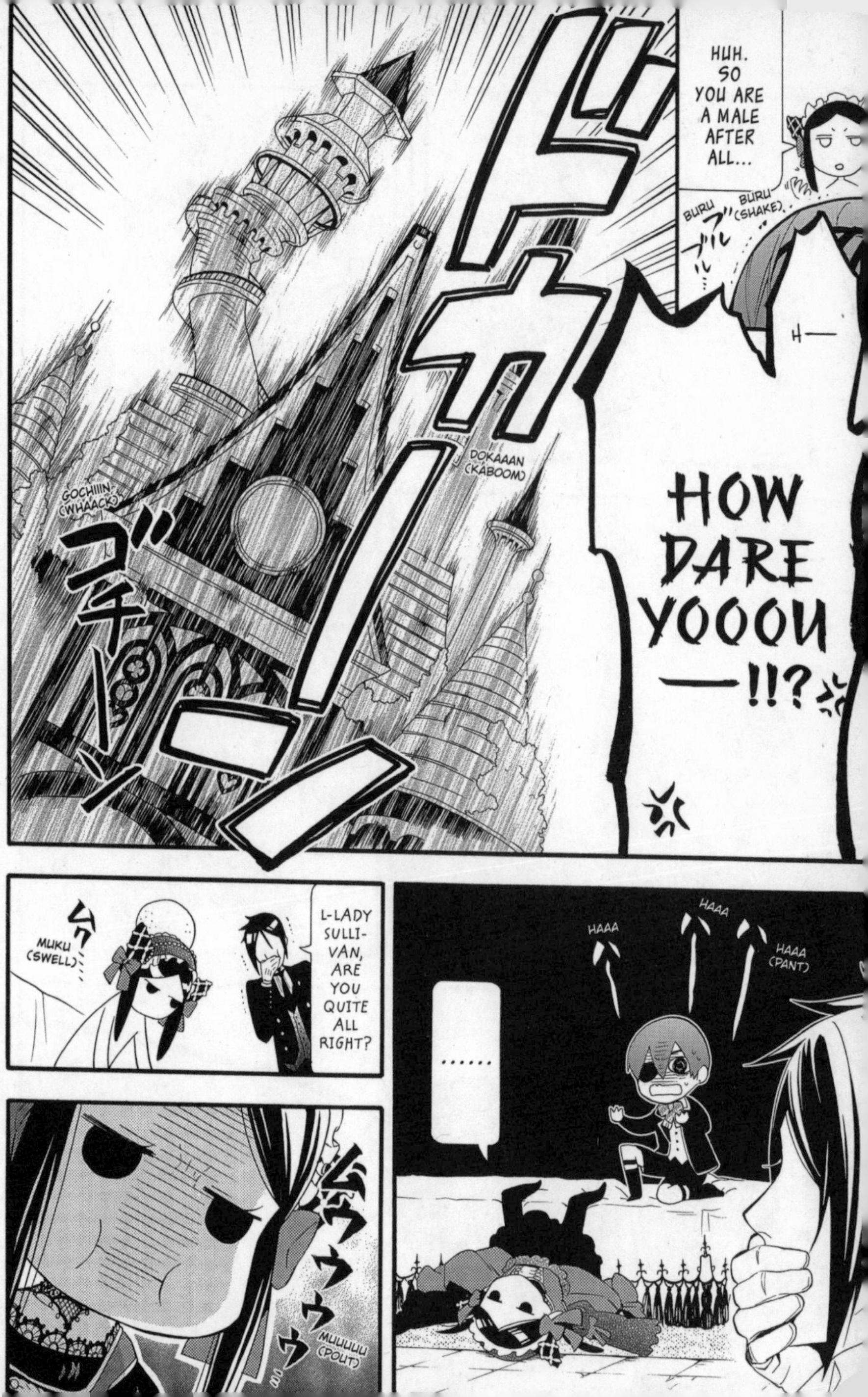
HUH. SO YOU ARE A MALE AFTER ALL...
BURU BURU (SHAKE)
H—
HOW DARE YOOOU—!!?
DOKAAAN (KABOOM)
GOCHIIN (WHAACK)
HAAA
HAAA
HAAA (PANT)
......
L-LADY SULLIVAN, ARE YOU QUITE ALL RIGHT?
MUKU (SWELL)
MUUUUU (POUT)

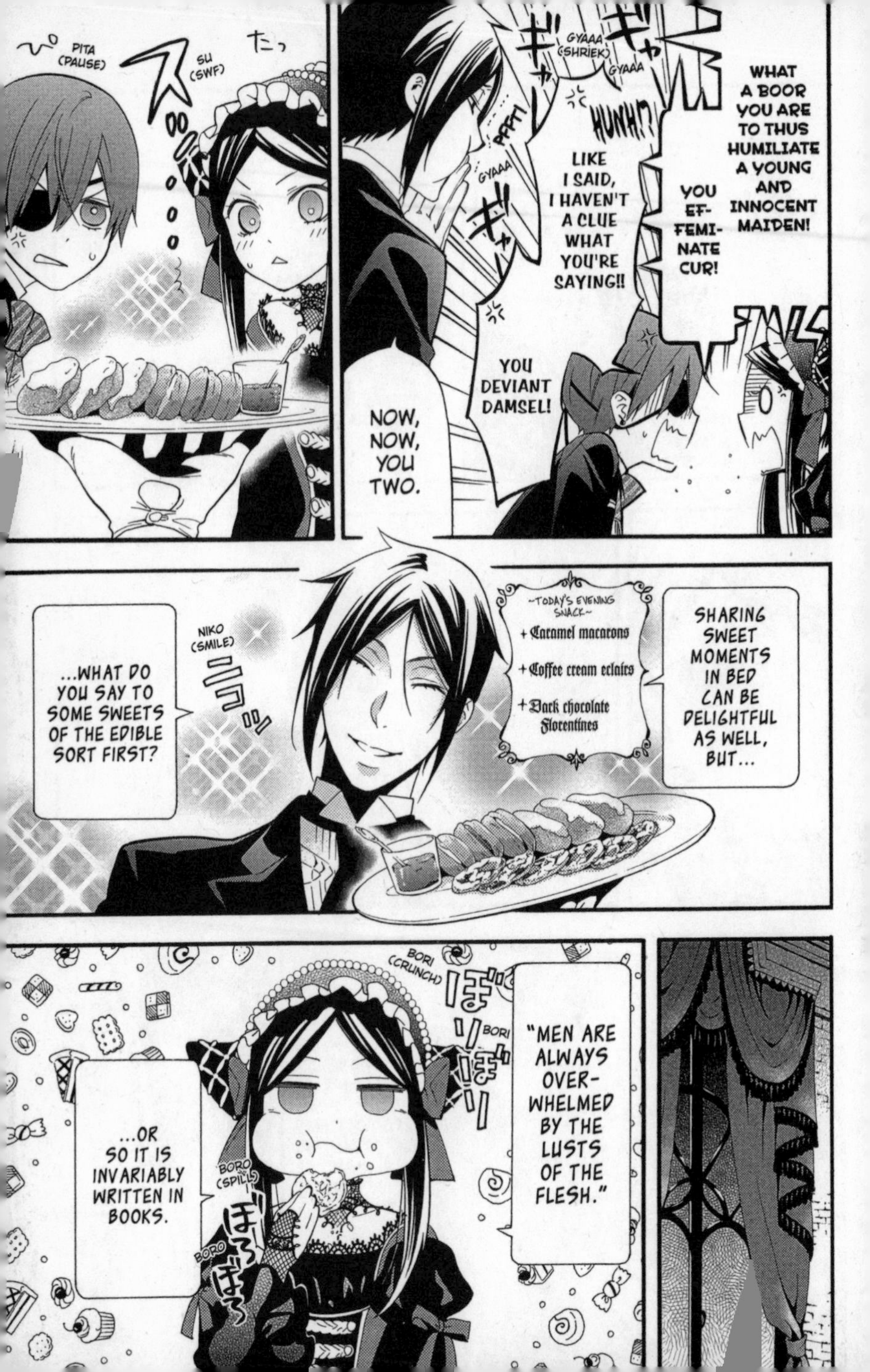
WHAT A BOOR YOU ARE TO THUS HUMILIATE A YOUNG AND INNOCENT MAIDEN!
YOU EF-FEMI-NATE CUR!
GYAAA (SHRIEK)
GYAAA
HUNH!?
LIKE I SAID, I HAVEN'T A CLUE WHAT YOU'RE SAYING!!
PFFT!
GYAAA
YOU DEVIANT DAMSEL!
NOW, NOW, YOU TWO.
SU (SWF)
PITA (PAUSE)
SHARING SWEET MOMENTS IN BED CAN BE DELIGHTFUL AS WELL, BUT...
~TODAY'S EVENING SNACK~
+ Caramel macarons
+ Coffee cream eclairs
+ Dark chocolate Florentines
NIKO (SMILE)
...WHAT DO YOU SAY TO SOME SWEETS OF THE EDIBLE SORT FIRST?
BORI (CRUNCH)
BORI
"MEN ARE ALWAYS OVER-WHELMED BY THE LUSTS OF THE FLESH."
...OR SO IT IS INVARIABLY WRITTEN IN BOOKS.
BORO (SPILL)
BORO

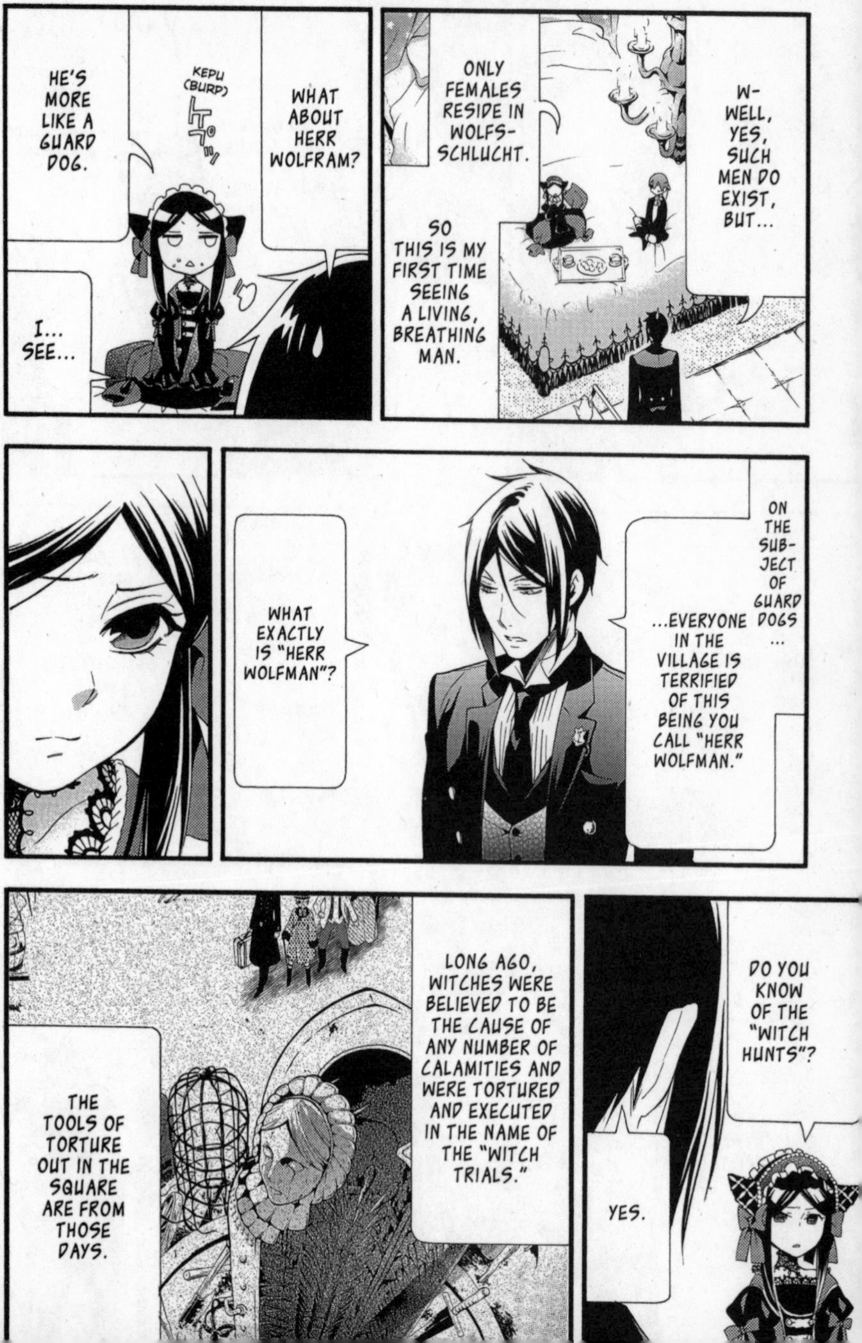
W-WELL, YES, SUCH MEN DO EXIST, BUT...
ONLY FEMALES RESIDE IN WOLFSSCHLUCHT.
SO THIS IS MY FIRST TIME SEEING A LIVING, BREATHING MAN.
WHAT ABOUT HERR WOLFRAM?
KEPU (BURP)
HE'S MORE LIKE A GUARD DOG.
I... SEE...
ON THE SUBJECT OF GUARD DOGS ...
...EVERYONE IN THE VILLAGE IS TERRIFIED OF THIS BEING YOU CALL "HERR WOLFMAN."
WHAT EXACTLY IS "HERR WOLFMAN"?
DO YOU KNOW OF THE "WITCH HUNTS"?
YES.
LONG AGO, WITCHES WERE BELIEVED TO BE THE CAUSE OF ANY NUMBER OF CALAMITIES AND WERE TORTURED AND EXECUTED IN THE NAME OF THE "WITCH TRIALS."
THE TOOLS OF TORTURE OUT IN THE SQUARE ARE FROM THOSE DAYS.

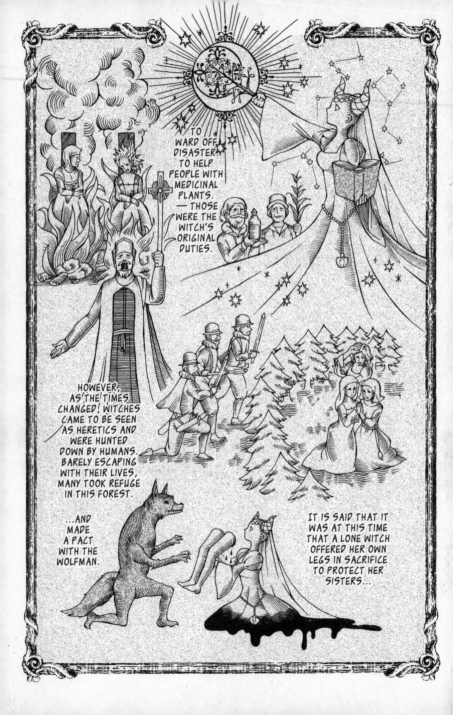

TO WARD OFF DISASTER. TO HELP PEOPLE WITH MEDICINAL PLANTS. —THOSE WERE THE WITCH'S ORIGINAL DUTIES.

HOWEVER, AS THE TIMES CHANGED, WITCHES CAME TO BE SEEN AS HERETICS AND WERE HUNTED DOWN BY HUMANS. BARELY ESCAPING WITH THEIR LIVES, MANY TOOK REFUGE IN THIS FOREST.

...AND MADE A PACT WITH THE WOLFMAN.

IT IS SAID THAT IT WAS AT THIS TIME THAT A LONE WITCH OFFERED HER OWN LEGS IN SACRIFICE TO PROTECT HER SISTERS...

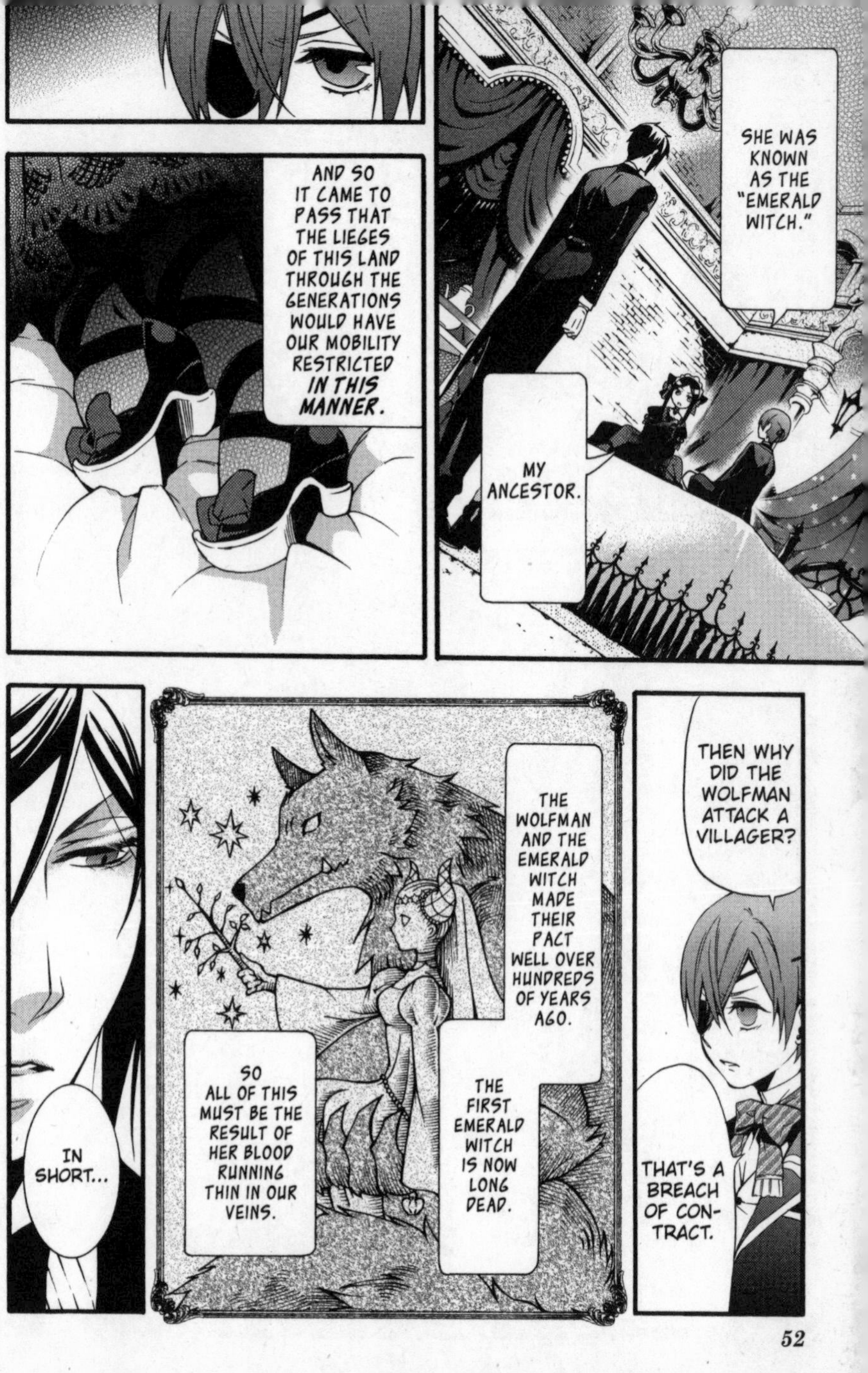
SHE WAS KNOWN AS THE "EMERALD WITCH."
MY ANCESTOR.
AND SO IT CAME TO PASS THAT THE LIEGES OF THIS LAND THROUGH THE GENERATIONS WOULD HAVE OUR MOBILITY RESTRICTED *IN THIS MANNER*.
THEN WHY DID THE WOLFMAN ATTACK A VILLAGER?
THAT'S A BREACH OF CONTRACT.
THE WOLFMAN AND THE EMERALD WITCH MADE THEIR PACT WELL OVER HUNDREDS OF YEARS AGO.
THE FIRST EMERALD WITCH IS NOW LONG DEAD.
SO ALL OF THIS MUST BE THE RESULT OF HER BLOOD RUNNING THIN IN OUR VEINS.
IN SHORT...

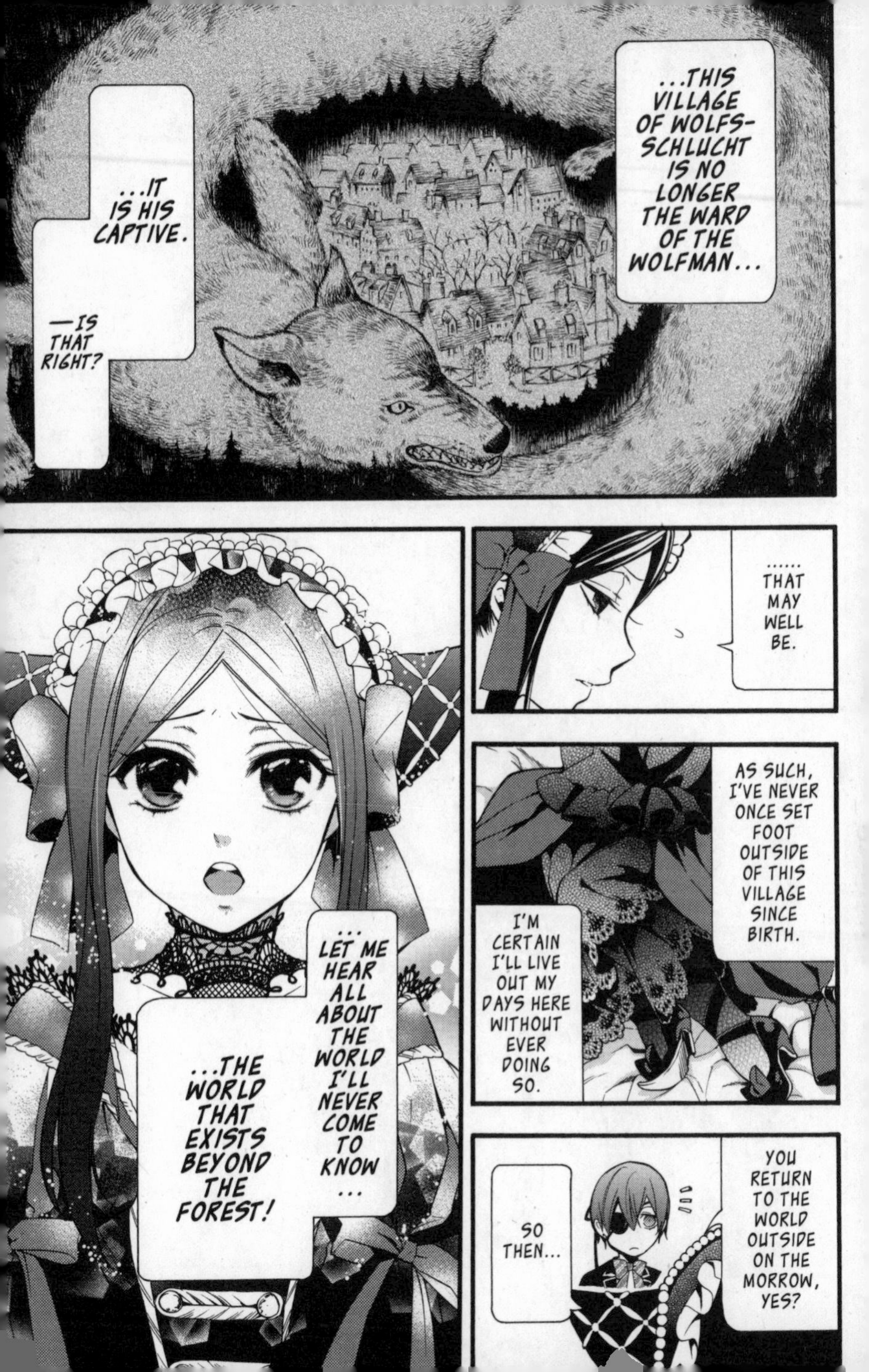
...THIS VILLAGE OF WOLFS-SCHLUCHT IS NO LONGER THE WARD OF THE WOLFMAN...
...IT IS HIS CAPTIVE.
—IS THAT RIGHT?
...... THAT MAY WELL BE.
AS SUCH, I'VE NEVER ONCE SET FOOT OUTSIDE OF THIS VILLAGE SINCE BIRTH.
I'M CERTAIN I'LL LIVE OUT MY DAYS HERE WITHOUT EVER DOING SO.
YOU RETURN TO THE WORLD OUTSIDE ON THE MORROW, YES?
SO THEN...
...LET ME HEAR ALL ABOUT THE WORLD I'LL NEVER COME TO KNOW...
...THE WORLD THAT EXISTS BEYOND THE FOREST!

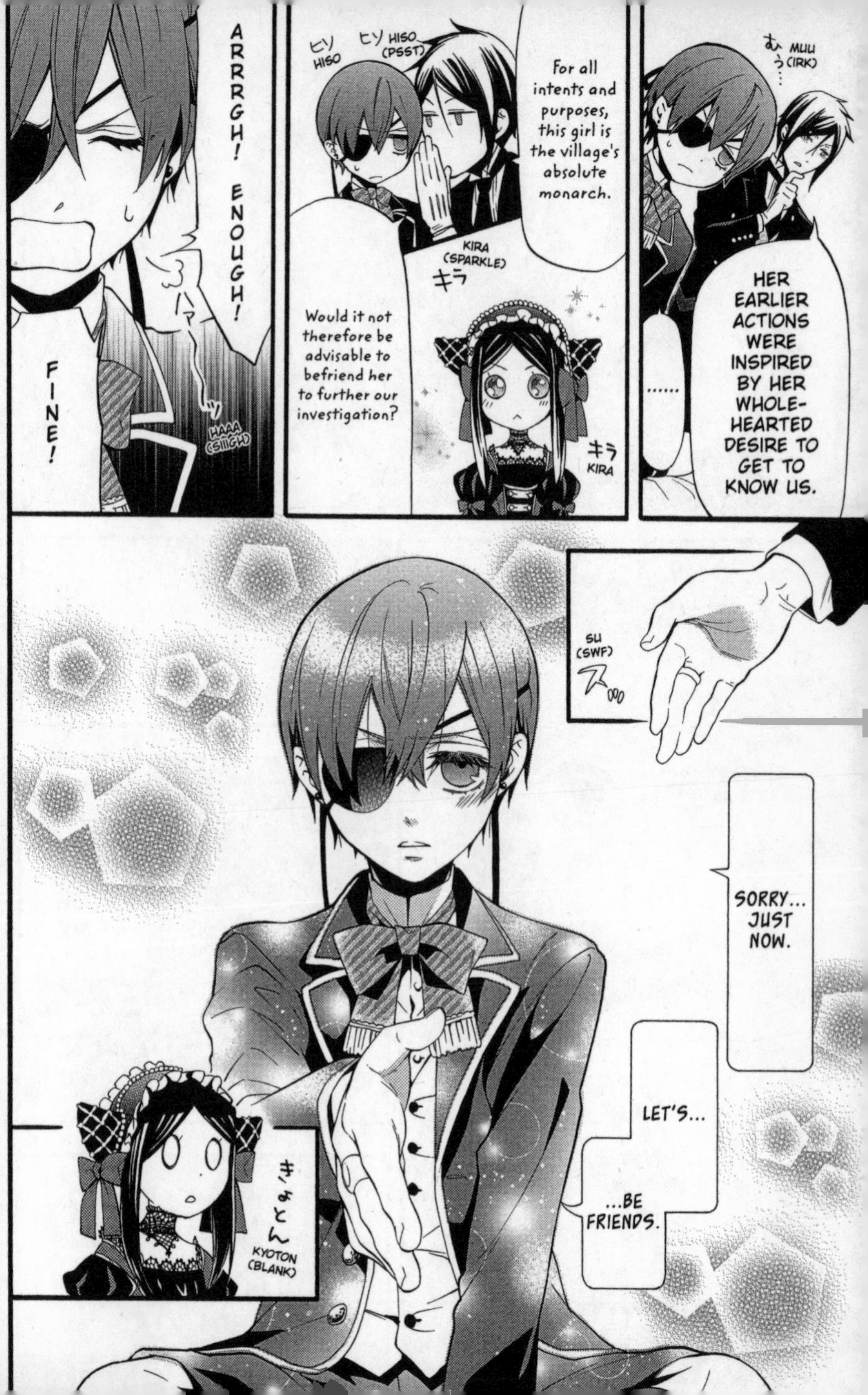

むぅ… MUU (IRK)
HER EARLIER ACTIONS WERE INSPIRED BY HER WHOLE-HEARTED DESIRE TO GET TO KNOW US.
......
ヒソ HISO
ヒソ HISO (PSST)
For all intents and purposes, this girl is the village's absolute monarch.
キラ KIRA (SPARKLE)
Would it not therefore be advisable to befriend her to further our investigation?
キラ KIRA
ARRRGH! ENOUGH!
ハァ HAAA (SIIIGH)
FINE!
ス SU (SWF)
SORRY... JUST NOW.
LET'S...
...BE FRIENDS.
きょとん KYOTON (BLANK)

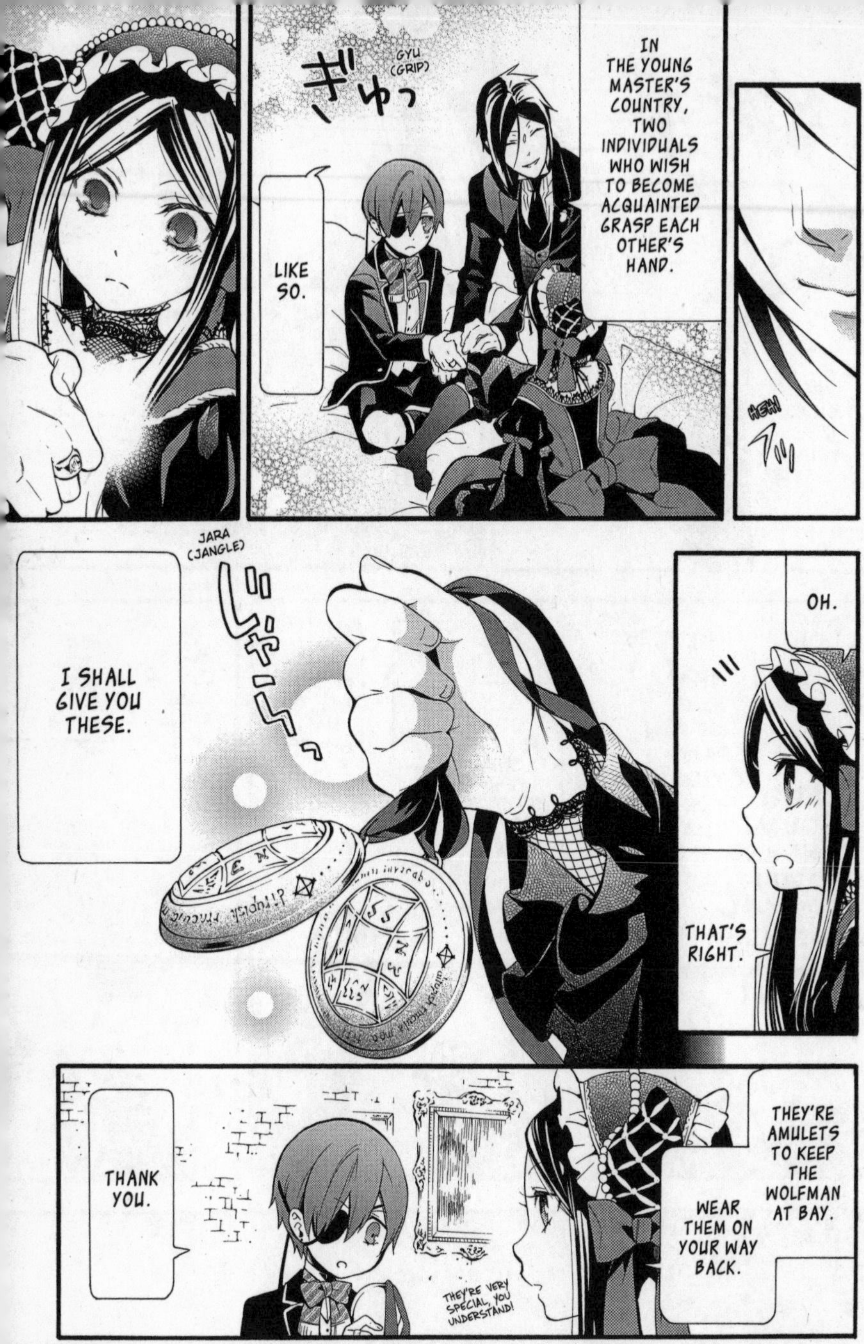
HEH!
IN THE YOUNG MASTER'S COUNTRY, TWO INDIVIDUALS WHO WISH TO BECOME ACQUAINTED GRASP EACH OTHER'S HAND.
ぎゅっ
GYU (GRIP)
LIKE SO.
OH.
THAT'S RIGHT.
じゃらっ
JARA (JANGLE)
I SHALL GIVE YOU THESE.
THEY'RE AMULETS TO KEEP THE WOLFMAN AT BAY.
WEAR THEM ON YOUR WAY BACK.
THEY'RE VERY SPECIAL, YOU UNDERSTAND!
THANK YOU.

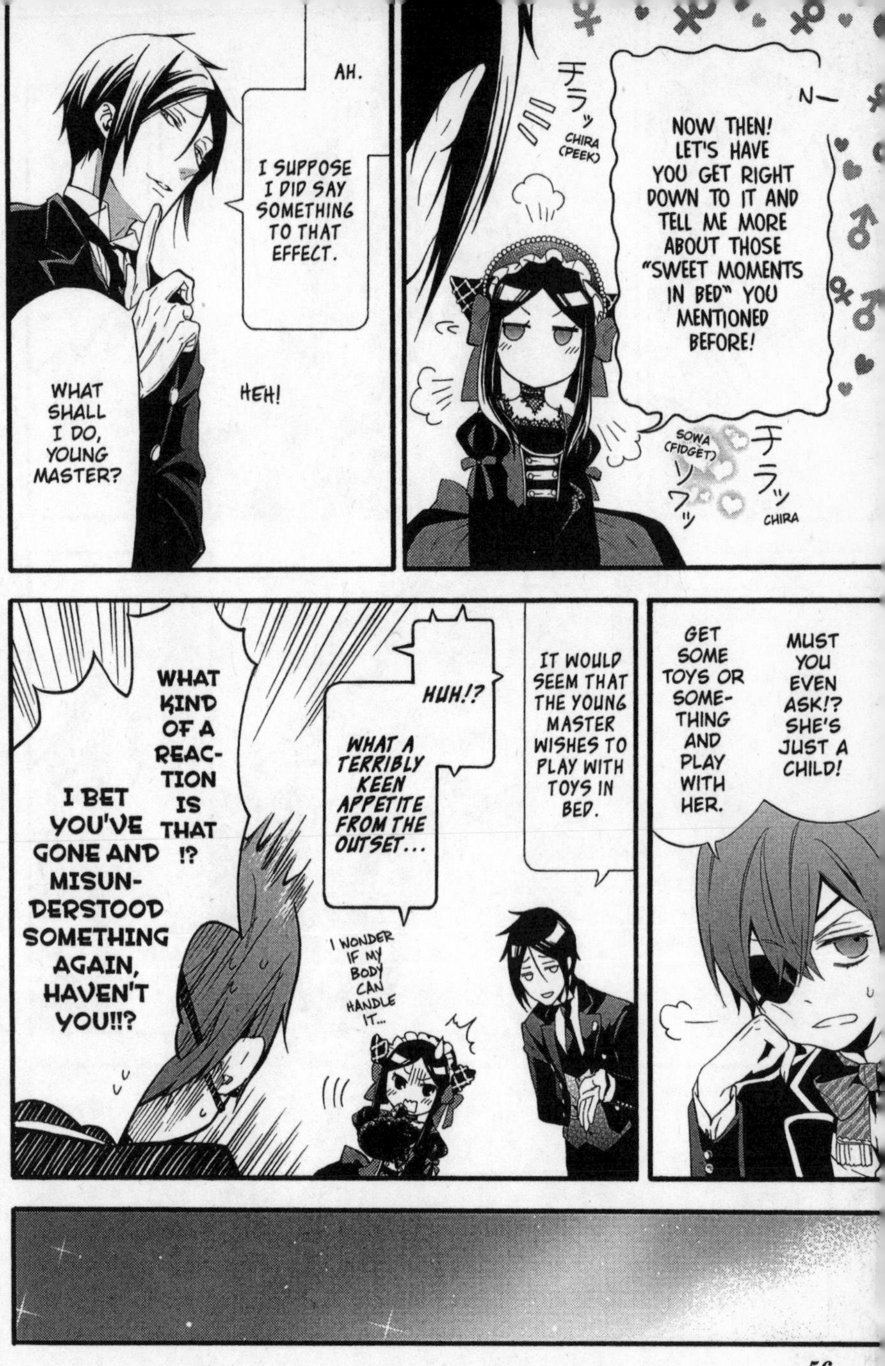
N—
NOW THEN! LET'S HAVE YOU GET RIGHT DOWN TO IT AND TELL ME MORE ABOUT THOSE "SWEET MOMENTS IN BED" YOU MENTIONED BEFORE!
チラッ
CHIRA (PEEK)
チラッ
CHIRA
ソワッ
SOWA (FIDGET)
AH.
I SUPPOSE I DID SAY SOMETHING TO THAT EFFECT.
HEH!
WHAT SHALL I DO, YOUNG MASTER?
MUST YOU EVEN ASK!? SHE'S JUST A CHILD!
GET SOME TOYS OR SOMETHING AND PLAY WITH HER.
IT WOULD SEEM THAT THE YOUNG MASTER WISHES TO PLAY WITH TOYS IN BED.
HUH!?
WHAT A TERRIBLY KEEN APPETITE FROM THE OUTSET...
I WONDER IF MY BODY CAN HANDLE IT...
WHAT KIND OF A REACTION IS THAT!?
I BET YOU'VE GONE AND MISUNDERSTOOD SOMETHING AGAIN, HAVEN'T YOU!!?

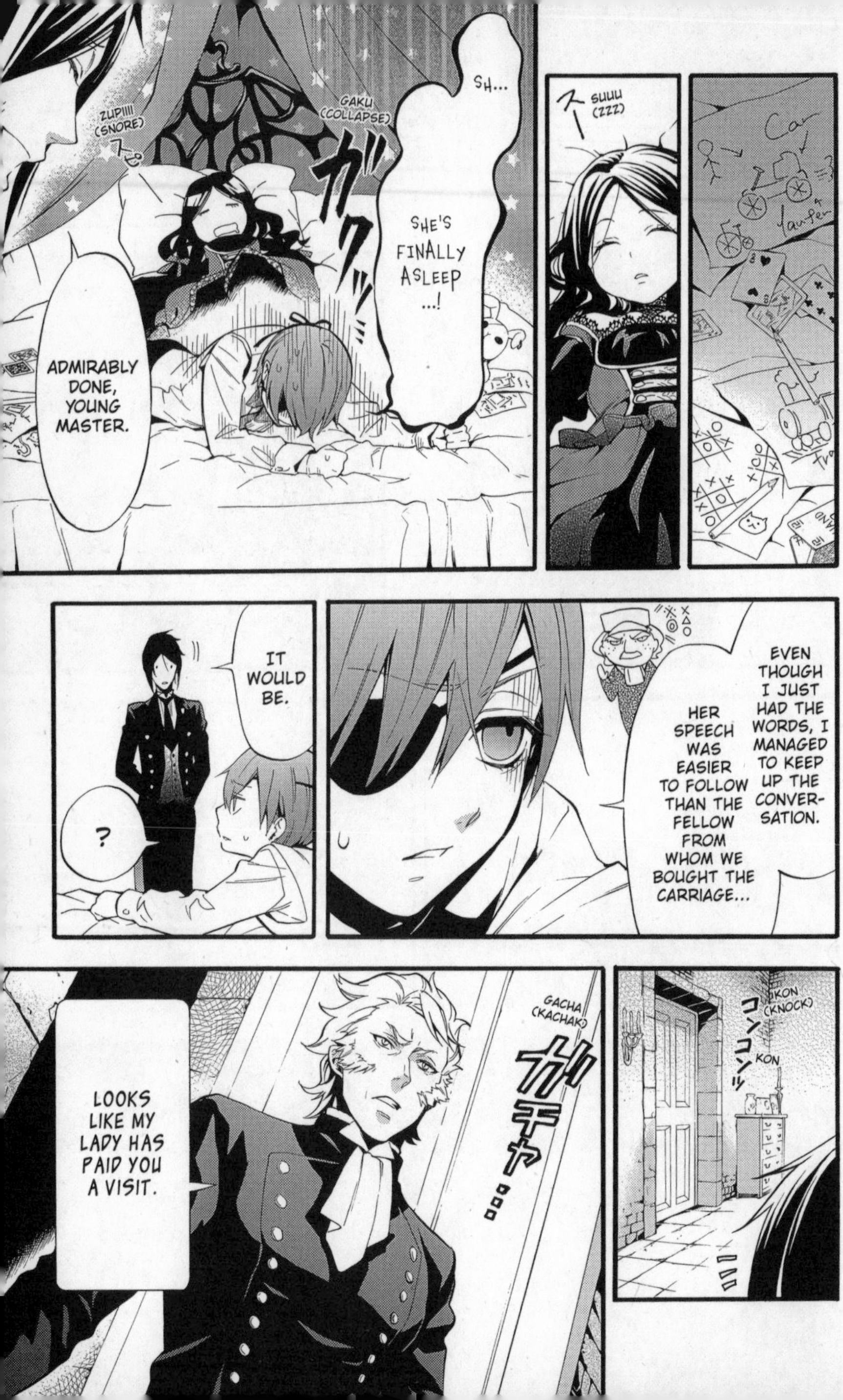
SUUU (ZZZ)
SH...
GAKU (COLLAPSE)
SHE'S FINALLY ASLEEP ...!
ZUPIIII (SNORE)
ADMIRABLY DONE, YOUNG MASTER.
EVEN THOUGH I JUST HAD THE WORDS, I MANAGED TO KEEP UP THE CONVERSATION.
HER SPEECH WAS EASIER TO FOLLOW THAN THE FELLOW FROM WHOM WE BOUGHT THE CARRIAGE...
IT WOULD BE.
?
KON (KNOCK)
KON
GACHA (KACHAK)
LOOKS LIKE MY LADY HAS PAID YOU A VISIT.

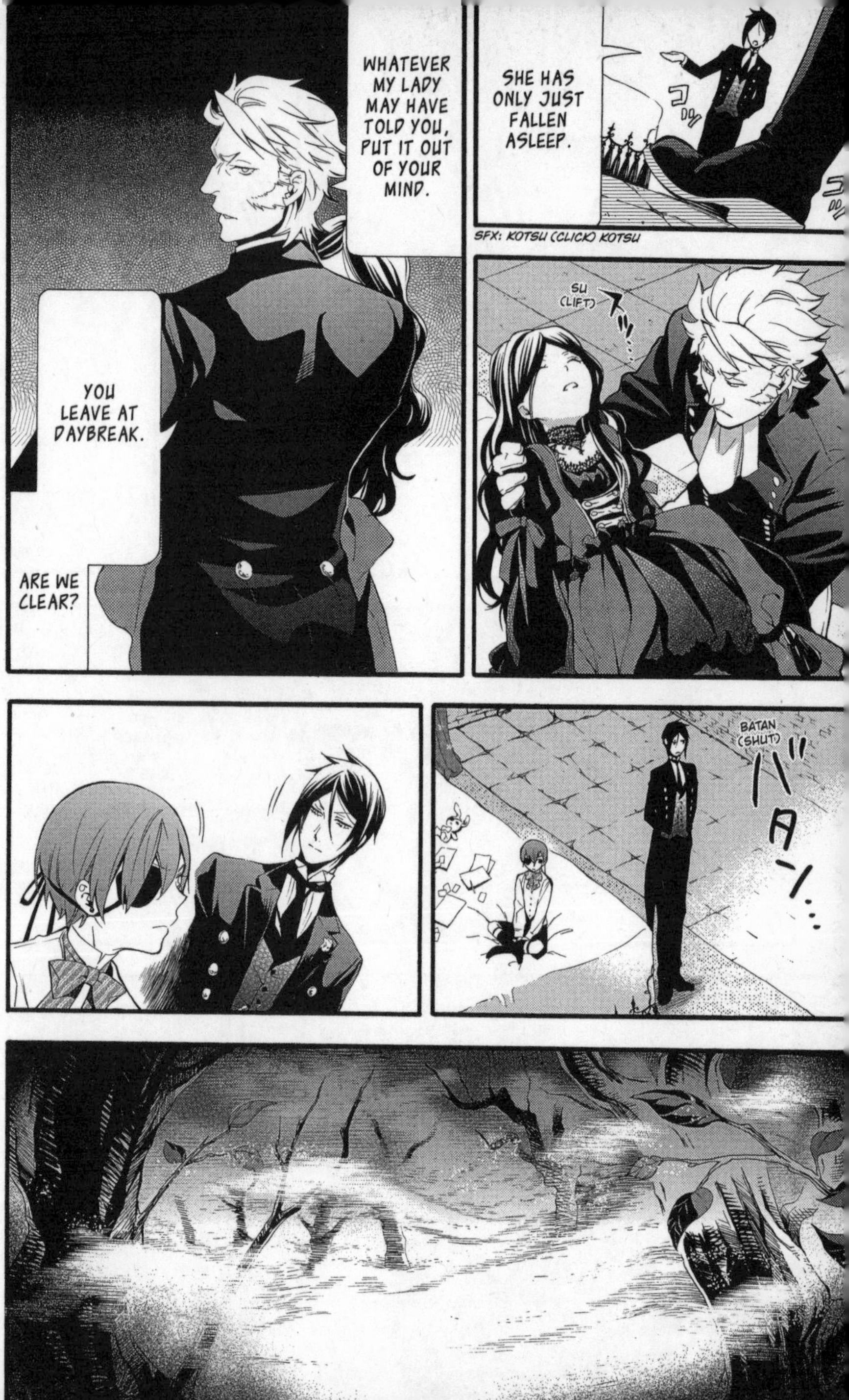
SHE HAS ONLY JUST FALLEN ASLEEP.
SFX: KOTSU (CLICK) KOTSU
SU (LIFT)
WHATEVER MY LADY MAY HAVE TOLD YOU, PUT IT OUT OF YOUR MIND.
YOU LEAVE AT DAYBREAK.
ARE WE CLEAR?
BATAN (SHUT)

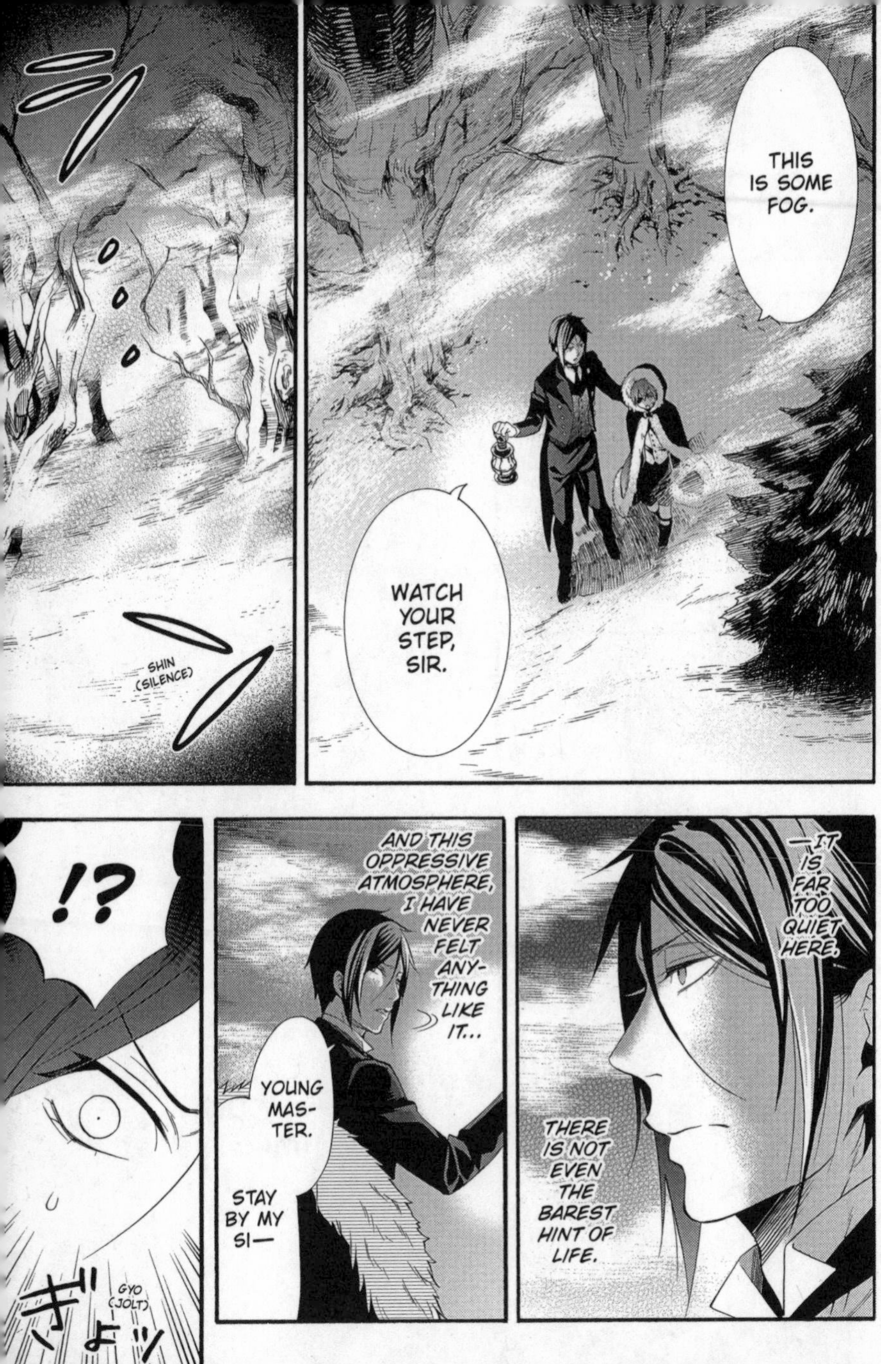
THIS IS SOME FOG.
WATCH YOUR STEP, SIR.
SHIN (SILENCE)
—IT IS FAR TOO QUIET HERE.
THERE IS NOT EVEN THE BAREST HINT OF LIFE.
AND THIS OPPRESSIVE ATMOSPHERE, I HAVE NEVER FELT ANYTHING LIKE IT...
YOUNG MASTER.
STAY BY MY SI—
!?
ぎょッ
GYO (JOLT)

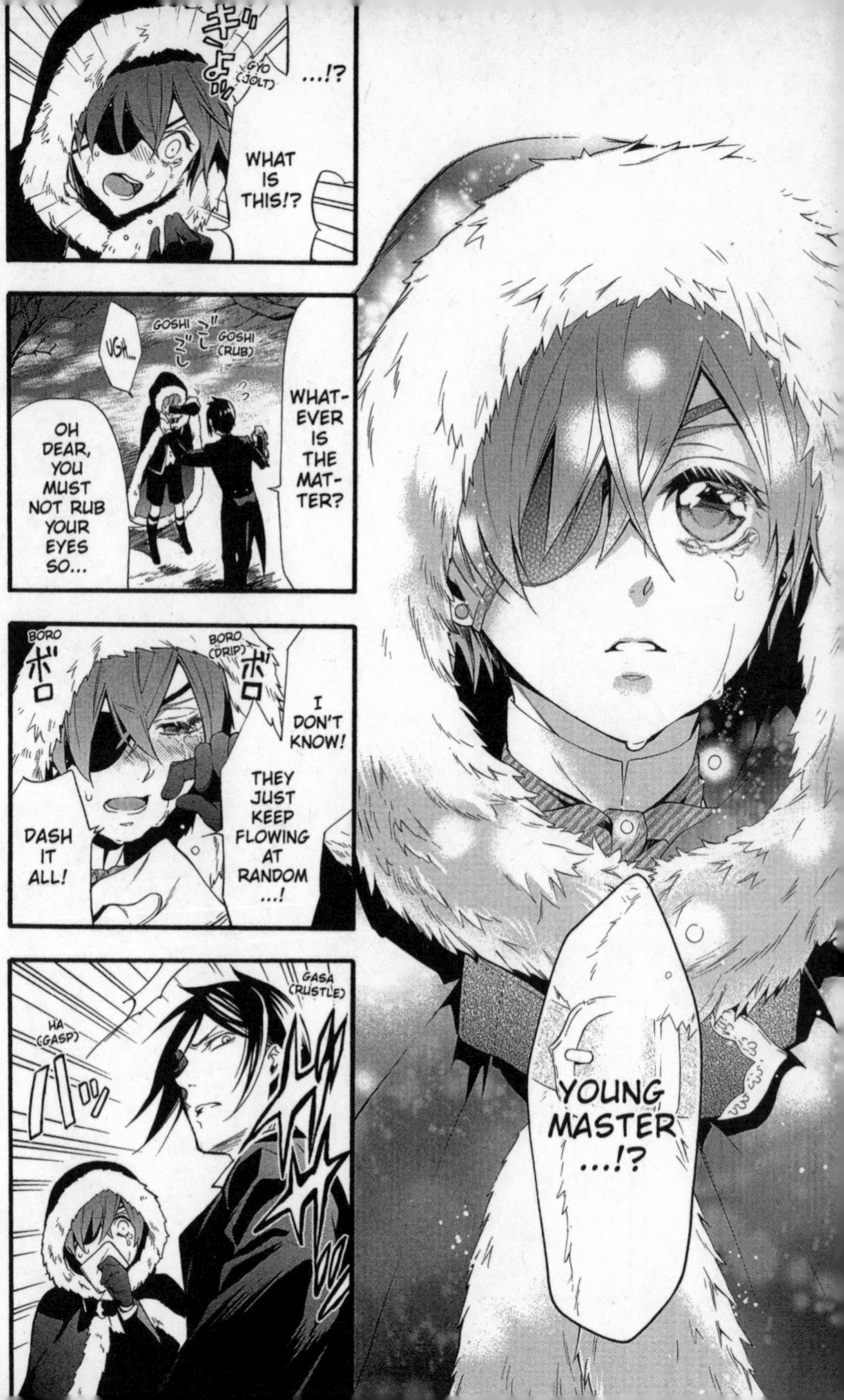
YOUNG MASTER ...!?
ぎょ
GYO (JOLT)
...!?
WHAT IS THIS!?
WHAT-EVER IS THE MAT-TER?
ごしごし
GOSHI GOSHI (RUB)
UGH...
OH DEAR, YOU MUST NOT RUB YOUR EYES SO...
ボロ
BORO (DRIP)
I DON'T KNOW!
THEY JUST KEEP FLOWING AT RANDOM ...!
ボロ
BORO
DASH IT ALL!
GASA (RUSTLE)
ハッ
HA (GASP)

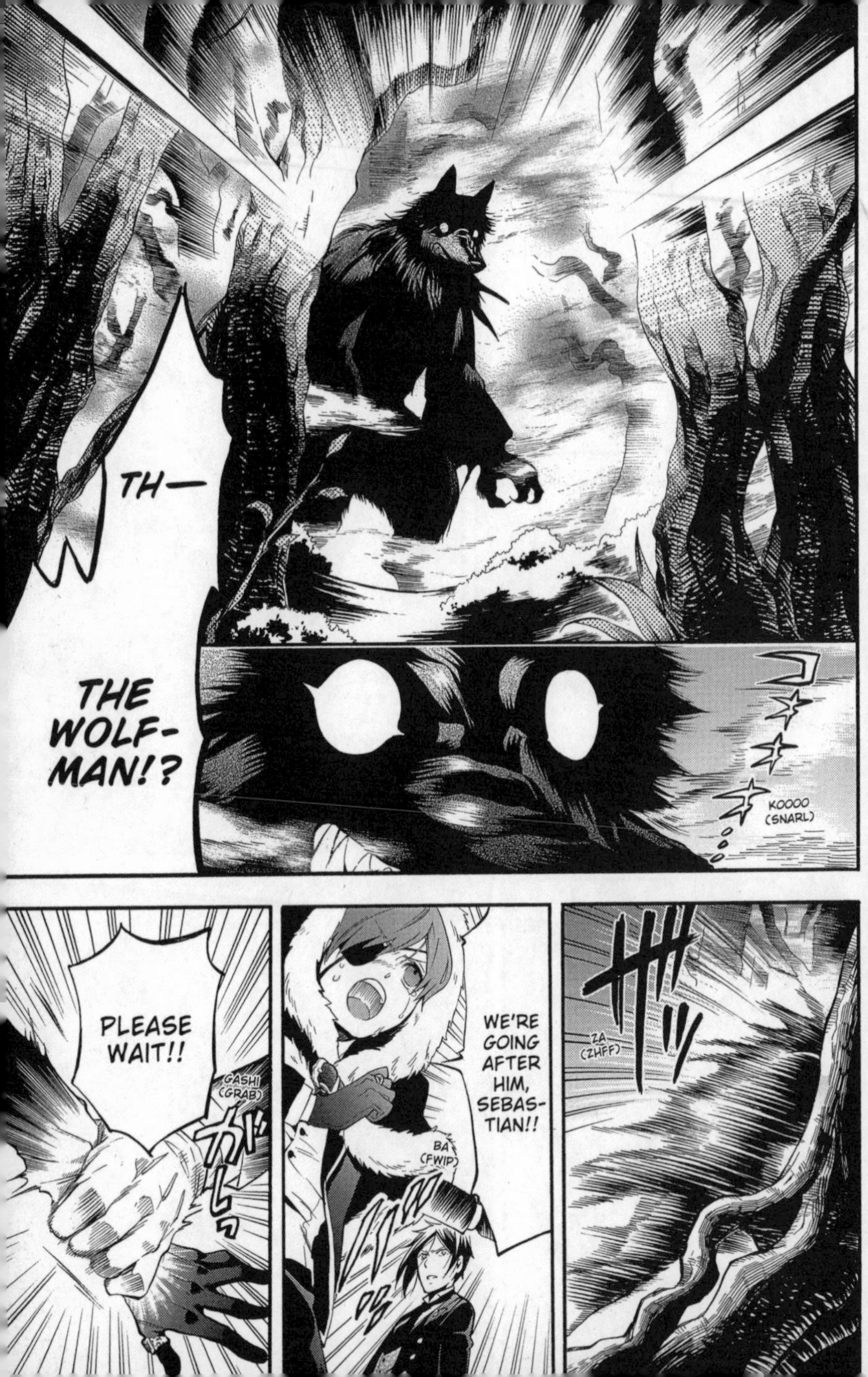
TH—
THE WOLF-MAN!?
KOOOO (SNARL)
ZA (ZHFF)
WE'RE GOING AFTER HIM, SEBASTIAN!!
BA (FWIP)
PLEASE WAIT!!
GASHI (GRAB)

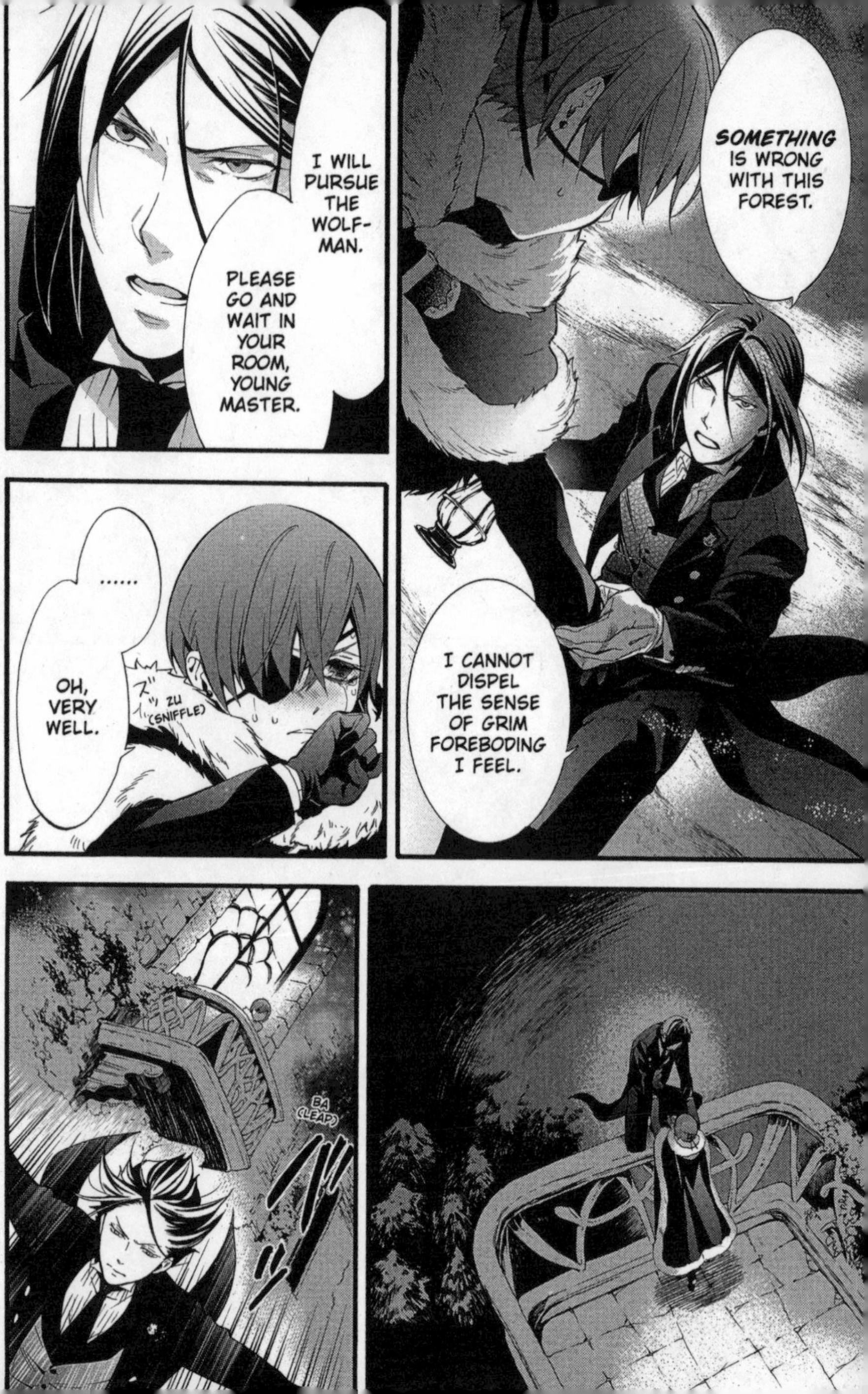
SOMETHING IS WRONG WITH THIS FOREST.
I CANNOT DISPEL THE SENSE OF GRIM FOREBODING I FEEL.
I WILL PURSUE THE WOLF-MAN.
PLEASE GO AND WAIT IN YOUR ROOM, YOUNG MASTER.
......
ズッ ZU (SNIFFLE)
OH, VERY WELL.
BA (LEAP)

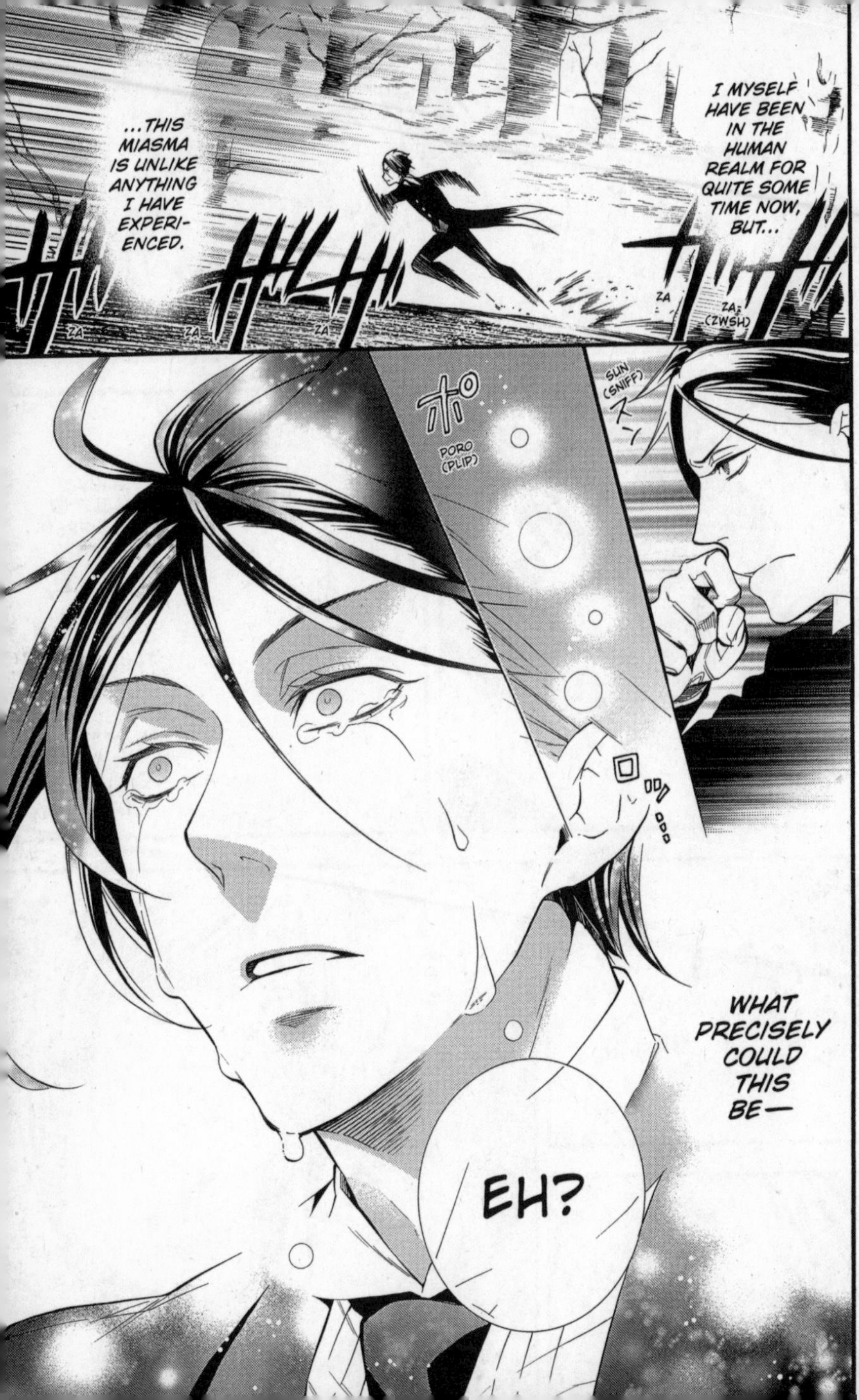
I MYSELF HAVE BEEN IN THE HUMAN REALM FOR QUITE SOME TIME NOW, BUT...
...THIS MIASMA IS UNLIKE ANYTHING I HAVE EXPERIENCED.
ZA (ZWSH)
ZA
ZA
ZA
ZA
SUN (SNIFF)
PORO (PLIP)
WHAT PRECISELY COULD THIS BE—
EH?

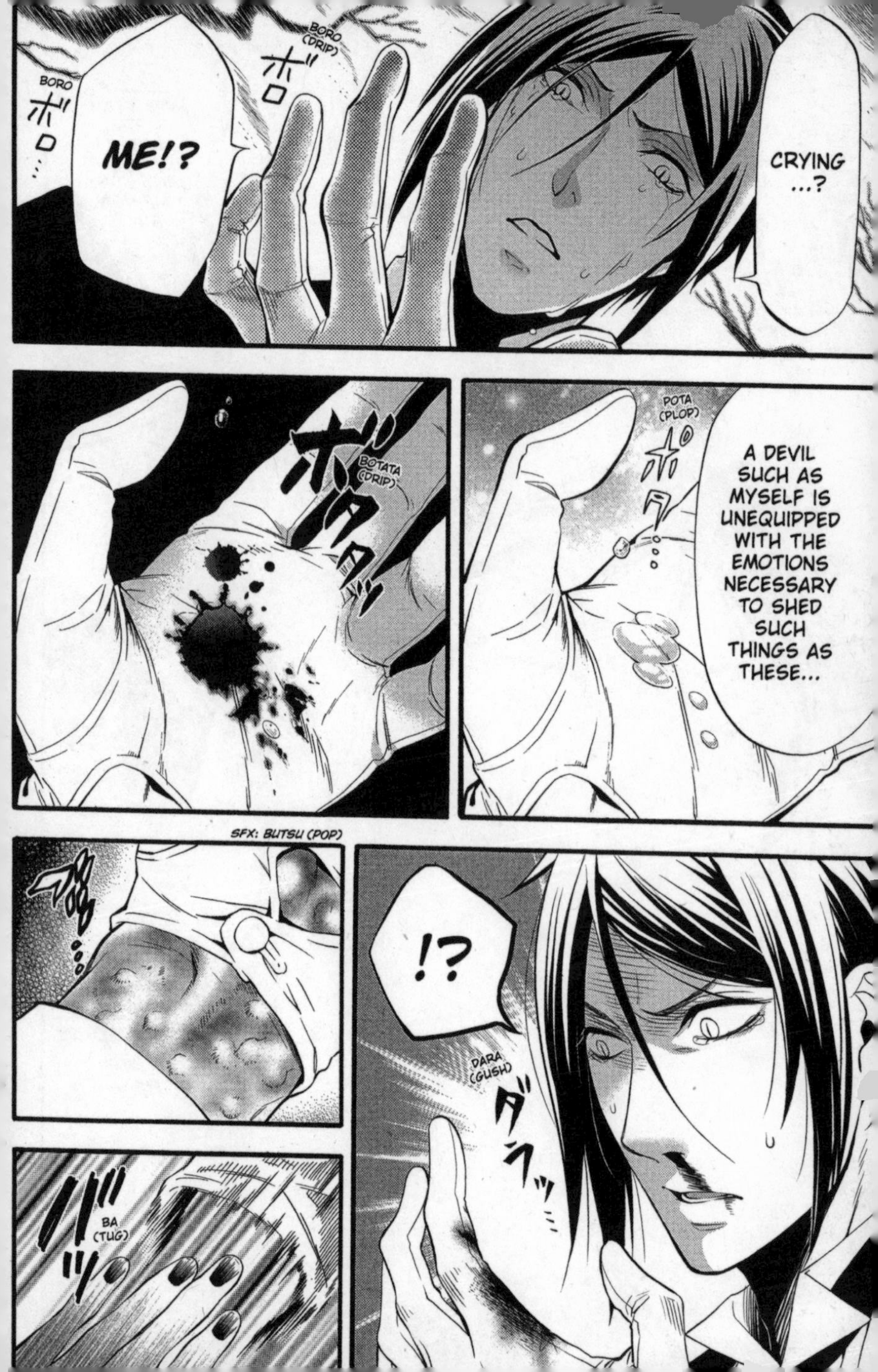
CRYING ...?
BORO (DRIP)
BORO
ME!?
POTA (PLOP)
A DEVIL SUCH AS MYSELF IS UNEQUIPPED WITH THE EMOTIONS NECESSARY TO SHED SUCH THINGS AS THESE...
BOTATA (DRIP)
SFX: BUTSU (POP)
!?
DARA (GUSH)
BA (TUG)

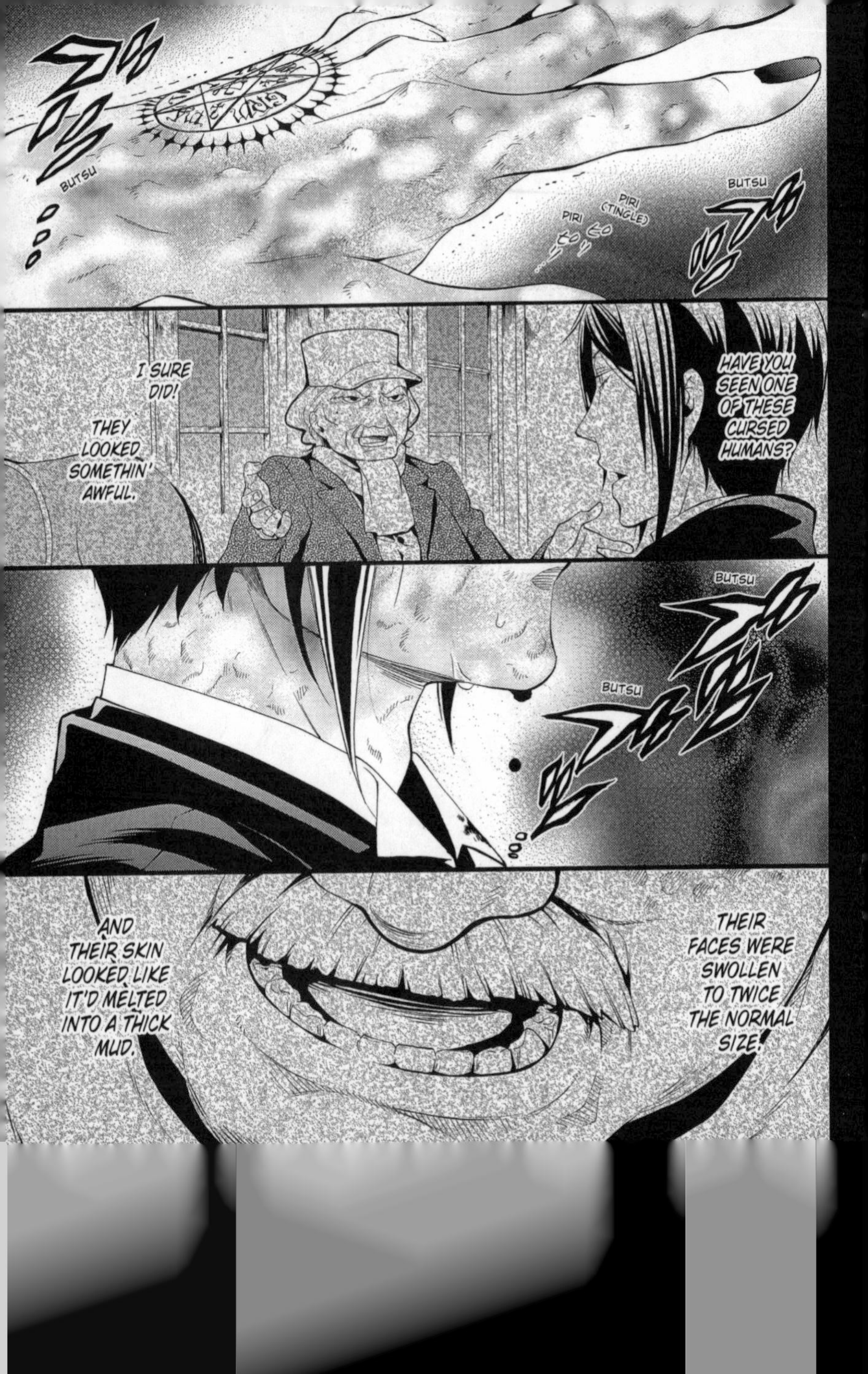
BUTSU
PIRI (TINGLE)
PIRI
BUTSU
HAVE YOU SEEN ONE OF THESE CURSED HUMANS?
I SURE DID!
THEY LOOKED SOMETHIN' AWFUL.
BUTSU
BUTSU
THEIR FACES WERE SWOLLEN TO TWICE THE NORMAL SIZE!
AND THEIR SKIN LOOKED LIKE IT'D MELTED INTO A THICK MUD.

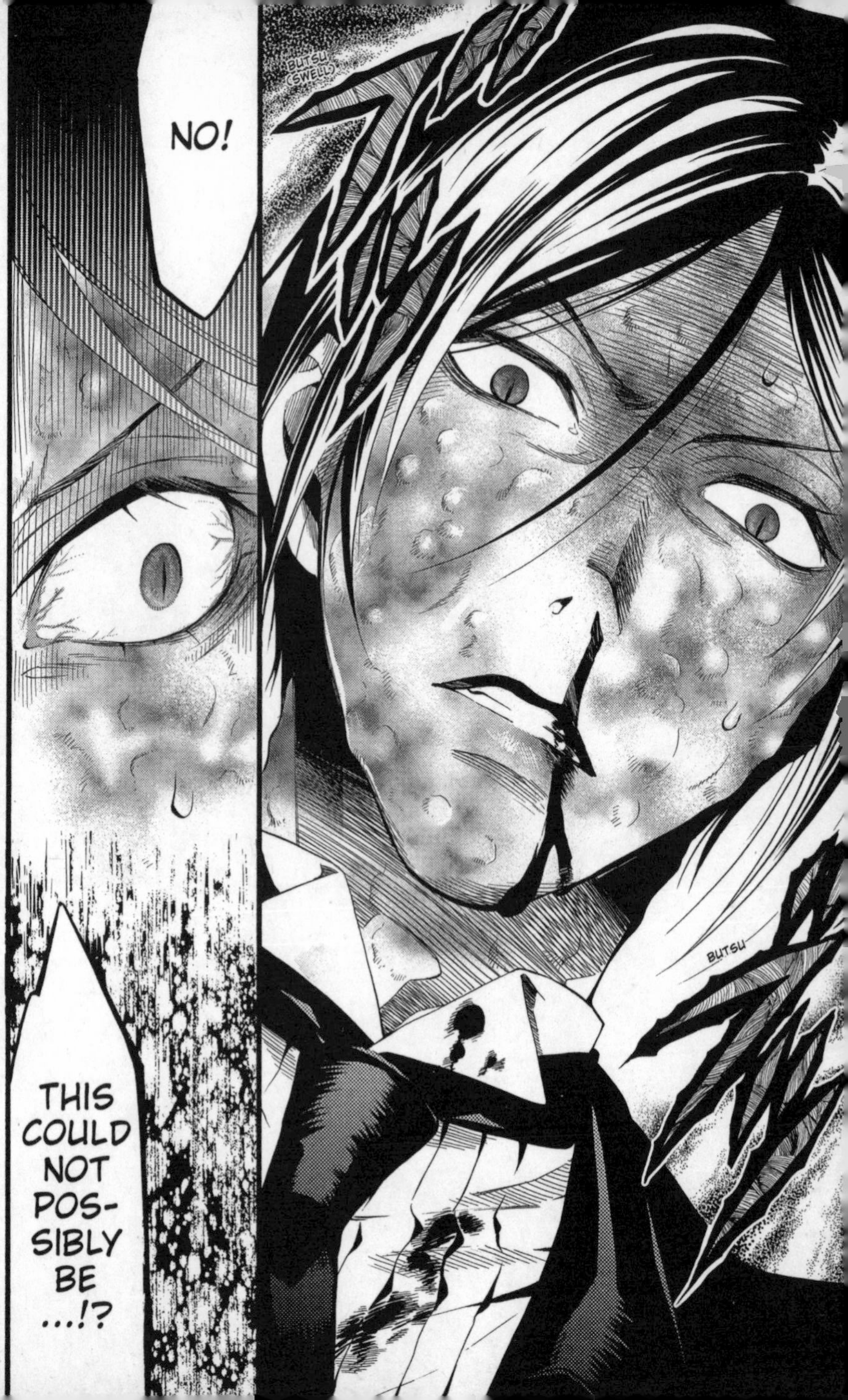
BUTSU (SWELL)
BUTSU
NO!
THIS COULD NOT POS-SIBLY BE ...!?

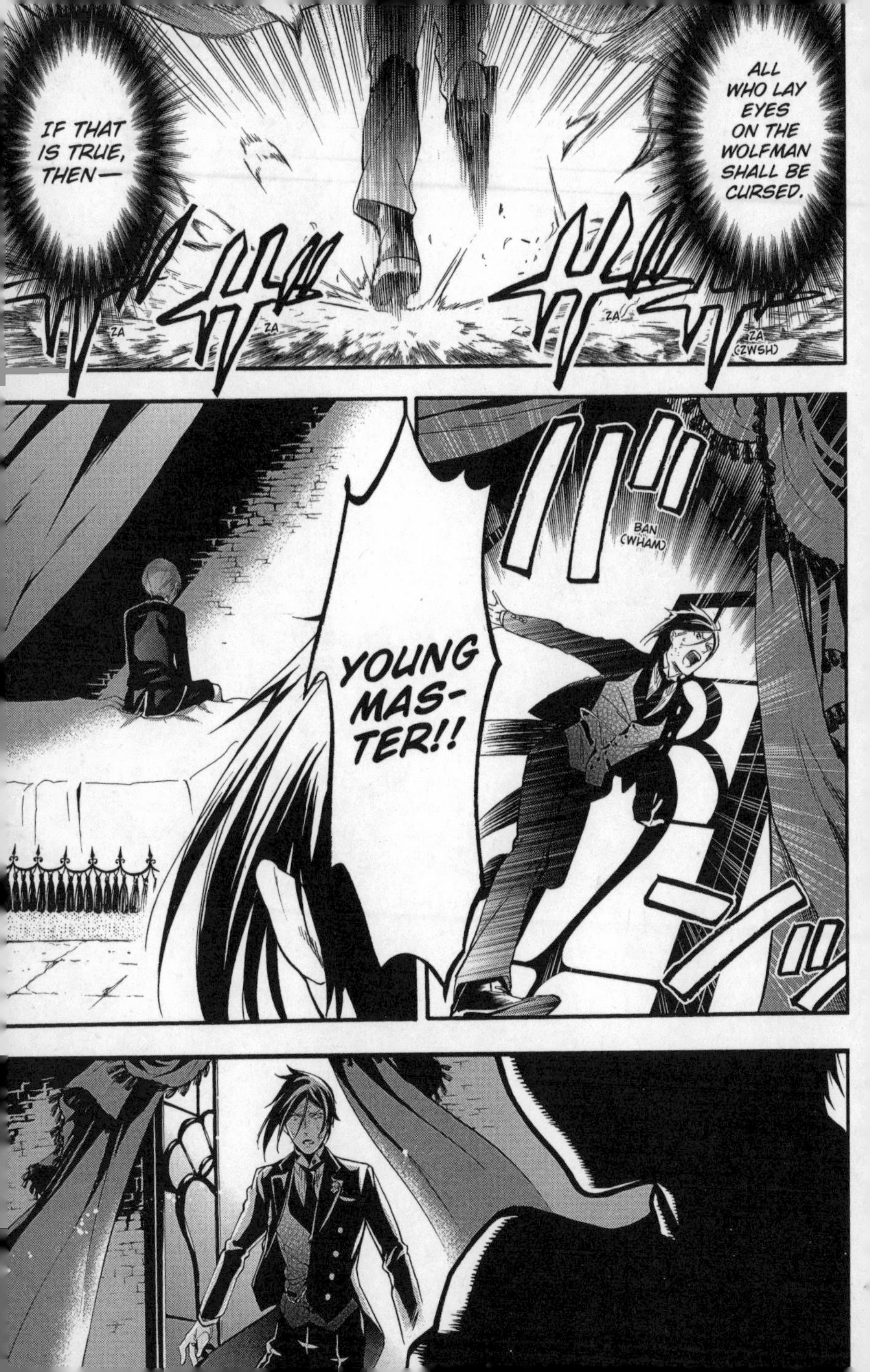
ALL WHO LAY EYES ON THE WOLFMAN SHALL BE CURSED.
IF THAT IS TRUE, THEN—
ZA (ZWSH)
ZA
ZA
ZA
BAN (WHAM)
YOUNG MAS-TER!!

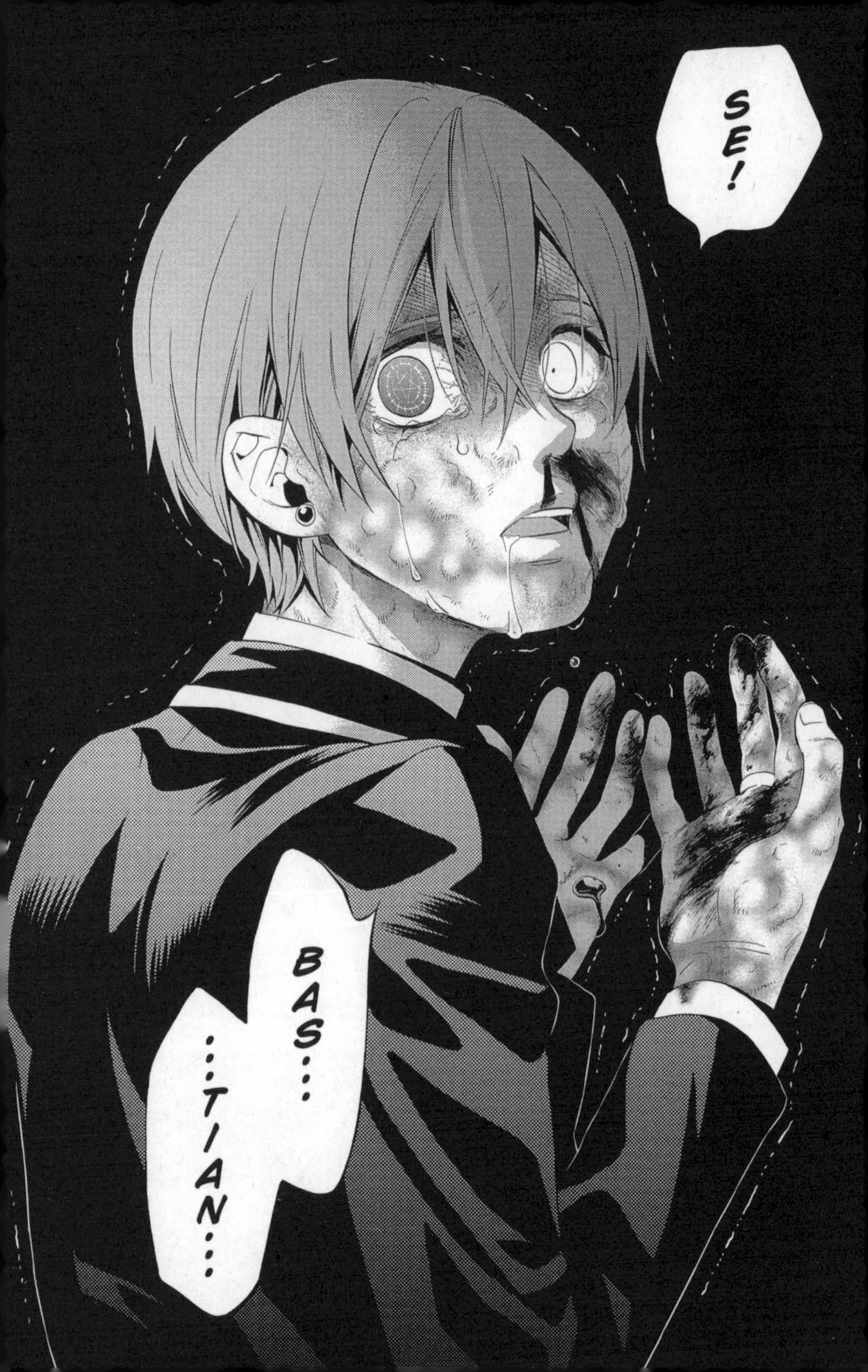
SE!
BAS...
...TIAN...

Black Butler

Chapter 90

In the afternoon : The Butler, On Loan

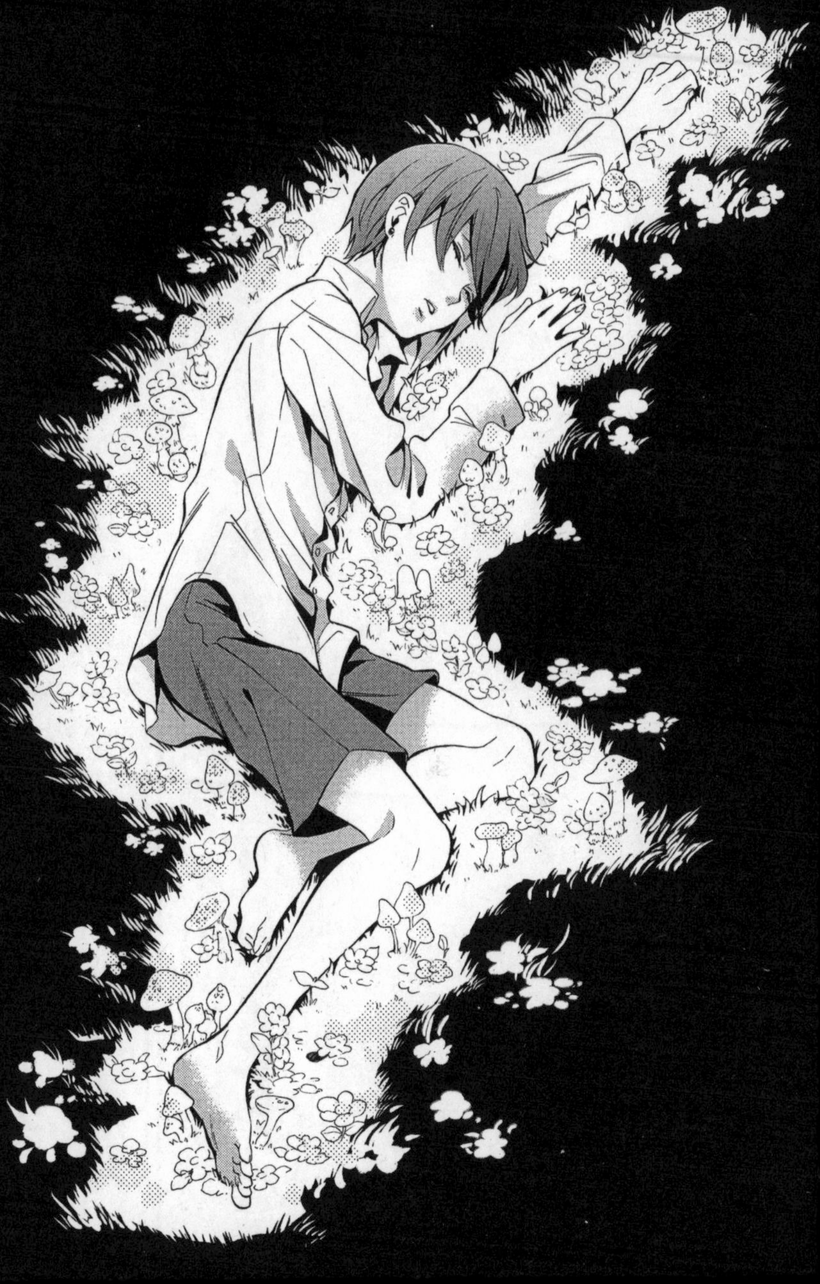

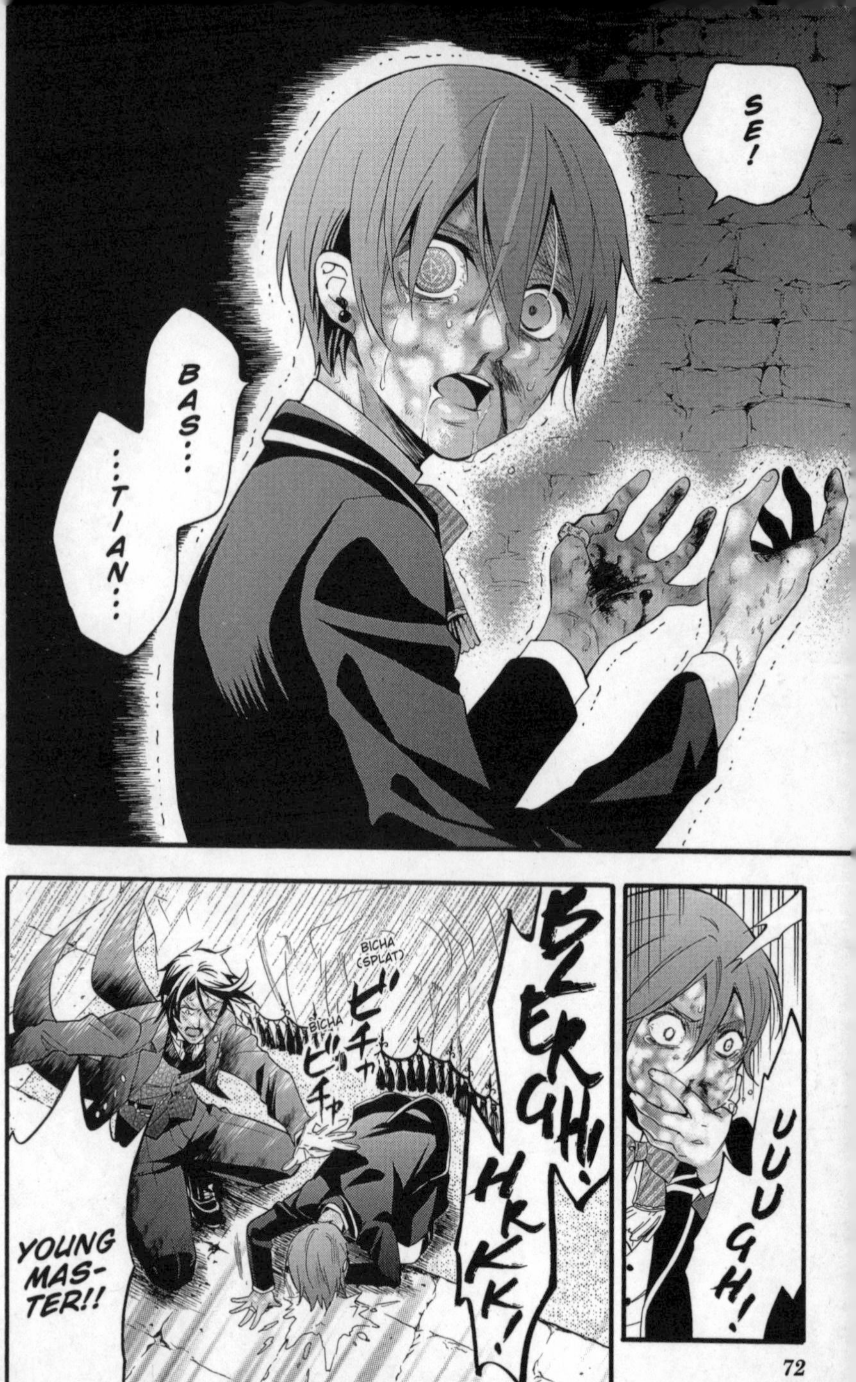
SE!
BAS...
...TIAN...
UUUUGH!
BLERGH!
HKKKK!
BICHA (SPLAT)
ビチャ
BICHA
ビチャ
YOUNG MAS-TER!!

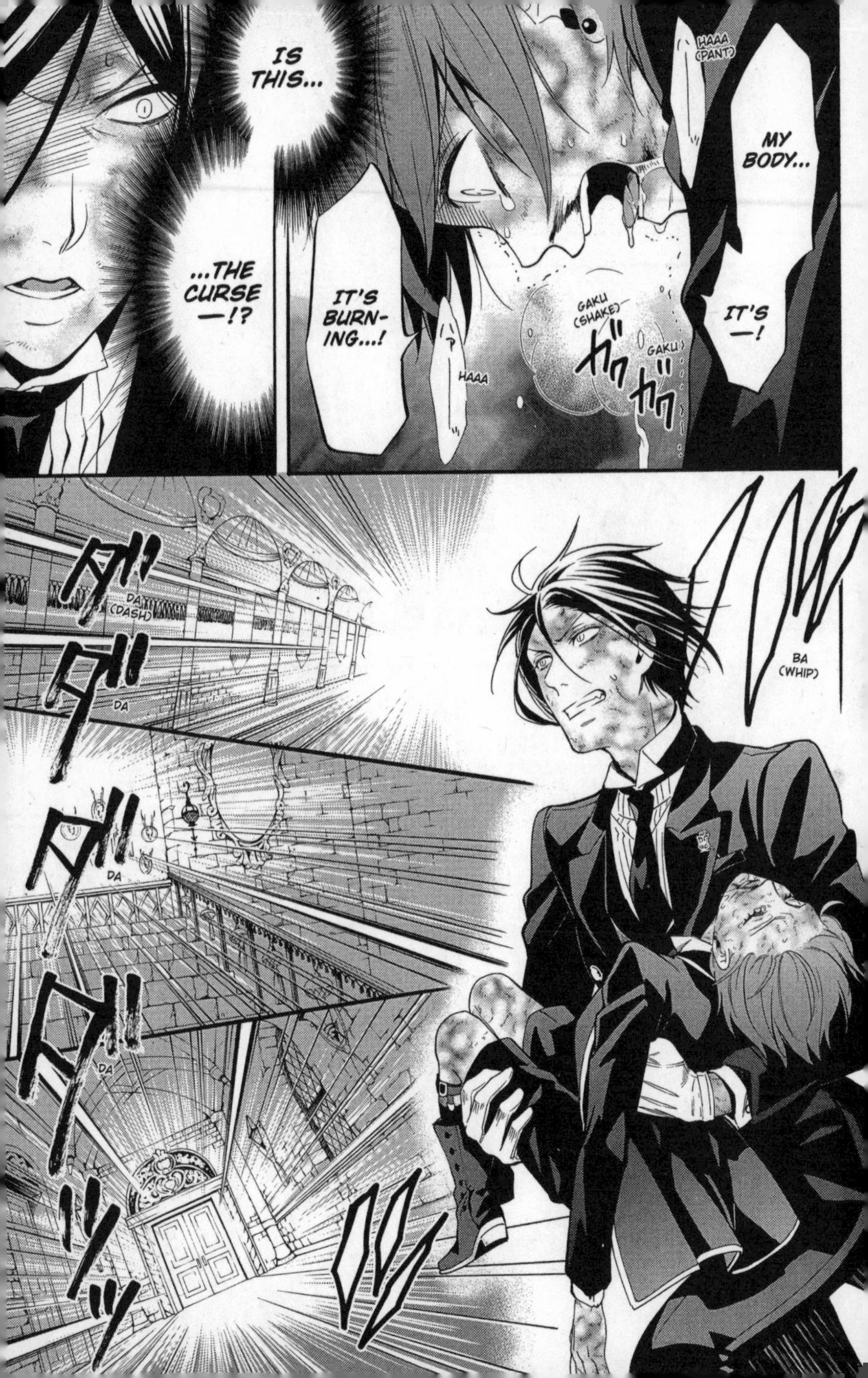
HAAA (PANT)
MY BODY...
IT'S —!
GAKU
GAKU (SHAKE)
IT'S BURNING...!
HAAA
IS THIS...
...THE CURSE —!?
BA (WHIP)
DA (DASH)
DA
DA
DA

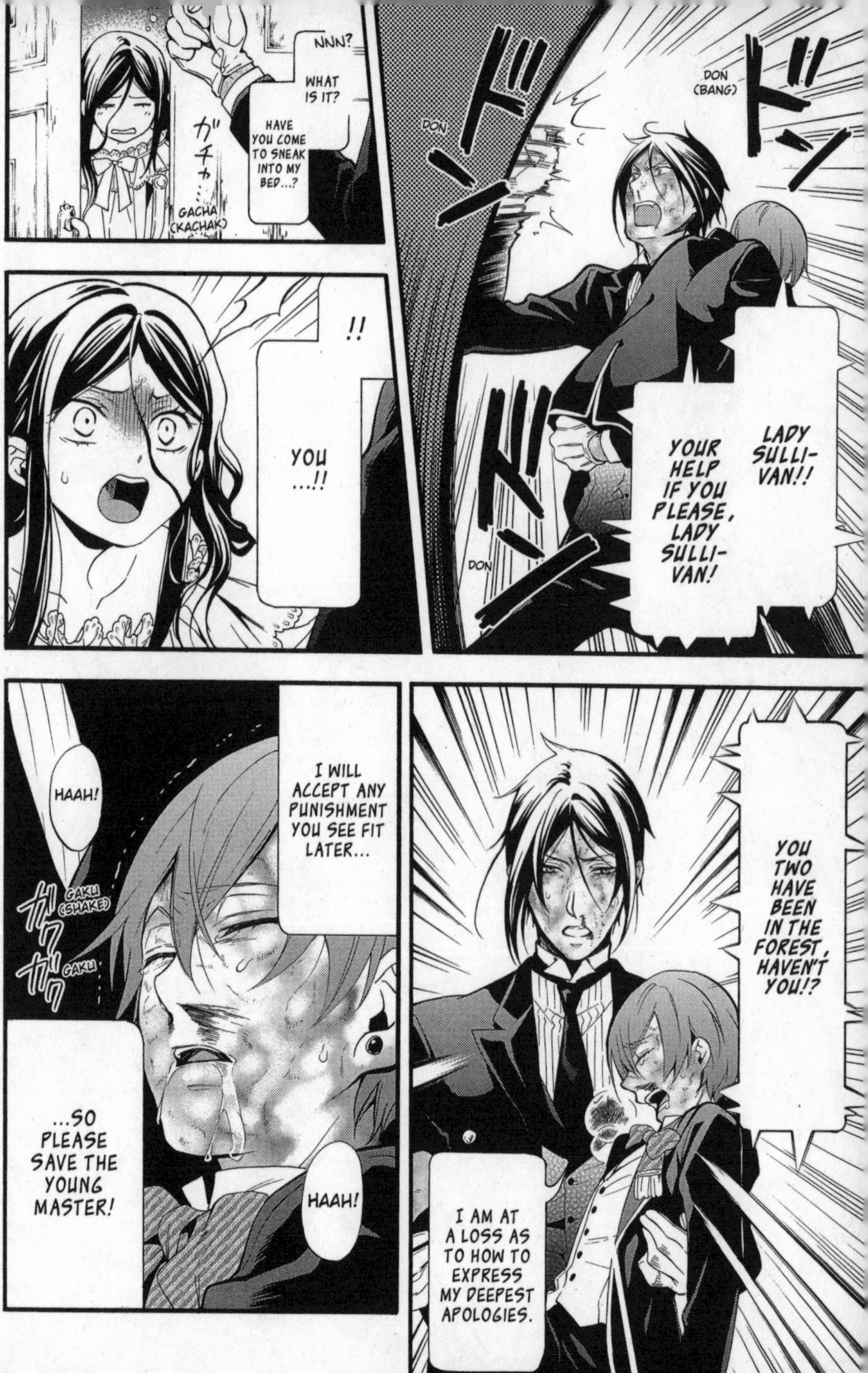
DON (BANG)
DON
DON
LADY SULLI-VAN!!
YOUR HELP IF YOU PLEASE, LADY SULLI-VAN!
NNN?
WHAT IS IT?
HAVE YOU COME TO SNEAK INTO MY BED...?
GACHA (KACHAK)
!!
YOU ...!!
YOU TWO HAVE BEEN IN THE FOREST, HAVEN'T YOU!?
I AM AT A LOSS AS TO HOW TO EXPRESS MY DEEPEST APOLOGIES.
I WILL ACCEPT ANY PUNISHMENT YOU SEE FIT LATER...
HAAH!
GAKU (SHAKE)
GAKU
...SO PLEASE SAVE THE YOUNG MASTER!
HAAH!

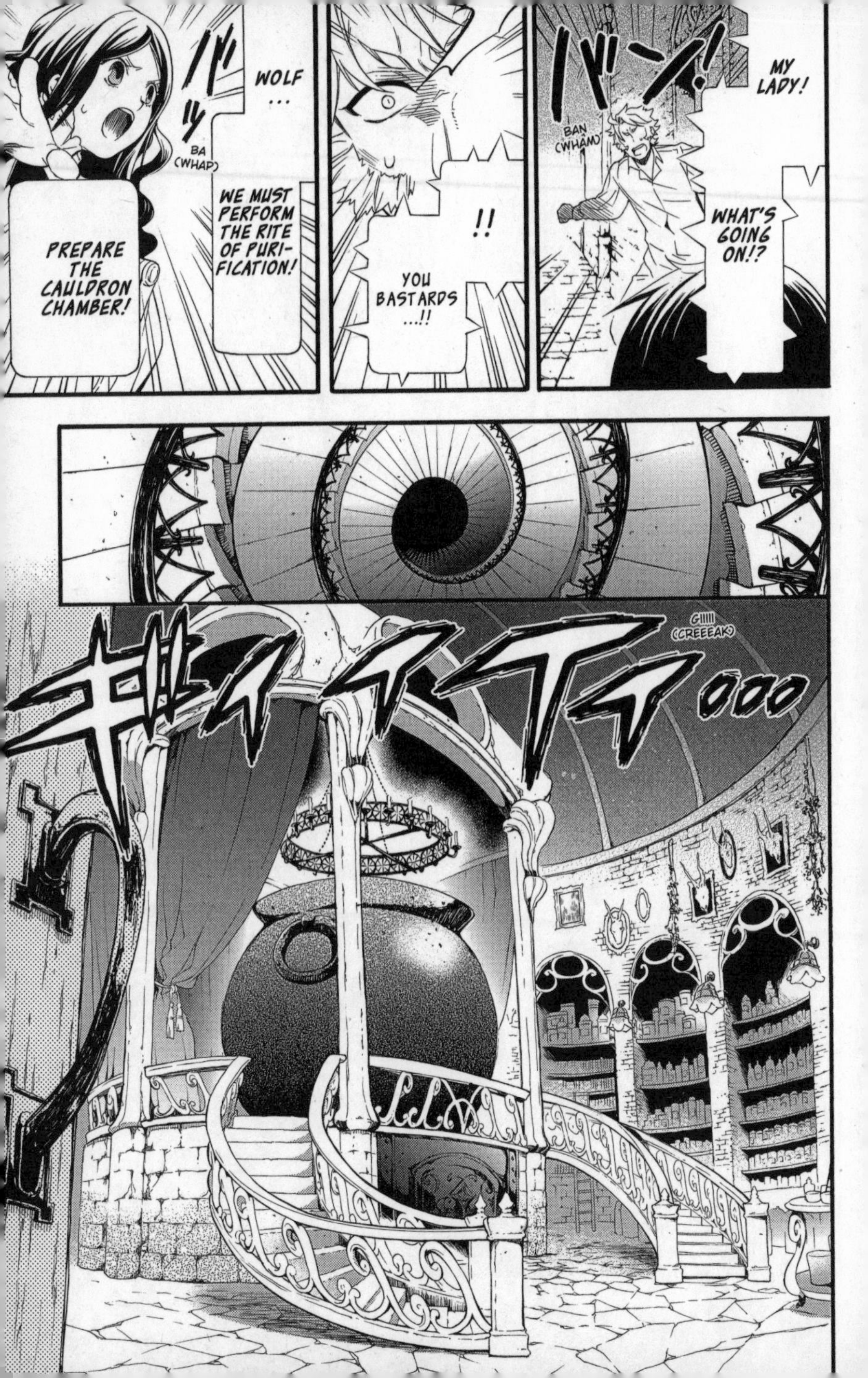
MY LADY!
BAN (WHAM)
WHAT'S GOING ON!?
!!
YOU BASTARDS ...!!
WOLF ...
WE MUST PERFORM THE RITE OF PURIFICATION!
BA (WHAP)
PREPARE THE CAULDRON CHAMBER!
GIIII (CREEEAK)

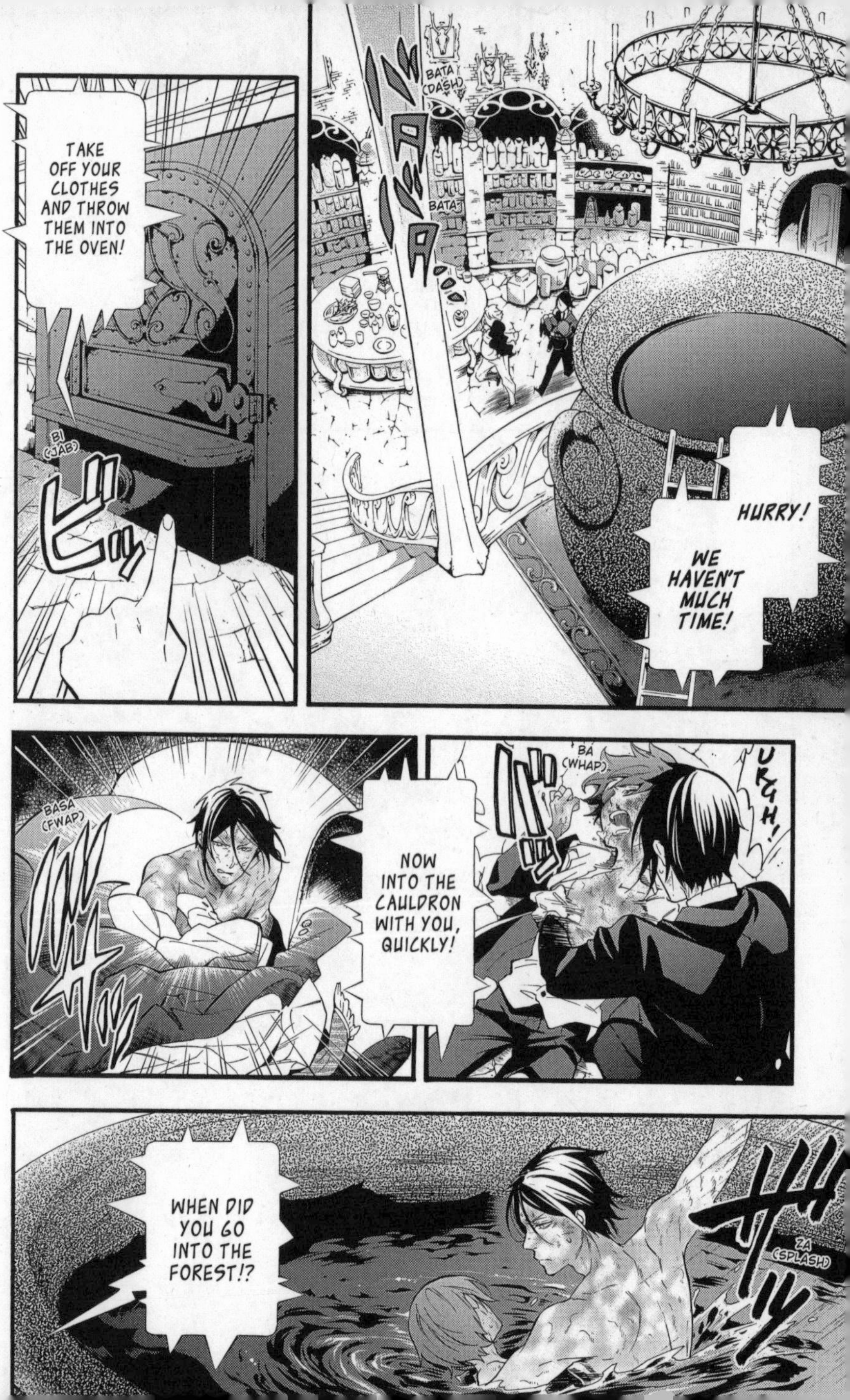
BATA (DASH)
BATA
HURRY!
WE HAVEN'T MUCH TIME!
TAKE OFF YOUR CLOTHES AND THROW THEM INTO THE OVEN!
BI (JAB)
BA (WHAP)
URGH!
NOW INTO THE CAULDRON WITH YOU, QUICKLY!
BASA (FWAP)
ZA (SPLASH)
WHEN DID YOU GO INTO THE FOREST!?

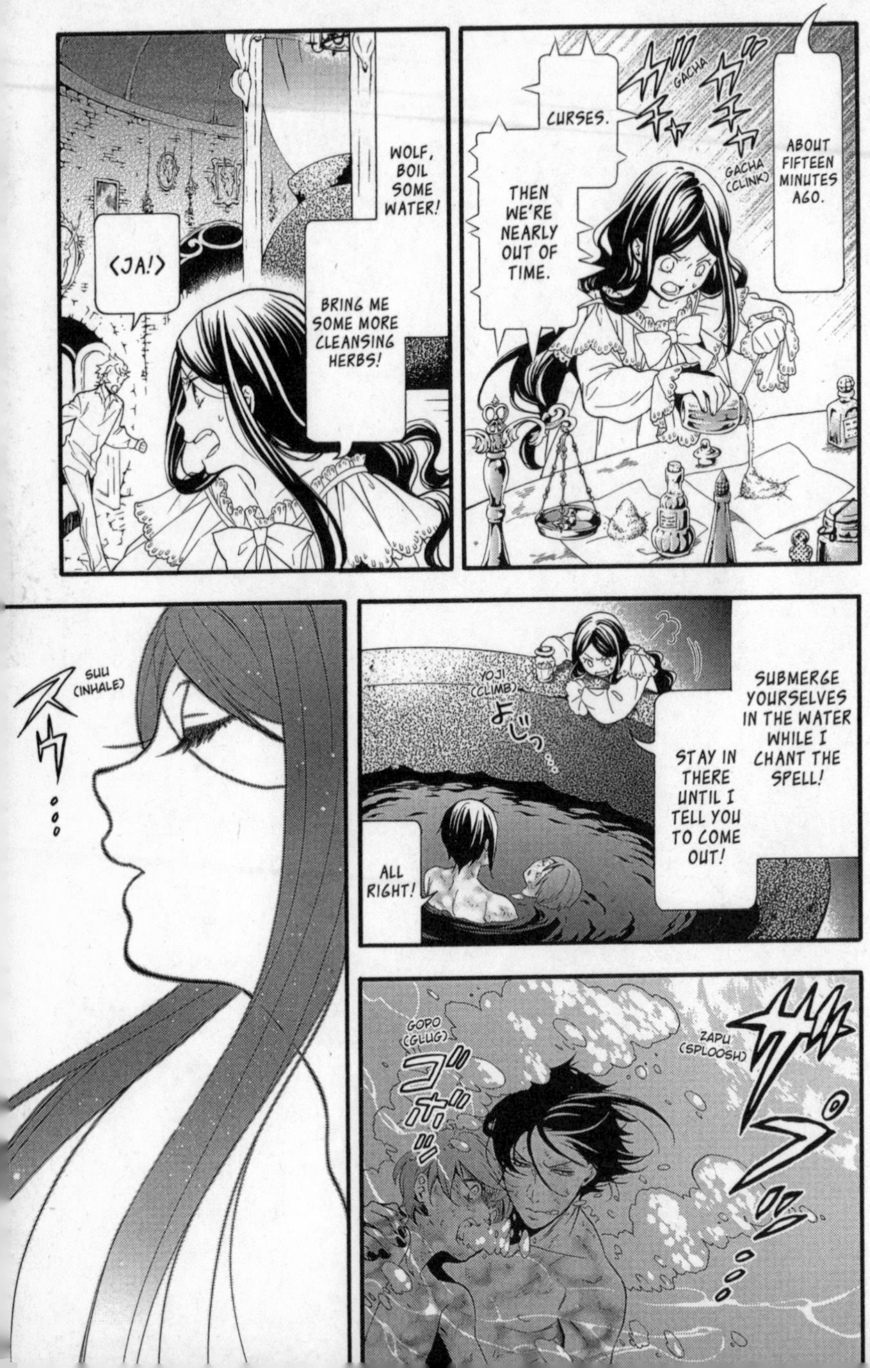
ABOUT FIFTEEN MINUTES AGO.
GACHA
GACHA (CLINK)
CURSES.
THEN WE'RE NEARLY OUT OF TIME.
WOLF, BOIL SOME WATER!
BRING ME SOME MORE CLEANSING HERBS!
⟨JA!⟩
SUBMERGE YOURSELVES IN THE WATER WHILE I CHANT THE SPELL!
STAY IN THERE UNTIL I TELL YOU TO COME OUT!
YOJI (CLIMB)
ALL RIGHT!
ZAPU (SPLOOSH)
GOPO (GLUG)
SUU (INHALE)

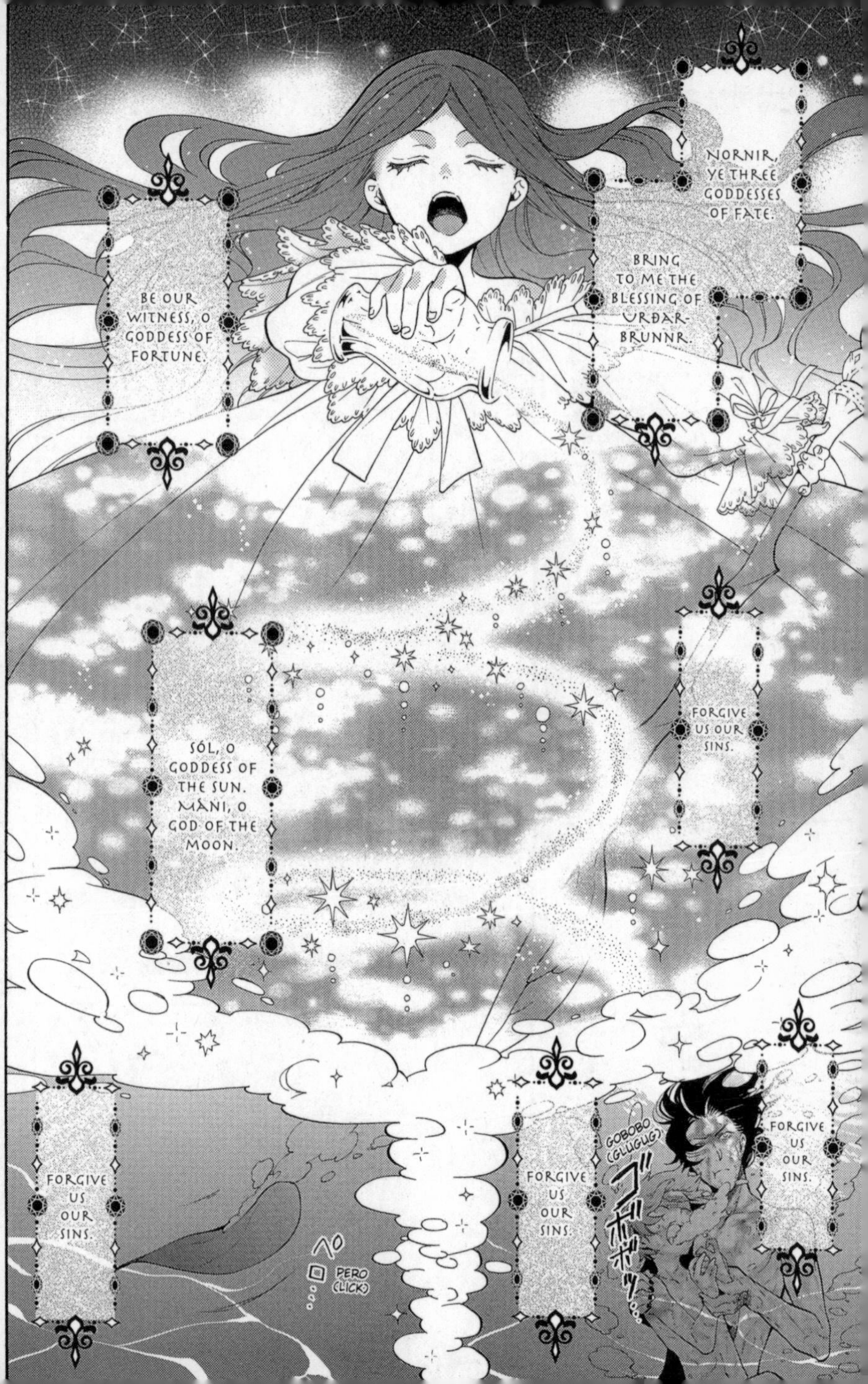
NORNIR, YE THREE GODDESSES OF FATE.
BRING TO ME THE BLESSING OF URDAR-BRUNNR.
BE OUR WITNESS, O GODDESS OF FORTUNE.
FORGIVE US OUR SINS.
SÓL, O GODDESS OF THE SUN. MANI, O GOD OF THE MOON.
FORGIVE US OUR SINS.
ゴボボッ…
GOBOBO (GLUGUG)
FORGIVE US OUR SINS.
ペロ
PERO (LICK)
FORGIVE US OUR SINS.

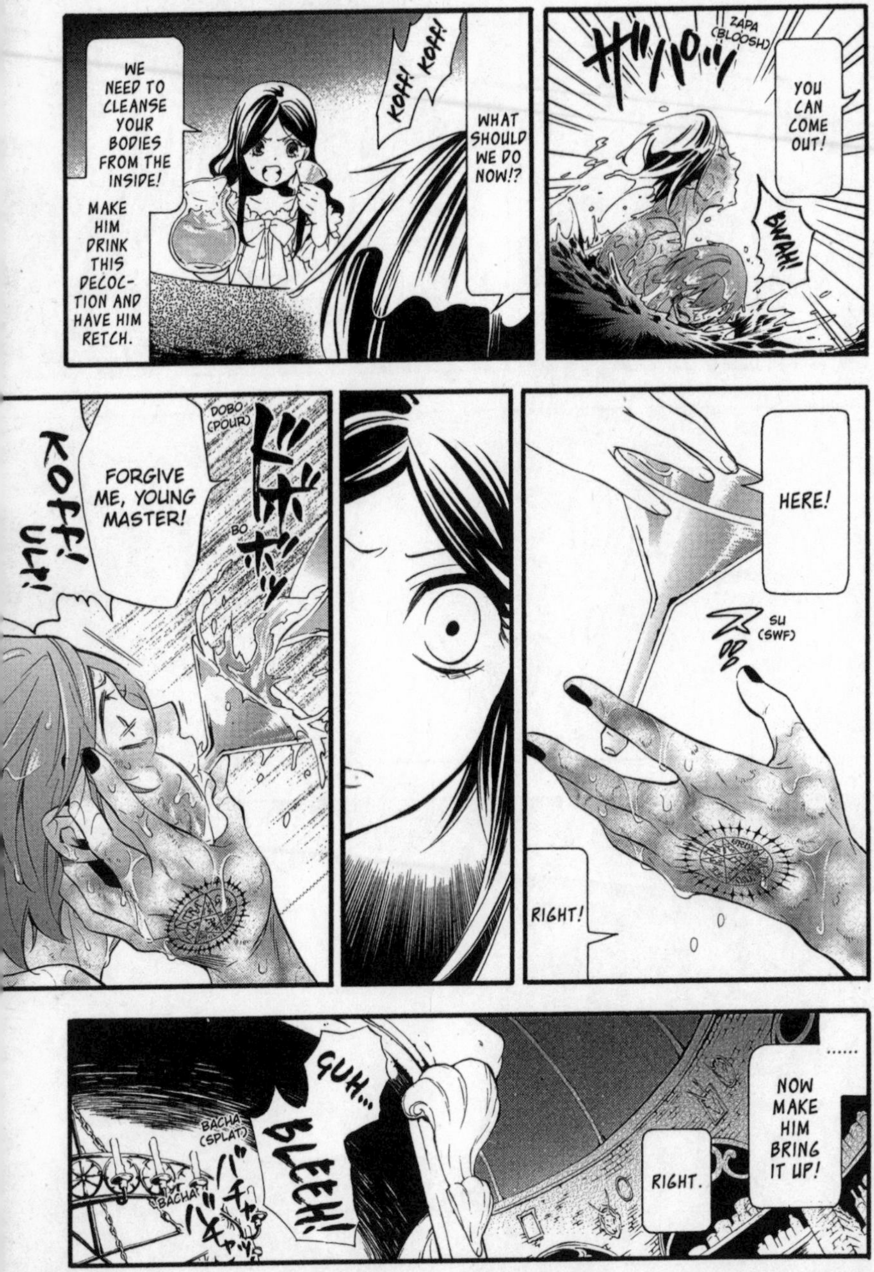
ZAPA (BLOOSH)
YOU CAN COME OUT!
BWAH!
KOFF! KOFF!
WHAT SHOULD WE DO NOW!?
WE NEED TO CLEANSE YOUR BODIES FROM THE INSIDE!
MAKE HIM DRINK THIS DECOCTION AND HAVE HIM RETCH.
HERE!
SU (SWF)
RIGHT!
DOBO (POUR)
BO
FORGIVE ME, YOUNG MASTER!
KOFF! ULP!
......
NOW MAKE HIM BRING IT UP!
RIGHT.
GUH...
BLEEH!
BACHA (SPLAT)
BACHA

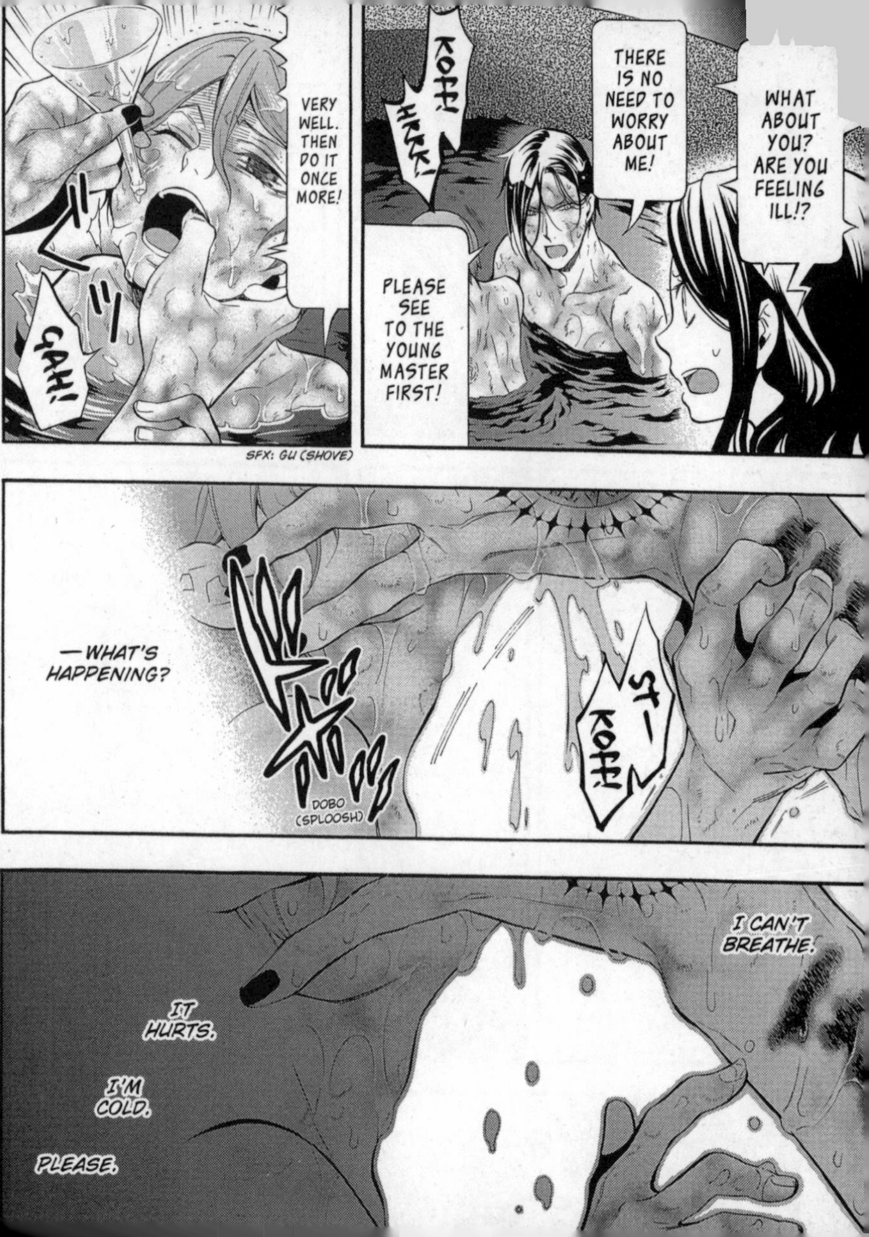
WHAT ABOUT YOU? ARE YOU FEELING ILL!?
THERE IS NO NEED TO WORRY ABOUT ME!
KOFF! HRKK!
PLEASE SEE TO THE YOUNG MASTER FIRST!
VERY WELL. THEN DO IT ONCE MORE!
GAH!
SFX: GU (SHOVE)
ST— KOFF!
DOBO (SPLOOSH)
—WHAT'S HAPPENING?
I CAN'T BREATHE.
IT HURTS.
I'M COLD.
PLEASE.

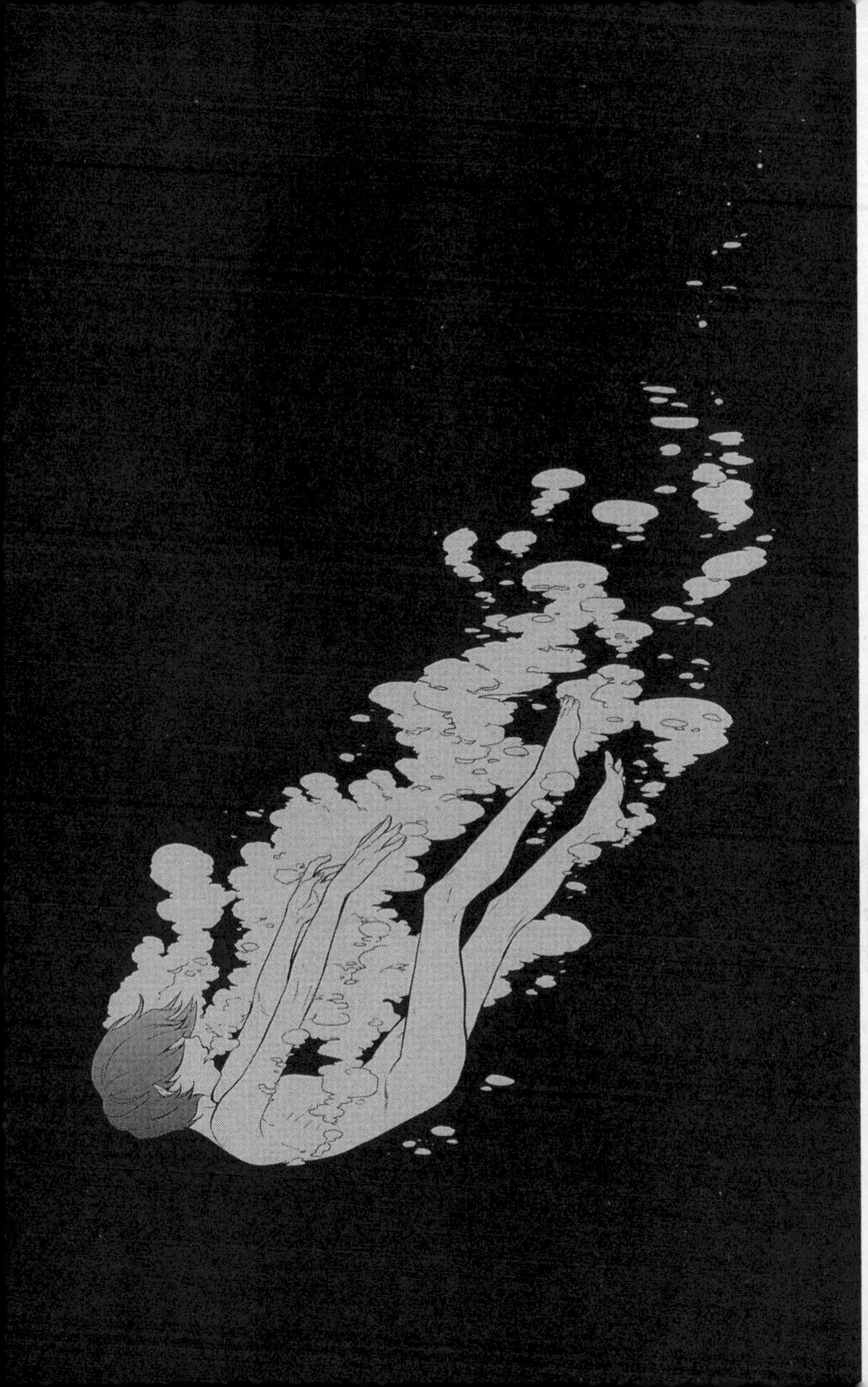

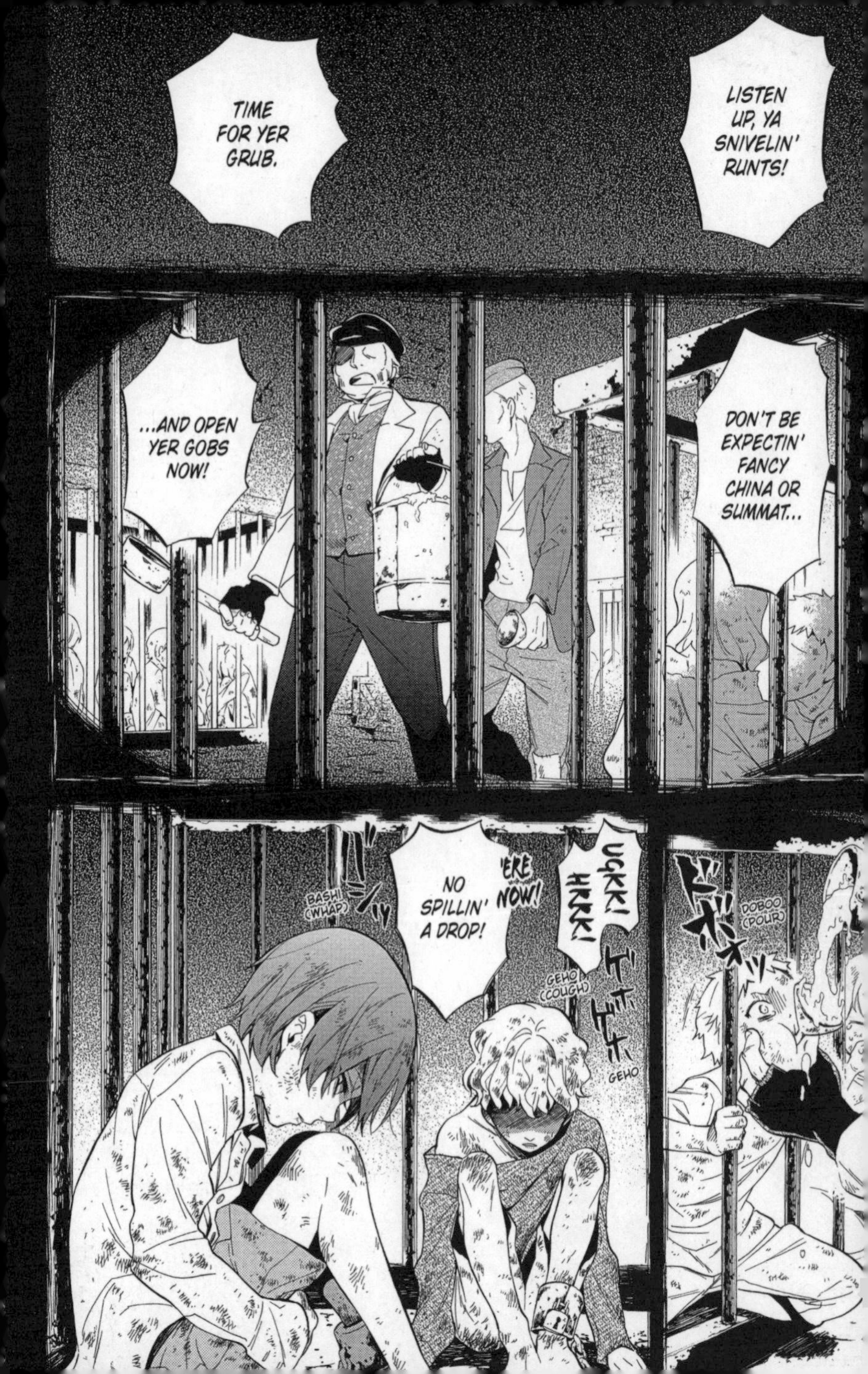
LISTEN UP, YA SNIVELIN' RUNTS!
TIME FOR YER GRUB.
DON'T BE EXPECTIN' FANCY CHINA OR SUMMAT...
...AND OPEN YER GOBS NOW!
DOBOO (POUR)
UGKK! HRKK!
'ERE NOW!
NO SPILLIN' A DROP!
BASHI (WHAP)
GEHO (COUGH)
GEHO

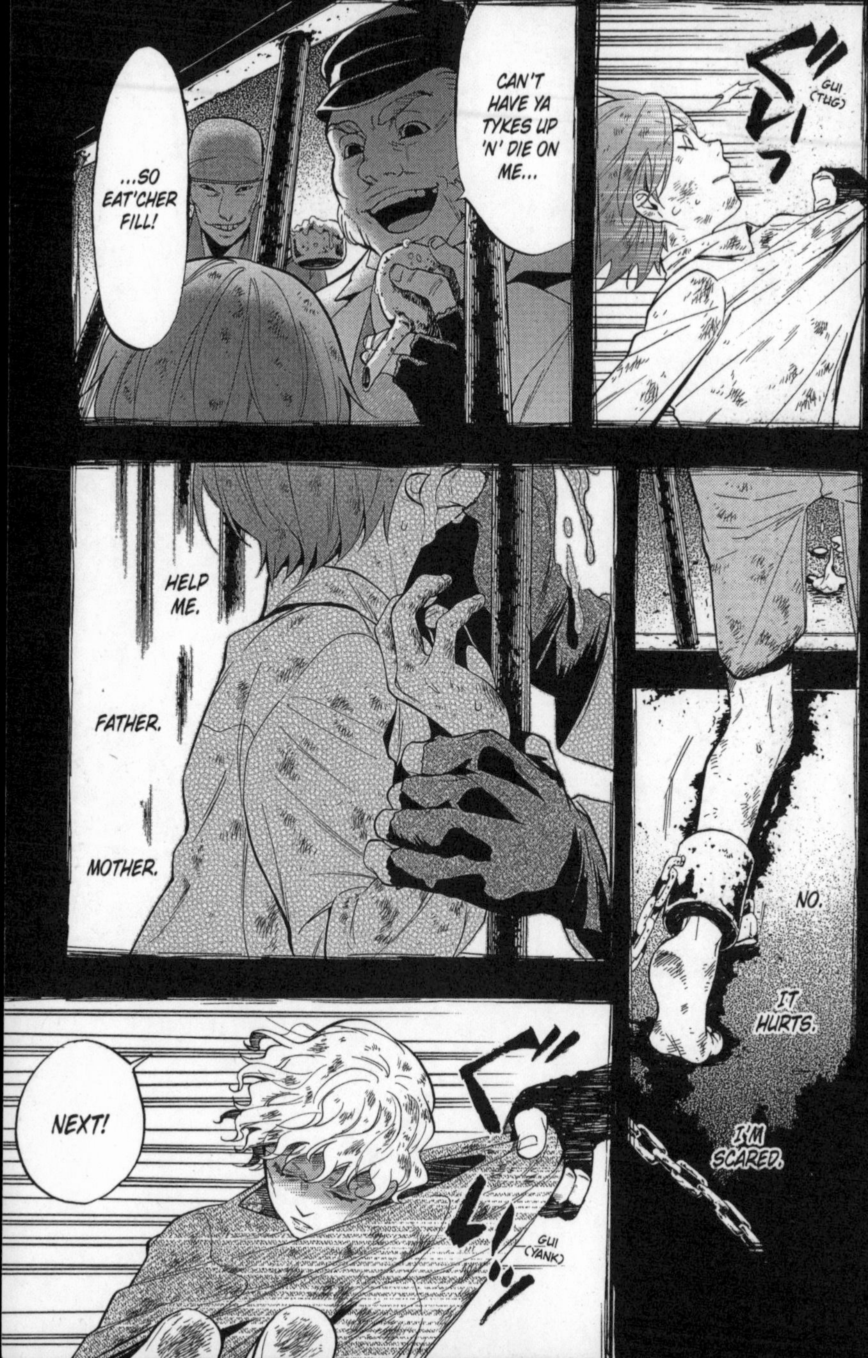
GUI (TUG)
CAN'T HAVE YA TYKES UP 'N' DIE ON ME...
...SO EAT'CHER FILL!
NO.
IT HURTS.
I'M SCARED.
HELP ME.
FATHER.
MOTHER.
NEXT!
GUI (YANK)

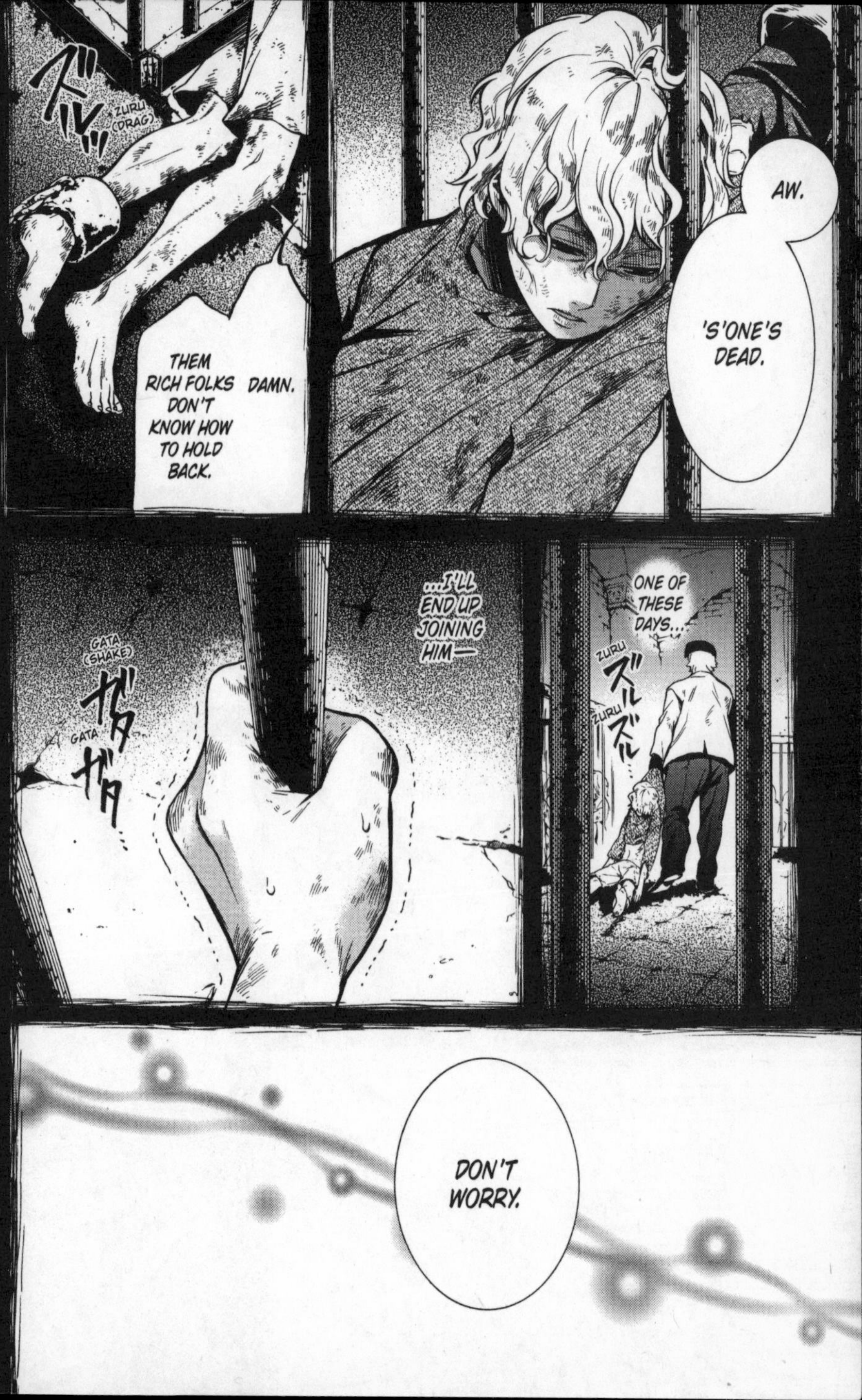
AW.
'S'ONE'S DEAD.
DAMN.
THEM RICH FOLKS DON'T KNOW HOW TO HOLD BACK.
ZURU (DRAG)
ONE OF THESE DAYS...
ZURU ZURU
...I'LL END UP JOINING HIM—
GATA (SHAKE) GATA
DON'T WORRY.

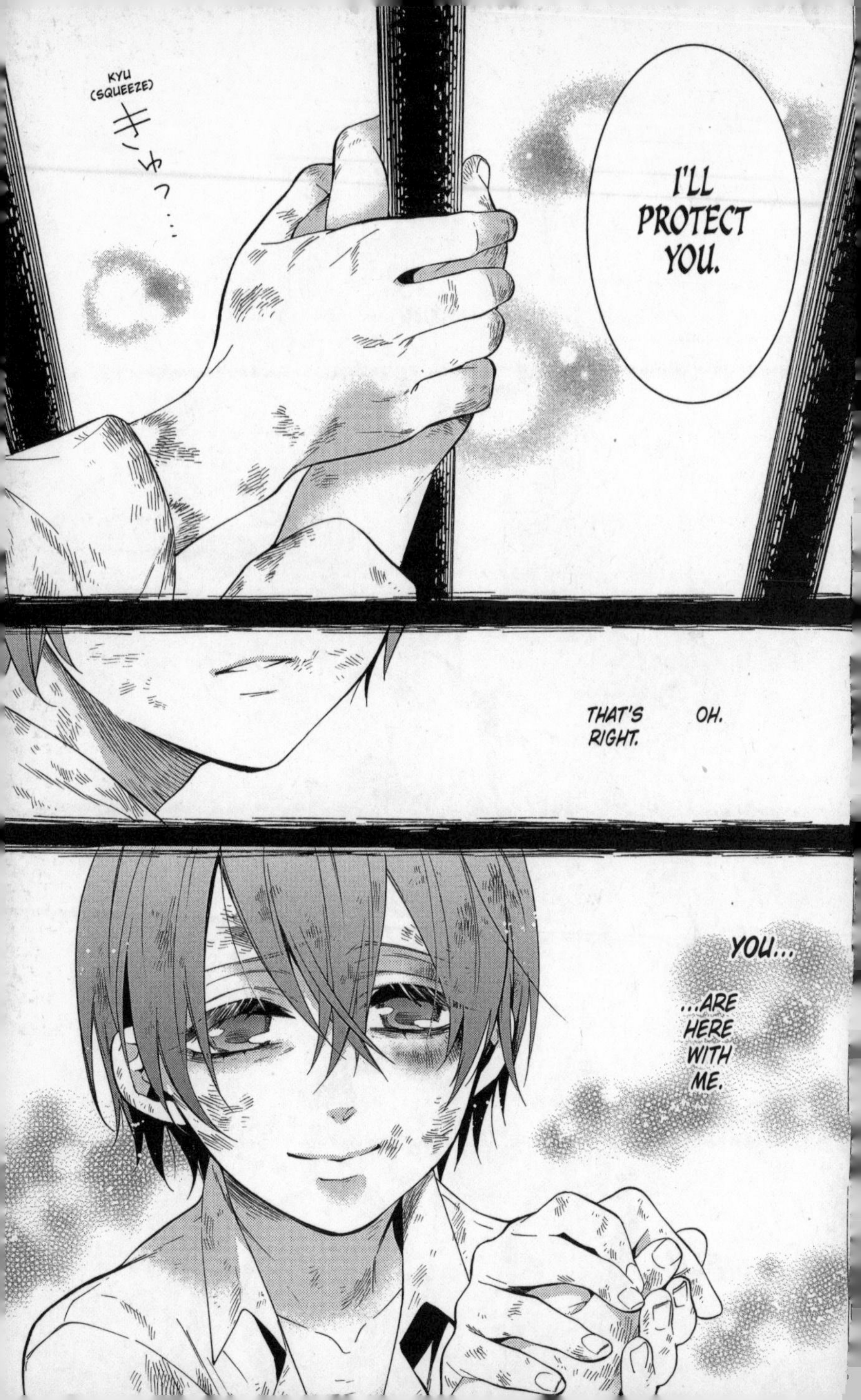
I'LL PROTECT YOU.
きゅっ…
KYU (SQUEEZE)
OH.
THAT'S RIGHT.
YOU...
...ARE HERE WITH ME.

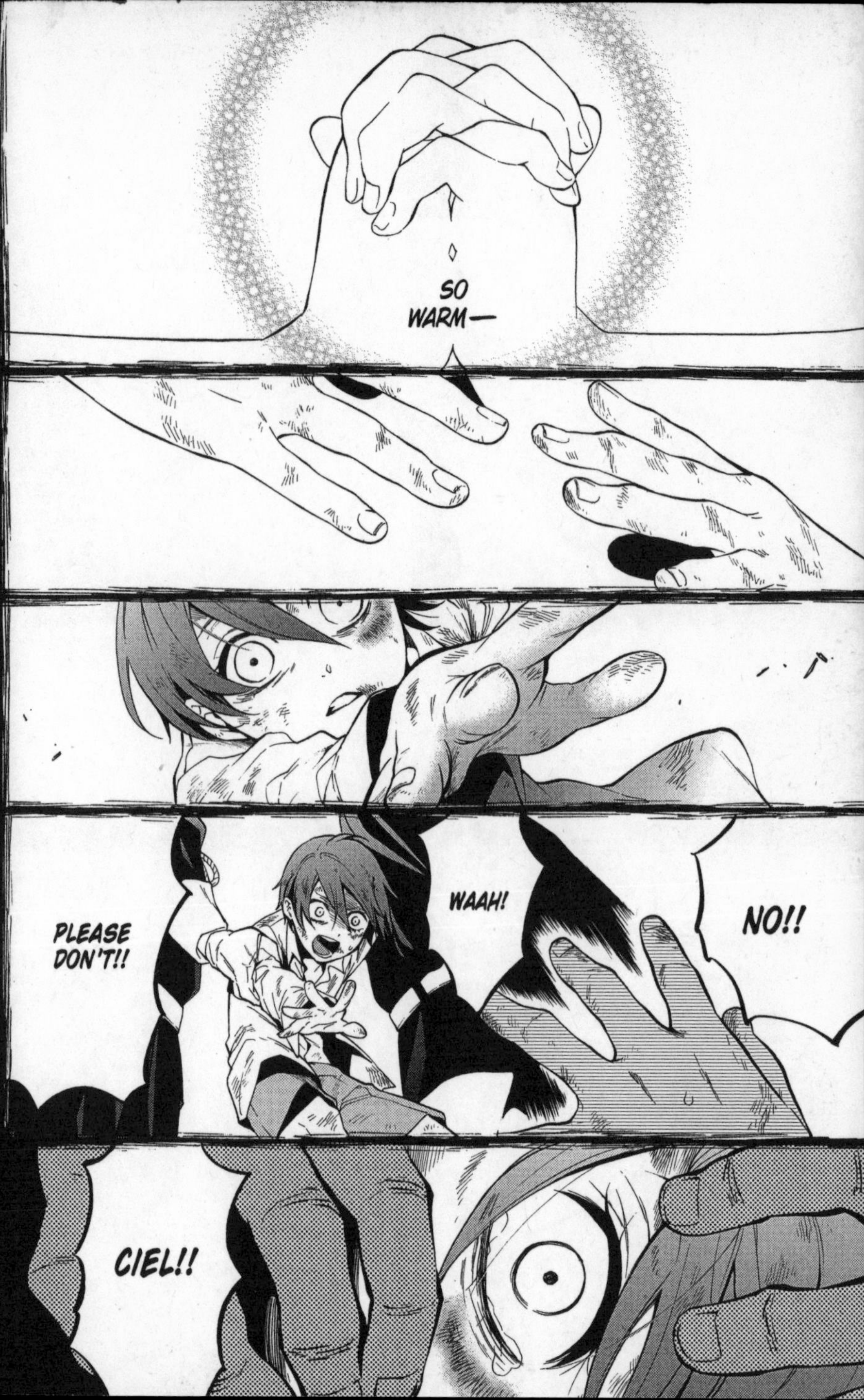
SO WARM—
NO!!
WAAH!
PLEASE DON'T!!
CIEL!!

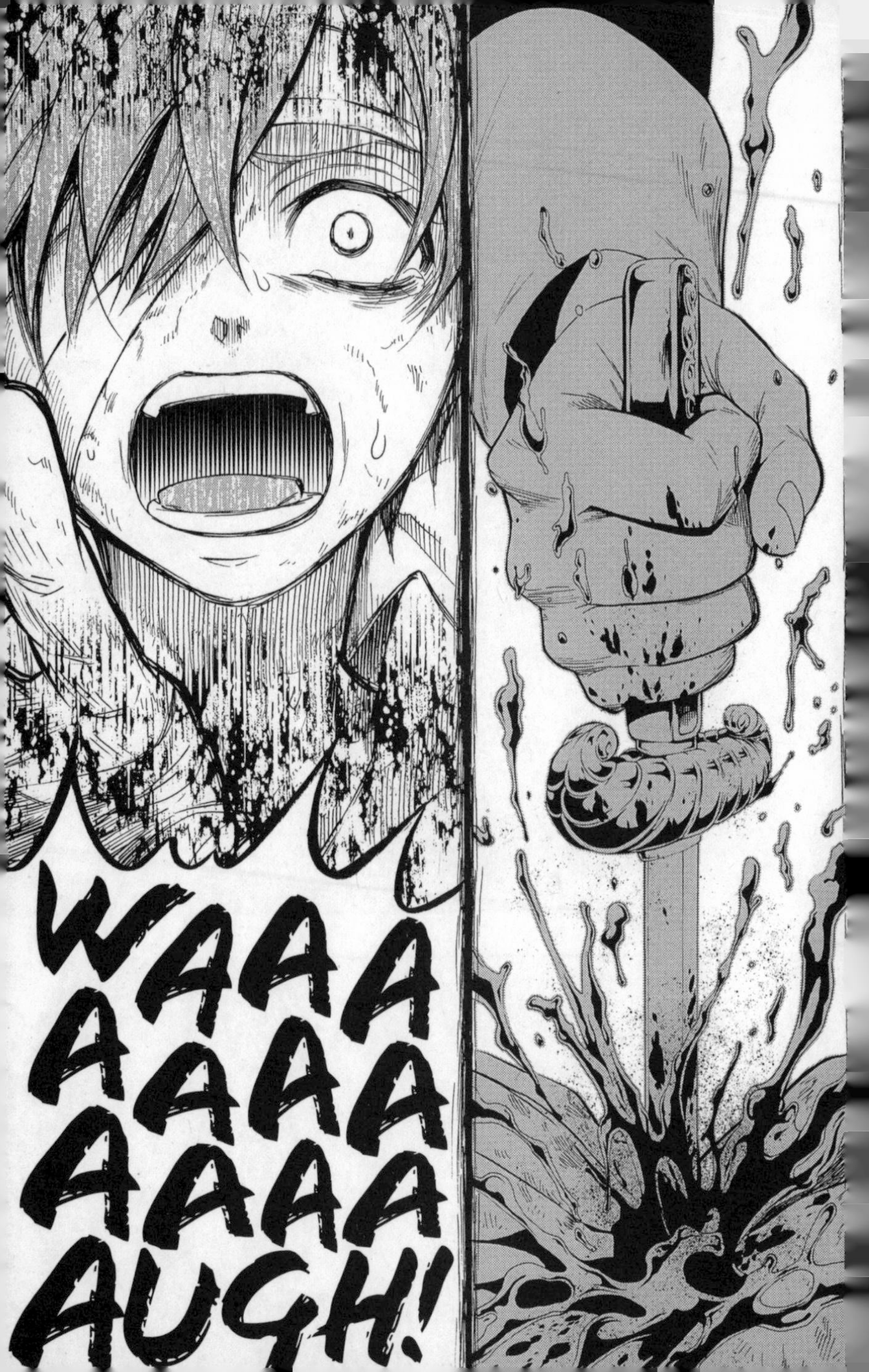
WAAAAAAAAAAAAUGH!

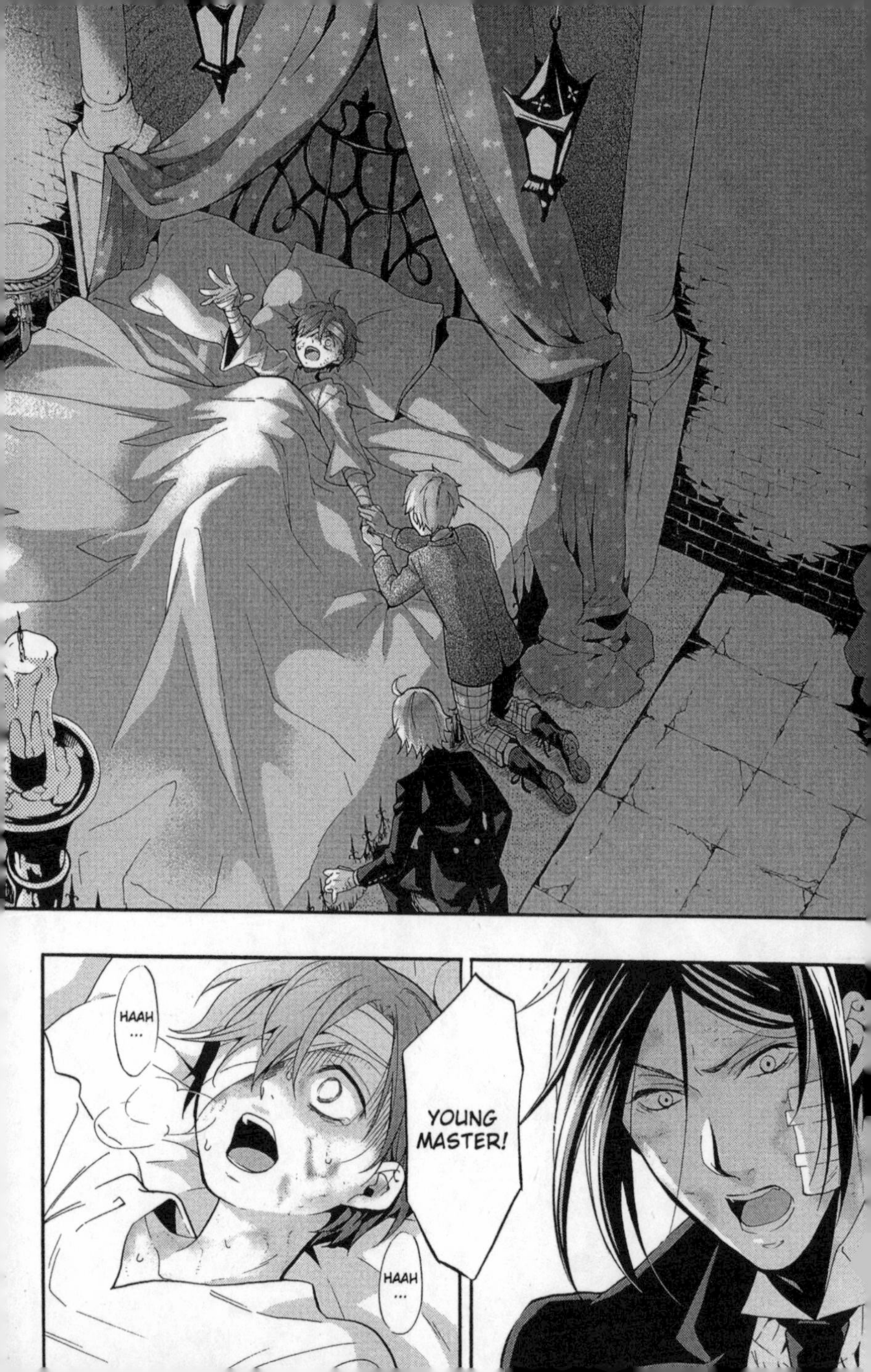
YOUNG MASTER!
HAAH ...
HAAH ...

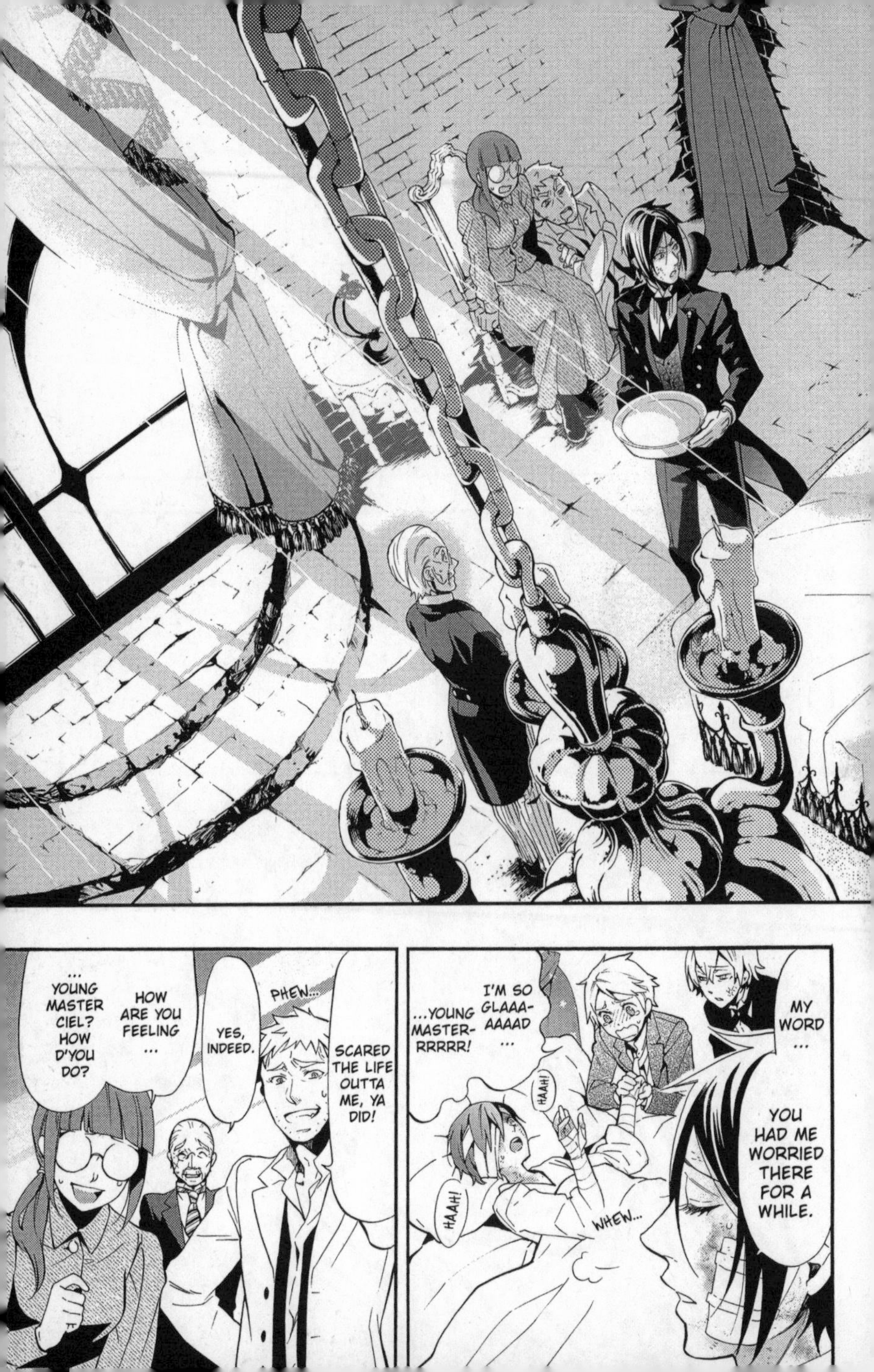
MY WORD ...
I'M SO GLAAA-AAAAD ...
...YOUNG MASTER-RRRRR!
YOU HAD ME WORRIED THERE FOR A WHILE.
HAAH!
WHEW...
HAAH!
SCARED THE LIFE OUTTA ME, YA DID!
PHEW...
YES, INDEED.
HOW ARE YOU FEELING ...
... YOUNG MASTER CIEL? HOW D'YOU DO?

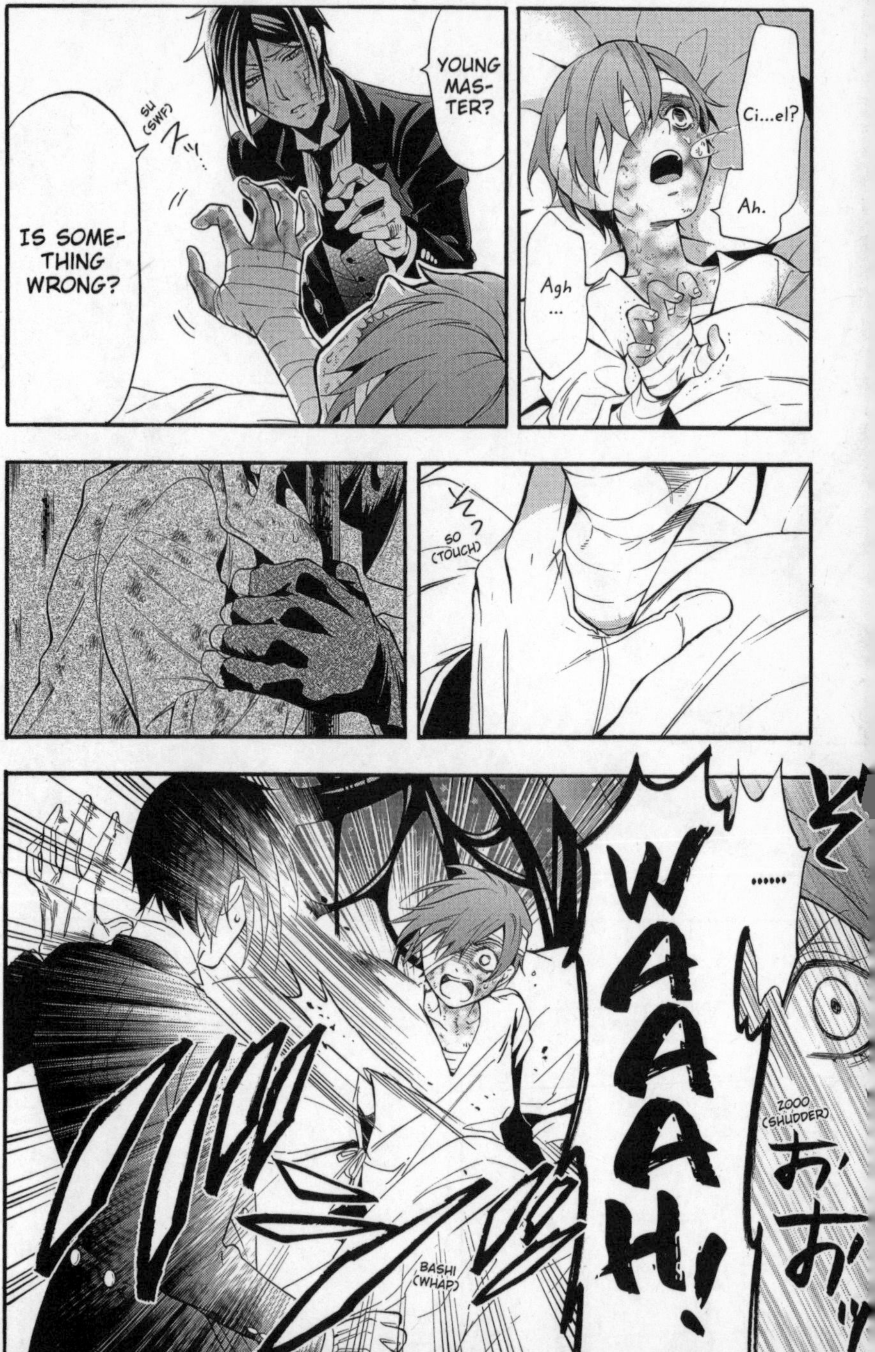
Ci...el?
Ah.
Agh ...
YOUNG MASTER?
SU (SWF)
IS SOMETHING WRONG?
SO (TOUCH)
......
WAAAH!
ZOOO (SHUDDER)
BASHI (WHAP)

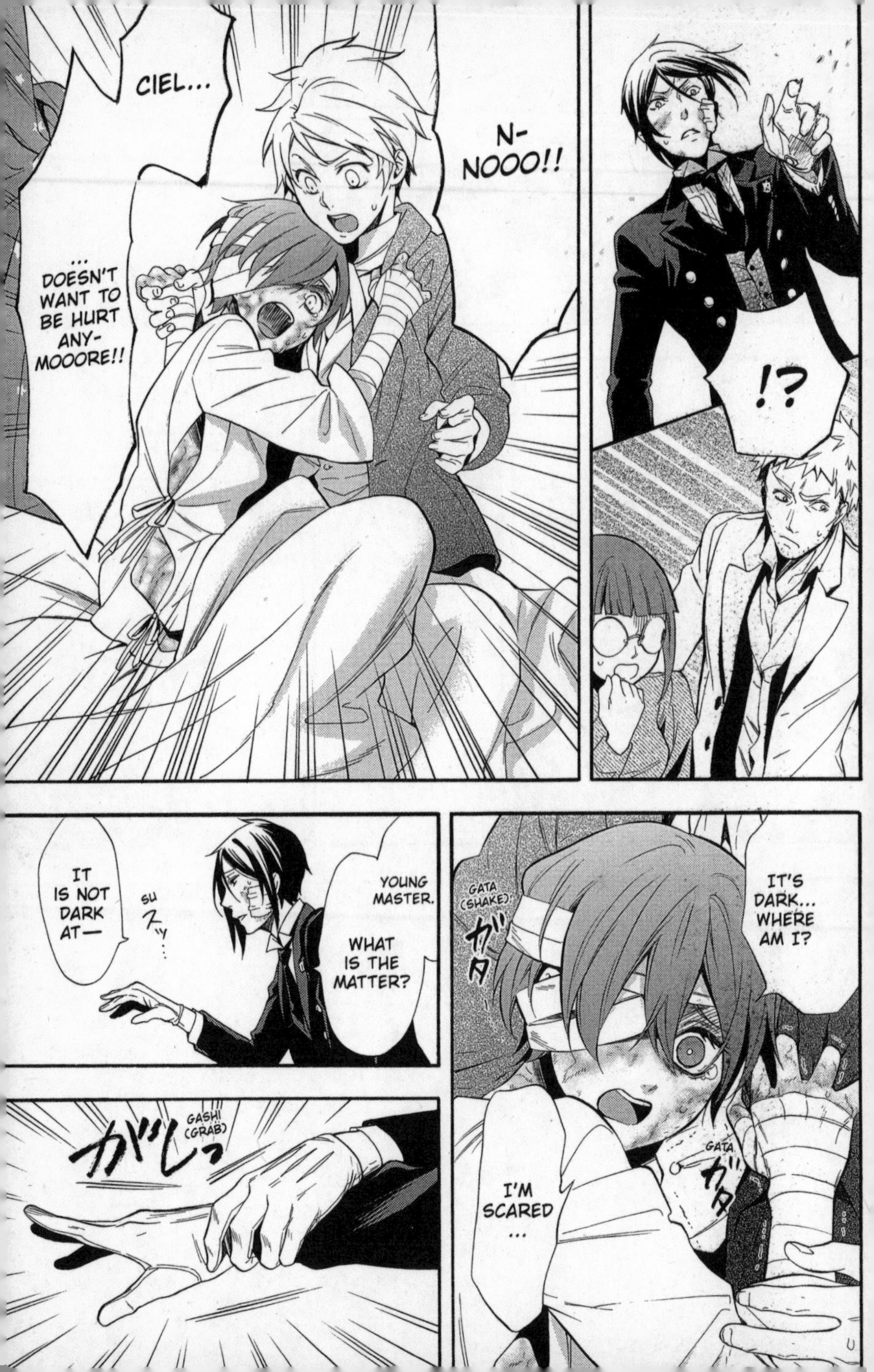
!?
N-NOOO!!
CIEL...
...DOESN'T WANT TO BE HURT ANY-MOOORE!!
IT'S DARK... WHERE AM I?
GATA (SHAKE)
ガタ
GATA
ガタ
I'M SCARED...
YOUNG MASTER.
WHAT IS THE MATTER?
SU
スッ...
IT IS NOT DARK AT—
GASHI (GRAB)
がしっ

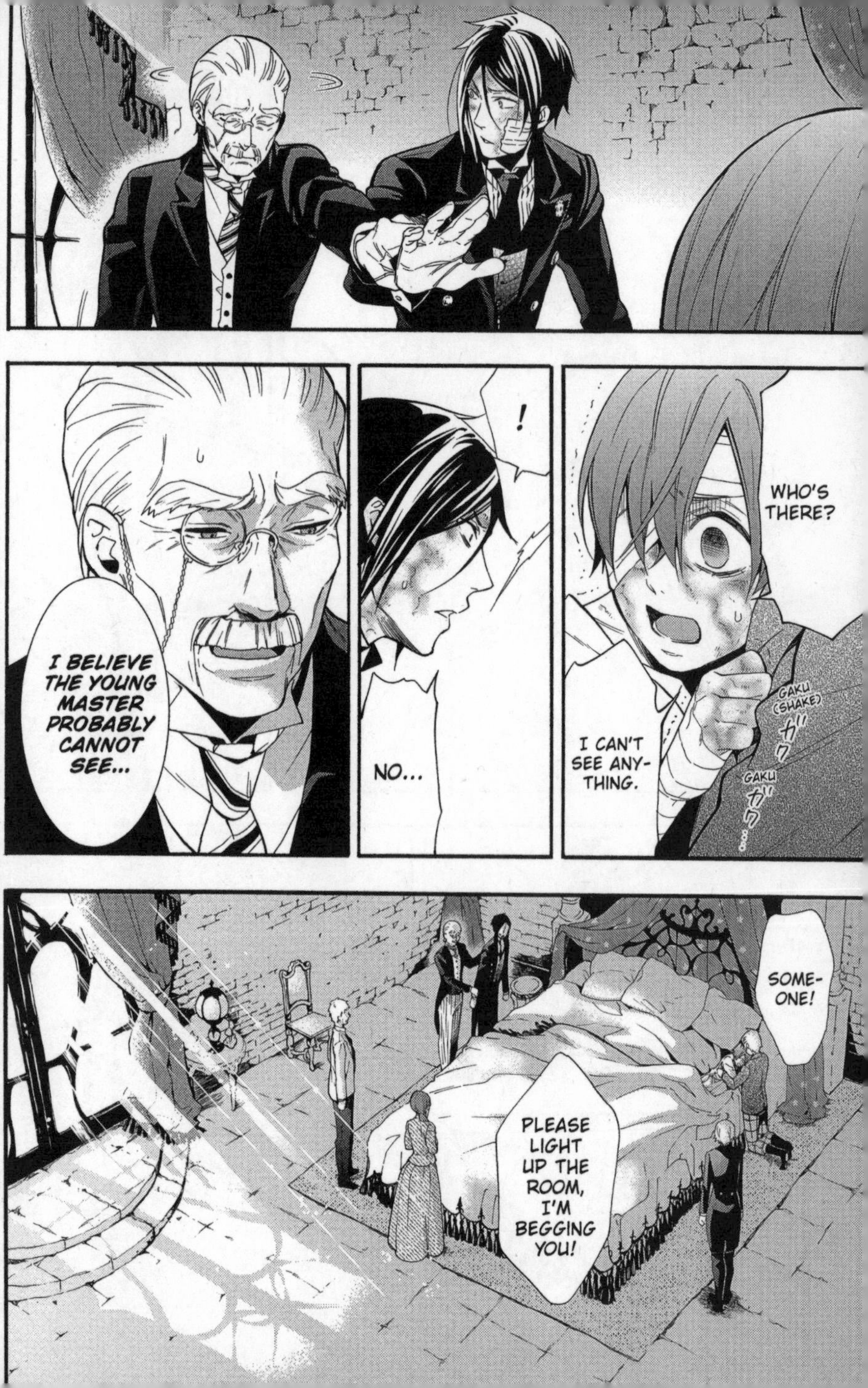
WHO'S THERE?
I CAN'T SEE ANY-THING.
GAKU (SHAKE)
ガク
GAKU
ガク…
!
NO...
I BELIEVE THE YOUNG MASTER PROBABLY CANNOT SEE...
SOME-ONE!
PLEASE LIGHT UP THE ROOM, I'M BEGGING YOU!

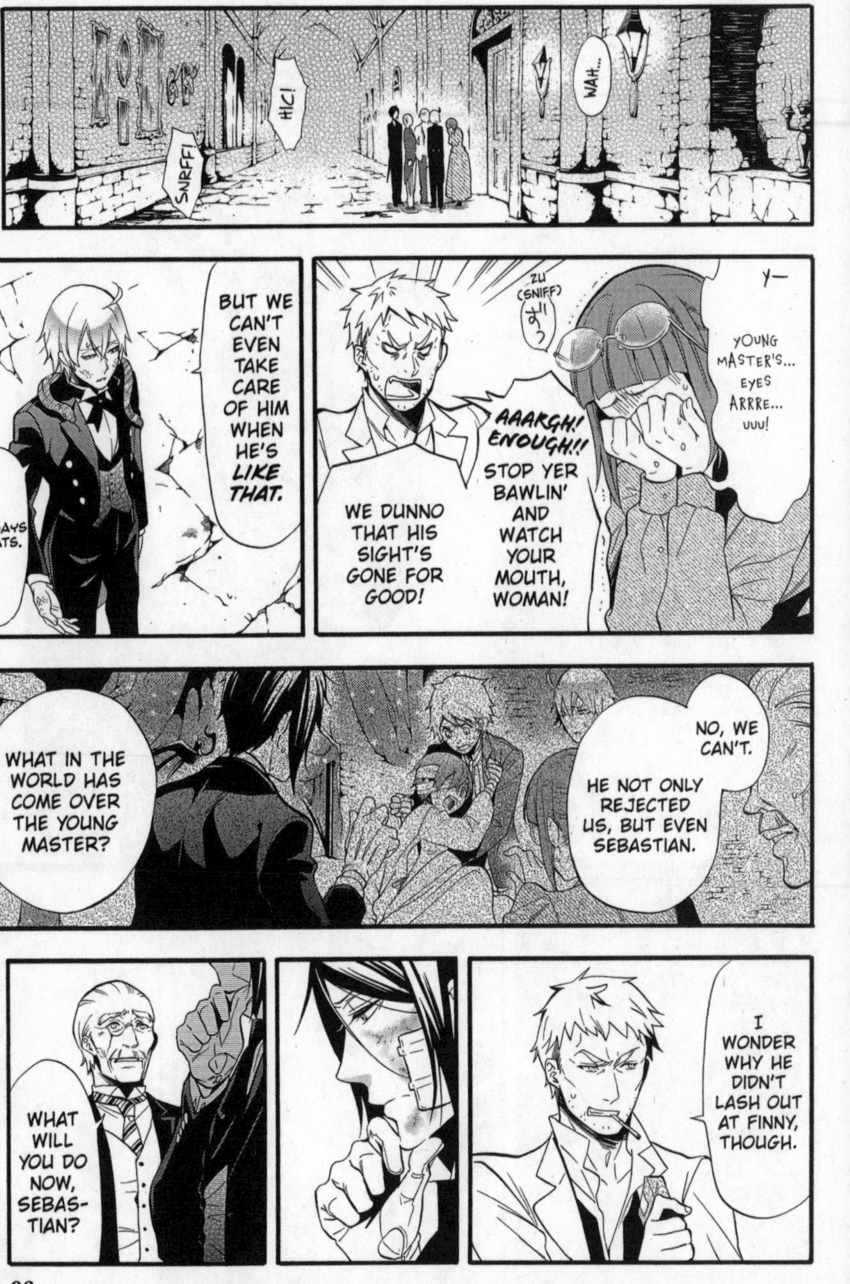
WAH...
HIC!
SNRFF!
Y—
YOUNG MASTER'S... EYES ARRRE... UUU!
ZU (SNIFF)
ずっ
AAARGH! ENOUGH!! STOP YER BAWLIN' AND WATCH YOUR MOUTH, WOMAN!
WE DUNNO THAT HIS SIGHT'S GONE FOR GOOD!
BUT WE CAN'T EVEN TAKE CARE OF HIM WHEN HE'S LIKE THAT.
—SAYS KEATS.
NO, WE CAN'T.
HE NOT ONLY REJECTED US, BUT EVEN SEBASTIAN.
WHAT IN THE WORLD HAS COME OVER THE YOUNG MASTER?
I WONDER WHY HE DIDN'T LASH OUT AT FINNY, THOUGH.
WHAT WILL YOU DO NOW, SEBAS-TIAN?

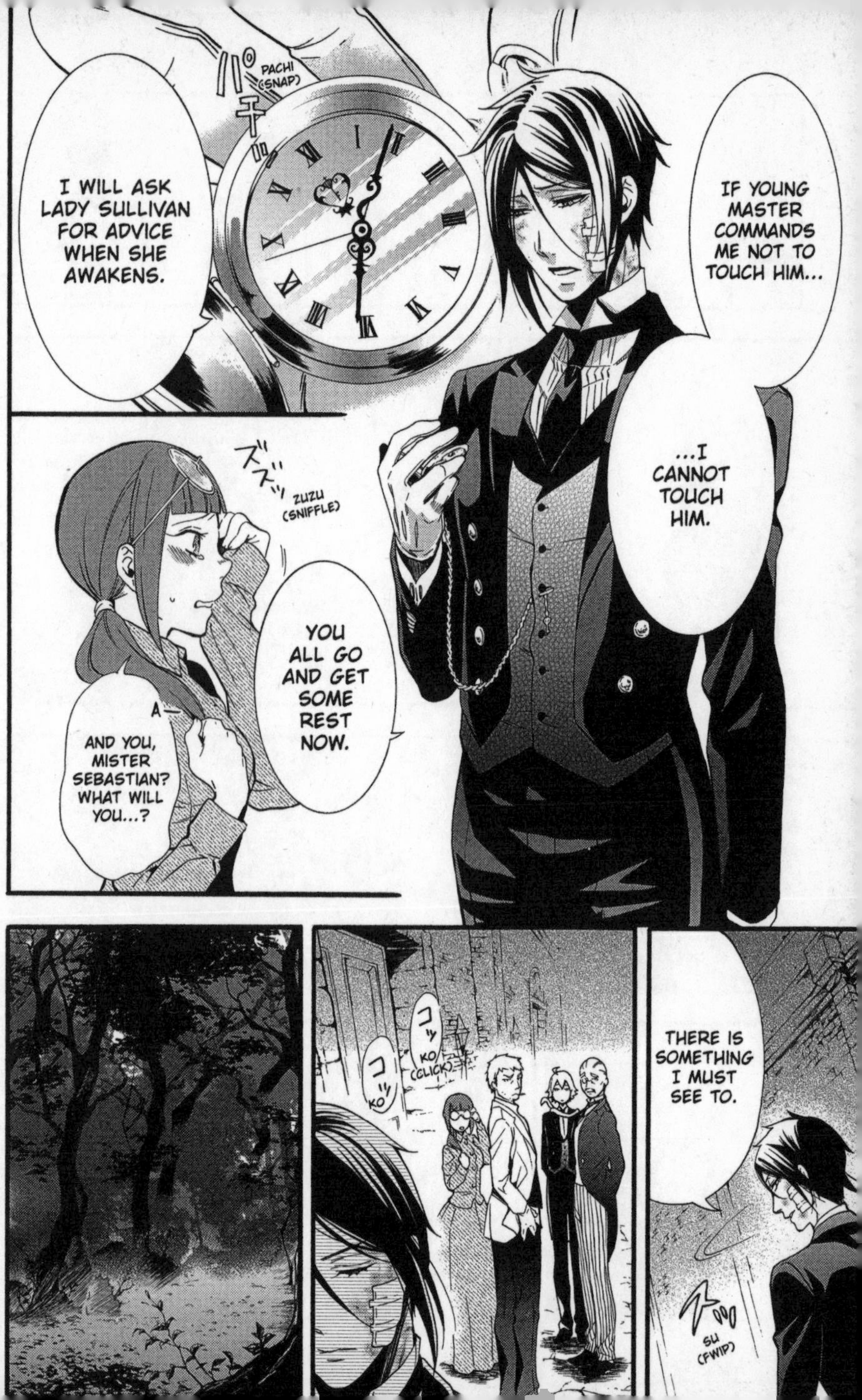
IF YOUNG MASTER COMMANDS ME NOT TO TOUCH HIM...
...I CANNOT TOUCH HIM.
PACHI (SNAP)
I WILL ASK LADY SULLIVAN FOR ADVICE WHEN SHE AWAKENS.
ZUZU (SNIFFLE)
YOU ALL GO AND GET SOME REST NOW.
A—
AND YOU, MISTER SEBASTIAN? WHAT WILL YOU...?
THERE IS SOMETHING I MUST SEE TO.
SU (FWIP)
KO (CLICK)
KO

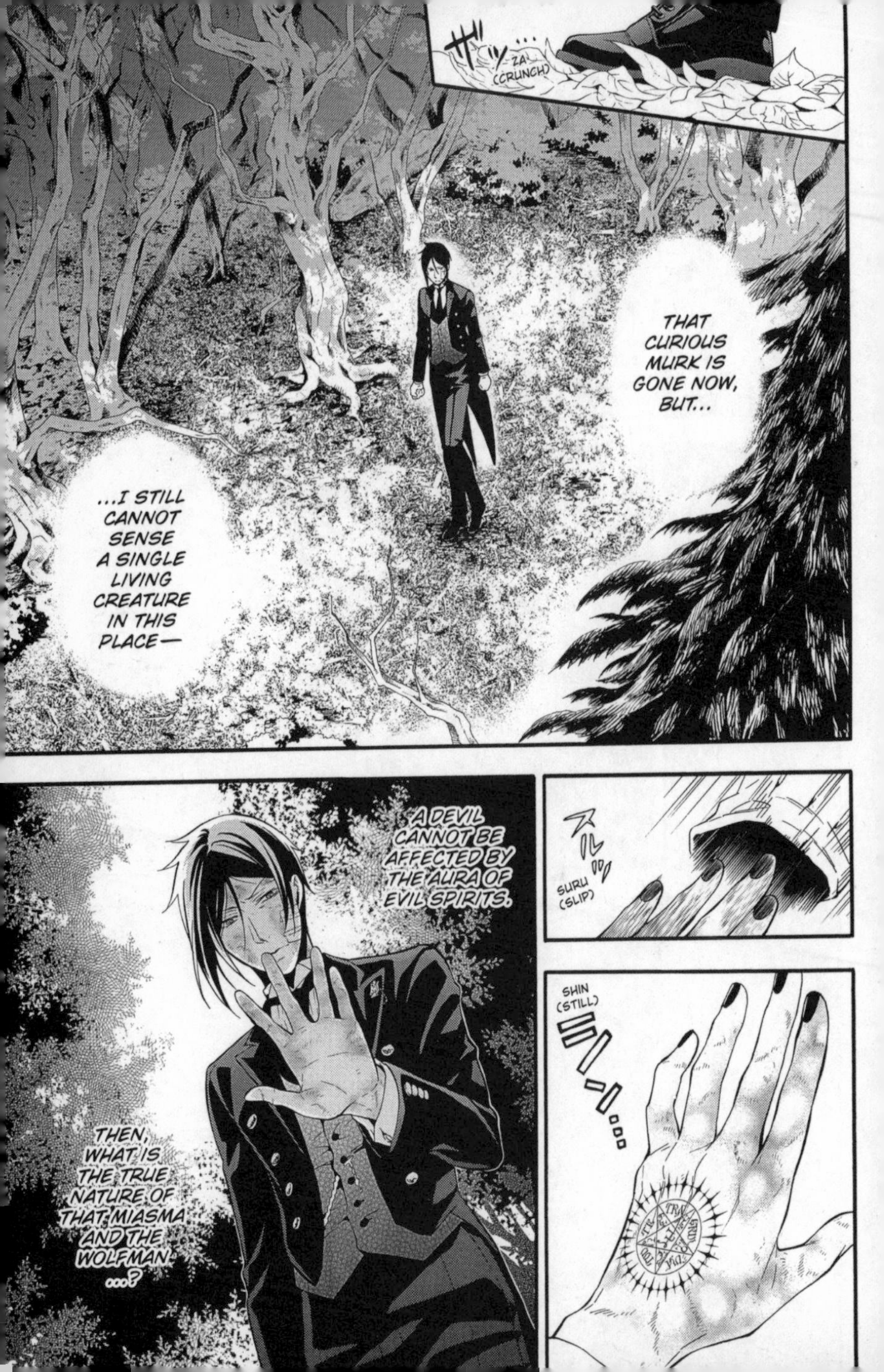
ザッ…
ZA (CRUNCH)
THAT CURIOUS MURK IS GONE NOW, BUT...
...I STILL CANNOT SENSE A SINGLE LIVING CREATURE IN THIS PLACE—
スルッ
SURU (SLIP)
A DEVIL CANNOT BE AFFECTED BY THE AURA OF EVIL SPIRITS.
SHIN (STILL)
THEN, WHAT IS THE TRUE NATURE OF THAT MIASMA AND THE WOLFMAN...?

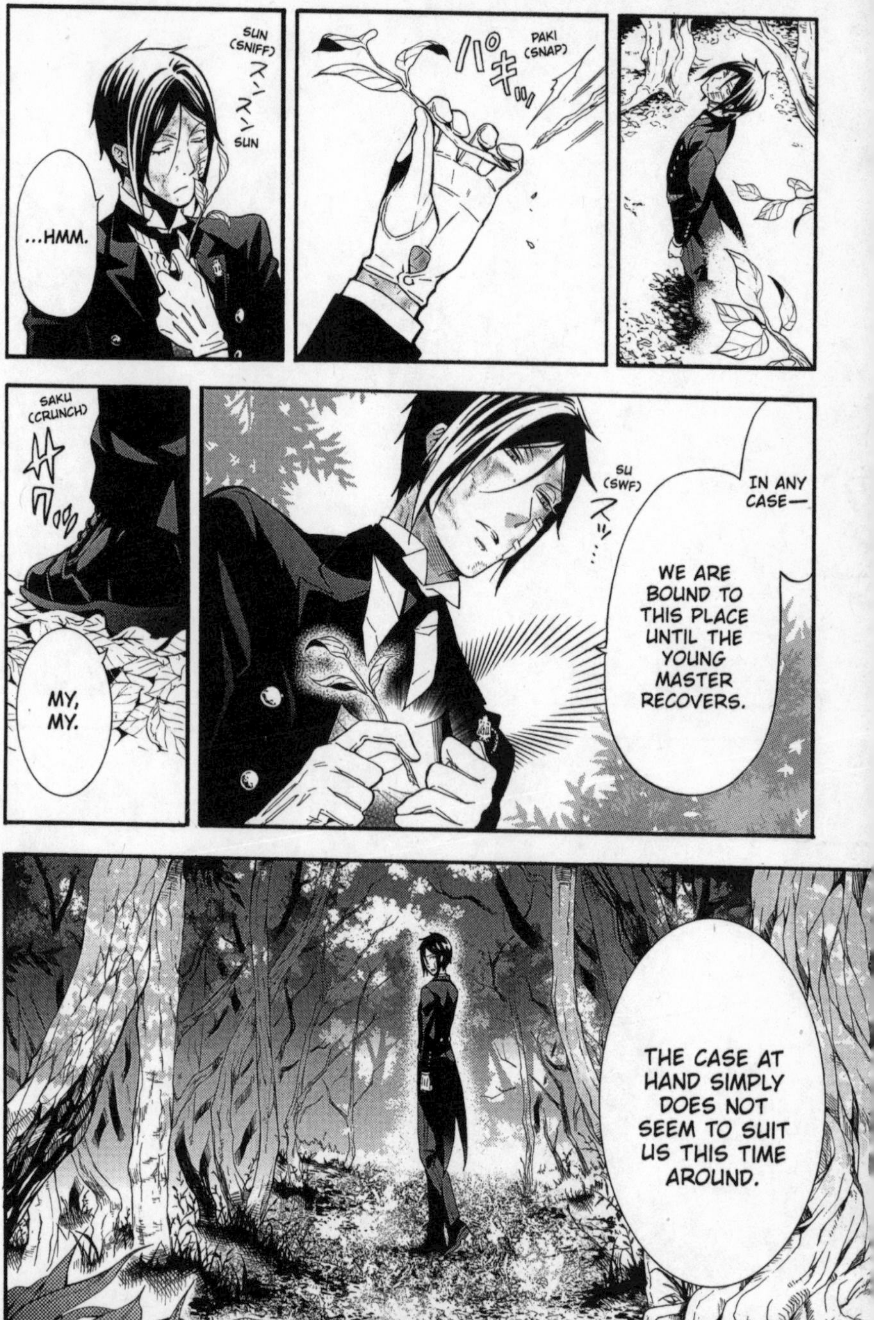
PAKI (SNAP)
パキッ
SUN (SNIFF)
スン スン
SUN
...HMM.
IN ANY CASE—
WE ARE BOUND TO THIS PLACE UNTIL THE YOUNG MASTER RECOVERS.
SU (SWF)
スッ...
SAKU (CRUNCH)
サクッ
MY, MY.
THE CASE AT HAND SIMPLY DOES NOT SEEM TO SUIT US THIS TIME AROUND.

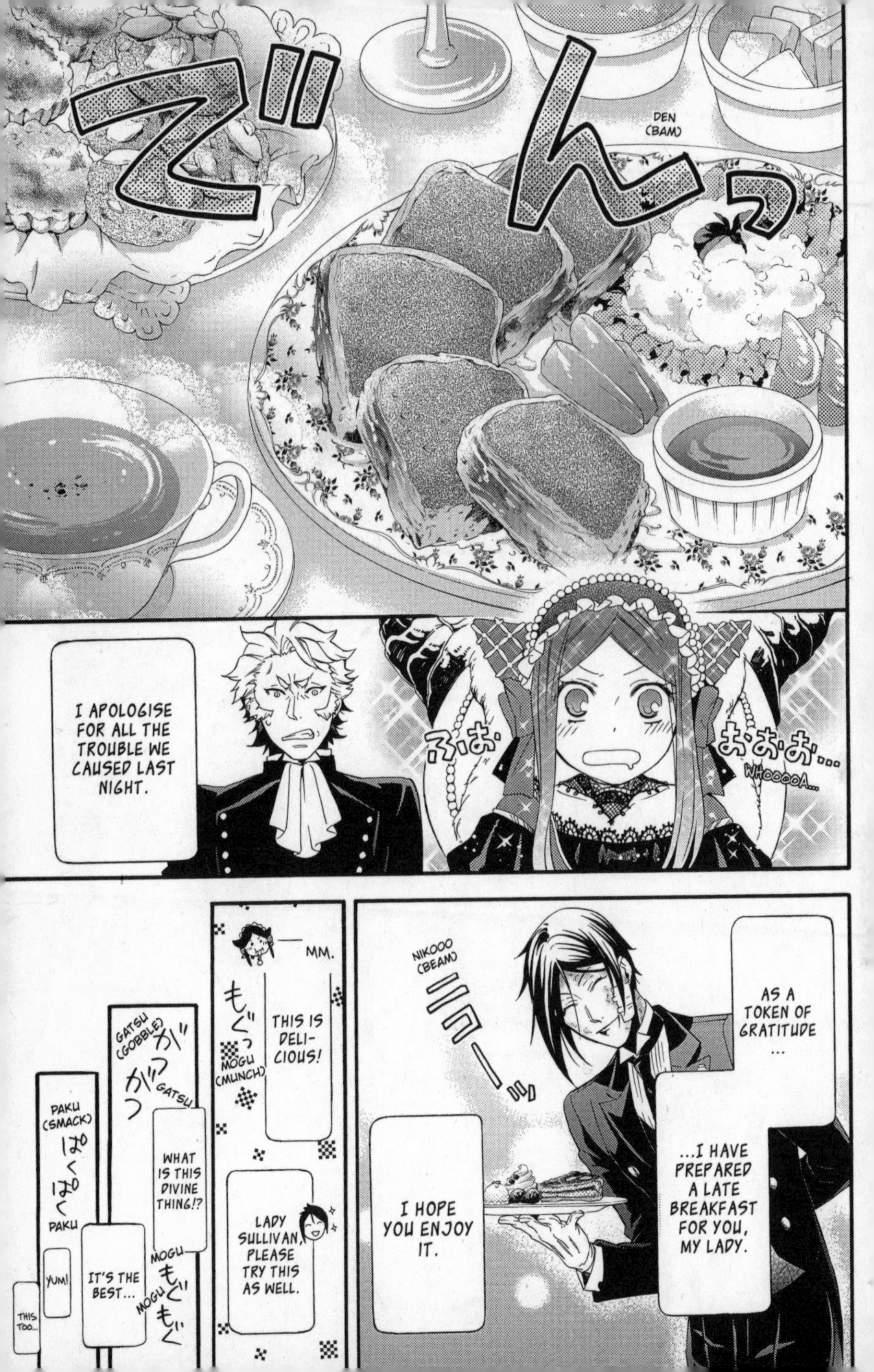
でんっ
DEN (BAM)
ふぉ
おおお…
WHOOOOA…
I APOLOGISE FOR ALL THE TROUBLE WE CAUSED LAST NIGHT.
AS A TOKEN OF GRATITUDE …
…I HAVE PREPARED A LATE BREAKFAST FOR YOU, MY LADY.
ニコー
NIKOOO (BEAM)
I HOPE YOU ENJOY IT.
—MM.
THIS IS DELI-CIOUS!
もぐっ
MOGU (MUNCH)
LADY SULLIVAN, PLEASE TRY THIS AS WELL.
がつ
GATSU (GOBBLE)
がつ
GATSU
WHAT IS THIS DIVINE THING!?
IT'S THE BEST…
もぐもぐ
MOGU MOGU
ぱくぱく
PAKU (SMACK)
PAKU
YUM!
THIS TOO…

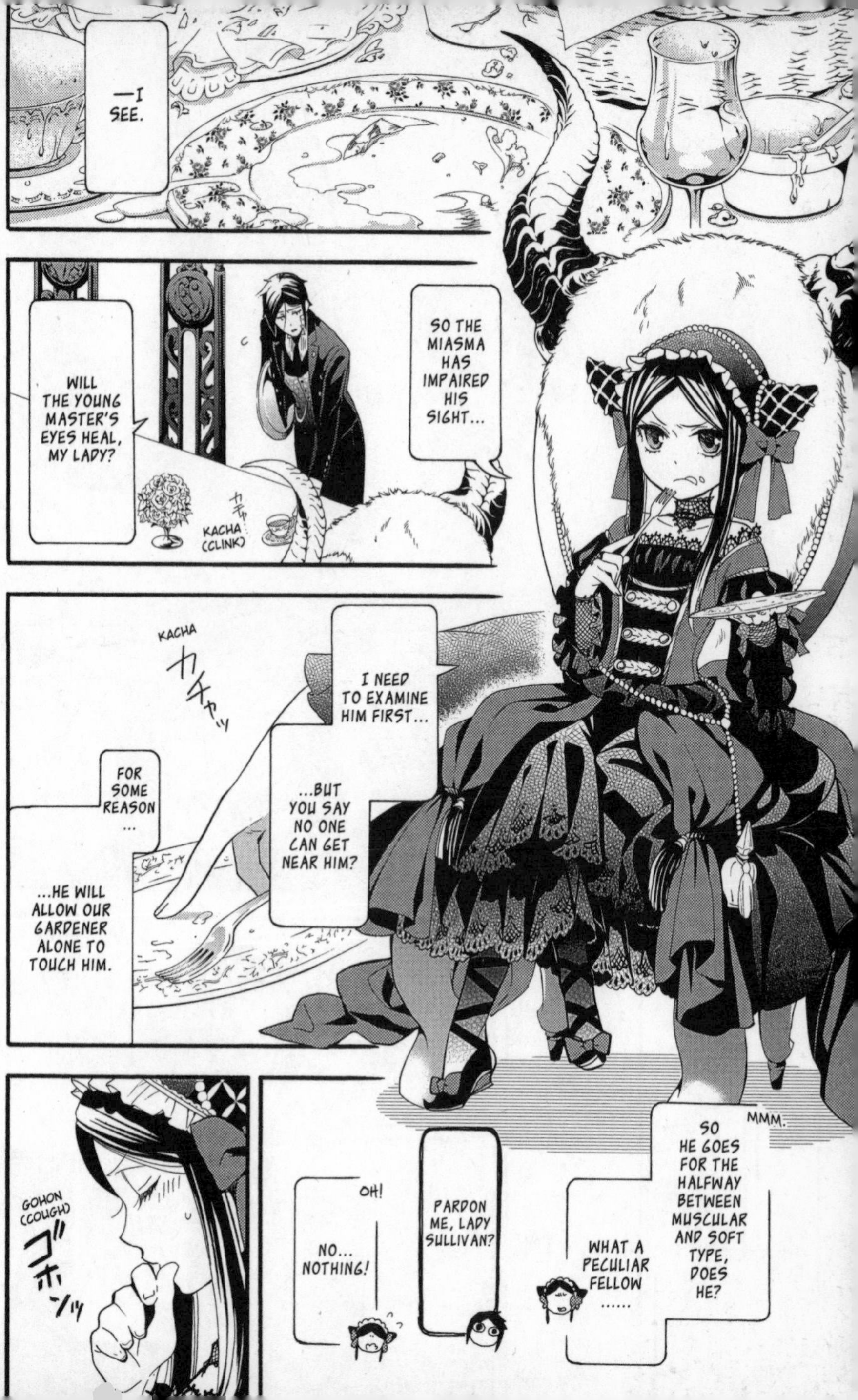
—I SEE.
SO THE MIASMA HAS IMPAIRED HIS SIGHT...
WILL THE YOUNG MASTER'S EYES HEAL, MY LADY?
カチャ
KACHA (CLINK)
I NEED TO EXAMINE HIM FIRST...
...BUT YOU SAY NO ONE CAN GET NEAR HIM?
KACHA
カチャッ
FOR SOME REASON...
...HE WILL ALLOW OUR GARDENER ALONE TO TOUCH HIM.
MMM.
SO HE GOES FOR THE HALFWAY BETWEEN MUSCULAR AND SOFT TYPE, DOES HE?
WHAT A PECULIAR FELLOW......
PARDON ME, LADY SULLIVAN?
OH!
NO... NOTHING!
GOHON (COUGH)
ゴホンッ

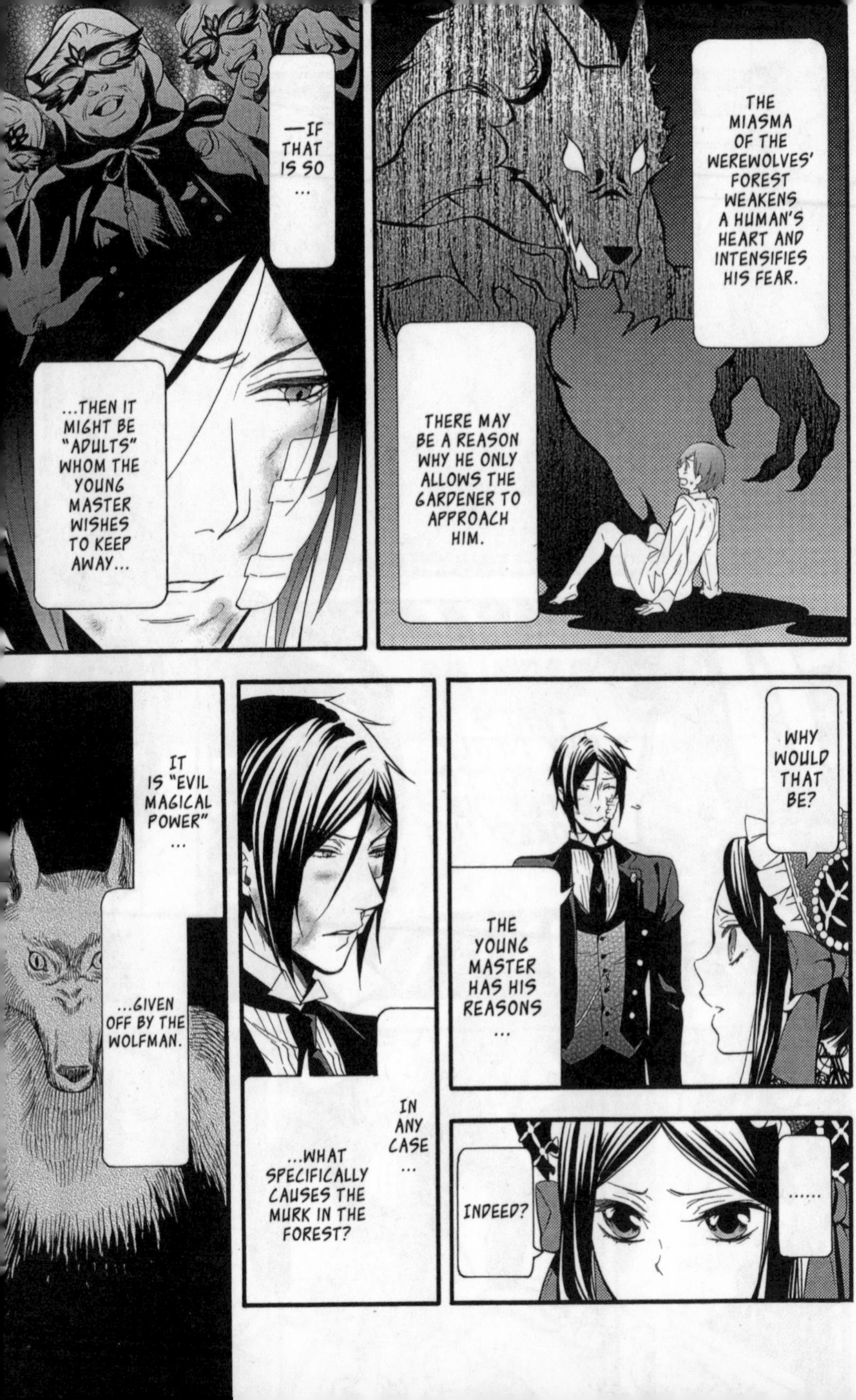
THE MIASMA OF THE WEREWOLVES' FOREST WEAKENS A HUMAN'S HEART AND INTENSIFIES HIS FEAR.
THERE MAY BE A REASON WHY HE ONLY ALLOWS THE GARDENER TO APPROACH HIM.
—IF THAT IS SO ...
...THEN IT MIGHT BE "ADULTS" WHOM THE YOUNG MASTER WISHES TO KEEP AWAY...
WHY WOULD THAT BE?
THE YOUNG MASTER HAS HIS REASONS ...
......
INDEED?
IN ANY CASE ...
...WHAT SPECIFICALLY CAUSES THE MURK IN THE FOREST?
IT IS "EVIL MAGICAL POWER" ...
...GIVEN OFF BY THE WOLFMAN.

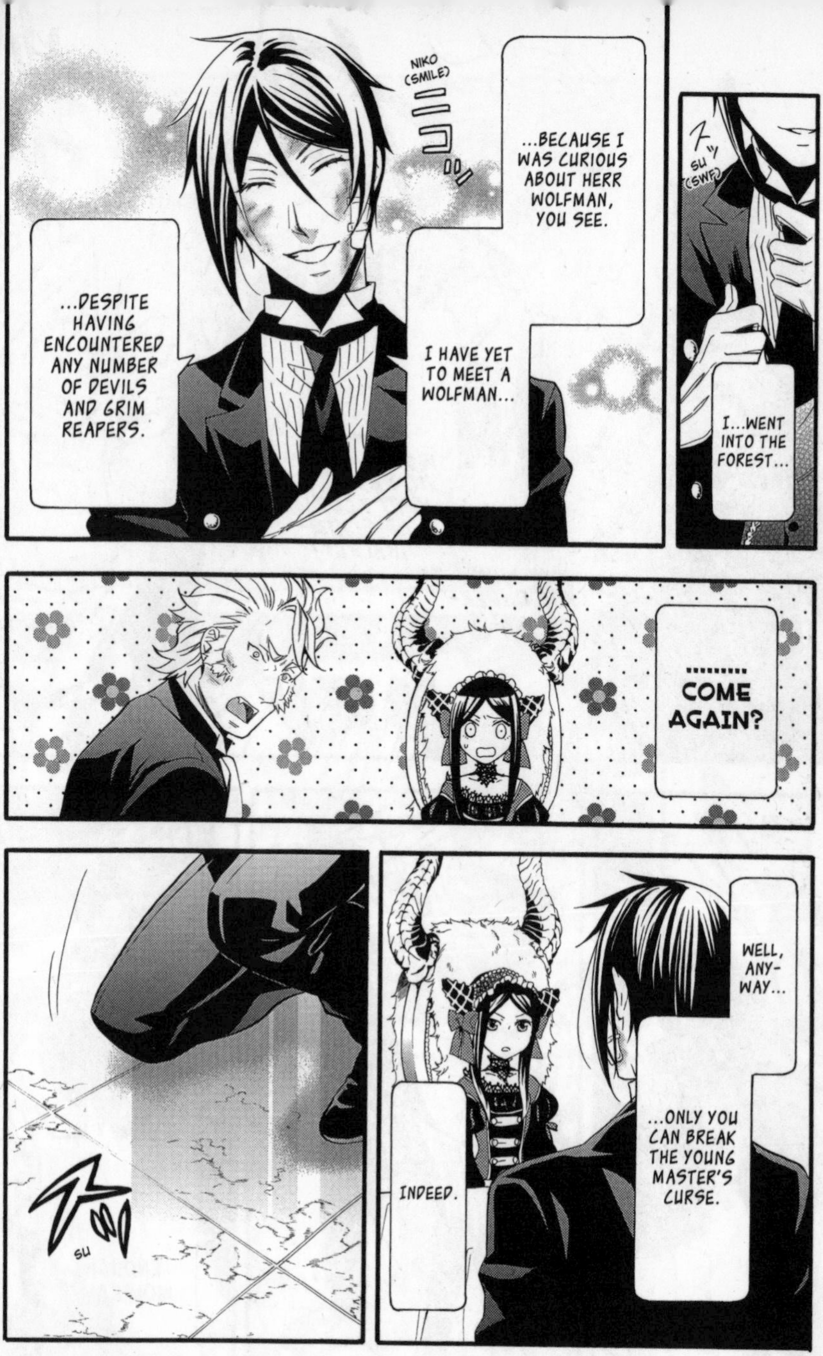

SU (SWF)
I...WENT INTO THE FOREST...
NIKO (SMILE)
...BECAUSE I WAS CURIOUS ABOUT HERR WOLFMAN, YOU SEE.
I HAVE YET TO MEET A WOLFMAN...
...DESPITE HAVING ENCOUNTERED ANY NUMBER OF DEVILS AND GRIM REAPERS.
....
COME AGAIN?
WELL, ANY-WAY...
...ONLY YOU CAN BREAK THE YOUNG MASTER'S CURSE.
INDEED.
SU

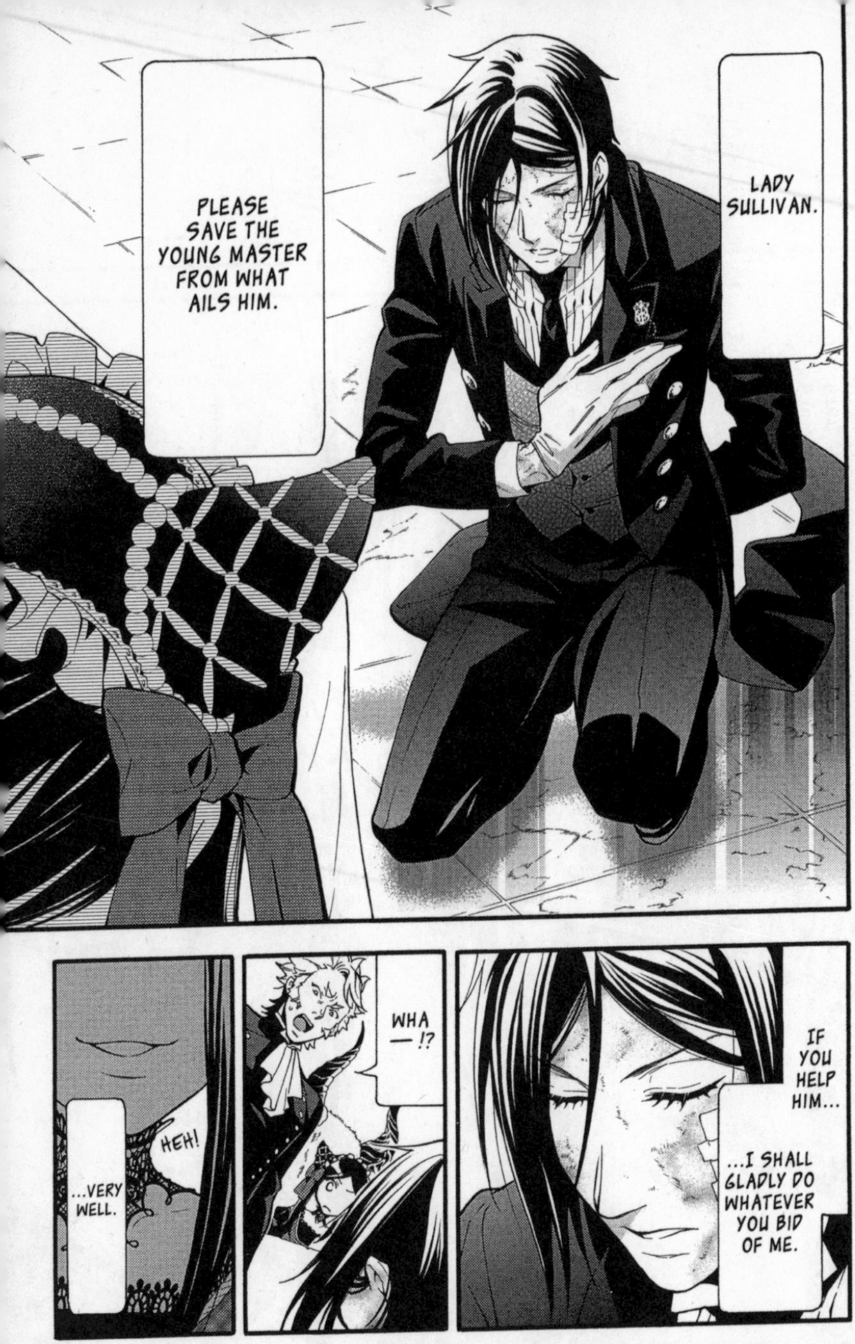
LADY SULLIVAN.
PLEASE SAVE THE YOUNG MASTER FROM WHAT AILS HIM.
IF YOU HELP HIM...
...I SHALL GLADLY DO WHATEVER YOU BID OF ME.
WHA—!?
HEH!
...VERY WELL.

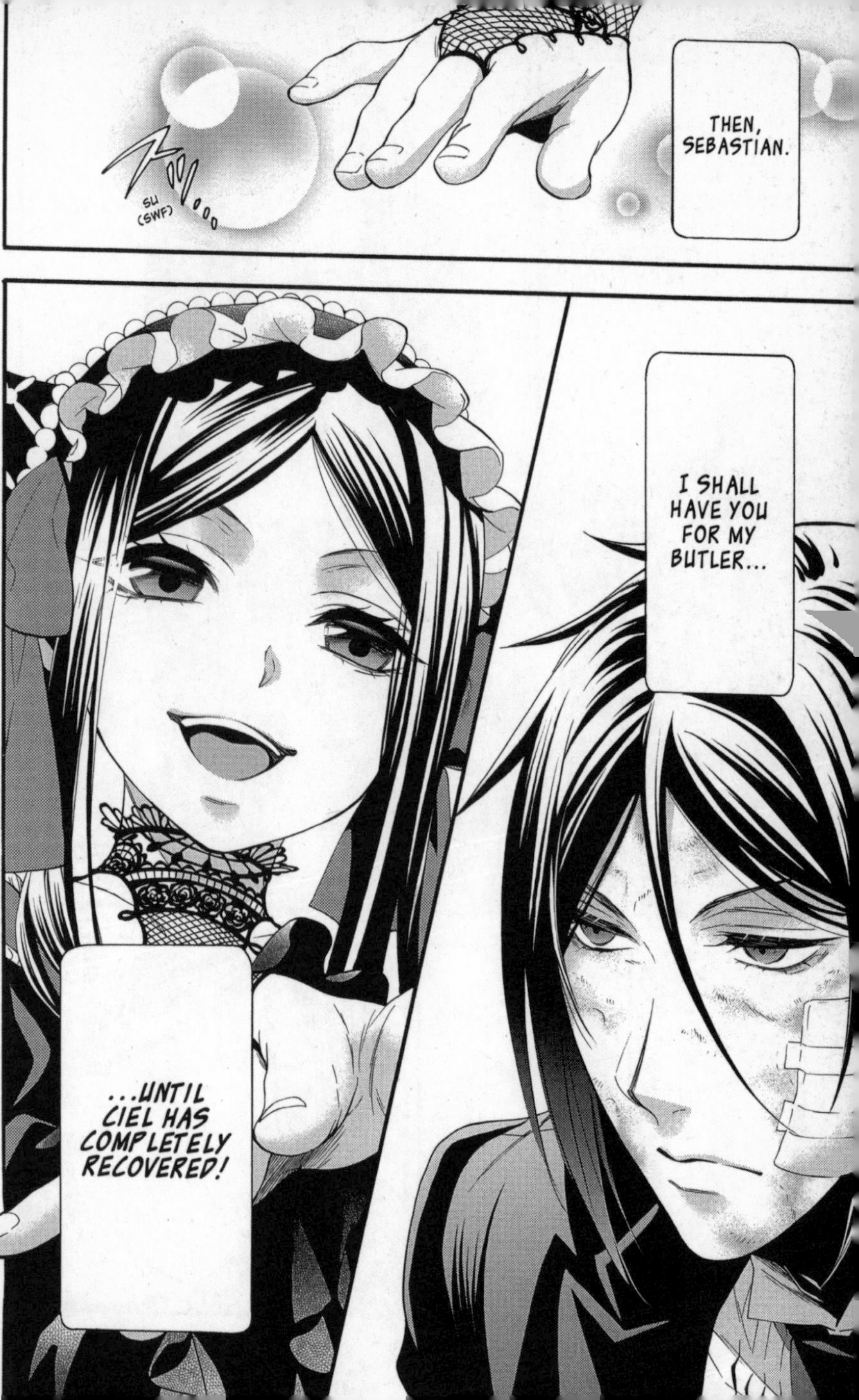
THEN, SEBASTIAN.
SU (SWF)
I SHALL HAVE YOU FOR MY BUTLER...
...UNTIL CIEL HAS COMPLETELY RECOVERED!

Black Butler

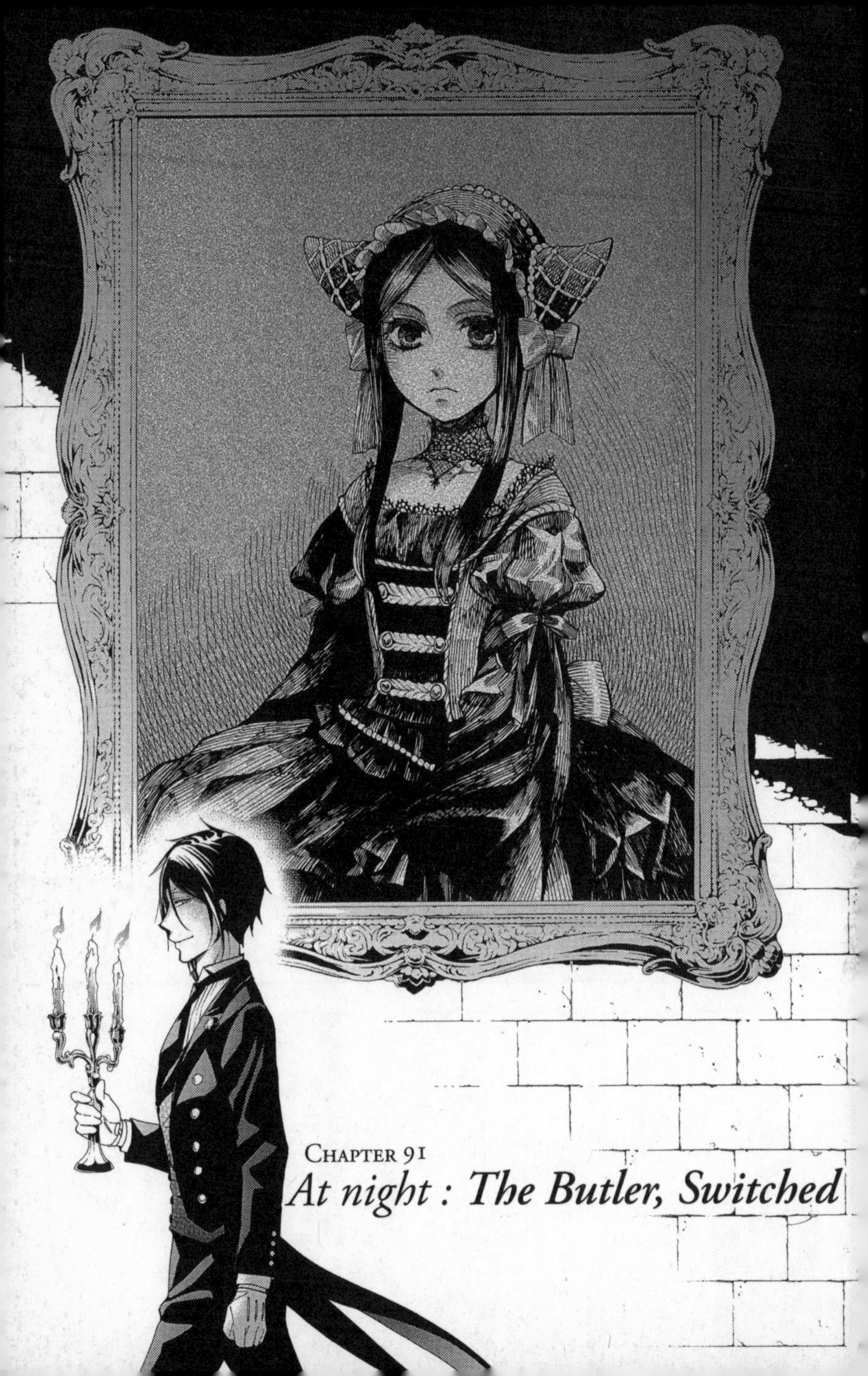
CHAPTER 91
At night : The Butler, Switched

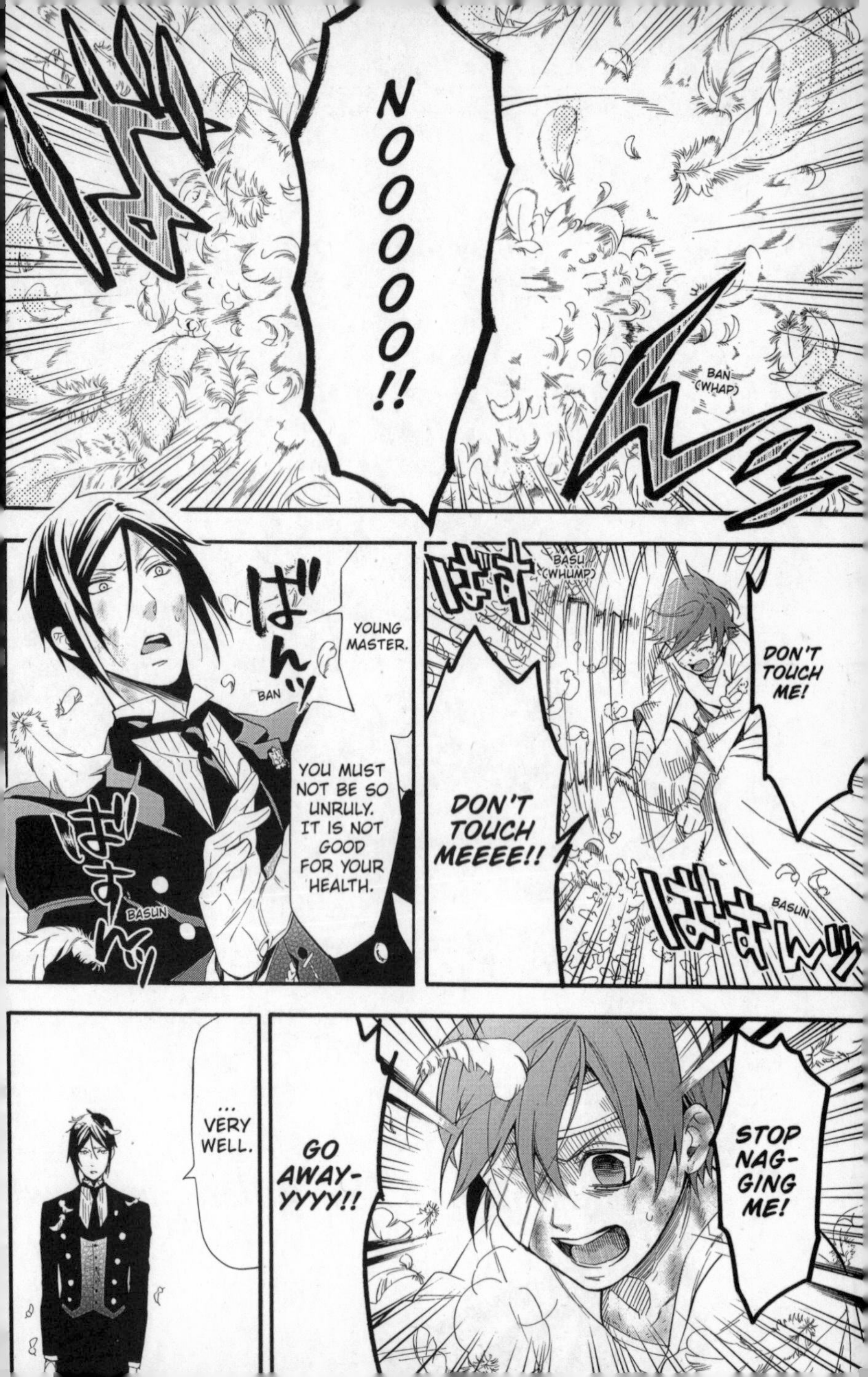
NOOOOOO!!
BAN (WHAP)
ばす
BASU (WHUMP)
DON'T TOUCH ME!
DON'T TOUCH MEEEE!!
ばすんッ
BASUN
ばんッ
BAN
YOUNG MASTER.
YOU MUST NOT BE SO UNRULY. IT IS NOT GOOD FOR YOUR HEALTH.
ばすんッ
BASUN
STOP NAG-GING ME!
GO AWAY-YYYY!!
...VERY WELL.

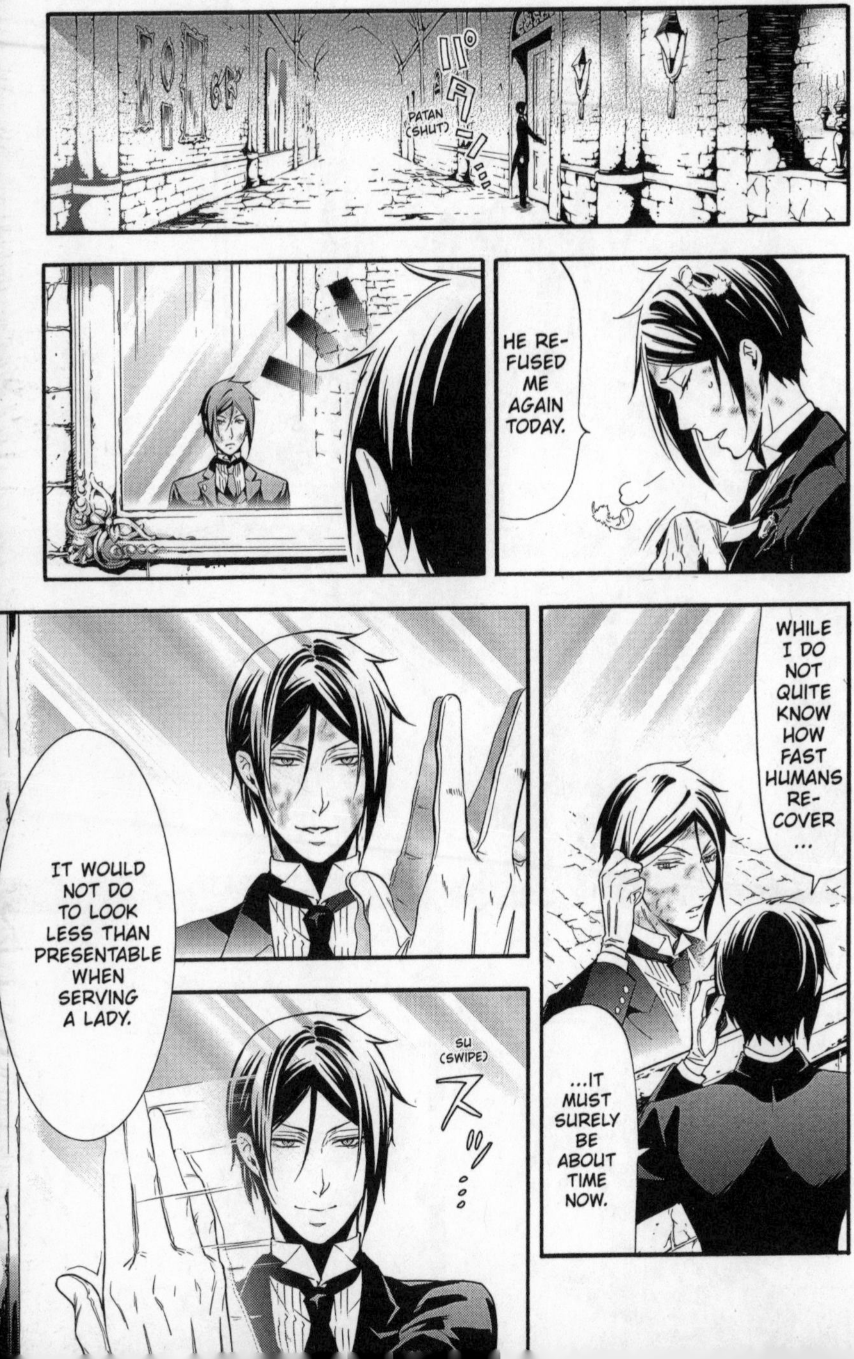
PATAN (SHUT)
HE RE-FUSED ME AGAIN TODAY.
WHILE I DO NOT QUITE KNOW HOW FAST HUMANS RE-COVER...
...IT MUST SURELY BE ABOUT TIME NOW.
IT WOULD NOT DO TO LOOK LESS THAN PRESENTABLE WHEN SERVING A LADY.
SU (SWIPE)

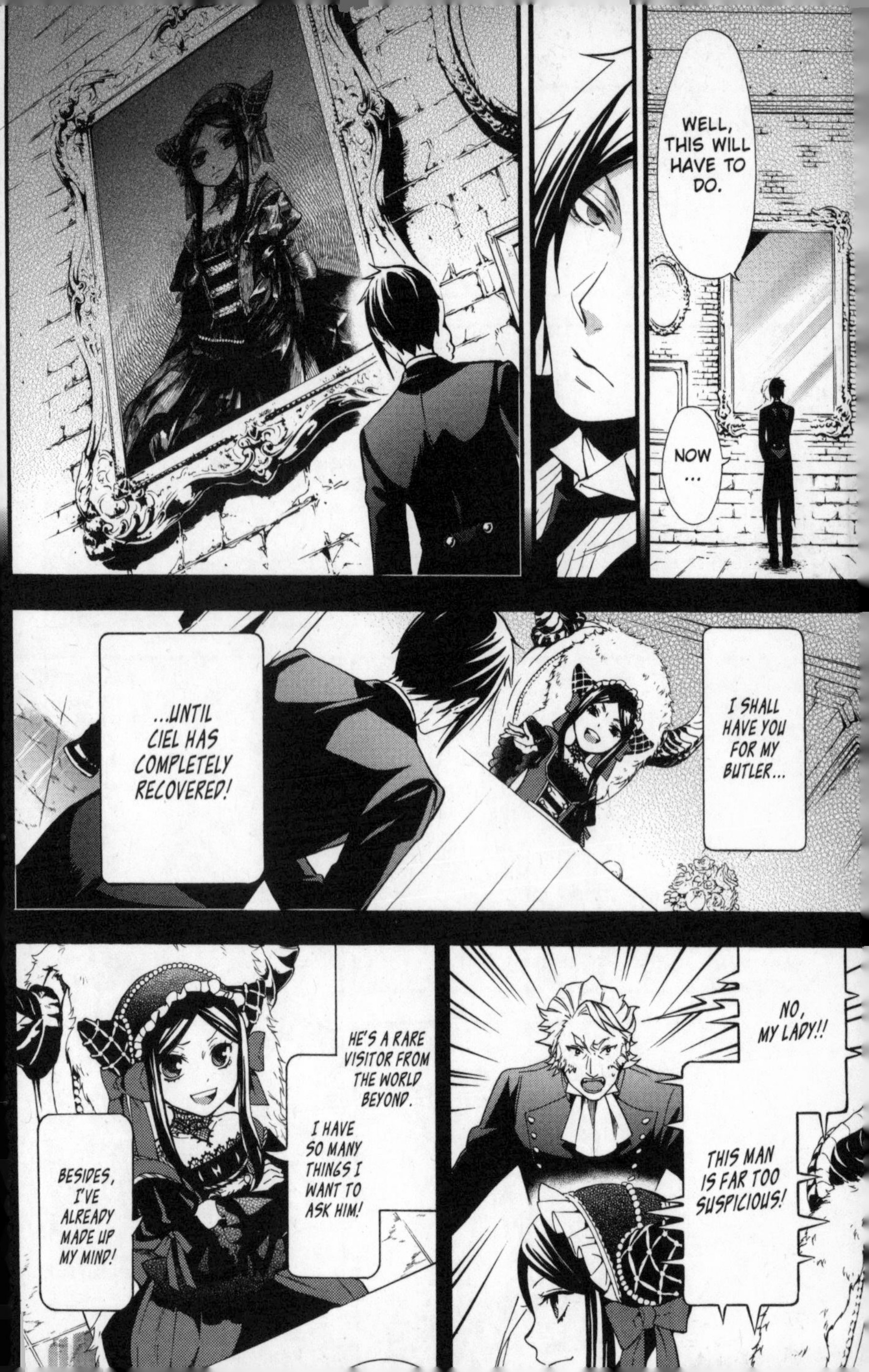
WELL, THIS WILL HAVE TO DO.
NOW ...
I SHALL HAVE YOU FOR MY BUTLER...
...UNTIL CIEL HAS COMPLETELY RECOVERED!
NO, MY LADY!!
THIS MAN IS FAR TOO SUSPICIOUS!
HE'S A RARE VISITOR FROM THE WORLD BEYOND.
I HAVE SO MANY THINGS I WANT TO ASK HIM!
BESIDES, I'VE ALREADY MADE UP MY MIND!

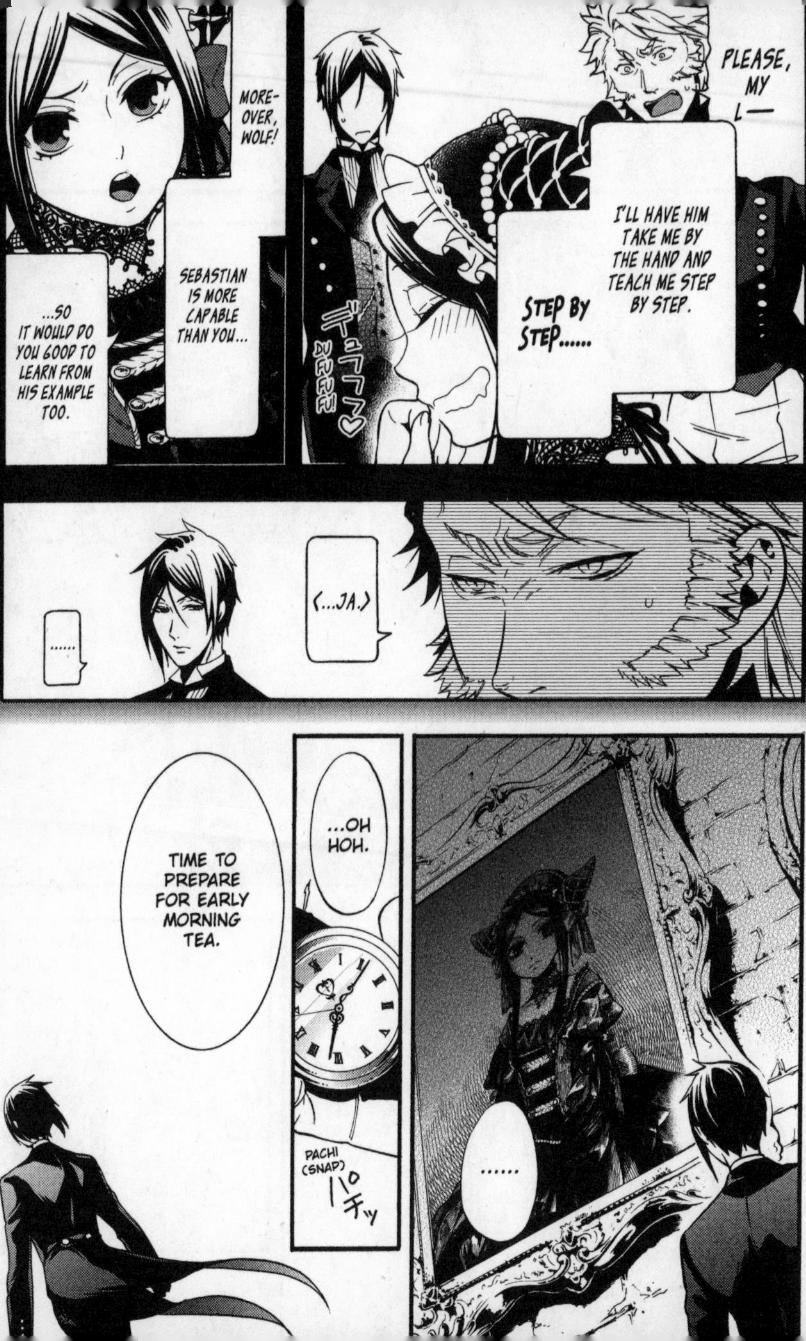
PLEASE, MY L—
I'LL HAVE HIM TAKE ME BY THE HAND AND TEACH ME STEP BY STEP.
STEP BY STEP......
デュフフ♡
DUFUFU!
MORE-OVER, WOLF!
SEBASTIAN IS MORE CAPABLE THAN YOU...
...SO IT WOULD DO YOU GOOD TO LEARN FROM HIS EXAMPLE TOO.
〈...JA.〉
......
......
...OH HOH.
パチッ
PACHI (SNAP)
TIME TO PREPARE FOR EARLY MORNING TEA.

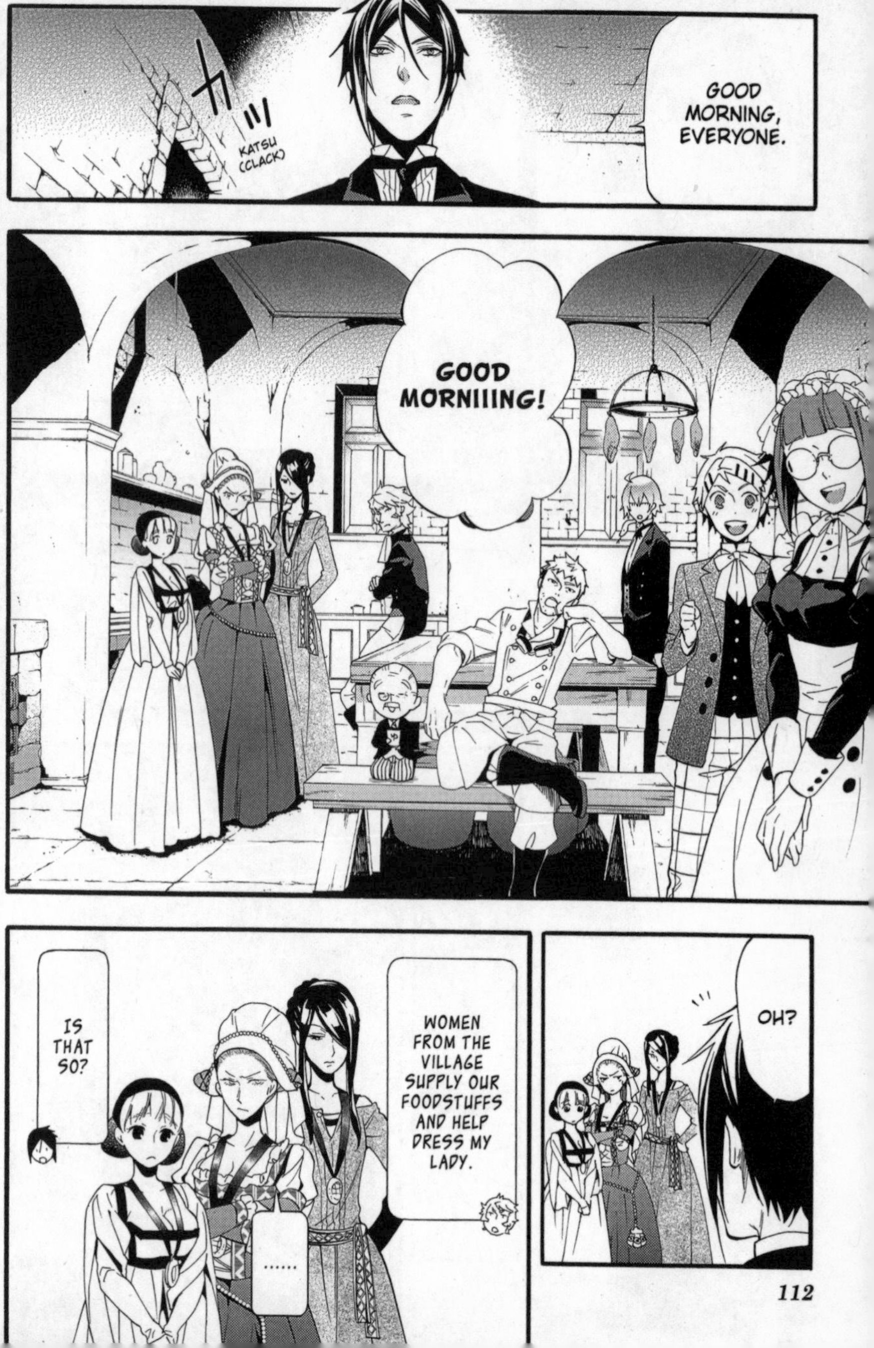
GOOD MORNING, EVERYONE.
カッ
KATSU (CLACK)
GOOD MORNIIING!
OH?
WOMEN FROM THE VILLAGE SUPPLY OUR FOODSTUFFS AND HELP DRESS MY LADY.
IS THAT SO?
......

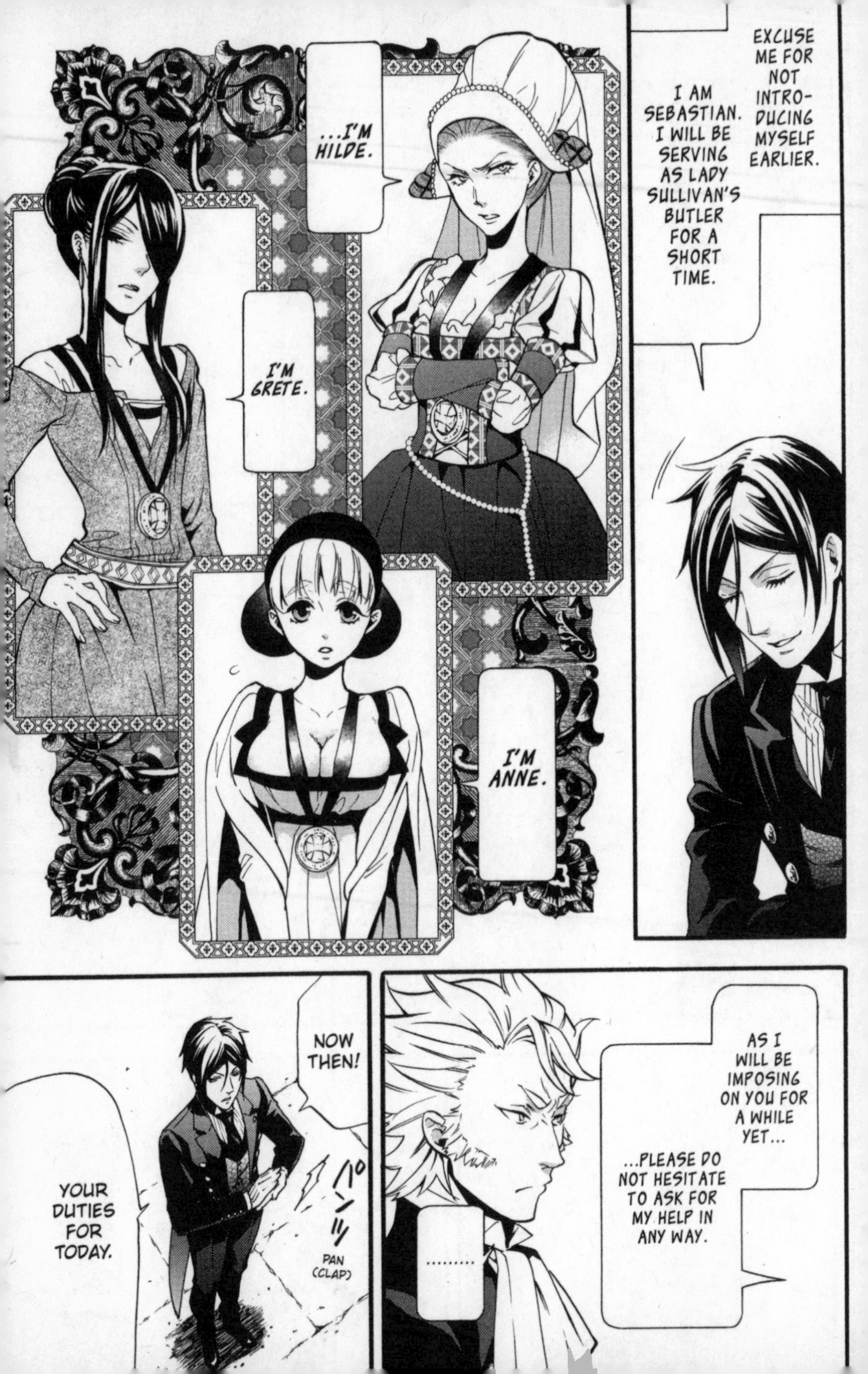
EXCUSE ME FOR NOT INTRODUCING MYSELF EARLIER.
I AM SEBASTIAN. I WILL BE SERVING AS LADY SULLIVAN'S BUTLER FOR A SHORT TIME.
...I'M HILDE.
I'M GRETE.
I'M ANNE.
AS I WILL BE IMPOSING ON YOU FOR A WHILE YET...
...PLEASE DO NOT HESITATE TO ASK FOR MY HELP IN ANY WAY.
....
NOW THEN!
PAN (CLAP)
YOUR DUTIES FOR TODAY.

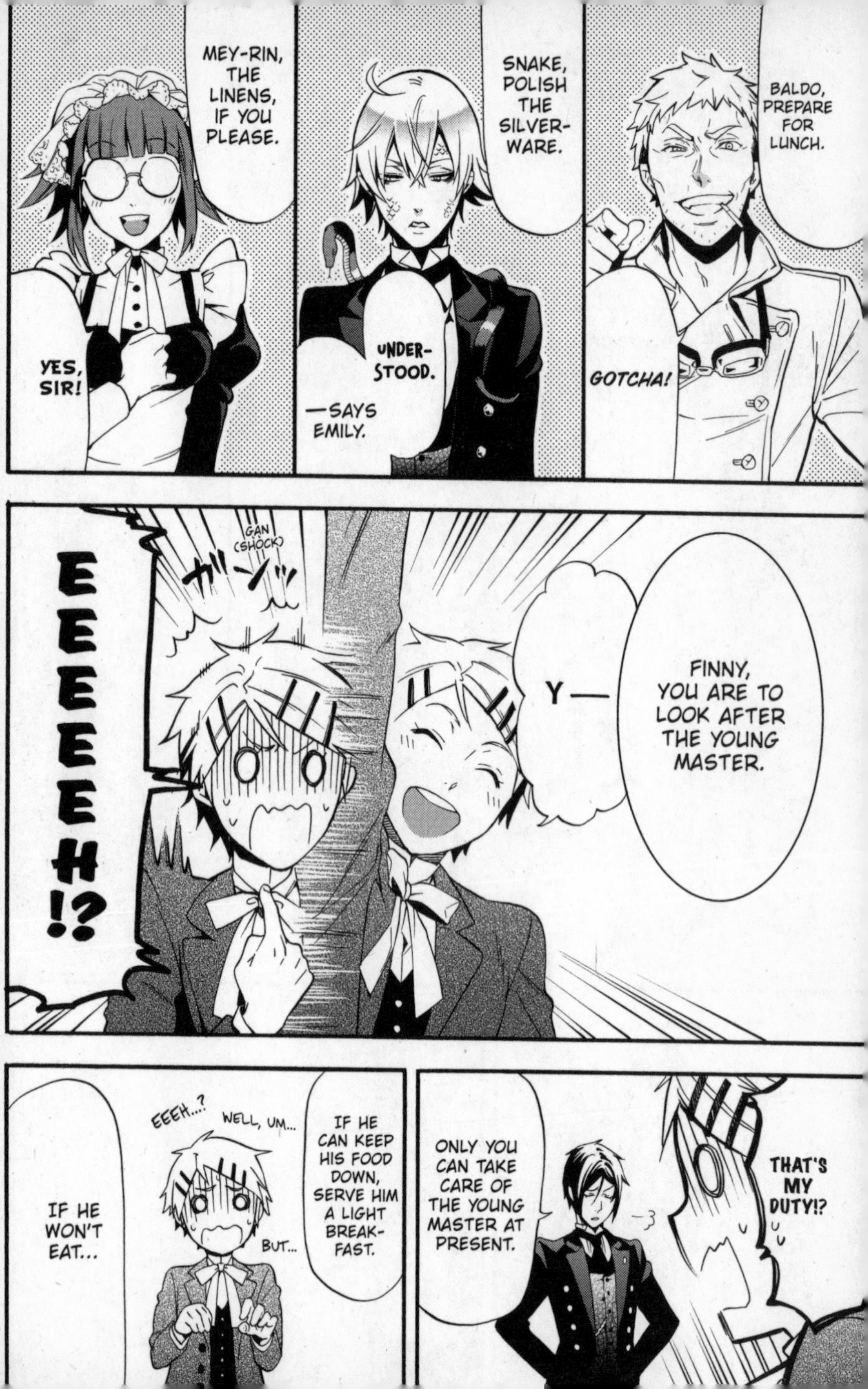
BALDO, PREPARE FOR LUNCH.
GOTCHA!
SNAKE, POLISH THE SILVER-WARE.
UNDER-STOOD.
—SAYS EMILY.
MEY-RIN, THE LINENS, IF YOU PLEASE.
YES, SIR!
FINNY, YOU ARE TO LOOK AFTER THE YOUNG MASTER.
Y—
GAN (SHOCK)
EEEEEEH!?
THAT'S MY DUTY!?
ONLY YOU CAN TAKE CARE OF THE YOUNG MASTER AT PRESENT.
IF HE CAN KEEP HIS FOOD DOWN, SERVE HIM A LIGHT BREAK-FAST.
EEEH...?
WELL, UM...
BUT...
IF HE WON'T EAT...

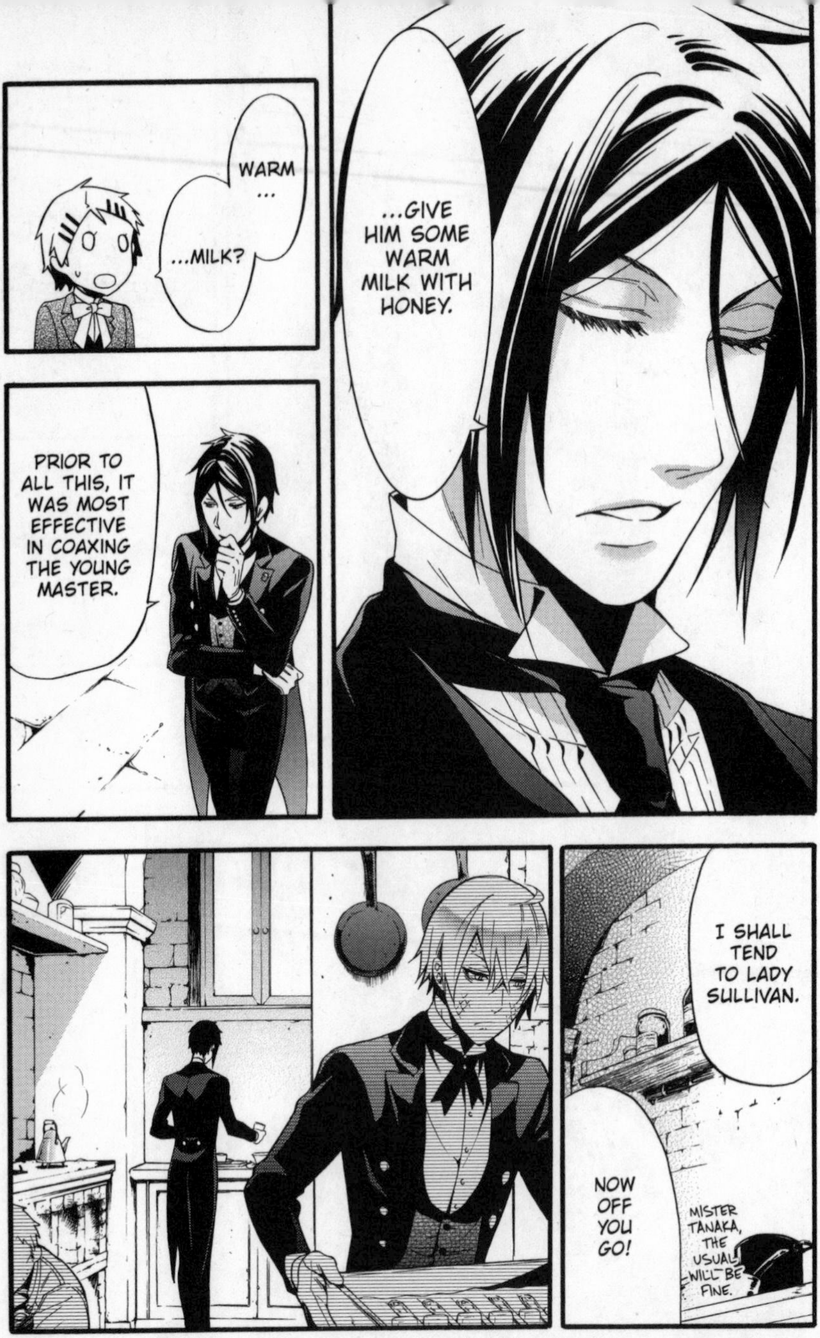
...GIVE HIM SOME WARM MILK WITH HONEY.
WARM...
...MILK?
PRIOR TO ALL THIS, IT WAS MOST EFFECTIVE IN COAXING THE YOUNG MASTER.
I SHALL TEND TO LADY SULLIVAN.
MISTER TANAKA, THE USUAL WILL BE FINE.
NOW OFF YOU GO!

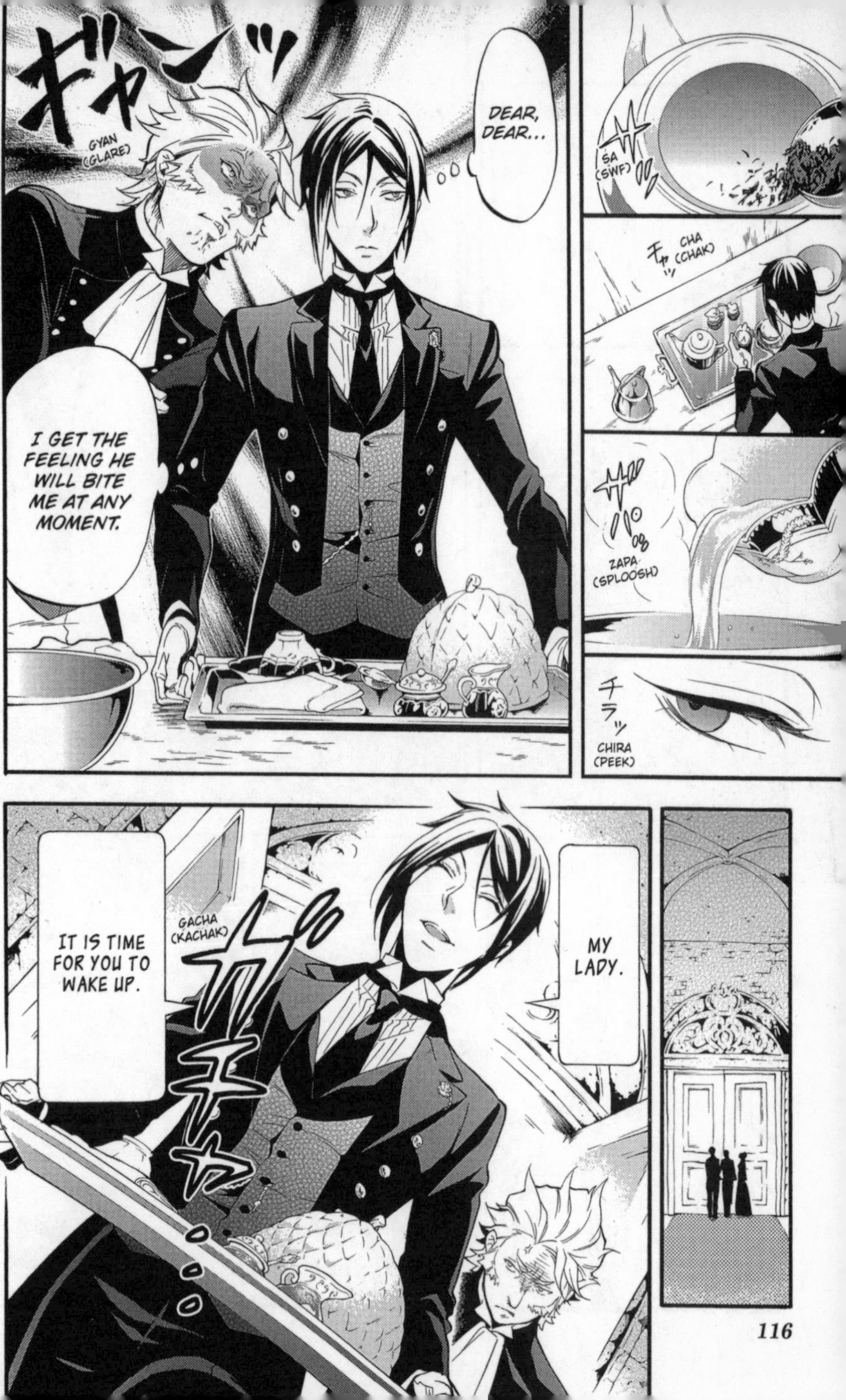

SA (SWF)
CHA (CHAK)
ZAPA (SPLOOSH)
チラッ
CHIRA (PEEK)
GYAN (GLARE)
DEAR, DEAR...
I GET THE FEELING HE WILL BITE ME AT ANY MOMENT.
MY LADY.
GACHA (KACHAK)
IT IS TIME FOR YOU TO WAKE UP.

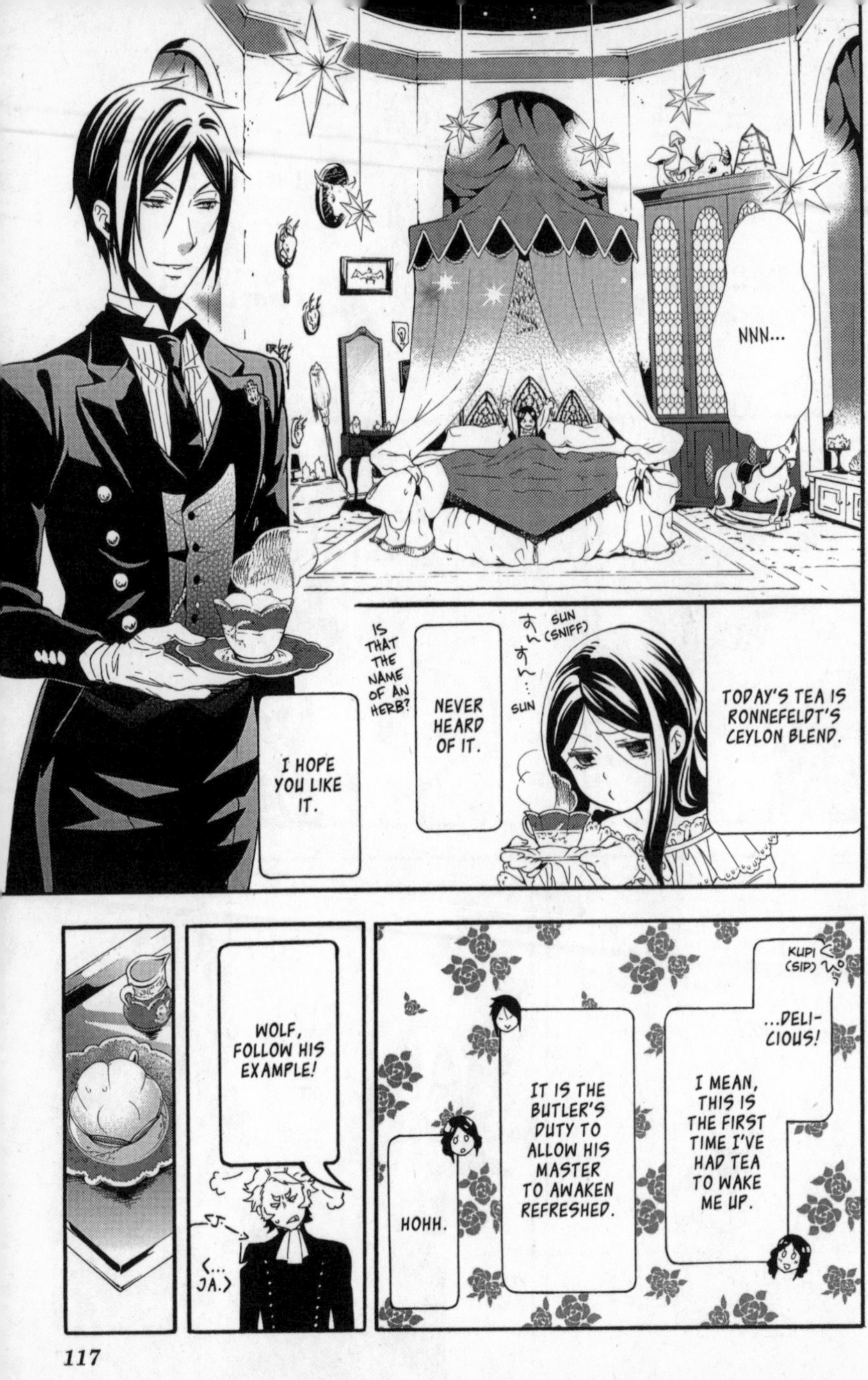
NNN...
TODAY'S TEA IS RONNEFELDT'S CEYLON BLEND.
すん すん…
SUN (SNIFF)
SUN
NEVER HEARD OF IT.
IS THAT THE NAME OF AN HERB?
I HOPE YOU LIKE IT.
くぴ
KUPI (SIP)
...DELI-CIOUS!
I MEAN, THIS IS THE FIRST TIME I'VE HAD TEA TO WAKE ME UP.
IT IS THE BUTLER'S DUTY TO ALLOW HIS MASTER TO AWAKEN REFRESHED.
HOHH.
WOLF, FOLLOW HIS EXAMPLE!
<J.>
<... JA.>

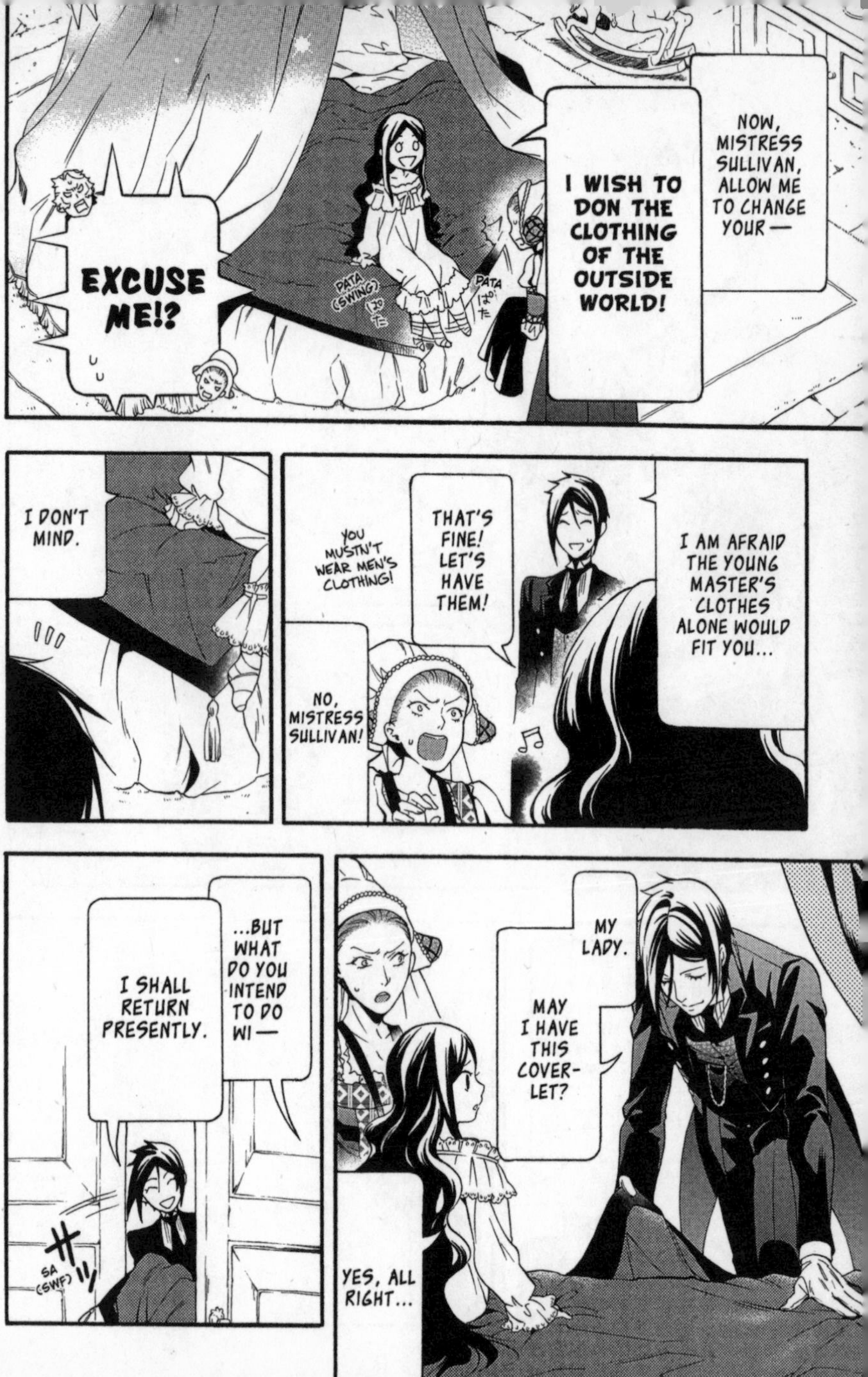
NOW, MISTRESS SULLIVAN, ALLOW ME TO CHANGE YOUR—
I WISH TO DON THE CLOTHING OF THE OUTSIDE WORLD!
PATA ぱた
PATA (SWING) ぱた
EXCUSE ME!?
I AM AFRAID THE YOUNG MASTER'S CLOTHES ALONE WOULD FIT YOU...
THAT'S FINE! LET'S HAVE THEM!
YOU MUSTN'T WEAR MEN'S CLOTHING!
NO, MISTRESS SULLIVAN!
I DON'T MIND.
MY LADY.
MAY I HAVE THIS COVER-LET?
YES, ALL RIGHT...
...BUT WHAT DO YOU INTEND TO DO WI—
I SHALL RETURN PRESENTLY.
SA (SWF)

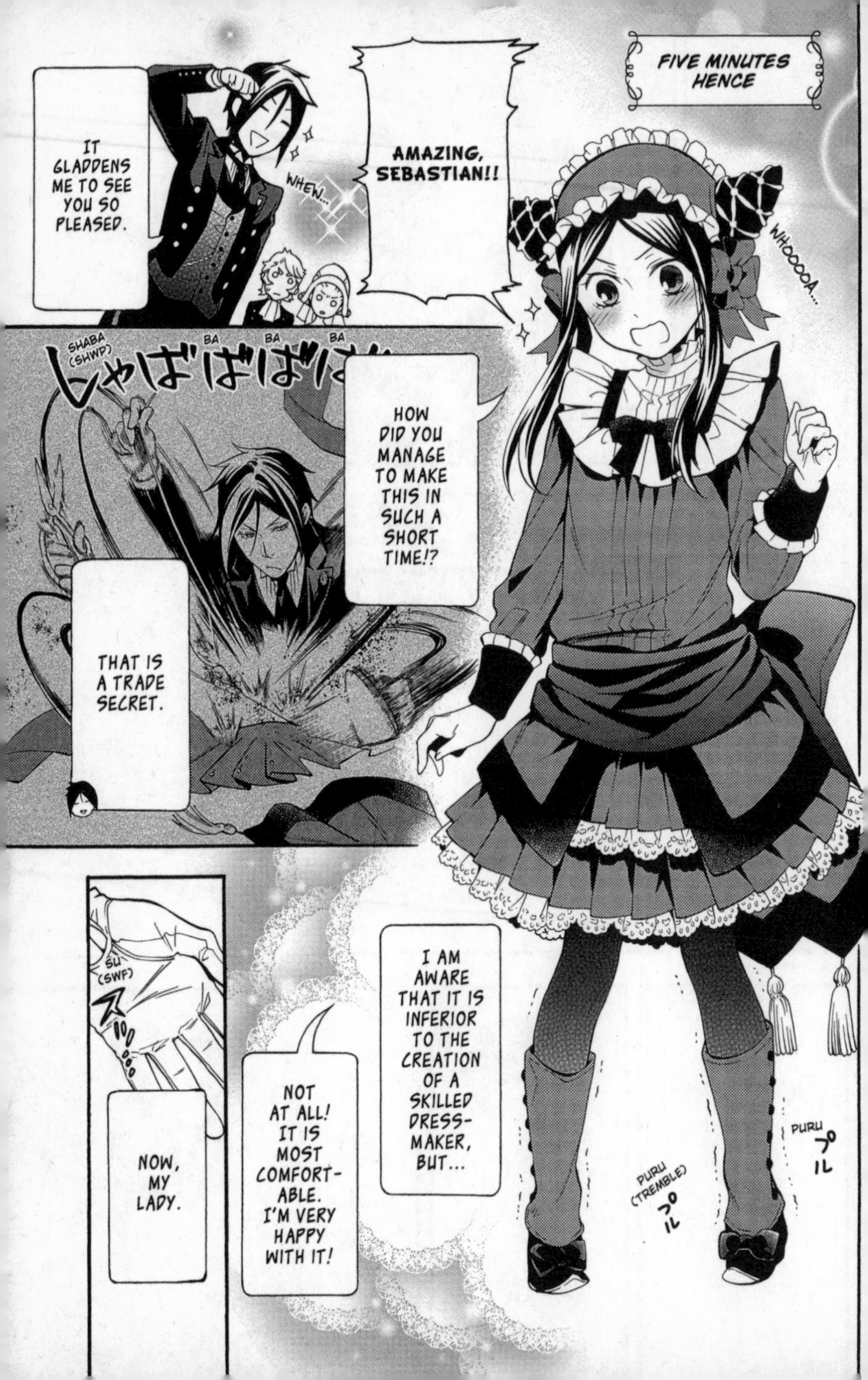
FIVE MINUTES HENCE
WHOOOOA...
AMAZING, SEBASTIAN!!
WHEW...
IT GLADDENS ME TO SEE YOU SO PLEASED.
SHABA (SHWP) BA BA BA
しゃばばばば
HOW DID YOU MANAGE TO MAKE THIS IN SUCH A SHORT TIME!?
THAT IS A TRADE SECRET.
I AM AWARE THAT IT IS INFERIOR TO THE CREATION OF A SKILLED DRESS-MAKER, BUT...
NOT AT ALL! IT IS MOST COMFORT-ABLE. I'M VERY HAPPY WITH IT!
PURU プル
PURU (TREMBLE) プル
SU (SWF)
NOW, MY LADY.

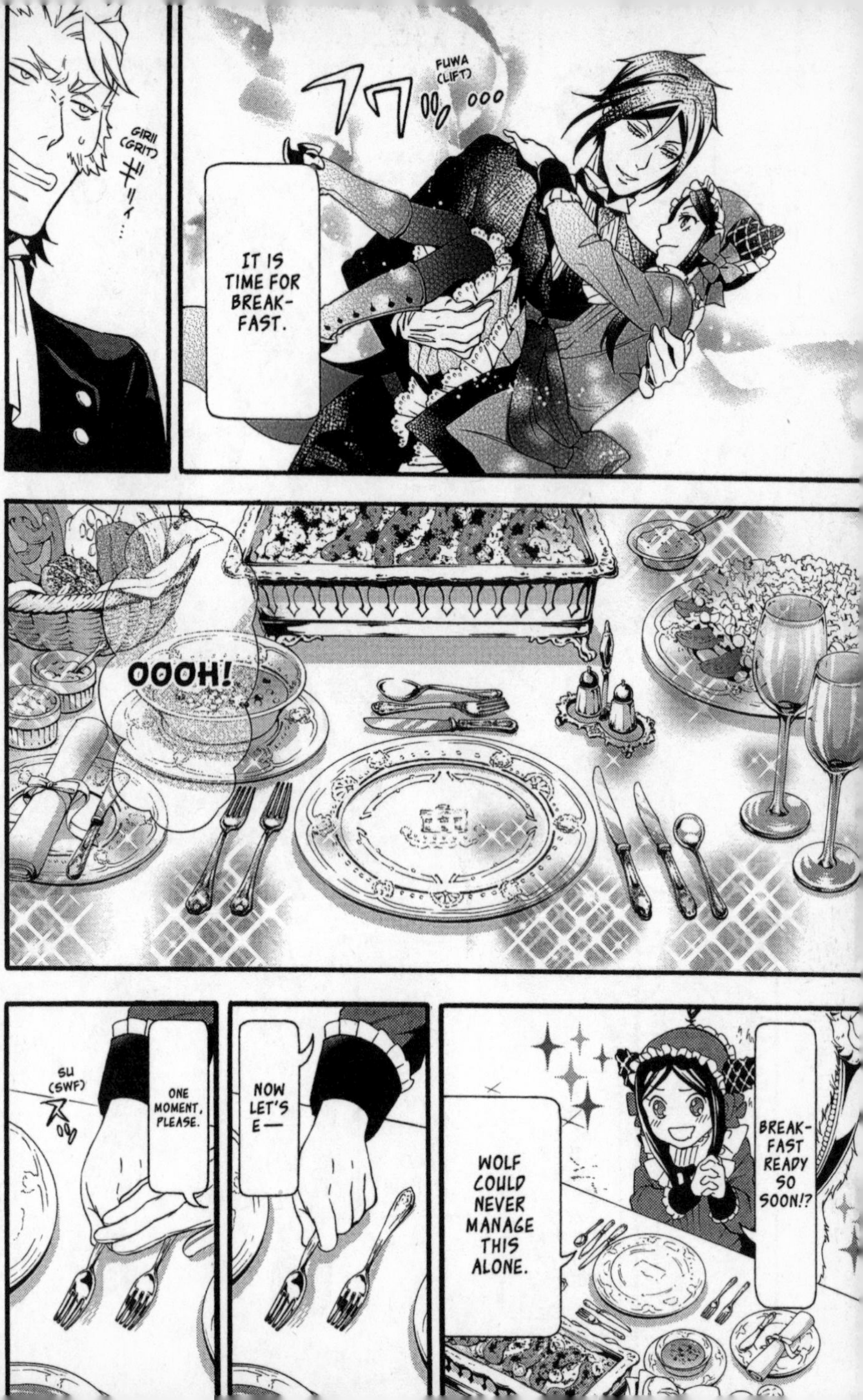
FUWA (LIFT)
フワ
IT IS TIME FOR BREAK-FAST.
GIRII (GRIT)
ギリィ…
OOOH!
BREAK-FAST READY SO SOON!?
WOLF COULD NEVER MANAGE THIS ALONE.
NOW LET'S E—
ONE MOMENT, PLEASE.
SU (SWF)
ス

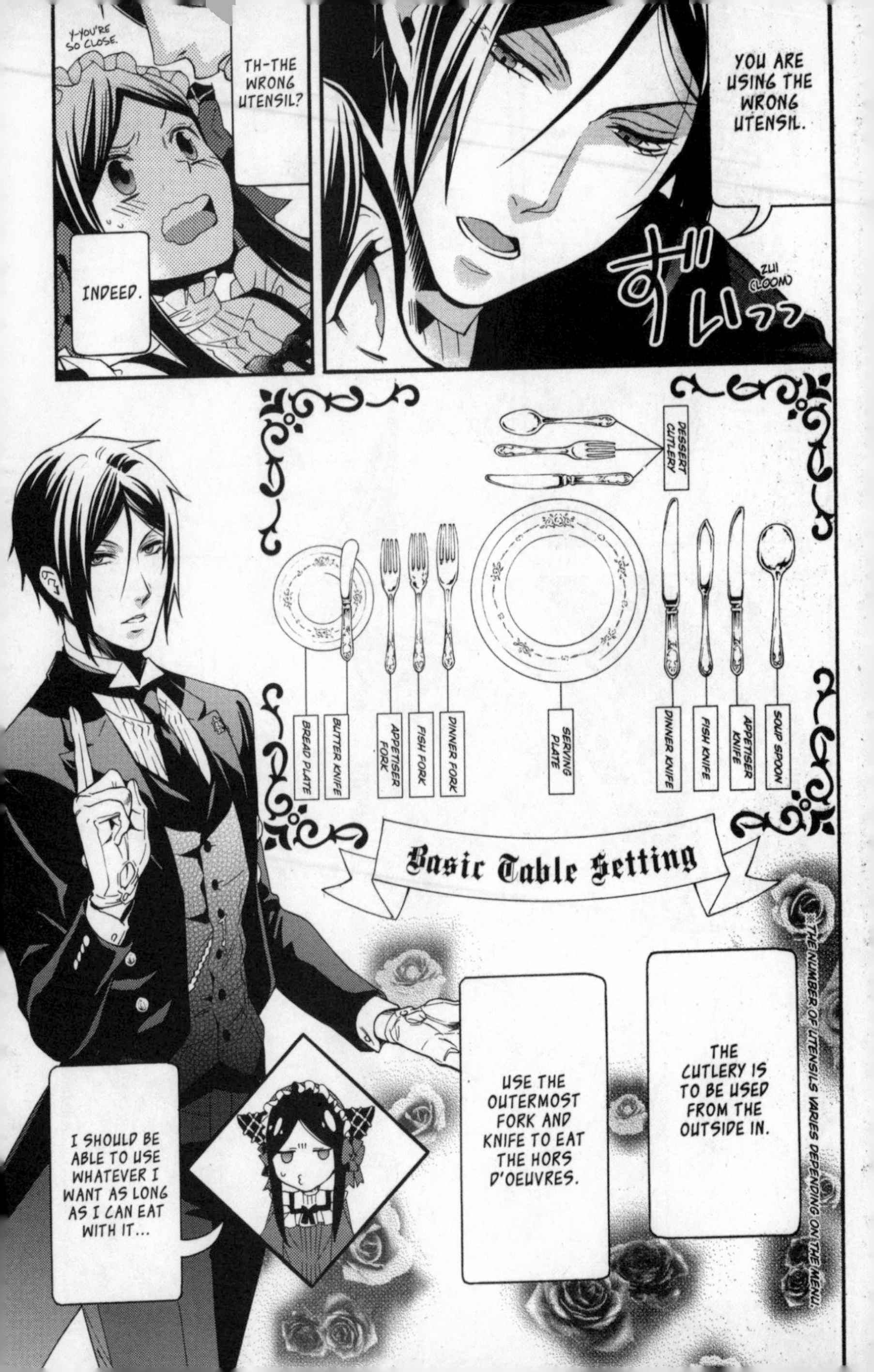
YOU ARE USING THE WRONG UTENSIL.
ZUI (LOOM)
TH-THE WRONG UTENSIL?
Y-YOU'RE SO CLOSE.
INDEED.
Basic Table Setting
DESSERT CUTLERY
SOUP SPOON
APPETISER KNIFE
FISH KNIFE
DINNER KNIFE
SERVING PLATE
DINNER FORK
FISH FORK
APPETISER FORK
BUTTER KNIFE
BREAD PLATE
THE NUMBER OF UTENSILS VARIES DEPENDING ON THE MENU.
THE CUTLERY IS TO BE USED FROM THE OUTSIDE IN.
USE THE OUTERMOST FORK AND KNIFE TO EAT THE HORS D'OEUVRES.
I SHOULD BE ABLE TO USE WHATEVER I WANT AS LONG AS I CAN EAT WITH IT...

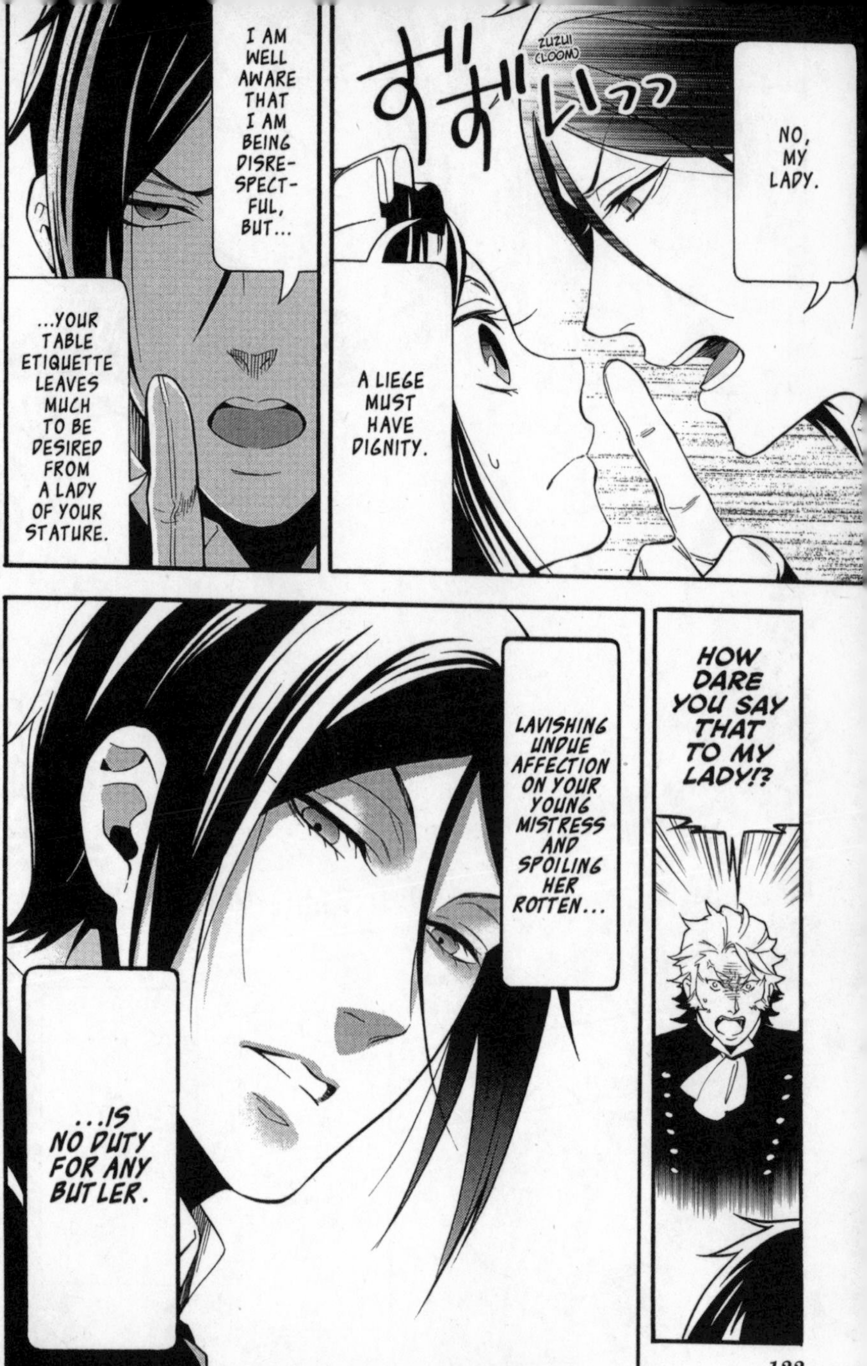
ZUZUI (LOOM)
NO, MY LADY.
A LIEGE MUST HAVE DIGNITY.
I AM WELL AWARE THAT I AM BEING DISRE-SPECT-FUL, BUT...
...YOUR TABLE ETIQUETTE LEAVES MUCH TO BE DESIRED FROM A LADY OF YOUR STATURE.
HOW DARE YOU SAY THAT TO MY LADY!?
LAVISHING UNDUE AFFECTION ON YOUR YOUNG MISTRESS AND SPOILING HER ROTTEN...
...IS NO DUTY FOR ANY BUTLER.

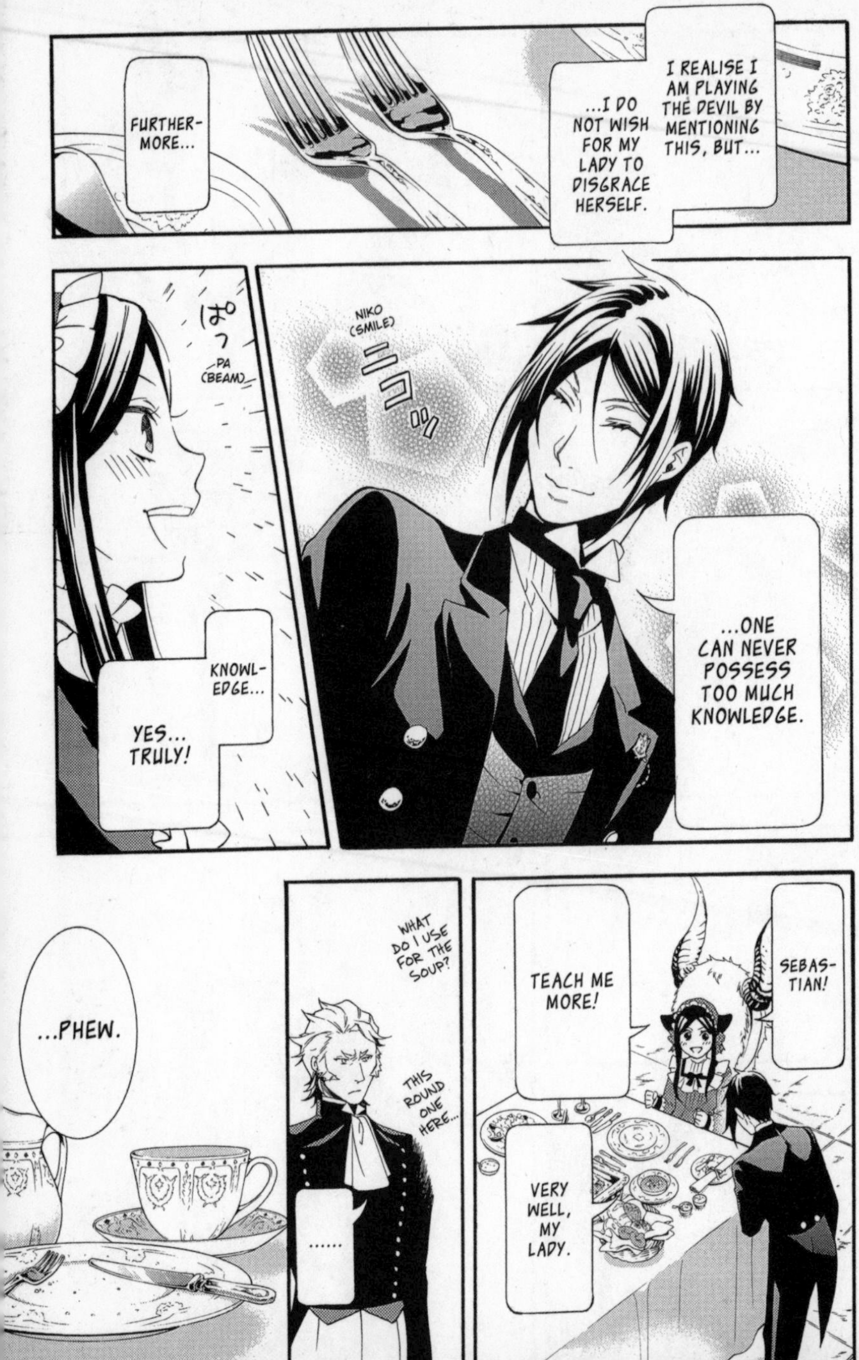
I REALISE I AM PLAYING THE DEVIL BY MENTIONING THIS, BUT...
...I DO NOT WISH FOR MY LADY TO DISGRACE HERSELF.
FURTHER-MORE...
NIKO (SMILE)
ニコッ
...ONE CAN NEVER POSSESS TOO MUCH KNOWLEDGE.
ぱっ
PA (BEAM)
KNOWL-EDGE...
YES... TRULY!
SEBAS-TIAN!
TEACH ME MORE!
VERY WELL, MY LADY.
WHAT DO I USE FOR THE SOUP?
THIS ROUND ONE HERE...
......
...PHEW.

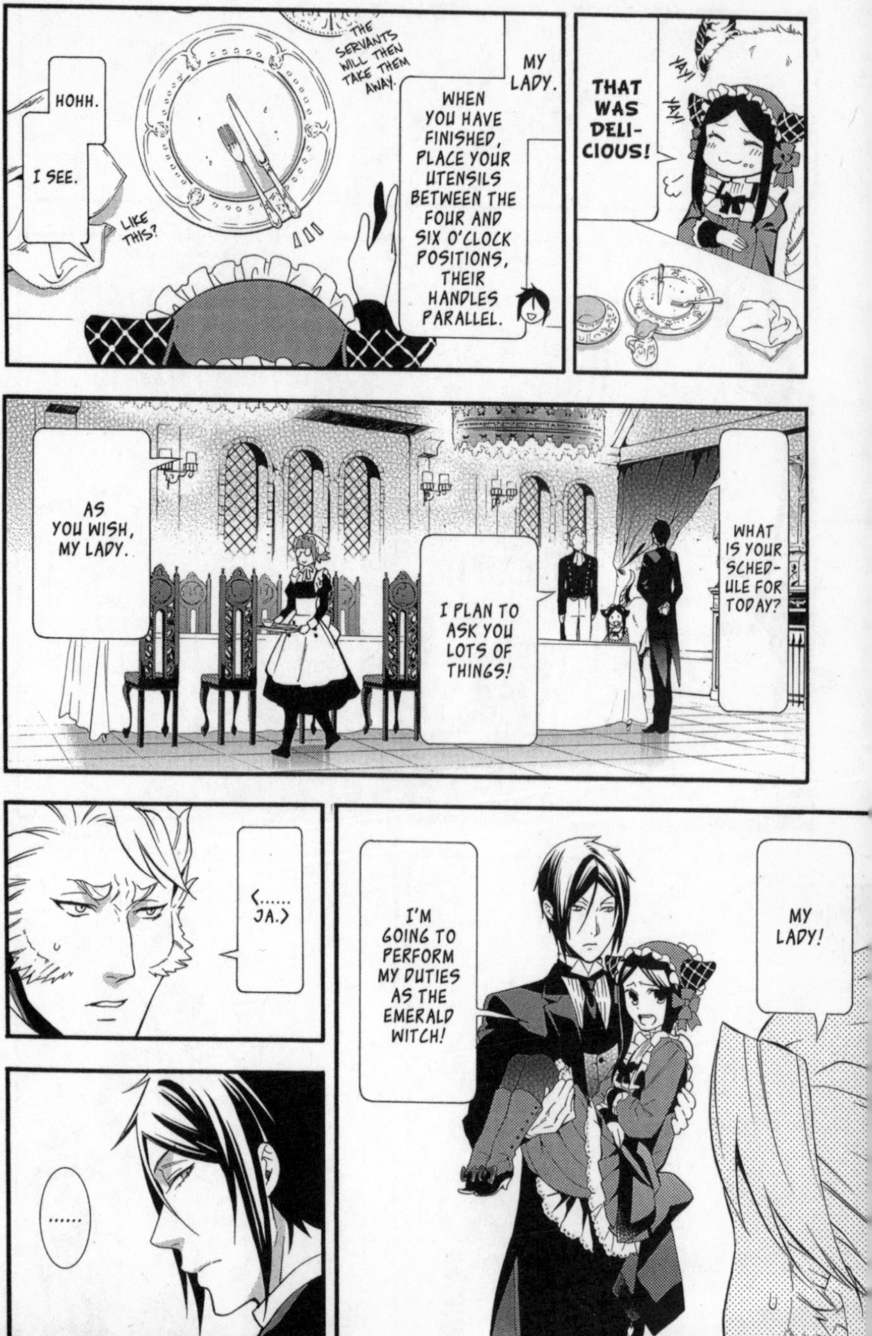
YAY! YAY!
THAT WAS DELICIOUS!
MY LADY.
WHEN YOU HAVE FINISHED, PLACE YOUR UTENSILS BETWEEN THE FOUR AND SIX O'CLOCK POSITIONS, THEIR HANDLES PARALLEL.
THE SERVANTS WILL THEN TAKE THEM AWAY.
HOHH.
I SEE.
LIKE THIS?
WHAT IS YOUR SCHEDULE FOR TODAY?
I PLAN TO ASK YOU LOTS OF THINGS!
AS YOU WISH, MY LADY.
MY LADY!
I'M GOING TO PERFORM MY DUTIES AS THE EMERALD WITCH!
<...... JA.>
......

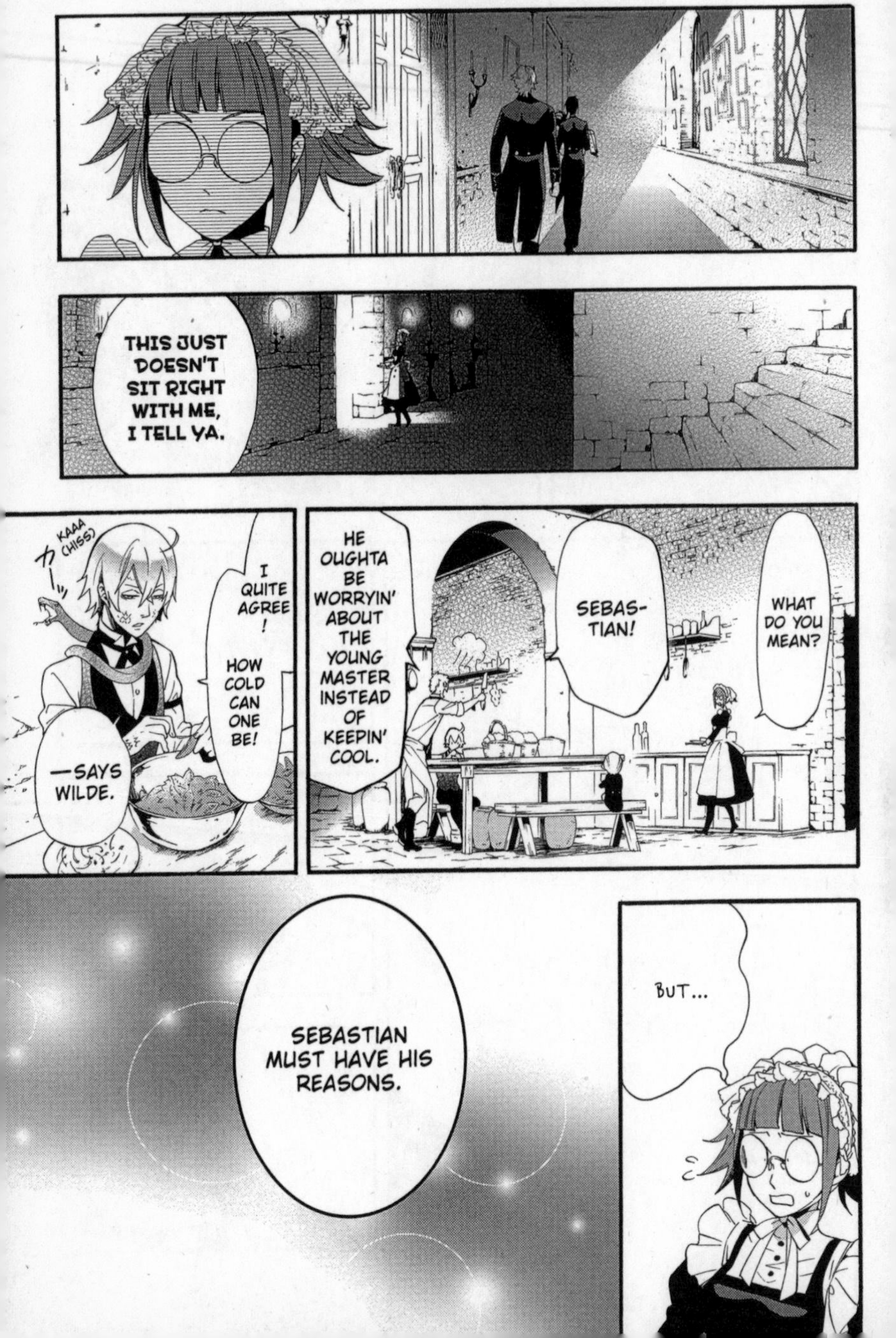
THIS JUST DOESN'T SIT RIGHT WITH ME, I TELL YA.
WHAT DO YOU MEAN?
SEBAS-TIAN!
HE OUGHTA BE WORRYIN' ABOUT THE YOUNG MASTER INSTEAD OF KEEPIN' COOL.
KAAA (HISS)
I QUITE AGREE! HOW COLD CAN ONE BE!
—SAYS WILDE.
BUT...
SEBASTIAN MUST HAVE HIS REASONS.

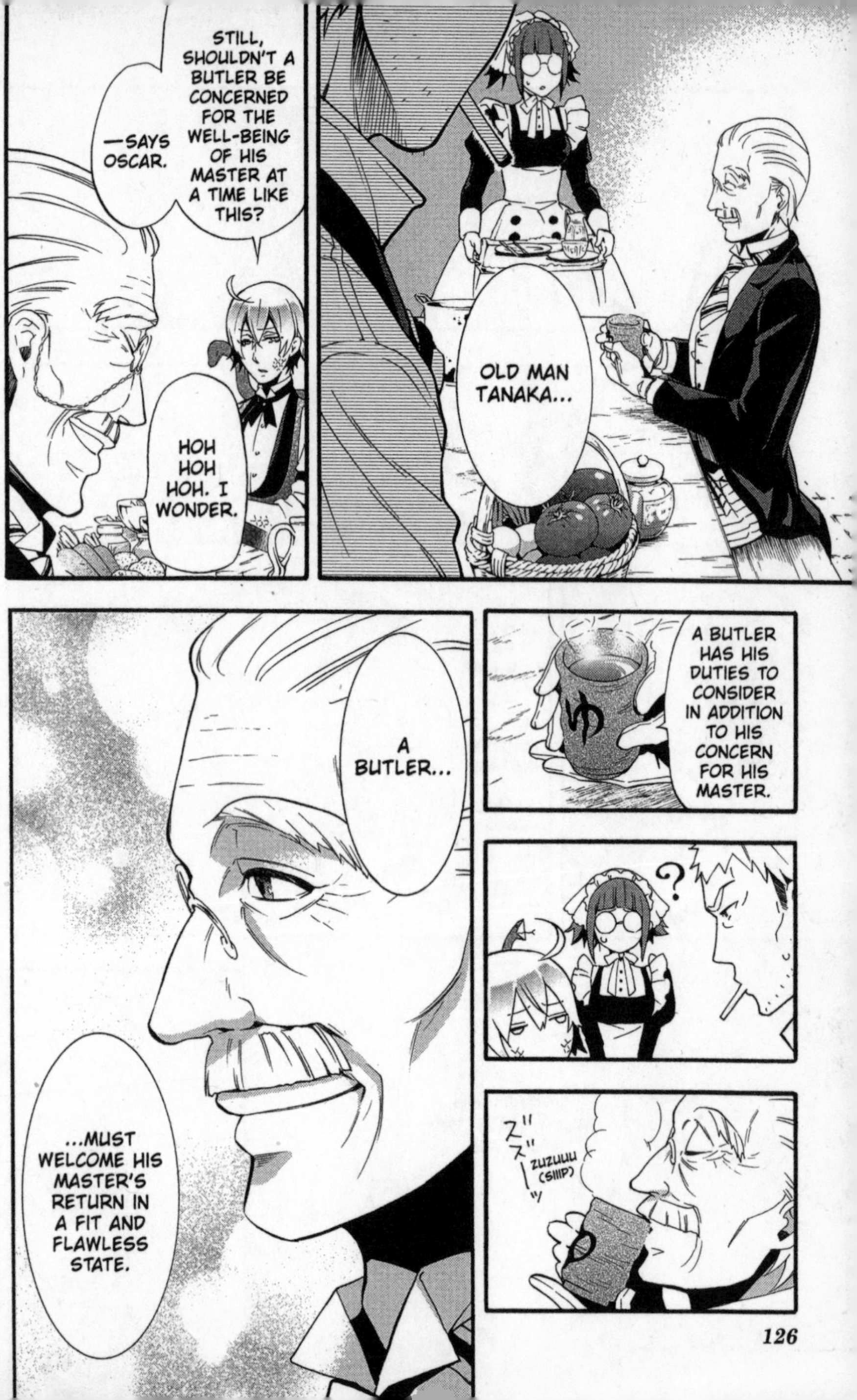
OLD MAN TANAKA...
STILL, SHOULDN'T A BUTLER BE CONCERNED FOR THE WELL-BEING OF HIS MASTER AT A TIME LIKE THIS?
—SAYS OSCAR.
HOH HOH HOH. I WONDER.
A BUTLER HAS HIS DUTIES TO CONSIDER IN ADDITION TO HIS CONCERN FOR HIS MASTER.
?
ズズーッ
ZUZUUU (SIIIP)
A BUTLER...
...MUST WELCOME HIS MASTER'S RETURN IN A FIT AND FLAWLESS STATE.

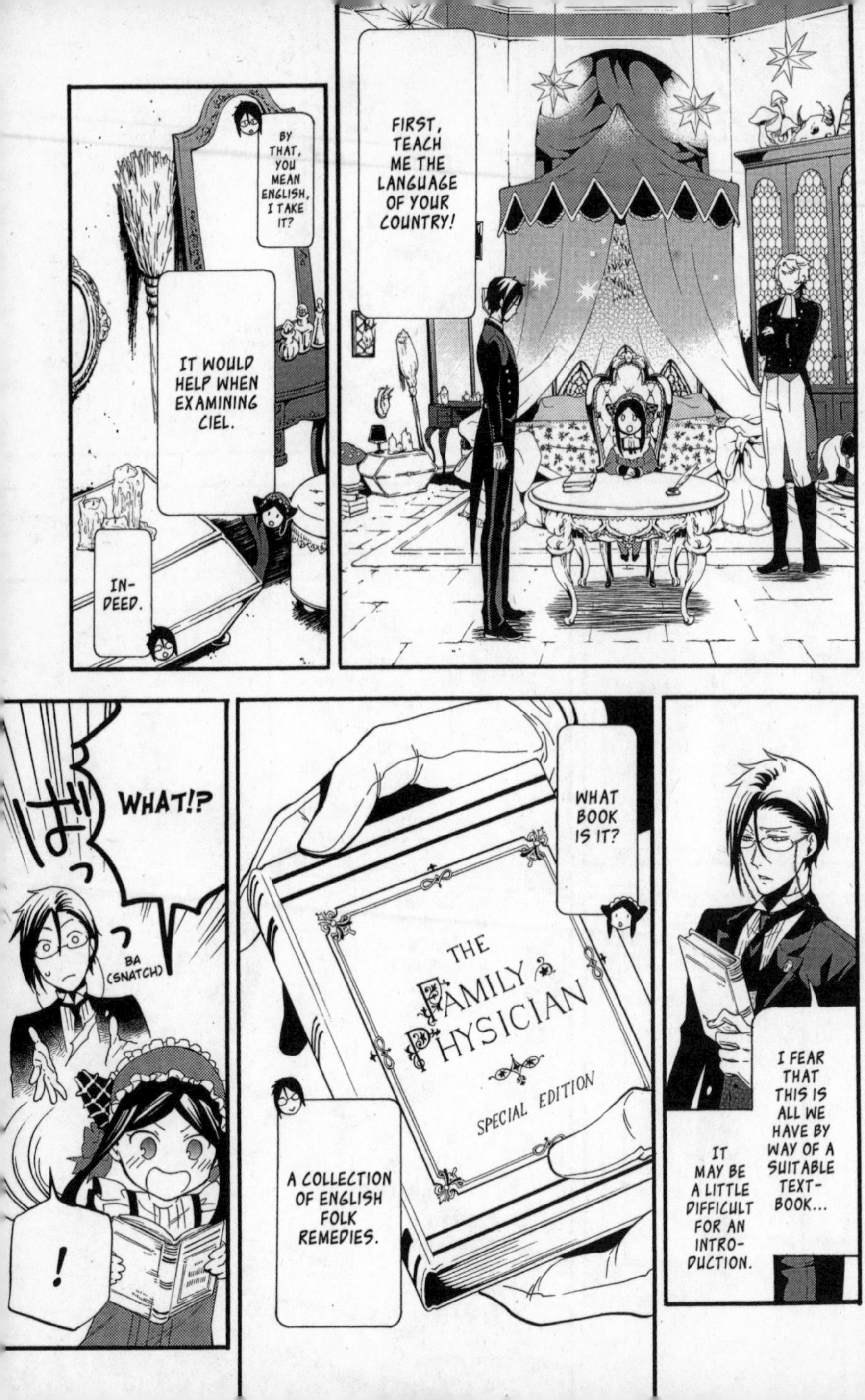
FIRST, TEACH ME THE LANGUAGE OF YOUR COUNTRY!
BY THAT, YOU MEAN ENGLISH, I TAKE IT?
IT WOULD HELP WHEN EXAMINING CIEL.
IN-DEED.
I FEAR THAT THIS IS ALL WE HAVE BY WAY OF A SUITABLE TEXT-BOOK...
IT MAY BE A LITTLE DIFFICULT FOR AN INTRO-DUCTION.
WHAT BOOK IS IT?
THE FAMILY PHYSICIAN
SPECIAL EDITION
A COLLECTION OF ENGLISH FOLK REMEDIES.
WHAT!?
ぱっ
BA (SNATCH)
!

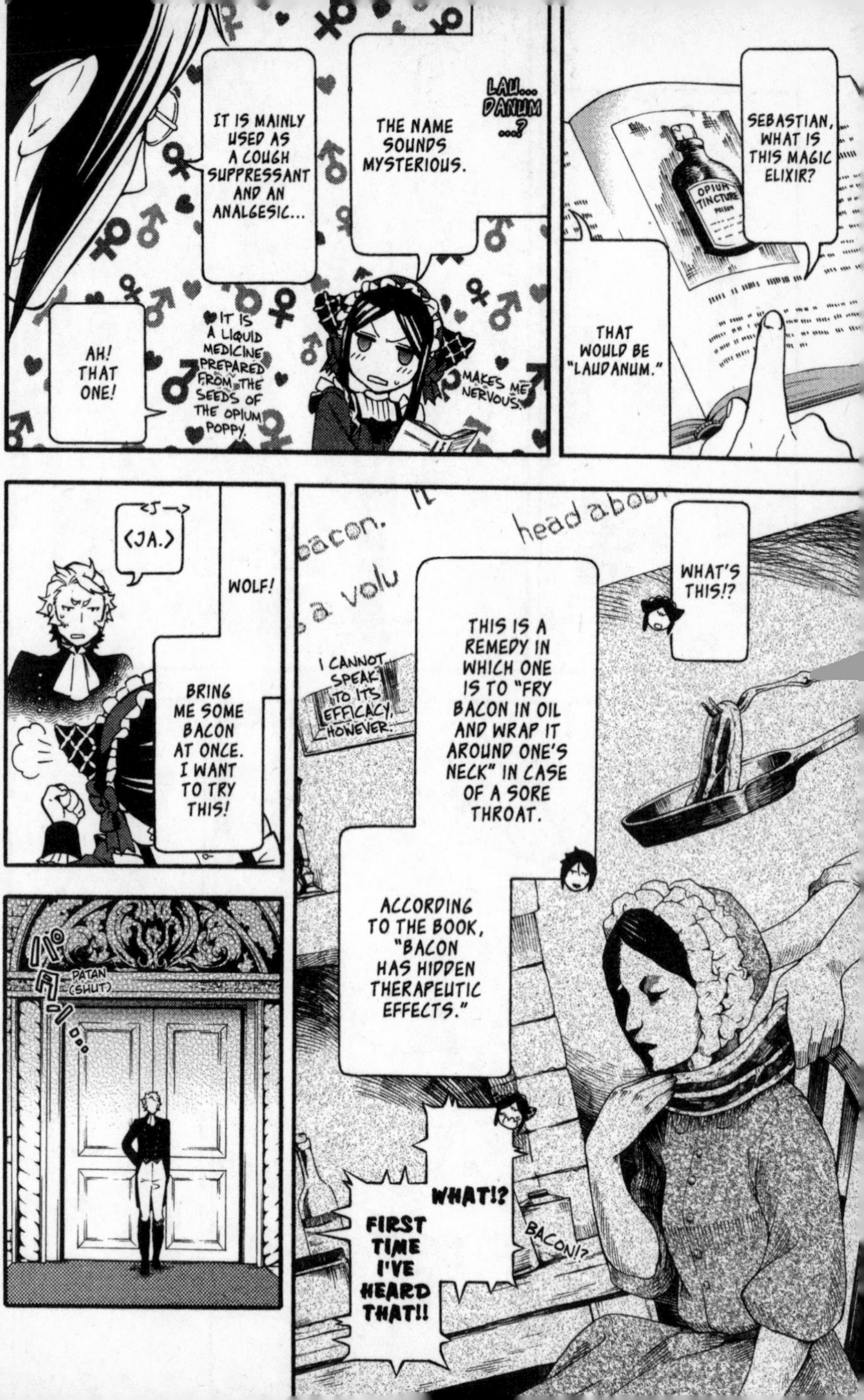
SEBASTIAN, WHAT IS THIS MAGIC ELIXIR?
OPIUM TINCTURE POISON
THAT WOULD BE "LAUDANUM."
LAU... DANUM ...?
THE NAME SOUNDS MYSTERIOUS.
MAKES ME NERVOUS.
IT IS MAINLY USED AS A COUGH SUPPRESSANT AND AN ANALGESIC...
IT IS A LIQUID MEDICINE PREPARED FROM THE SEEDS OF THE OPIUM POPPY.
AH! THAT ONE!
WHAT'S THIS!?
THIS IS A REMEDY IN WHICH ONE IS TO "FRY BACON IN OIL AND WRAP IT AROUND ONE'S NECK" IN CASE OF A SORE THROAT.
I CANNOT SPEAK TO ITS EFFICACY, HOWEVER.
ACCORDING TO THE BOOK, "BACON HAS HIDDEN THERAPEUTIC EFFECTS."
BACON!?
WHAT!?
FIRST TIME I'VE HEARD THAT!!
WOLF!
BRING ME SOME BACON AT ONCE. I WANT TO TRY THIS!
<J>
<JA.>
PATAN (SHUT)

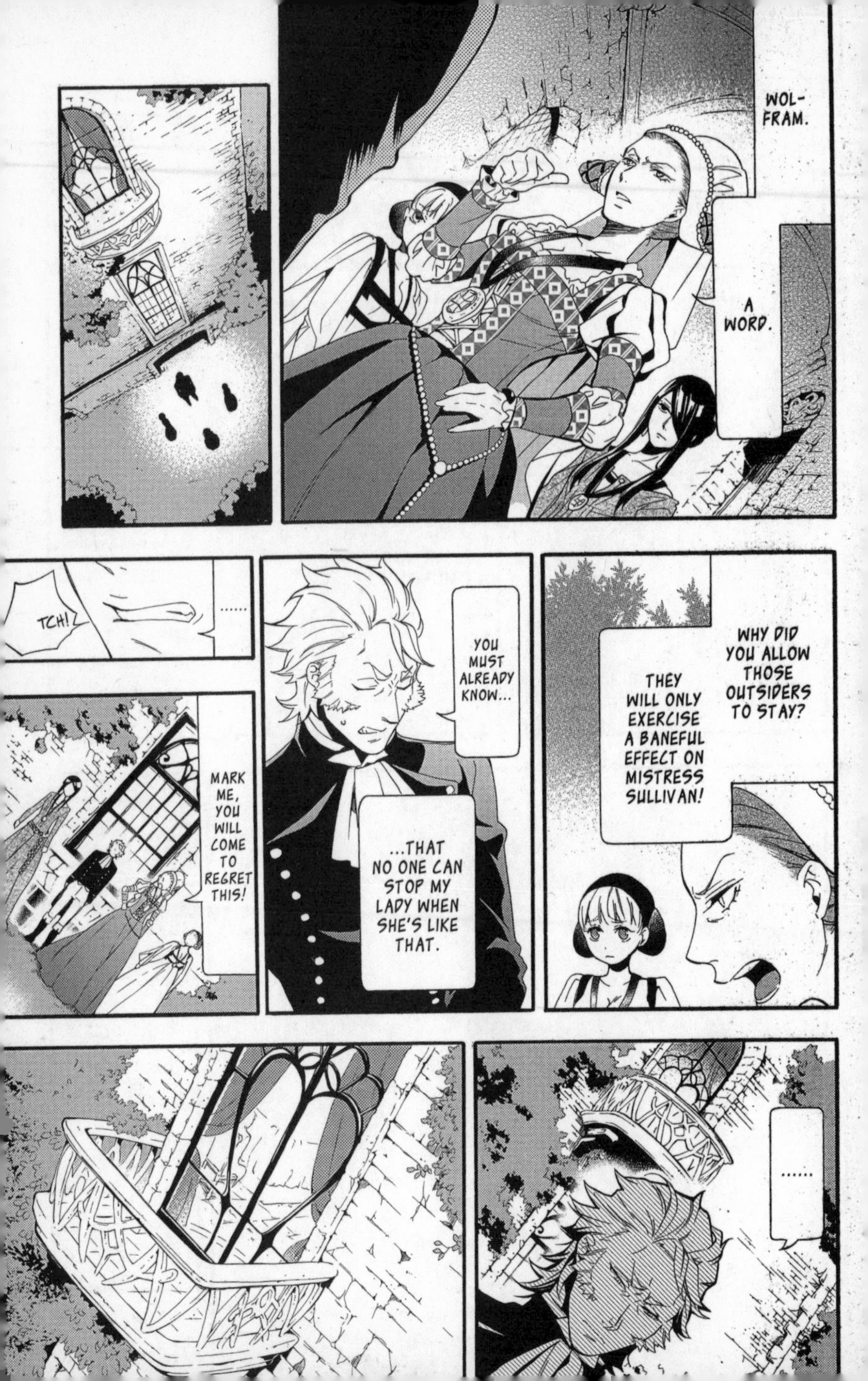
WOL-FRAM.
A WORD.
WHY DID YOU ALLOW THOSE OUTSIDERS TO STAY?
THEY WILL ONLY EXERCISE A BANEFUL EFFECT ON MISTRESS SULLIVAN!
YOU MUST ALREADY KNOW...
...THAT NO ONE CAN STOP MY LADY WHEN SHE'S LIKE THAT.
......
TCH!
MARK ME, YOU WILL COME TO REGRET THIS!
......

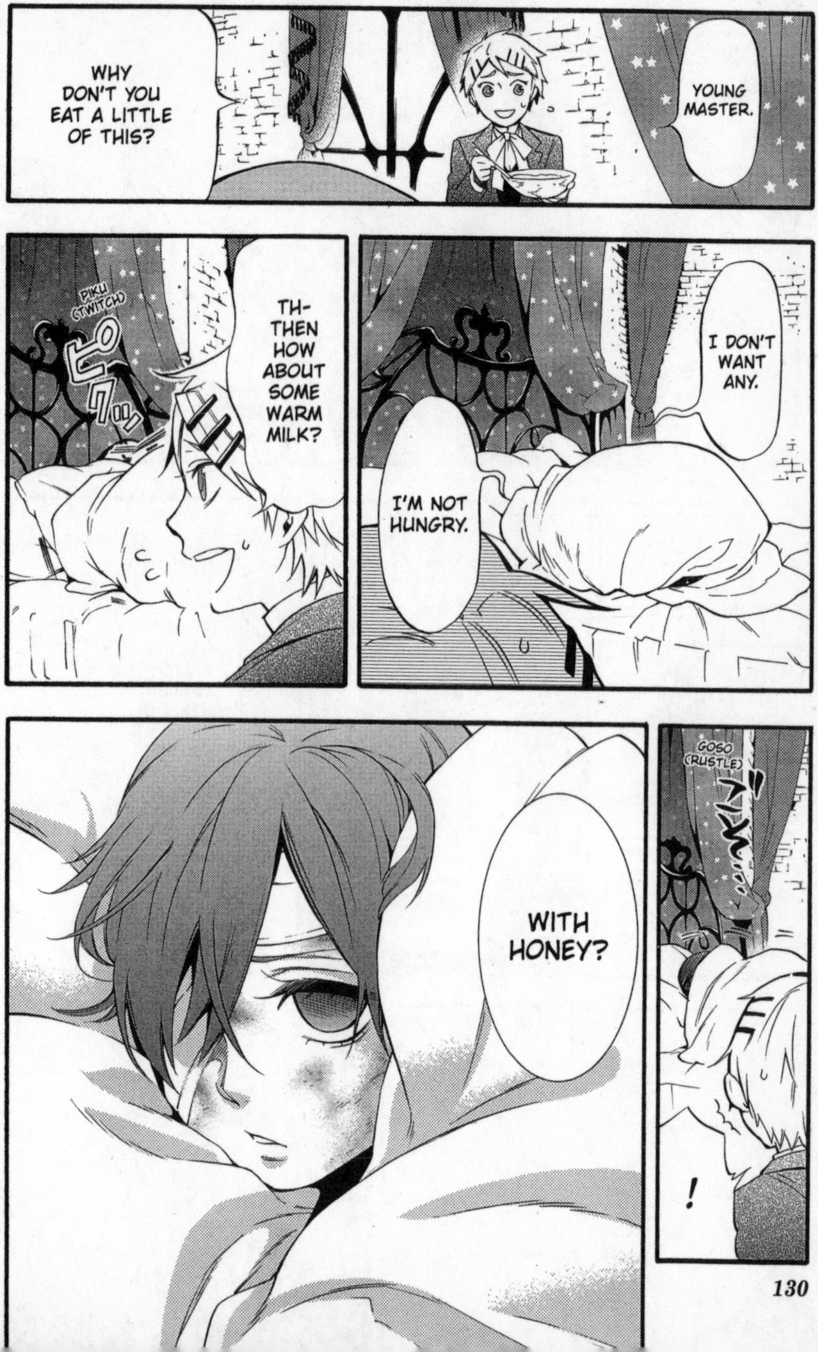
YOUNG MASTER.
WHY DON'T YOU EAT A LITTLE OF THIS?
I DON'T WANT ANY.
I'M NOT HUNGRY.
TH-THEN HOW ABOUT SOME WARM MILK?
PIKU (TWITCH)
GOSO (RUSTLE)
!
WITH HONEY?

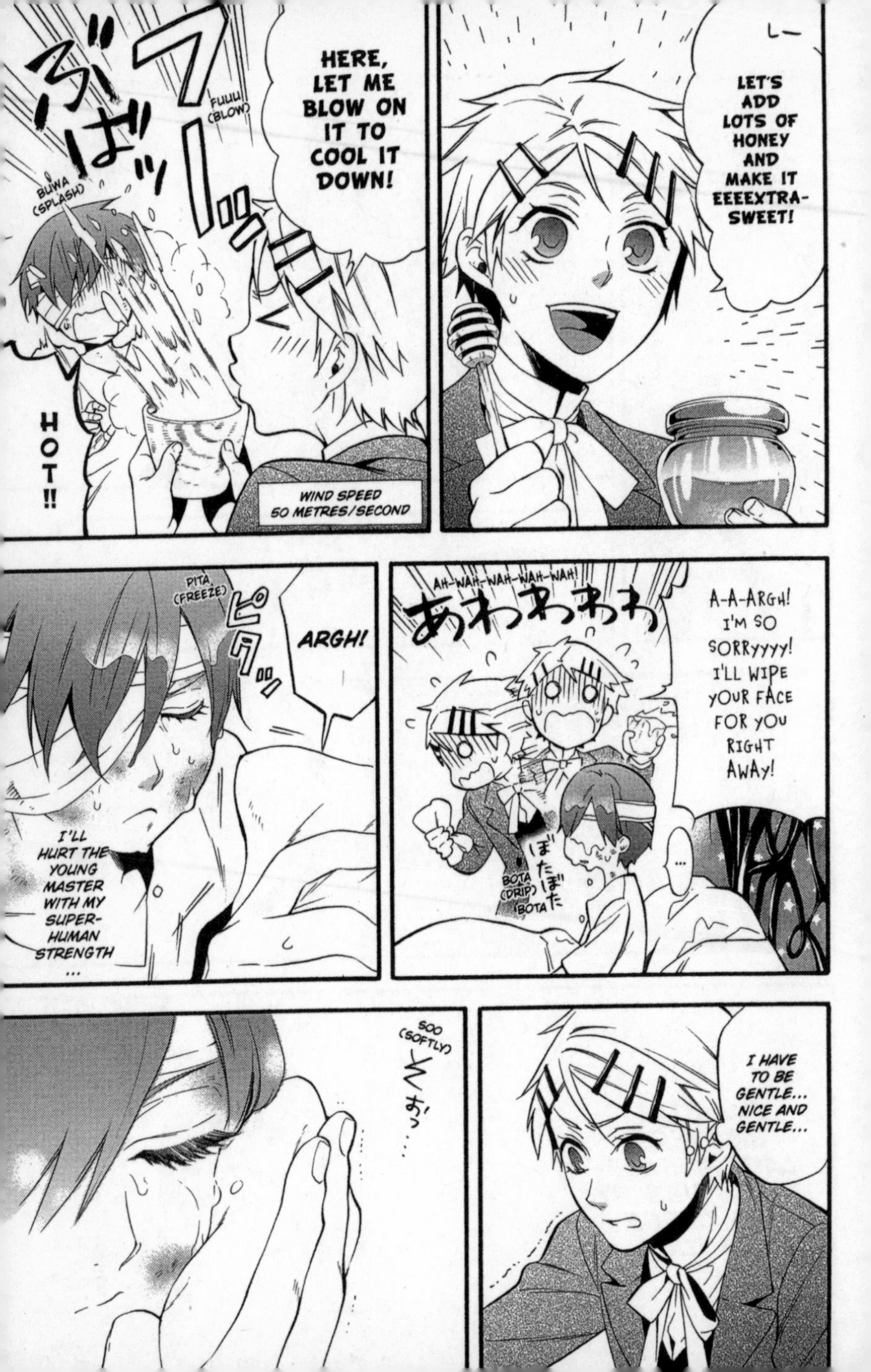
LET'S ADD LOTS OF HONEY AND MAKE IT EEEEXTRA-SWEET!
HERE, LET ME BLOW ON IT TO COOL IT DOWN!
FUUU (BLOW)
BUWA (SPLASH)
HOT!!
WIND SPEED 50 METRES/SECOND
AH-WAH-WAH-WAH-WAH!
あわわわわ
A-A-ARGH! I'M SO SORRYYYY! I'LL WIPE YOUR FACE FOR YOU RIGHT AWAY!
...
BOTA (DRIP) BOTA
ぼたぼた
PITA (FREEZE)
ピタッ
ARGH!
I'LL HURT THE YOUNG MASTER WITH MY SUPER-HUMAN STRENGTH ...
I HAVE TO BE GENTLE... NICE AND GENTLE...
SOO (SOFTLY)
そおっ...

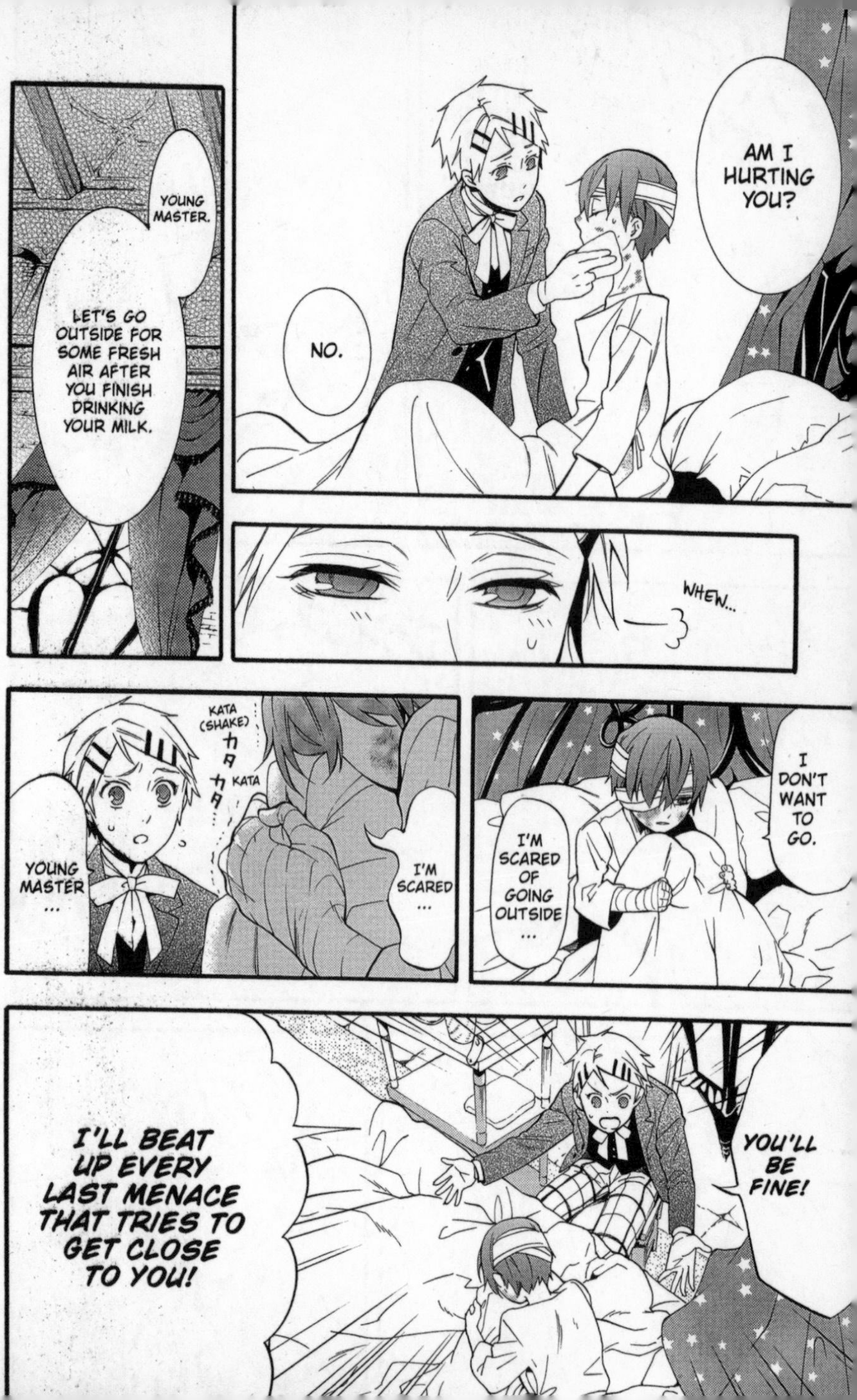
AM I HURTING YOU?
NO.
WHEW...
YOUNG MASTER.
LET'S GO OUTSIDE FOR SOME FRESH AIR AFTER YOU FINISH DRINKING YOUR MILK.
I DON'T WANT TO GO.
I'M SCARED OF GOING OUTSIDE ...
KATA (SHAKE) カタ
KATA カタ...
I'M SCARED ...
YOUNG MASTER ...
YOU'LL BE FINE!
I'LL BEAT UP EVERY LAST MENACE THAT TRIES TO GET CLOSE TO YOU!

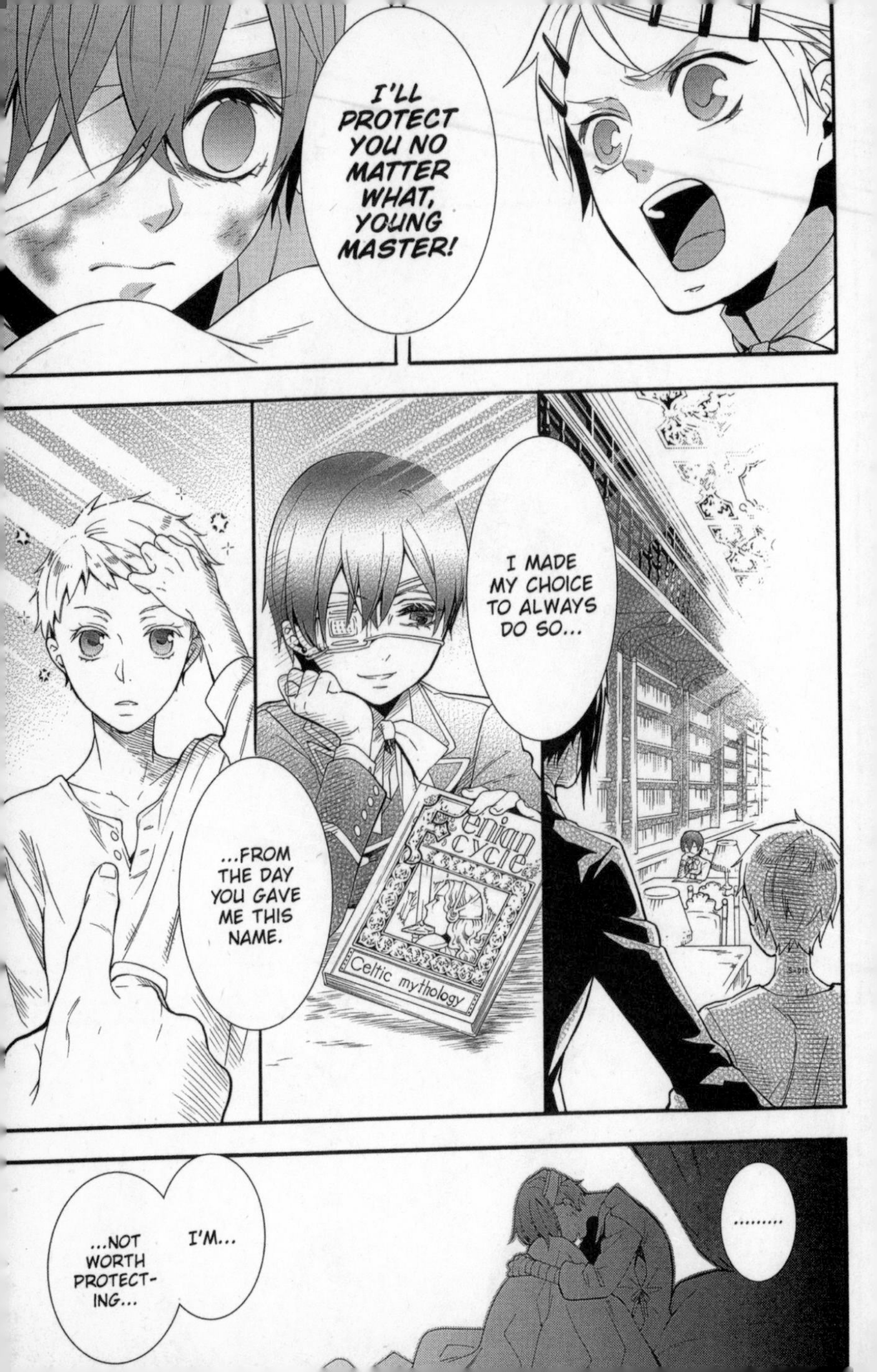
I'LL PROTECT YOU NO MATTER WHAT, YOUNG MASTER!
I MADE MY CHOICE TO ALWAYS DO SO...
...FROM THE DAY YOU GAVE ME THIS NAME.
Fenian Cycle
Celtic mythology
....
I'M...
...NOT WORTH PROTECT-ING...

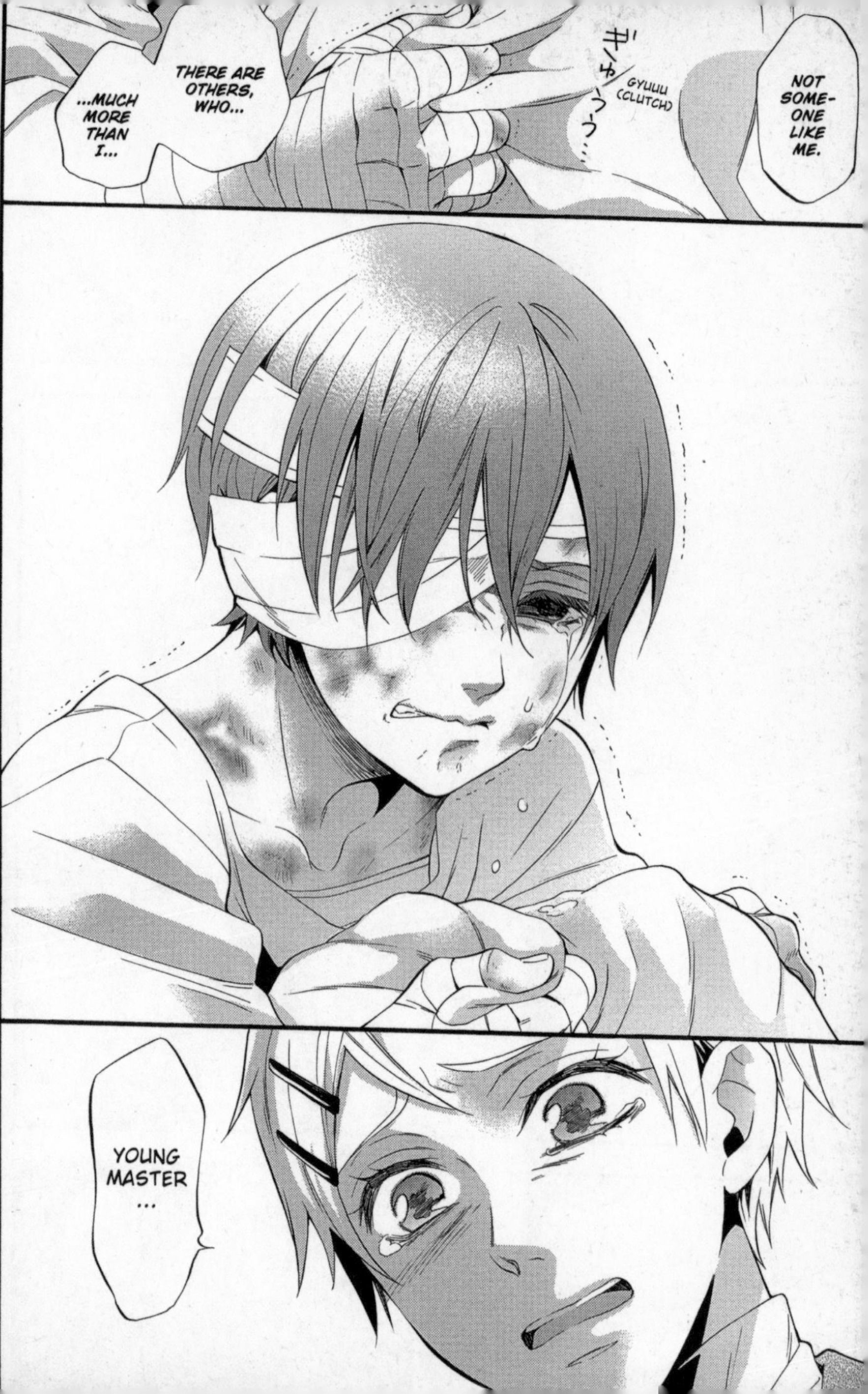
NOT SOME-ONE LIKE ME.
GYUUU (CLUTCH)
THERE ARE OTHERS, WHO...
...MUCH MORE THAN I...
YOUNG MASTER ...

Black Butler

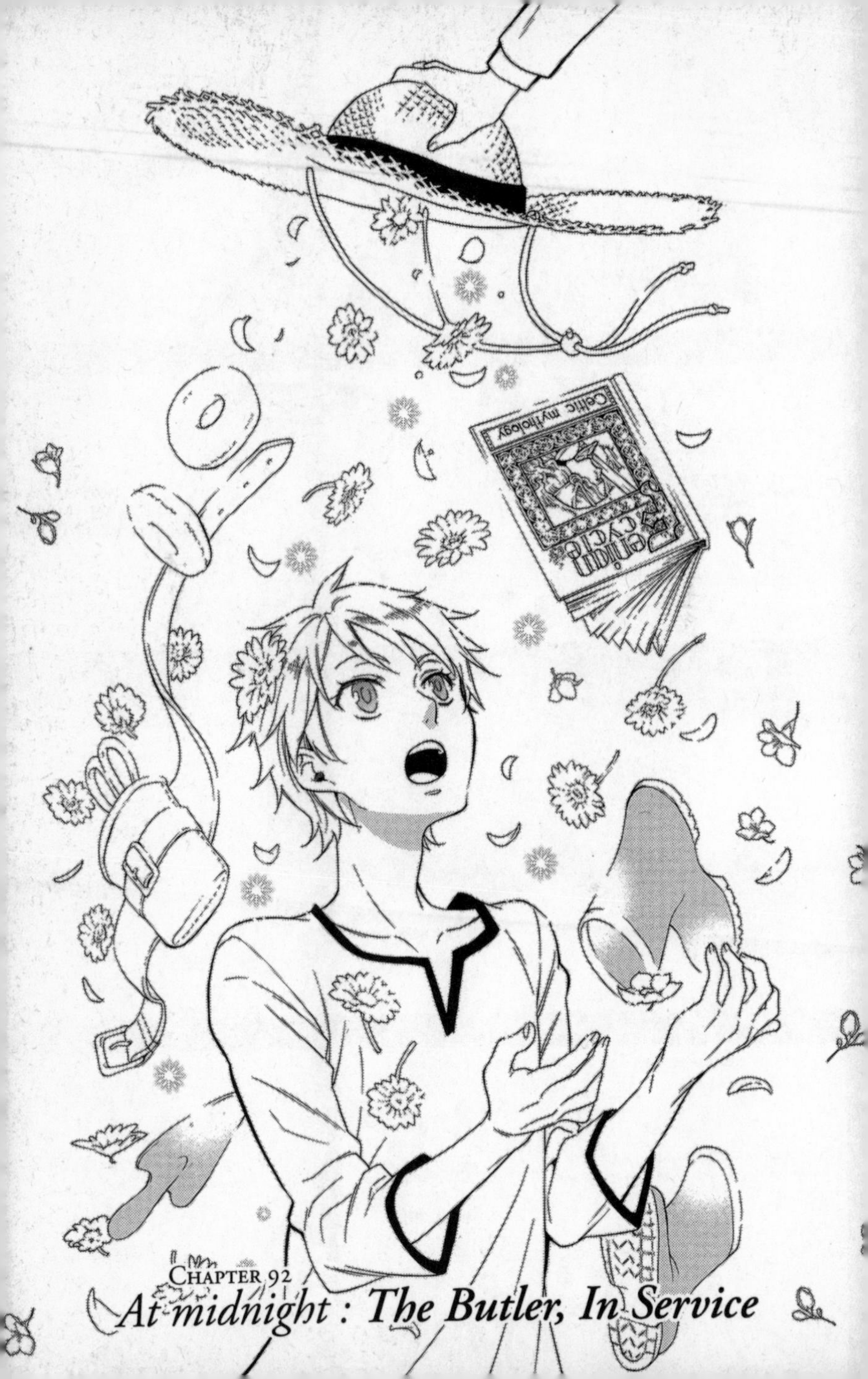
Celtic mythology
Fenian Cycle

Chapter 92

At midnight : The Butler, In Service

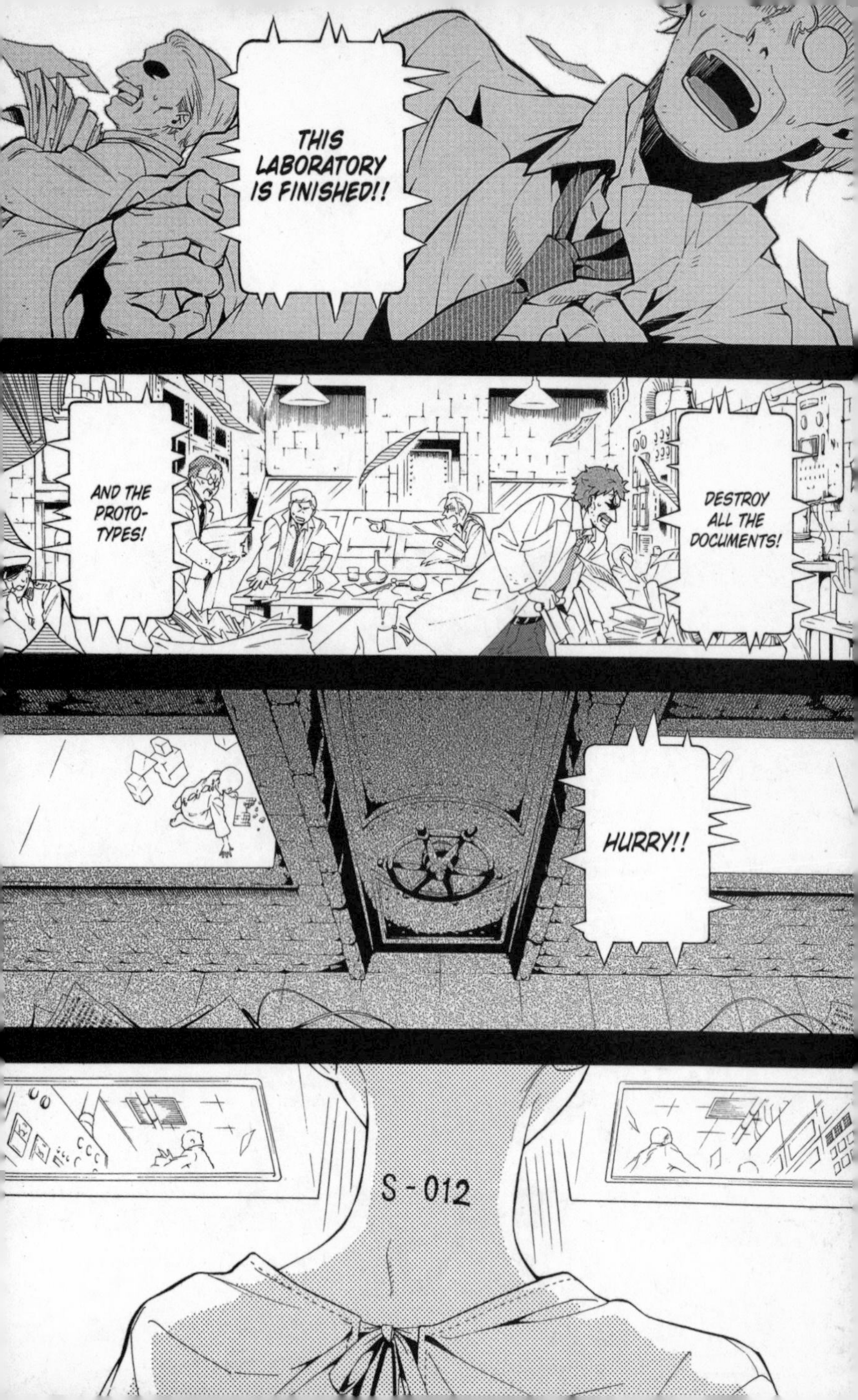
THIS LABORATORY IS FINISHED!!
DESTROY ALL THE DOCUMENTS!
AND THE PROTO-TYPES!
HURRY!!
S-012

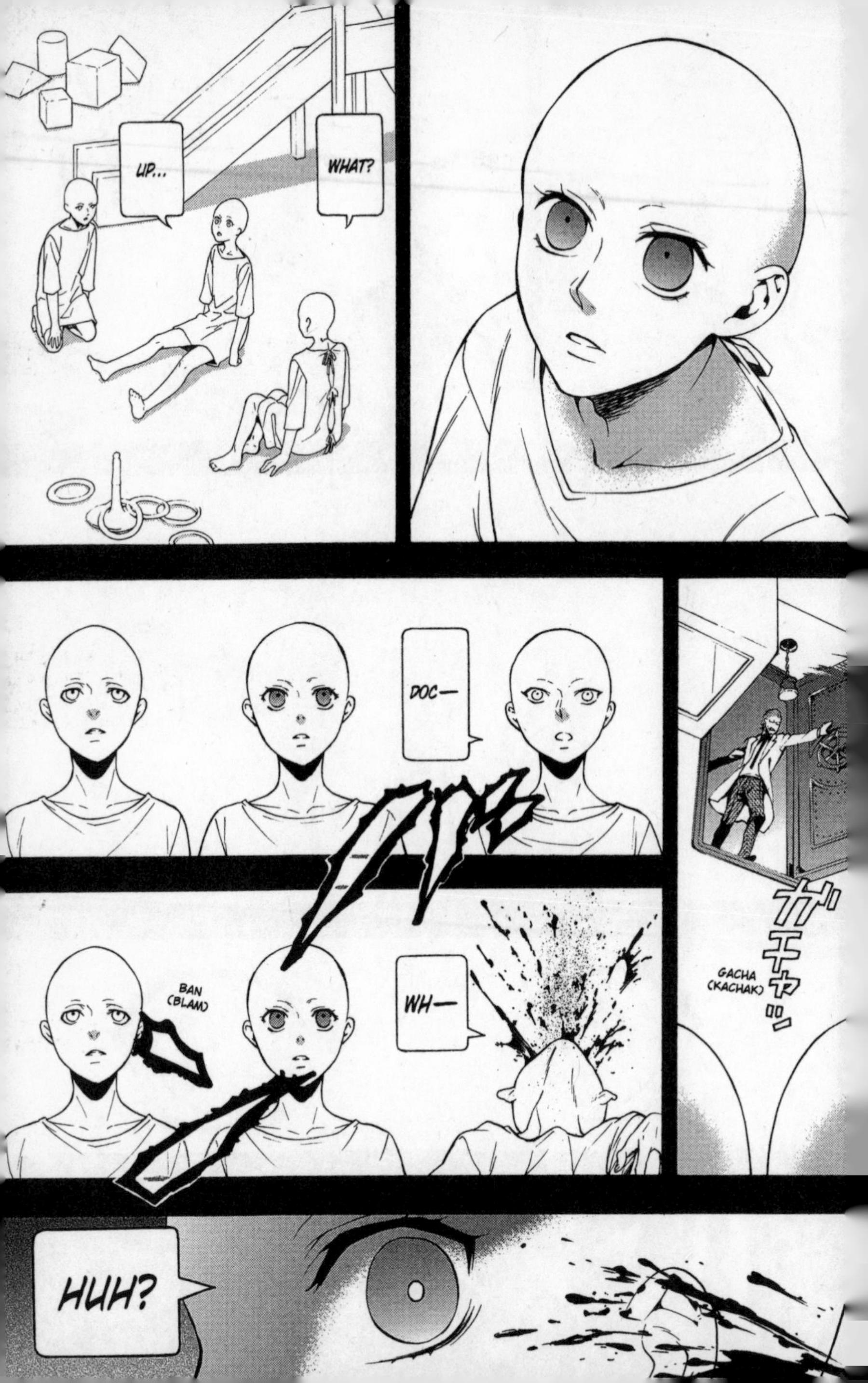
WHAT?
UP...
ガチャッ
GACHA (KACHAK)
DOC—
WH—
BAN (BLAM)
HUH?

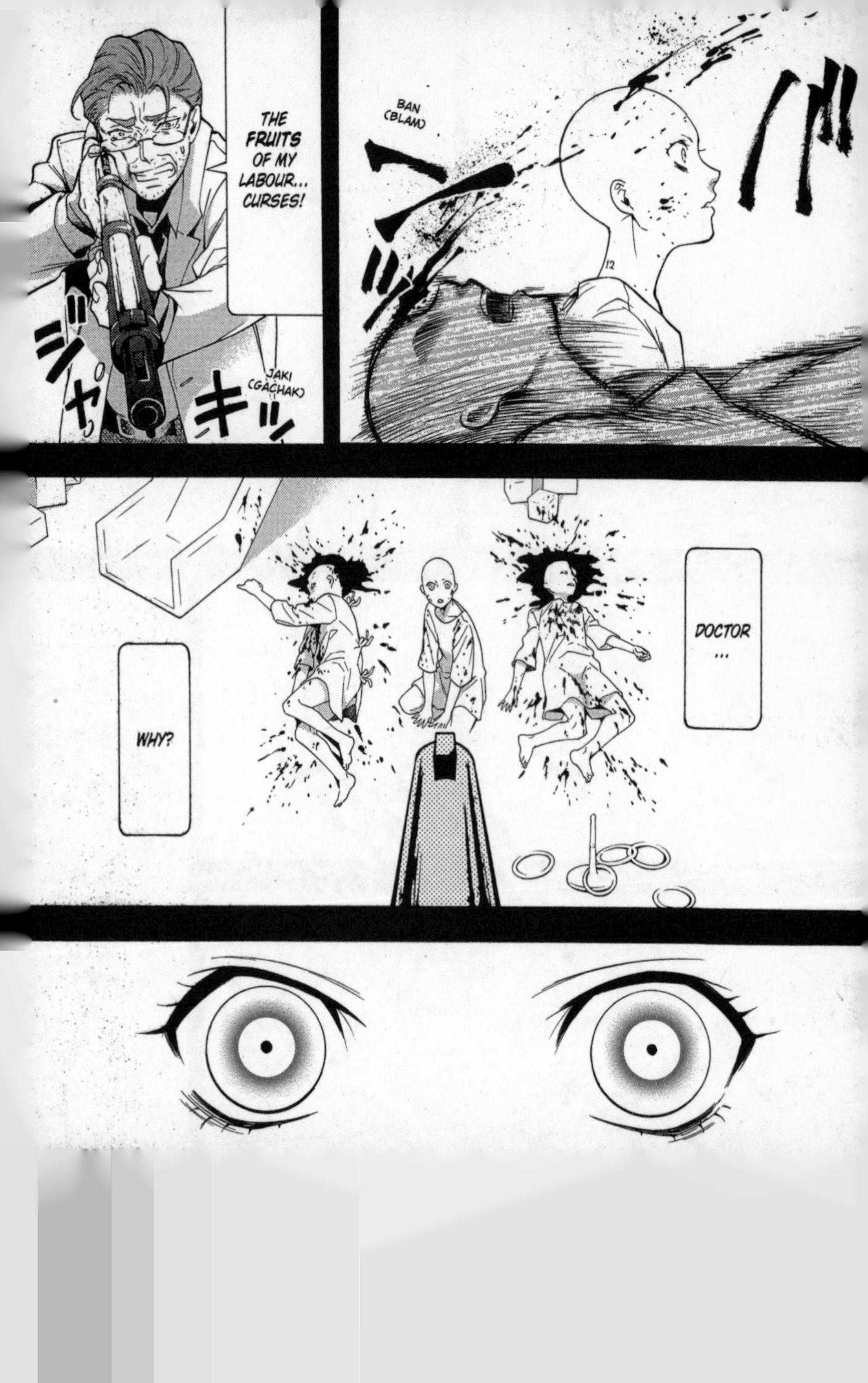
BAN
(BLAM)
THE FRUITS OF MY LABOUR... CURSES!
JAKI
(GACHAK)
DOCTOR ...
WHY?

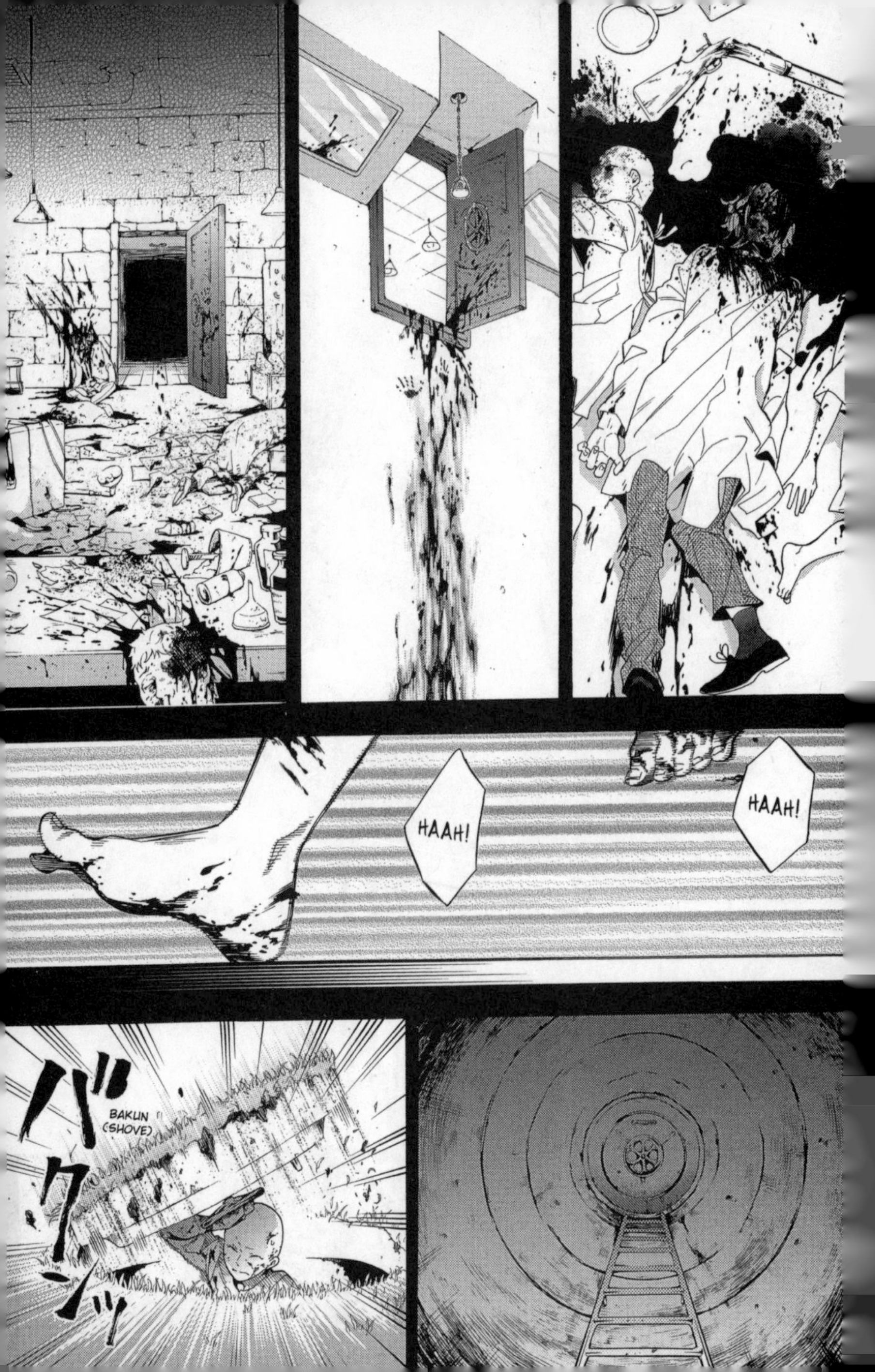
HAAH!
HAAH!
バクッ
BAKUN (SHOVE)

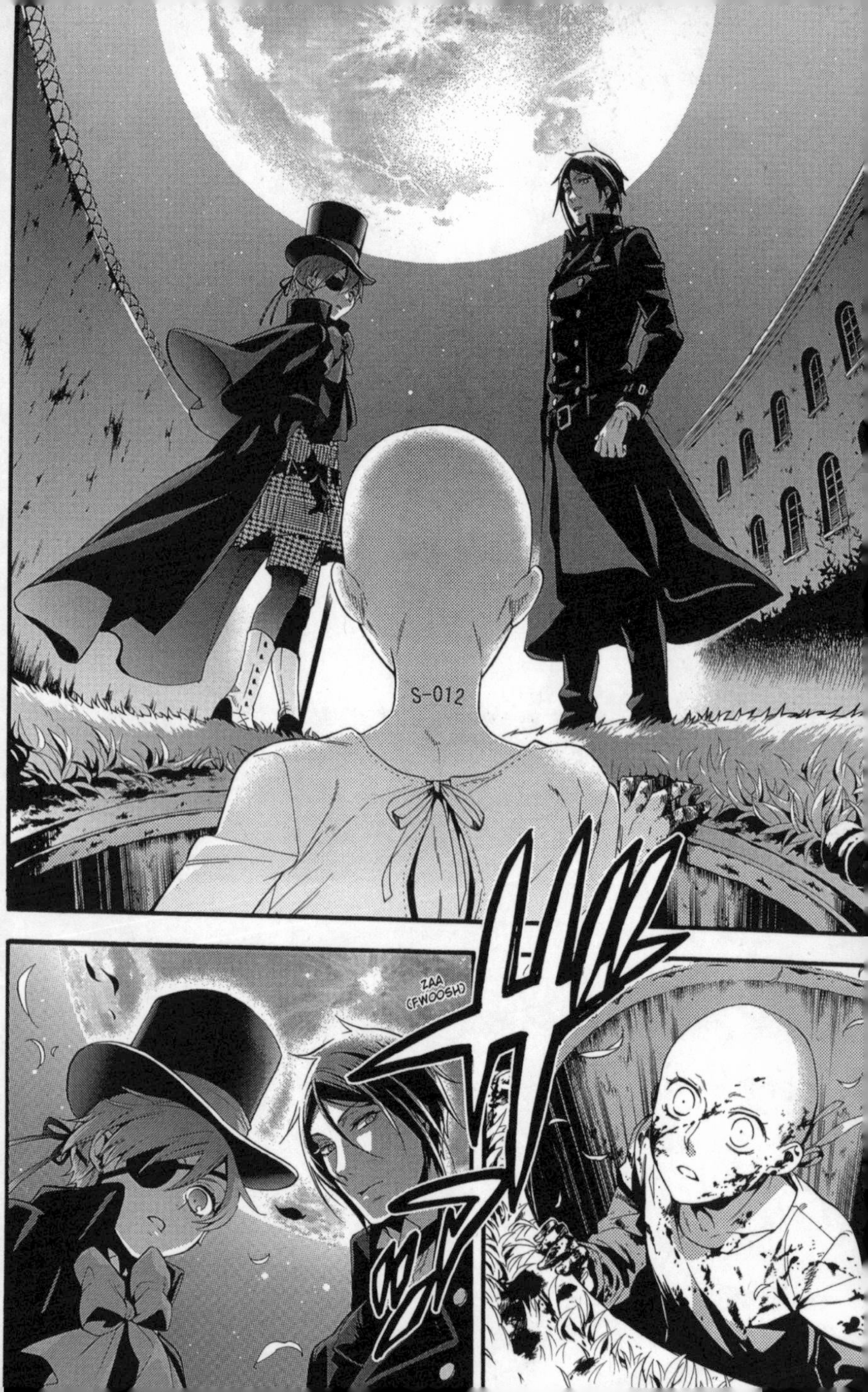
S-012
ZAA
(FWOOSH)

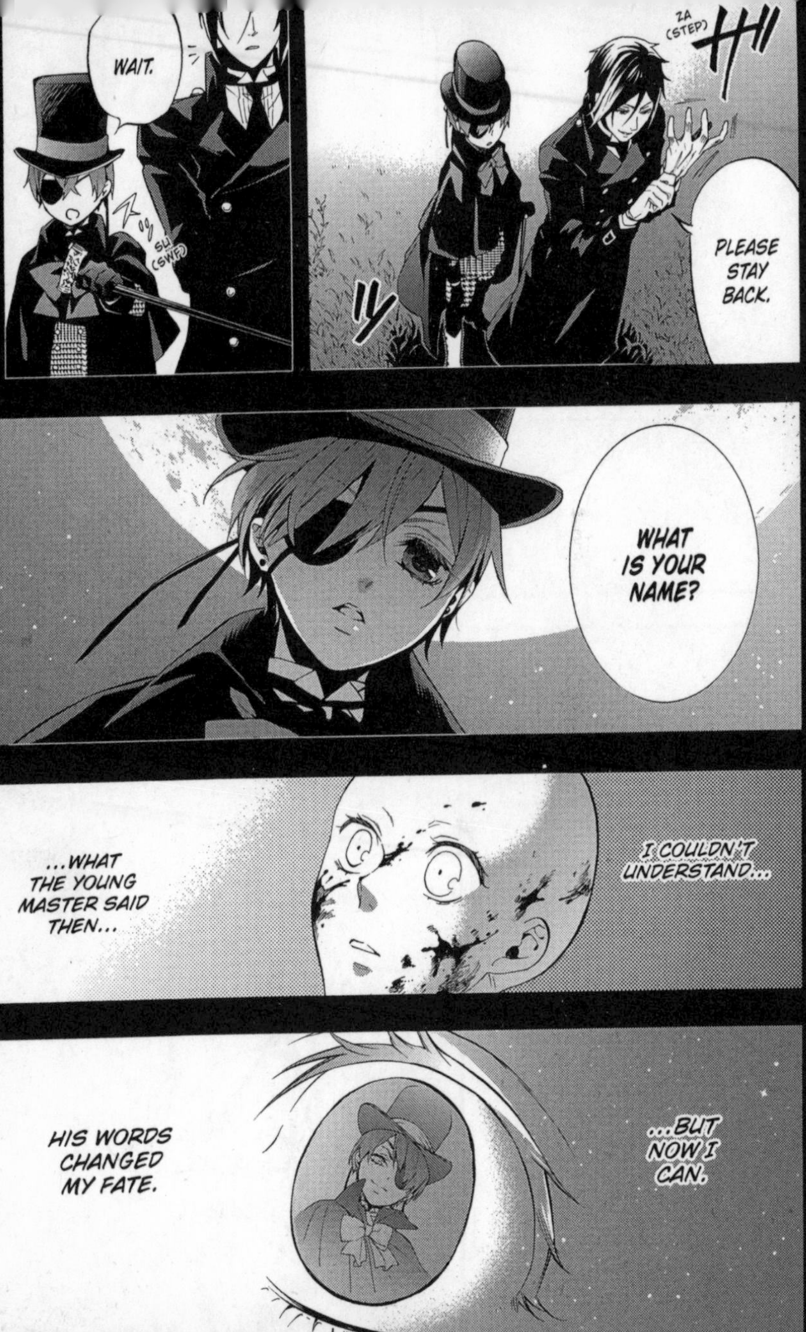
ZA (STEP)
PLEASE STAY BACK.
WAIT.
SLI (SWF)
WHAT IS YOUR NAME?
I COULDN'T UNDERSTAND...
...WHAT THE YOUNG MASTER SAID THEN...
...BUT NOW I CAN.
HIS WORDS CHANGED MY FATE.

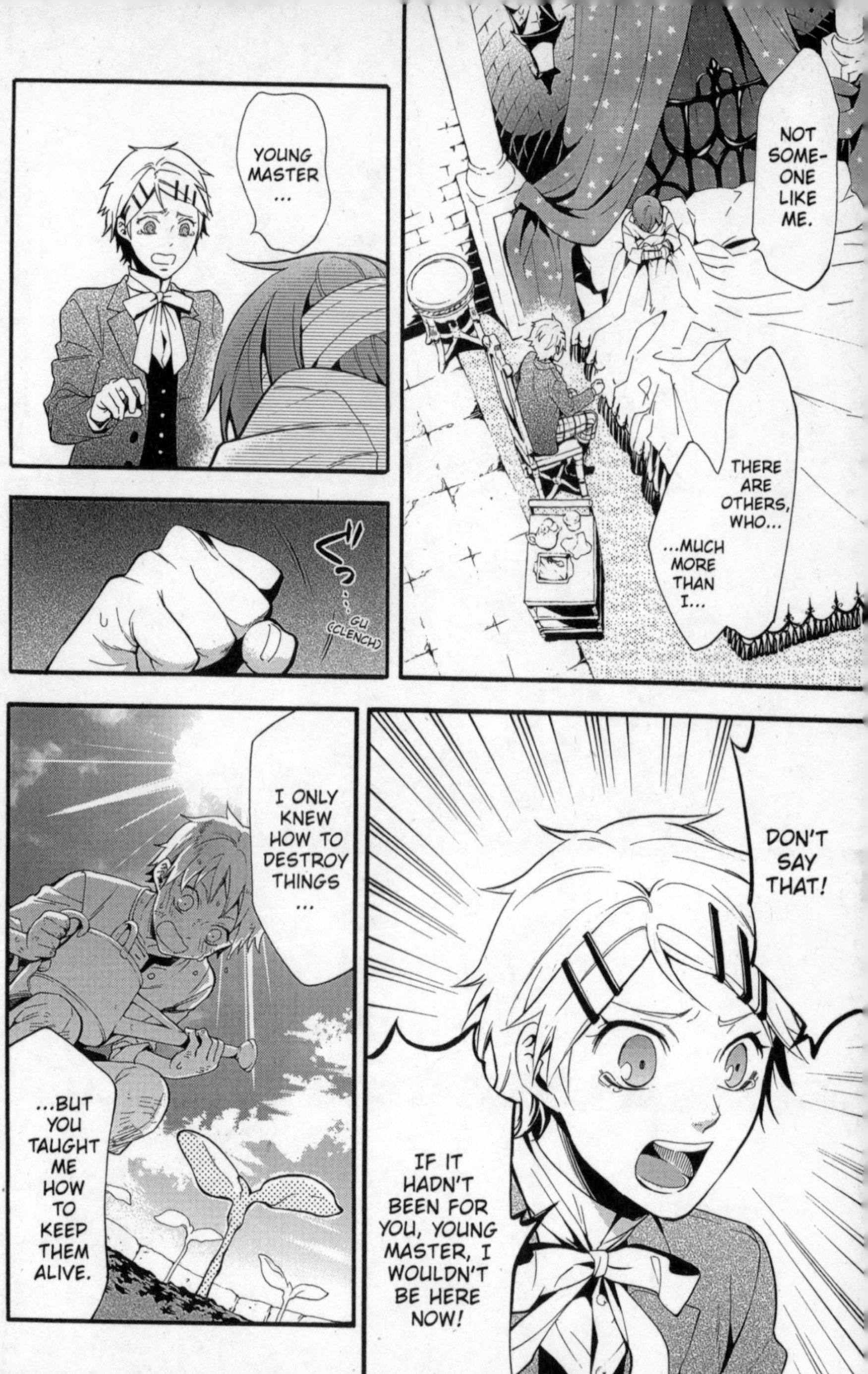
NOT SOME-ONE LIKE ME.
THERE ARE OTHERS, WHO...
...MUCH MORE THAN I...
YOUNG MASTER ...
GU (CLENCH)
DON'T SAY THAT!
IF IT HADN'T BEEN FOR YOU, YOUNG MASTER, I WOULDN'T BE HERE NOW!
I ONLY KNEW HOW TO DESTROY THINGS ...
...BUT YOU TAUGHT ME HOW TO KEEP THEM ALIVE.

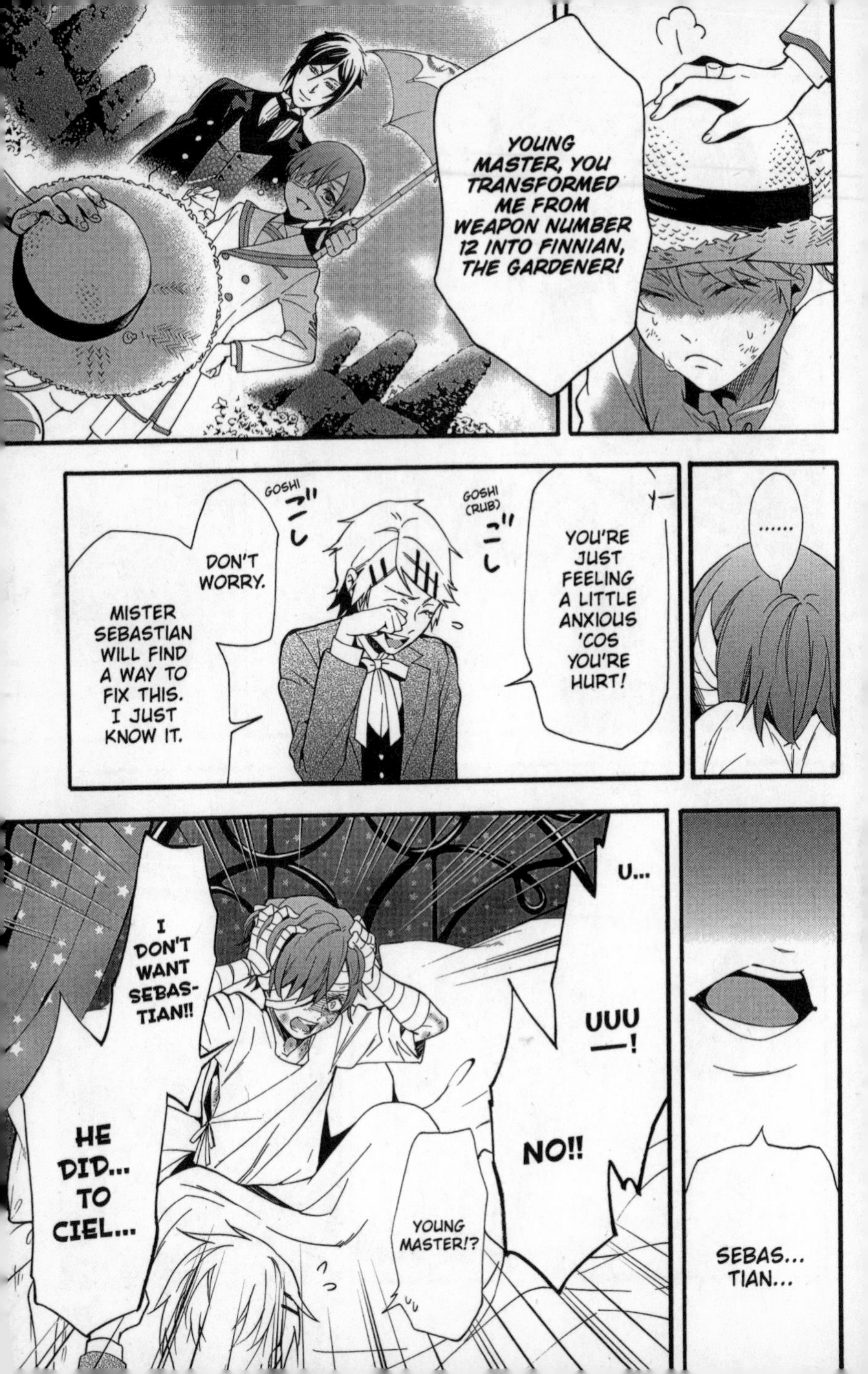

YOUNG MASTER, YOU TRANSFORMED ME FROM WEAPON NUMBER 12 INTO FINNIAN, THE GARDENER!
......
Y—
YOU'RE JUST FEELING A LITTLE ANXIOUS 'COS YOU'RE HURT!
GOSHI (RUB)
GOSHI
DON'T WORRY.
MISTER SEBASTIAN WILL FIND A WAY TO FIX THIS. I JUST KNOW IT.
SEBAS... TIAN...
U...
UUU—!
NO!!
I DON'T WANT SEBAS-TIAN!!
YOUNG MASTER!?
HE DID... TO CIEL...

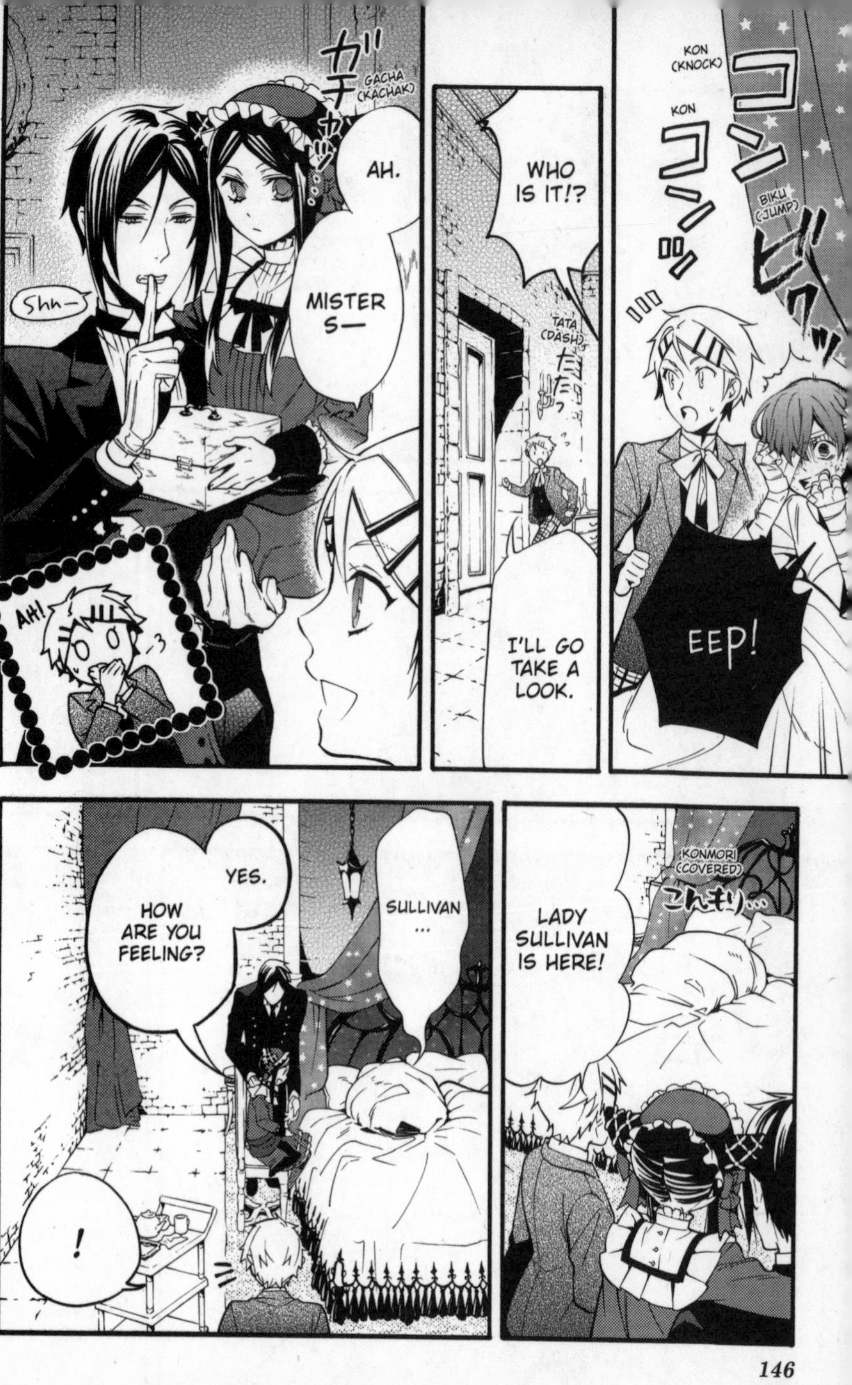
KON (KNOCK)
KON
BIKU (JUMP)
EEP!
WHO IS IT!?
TATA (DASH)
I'LL GO TAKE A LOOK.
GACHA (KACHAK)
AH.
MISTER S—
Shh—
AH!
KONMORI (COVERED)
こんもり…
LADY SULLIVAN IS HERE!
SULLIVAN ...
YES.
HOW ARE YOU FEELING?
!

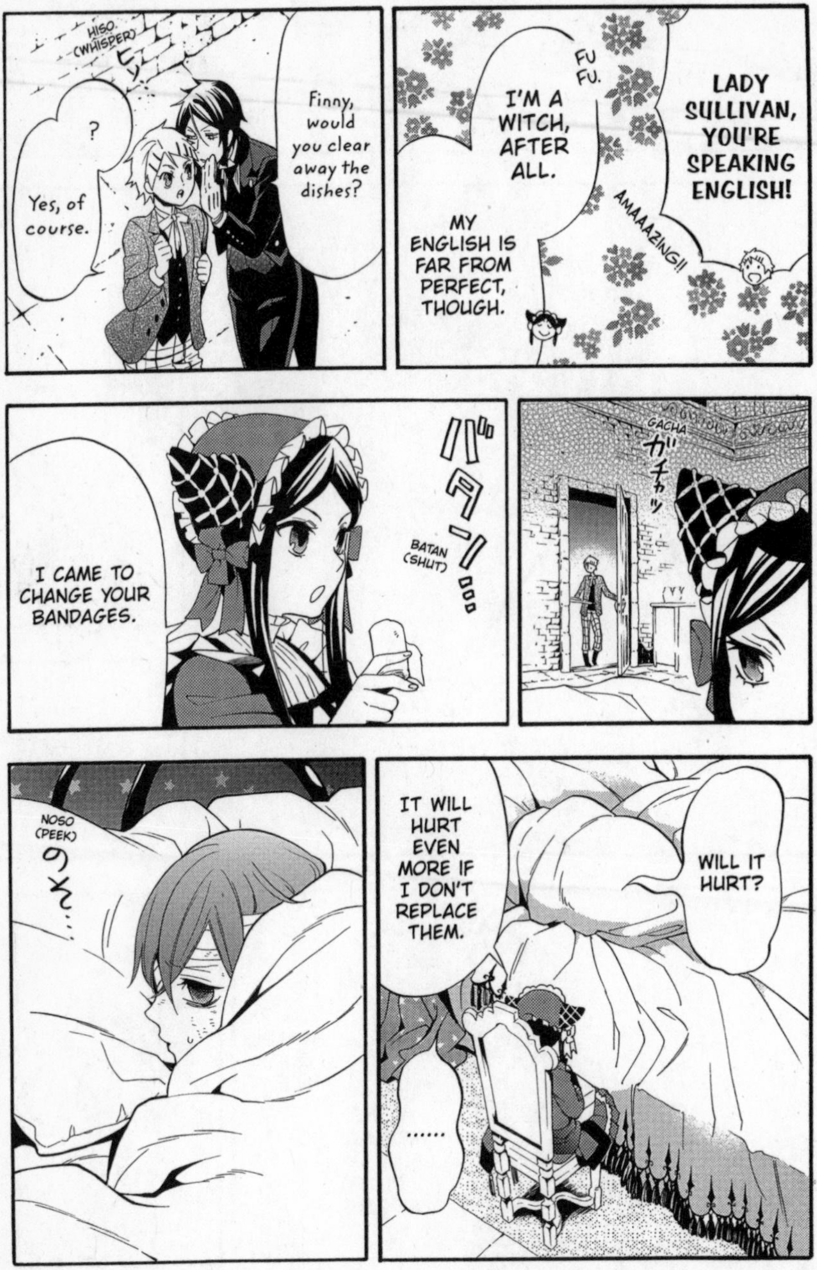
LADY SULLIVAN, YOU'RE SPEAKING ENGLISH!
AMAAAZING!!
FU FU.
I'M A WITCH, AFTER ALL.
MY ENGLISH IS FAR FROM PERFECT, THOUGH.
Finny, would you clear away the dishes?
HISO. (WHISPER)
?
Yes, of course.
GACHA
BATAN (SHUT)
I CAME TO CHANGE YOUR BANDAGES.
WILL IT HURT?
IT WILL HURT EVEN MORE IF I DON'T REPLACE THEM.
......
NOSO (PEEK)

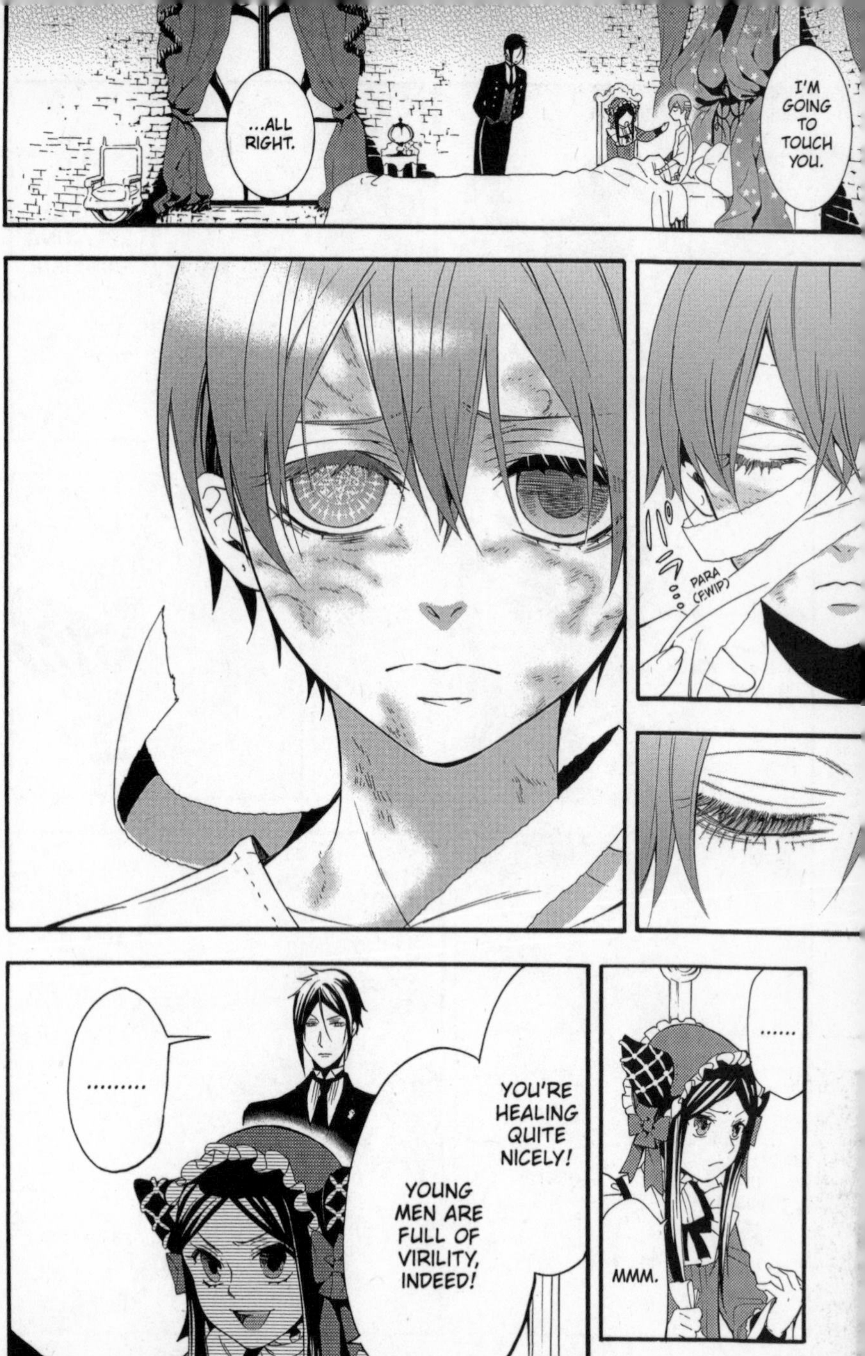
I'M GOING TO TOUCH YOU.
...ALL RIGHT.
PARA (F.WIP)
......
MMM.
YOU'RE HEALING QUITE NICELY!
YOUNG MEN ARE FULL OF VIRILITY, INDEED!
....

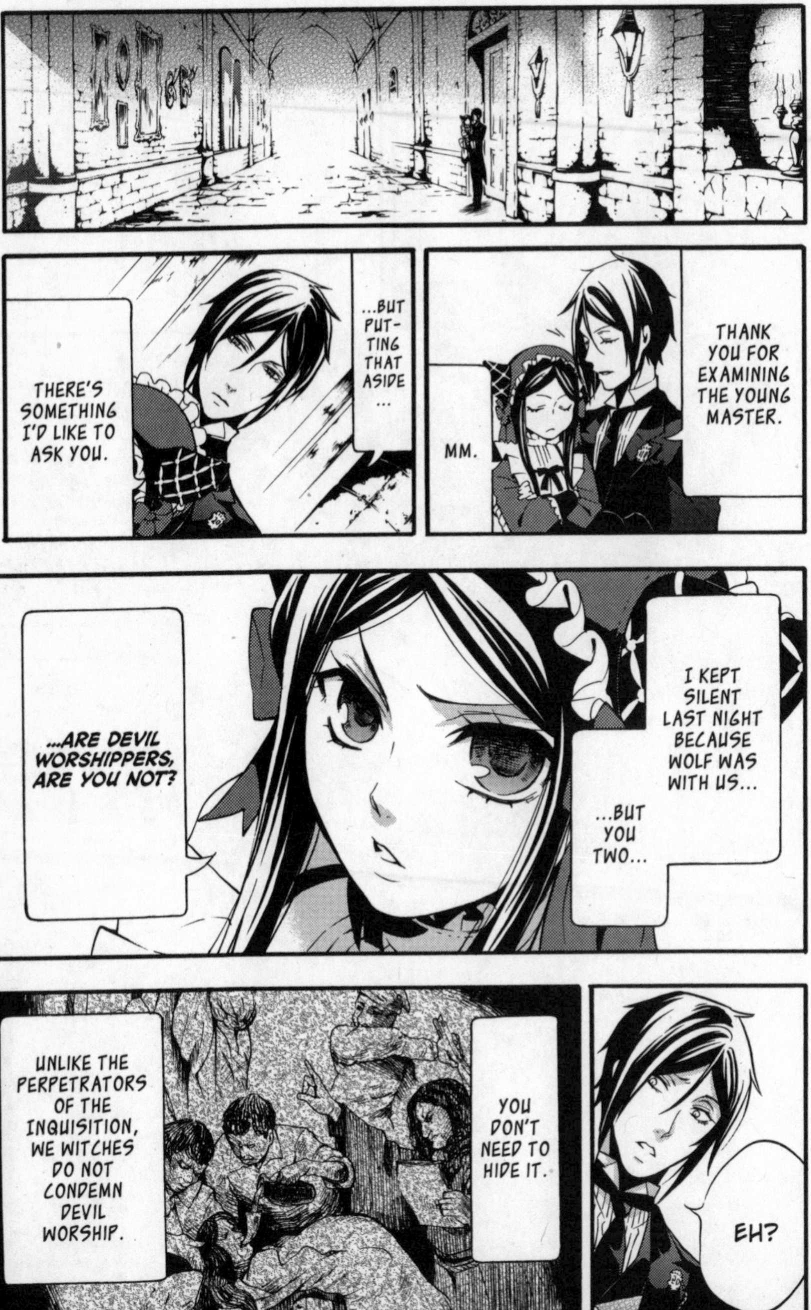
THANK YOU FOR EXAMINING THE YOUNG MASTER.
MM.
...BUT PUTTING THAT ASIDE ...
THERE'S SOMETHING I'D LIKE TO ASK YOU.
I KEPT SILENT LAST NIGHT BECAUSE WOLF WAS WITH US...
...BUT YOU TWO...
...ARE DEVIL WORSHIPPERS, ARE YOU NOT?
EH?
YOU DON'T NEED TO HIDE IT.
UNLIKE THE PERPETRATORS OF THE INQUISITION, WE WITCHES DO NOT CONDEMN DEVIL WORSHIP.

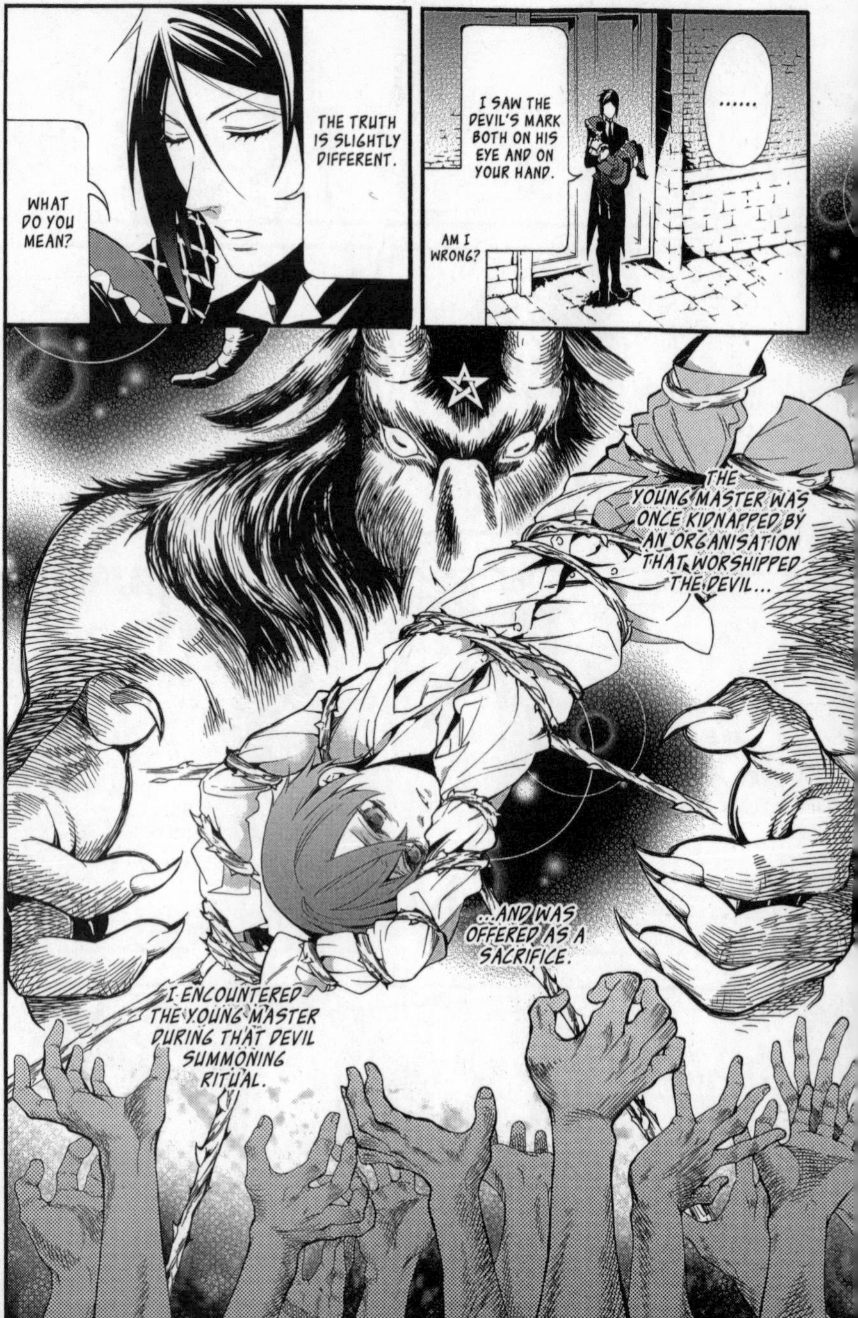
......
I SAW THE DEVIL'S MARK BOTH ON HIS EYE AND ON YOUR HAND.
AM I WRONG?
THE TRUTH IS SLIGHTLY DIFFERENT.
WHAT DO YOU MEAN?
THE YOUNG MASTER WAS ONCE KIDNAPPED BY AN ORGANISATION THAT WORSHIPPED THE DEVIL...
...AND WAS OFFERED AS A SACRIFICE.
I ENCOUNTERED THE YOUNG MASTER DURING THAT DEVIL SUMMONING RITUAL.

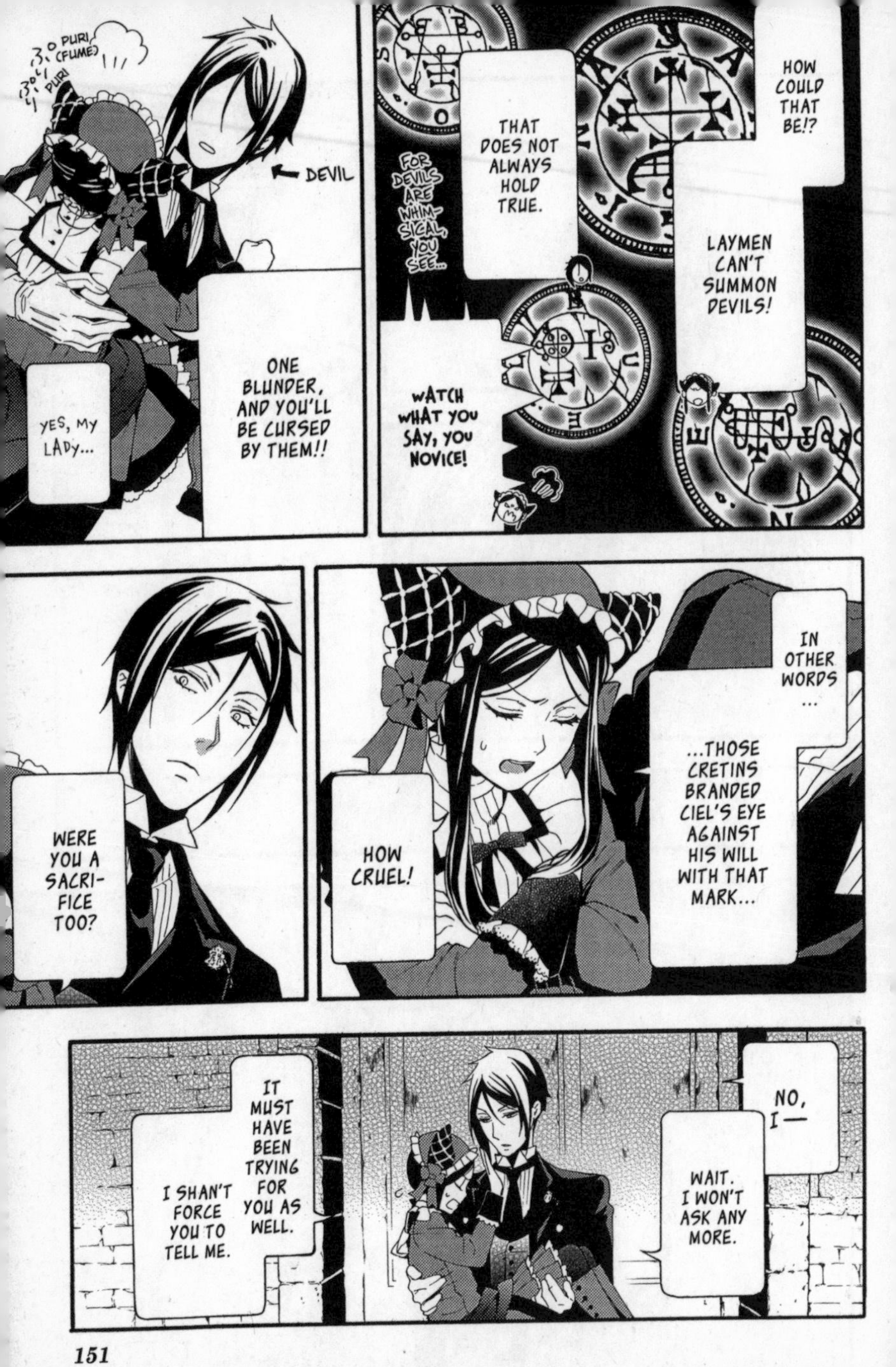
HOW COULD THAT BE!?
LAYMEN CAN'T SUMMON DEVILS!
THAT DOES NOT ALWAYS HOLD TRUE.
FOR DEVILS ARE WHIMSICAL, YOU SEE...
WATCH WHAT YOU SAY, YOU NOVICE!
PURI (FUME)
PURI
DEVIL
ONE BLUNDER, AND YOU'LL BE CURSED BY THEM!!
YES, MY LADY...
IN OTHER WORDS...
...THOSE CRETINS BRANDED CIEL'S EYE AGAINST HIS WILL WITH THAT MARK...
HOW CRUEL!
WERE YOU A SACRIFICE TOO?
NO, I—
WAIT. I WON'T ASK ANY MORE.
IT MUST HAVE BEEN TRYING FOR YOU AS WELL.
I SHAN'T FORCE YOU TO TELL ME.

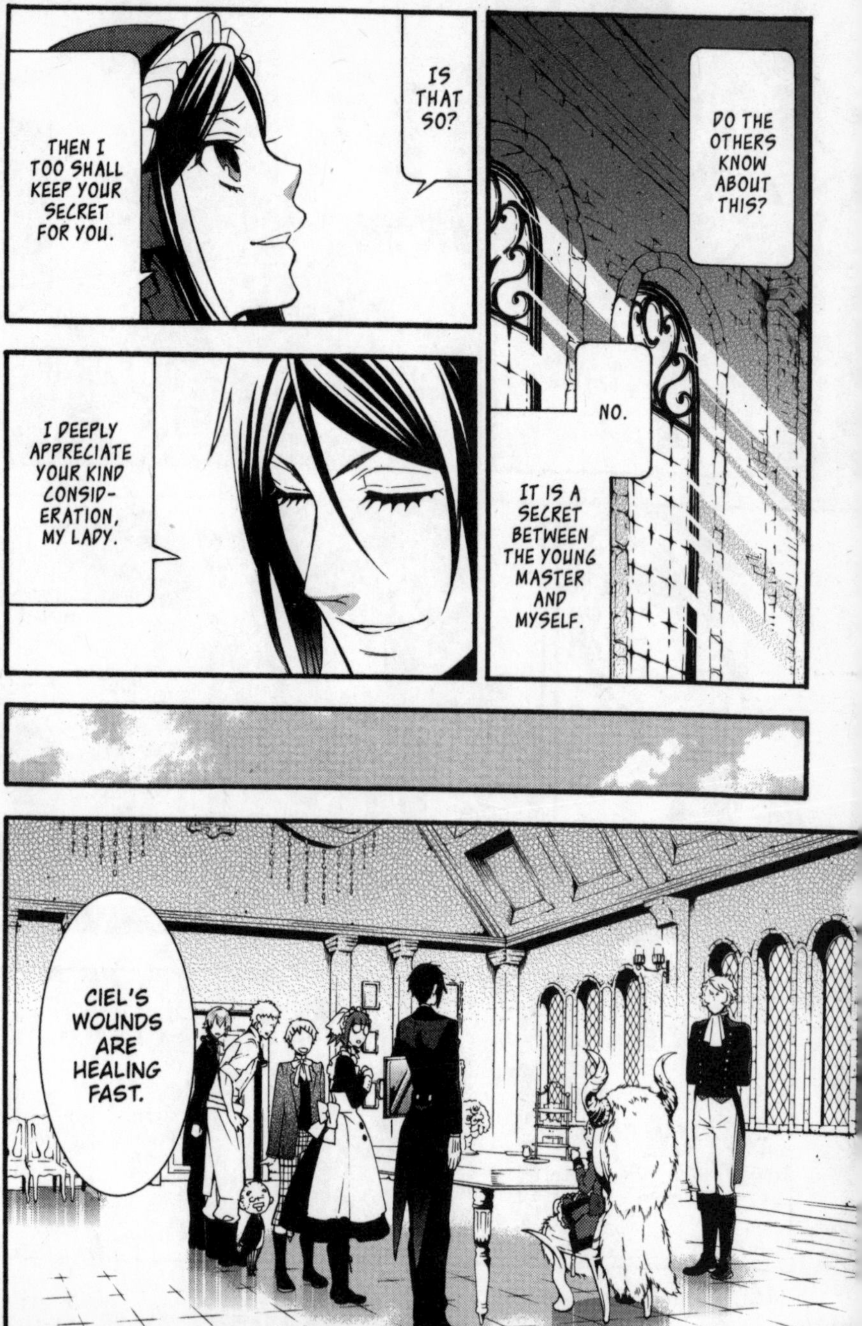

DO THE OTHERS KNOW ABOUT THIS?
NO.
IT IS A SECRET BETWEEN THE YOUNG MASTER AND MYSELF.
IS THAT SO?
THEN I TOO SHALL KEEP YOUR SECRET FOR YOU.
I DEEPLY APPRECIATE YOUR KIND CONSID-ERATION, MY LADY.
CIEL'S WOUNDS ARE HEALING FAST.

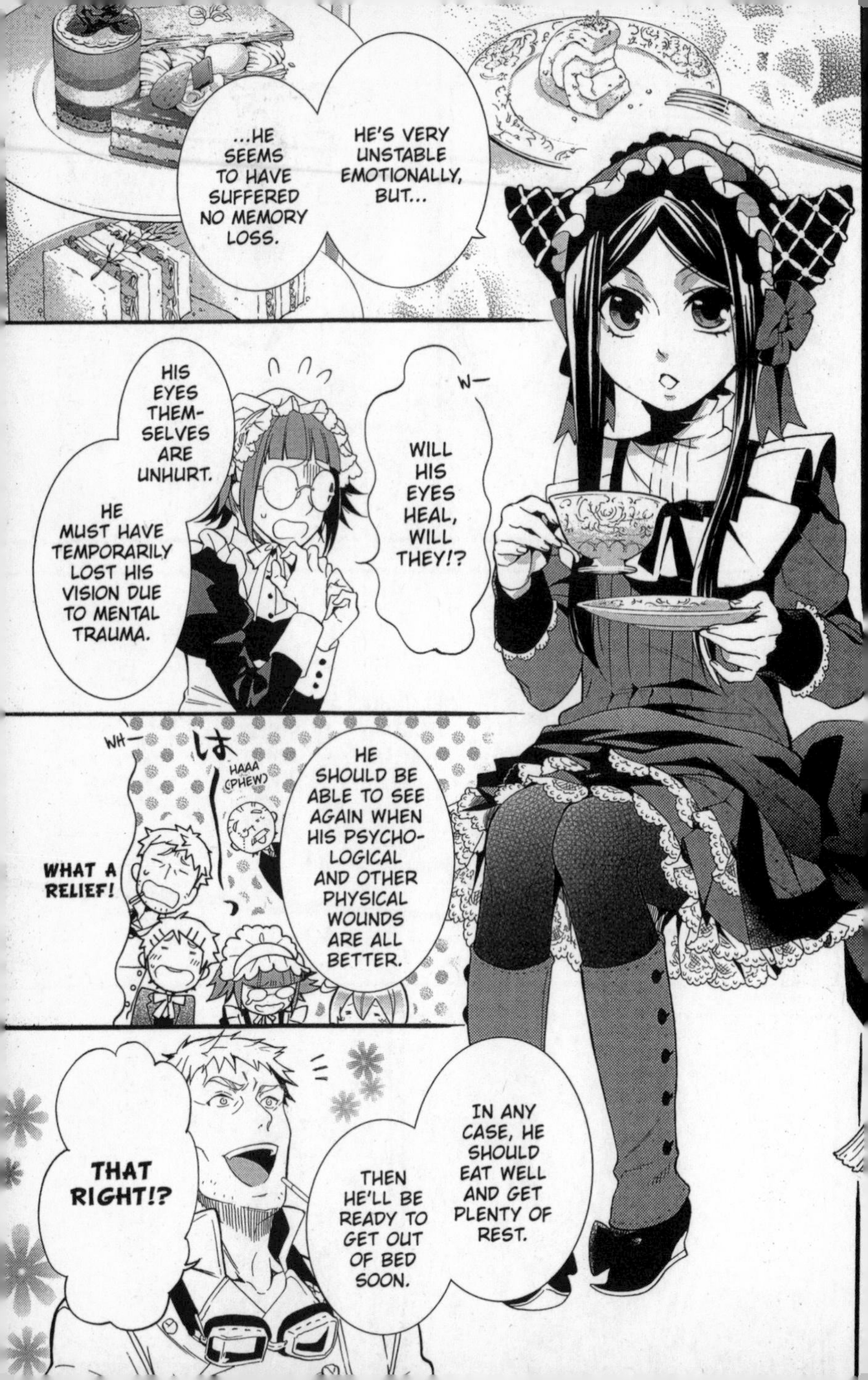
HE'S VERY UNSTABLE EMOTIONALLY, BUT...
...HE SEEMS TO HAVE SUFFERED NO MEMORY LOSS.
W—
WILL HIS EYES HEAL, WILL THEY!?
HIS EYES THEM-SELVES ARE UNHURT.
HE MUST HAVE TEMPORARILY LOST HIS VISION DUE TO MENTAL TRAUMA.
HE SHOULD BE ABLE TO SEE AGAIN WHEN HIS PSYCHO-LOGICAL AND OTHER PHYSICAL WOUNDS ARE ALL BETTER.
HAAA (PHEW)
は
WH—
WHAT A RELIEF!
IN ANY CASE, HE SHOULD EAT WELL AND GET PLENTY OF REST.
THEN HE'LL BE READY TO GET OUT OF BED SOON.
THAT RIGHT!?

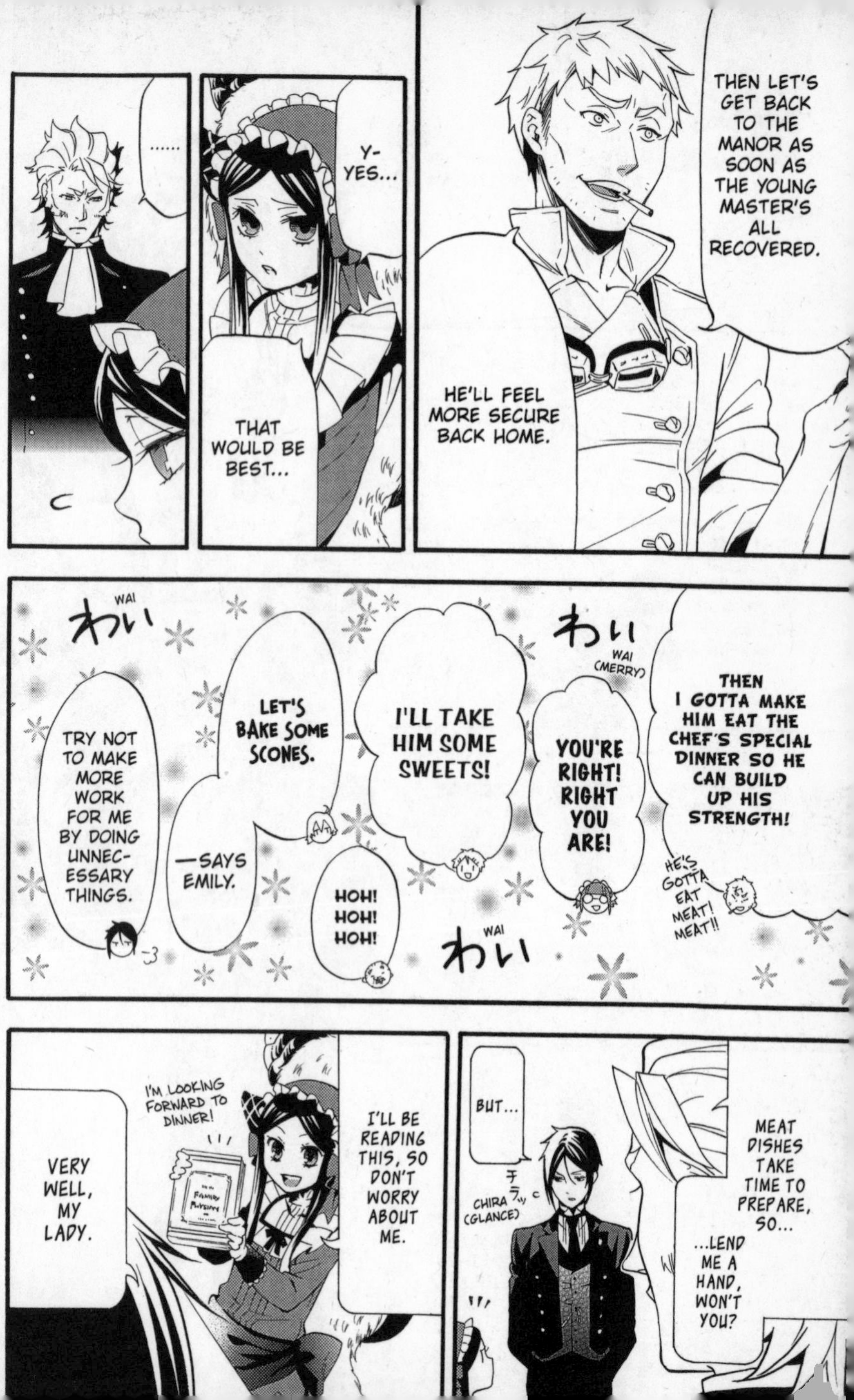
THEN LET'S GET BACK TO THE MANOR AS SOON AS THE YOUNG MASTER'S ALL RECOVERED.
HE'LL FEEL MORE SECURE BACK HOME.
Y-YES...
THAT WOULD BE BEST...
......
THEN I GOTTA MAKE HIM EAT THE CHEF'S SPECIAL DINNER SO HE CAN BUILD UP HIS STRENGTH!
HE'S GOTTA EAT MEAT! MEAT!!
わい
WAI (MERRY)
YOU'RE RIGHT! RIGHT YOU ARE!
I'LL TAKE HIM SOME SWEETS!
HOH! HOH! HOH!
わい
WAI
LET'S BAKE SOME SCONES.
—SAYS EMILY.
わい
WAI
TRY NOT TO MAKE MORE WORK FOR ME BY DOING UNNEC-ESSARY THINGS.
MEAT DISHES TAKE TIME TO PREPARE, SO...
...LEND ME A HAND, WON'T YOU?
BUT...
チラッ
CHIRA (GLANCE)
I'LL BE READING THIS, SO DON'T WORRY ABOUT ME.
I'M LOOKING FORWARD TO DINNER!
VERY WELL, MY LADY.

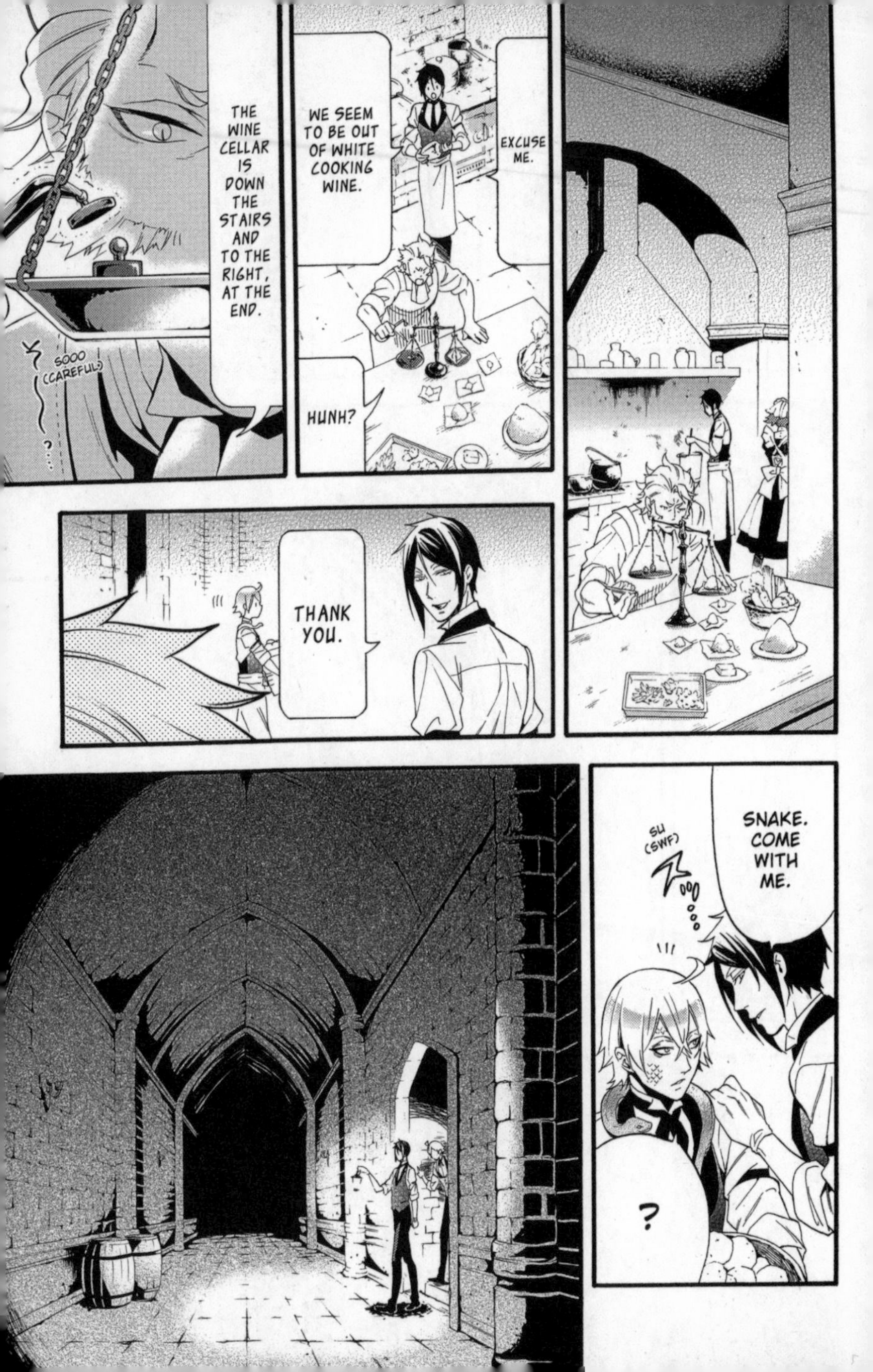
EXCUSE ME.
WE SEEM TO BE OUT OF WHITE COOKING WINE.
HUNH?
THE WINE CELLAR IS DOWN THE STAIRS AND TO THE RIGHT, AT THE END.
SOOO (CAREFUL)
?...
THANK YOU.
SNAKE. COME WITH ME.
SU (SWF)
?

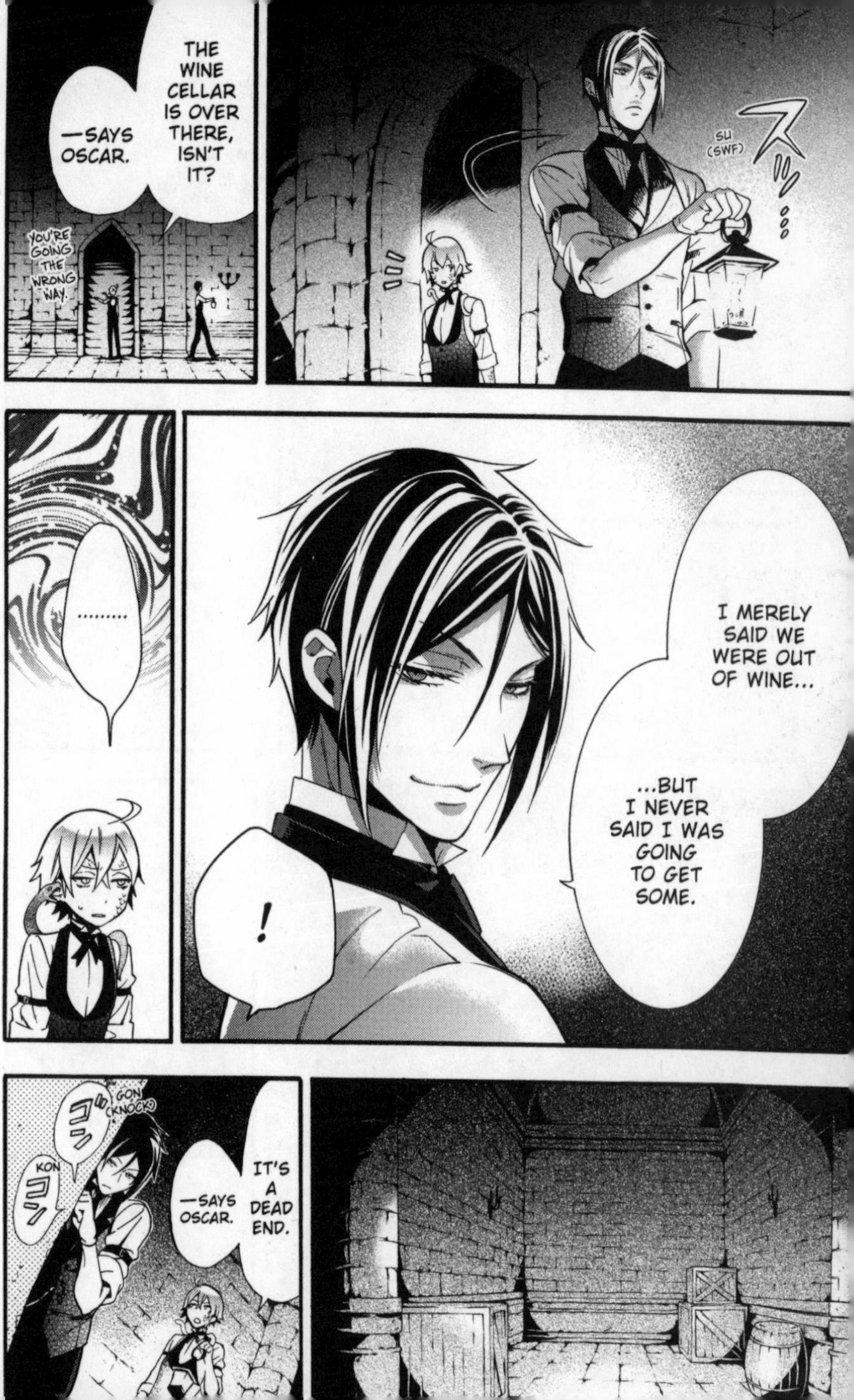
SU (SWF)
THE WINE CELLAR IS OVER THERE, ISN'T IT?
—SAYS OSCAR.
YOU'RE GOING THE WRONG WAY.
I MERELY SAID WE WERE OUT OF WINE...
...BUT I NEVER SAID I WAS GOING TO GET SOME.
!
....
IT'S A DEAD END.
—SAYS OSCAR.
GON (KNOCK)
KON

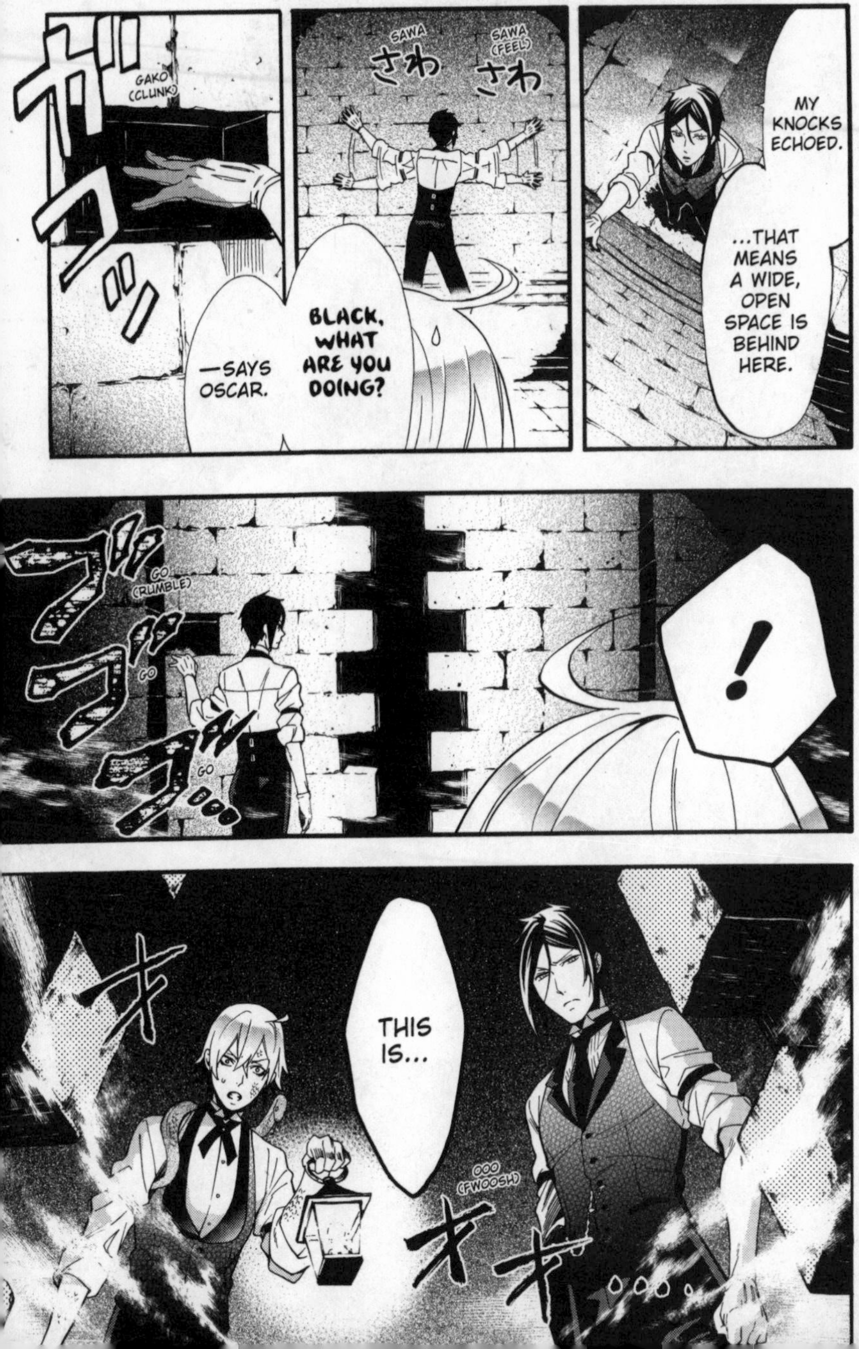
MY KNOCKS ECHOED.
...THAT MEANS A WIDE, OPEN SPACE IS BEHIND HERE.
SAWA
SAWA (FEEL)
さわ さわ
BLACK, WHAT ARE YOU DOING?
—SAYS OSCAR.
GAKO (CLUNK)
!
GO (RUMBLE)
GO
GO
THIS IS...
OOO (FWOOSH)

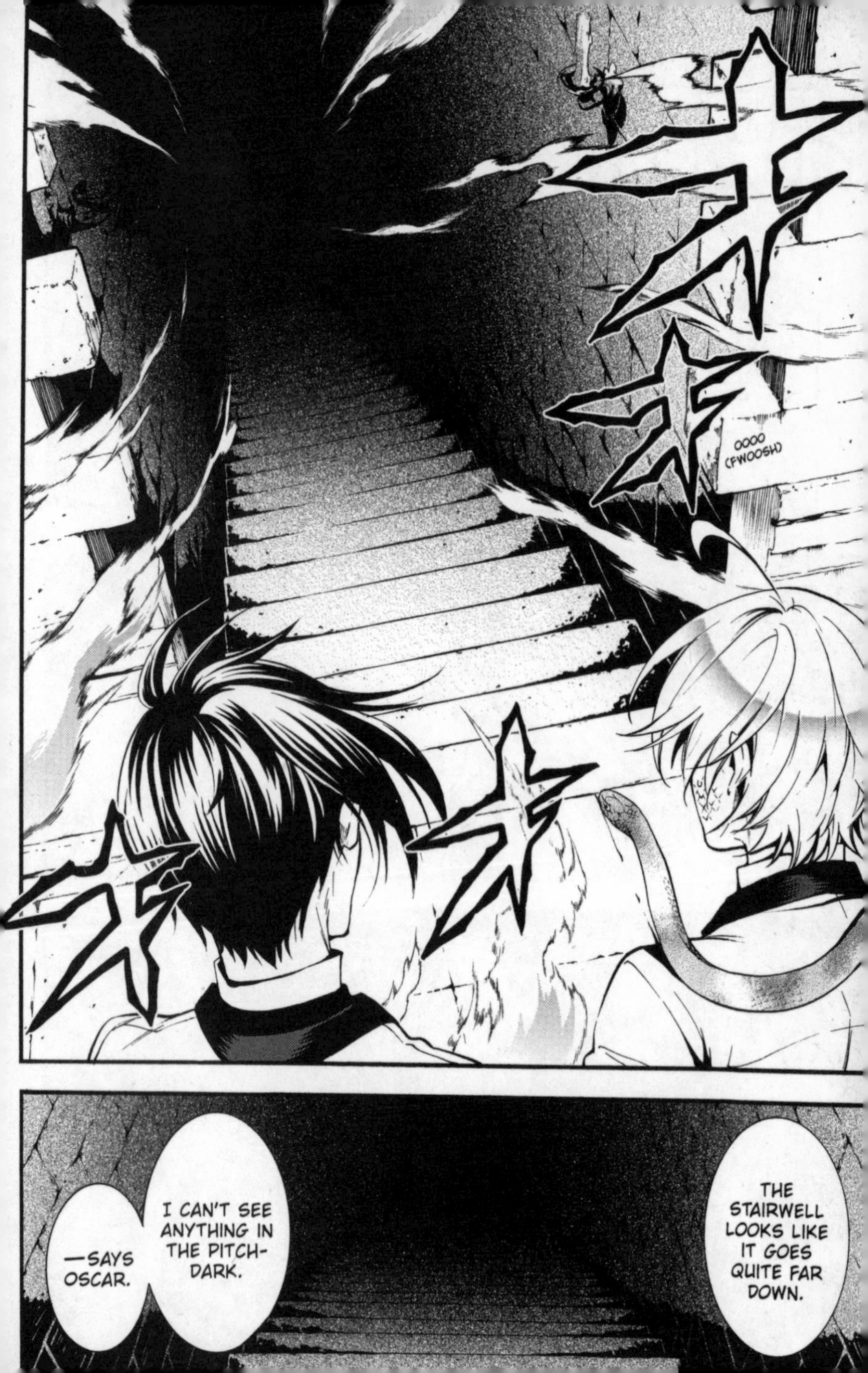
OOOO (FWOOSH)
THE STAIRWELL LOOKS LIKE IT GOES QUITE FAR DOWN.
I CAN'T SEE ANYTHING IN THE PITCH-DARK.
—SAYS OSCAR.

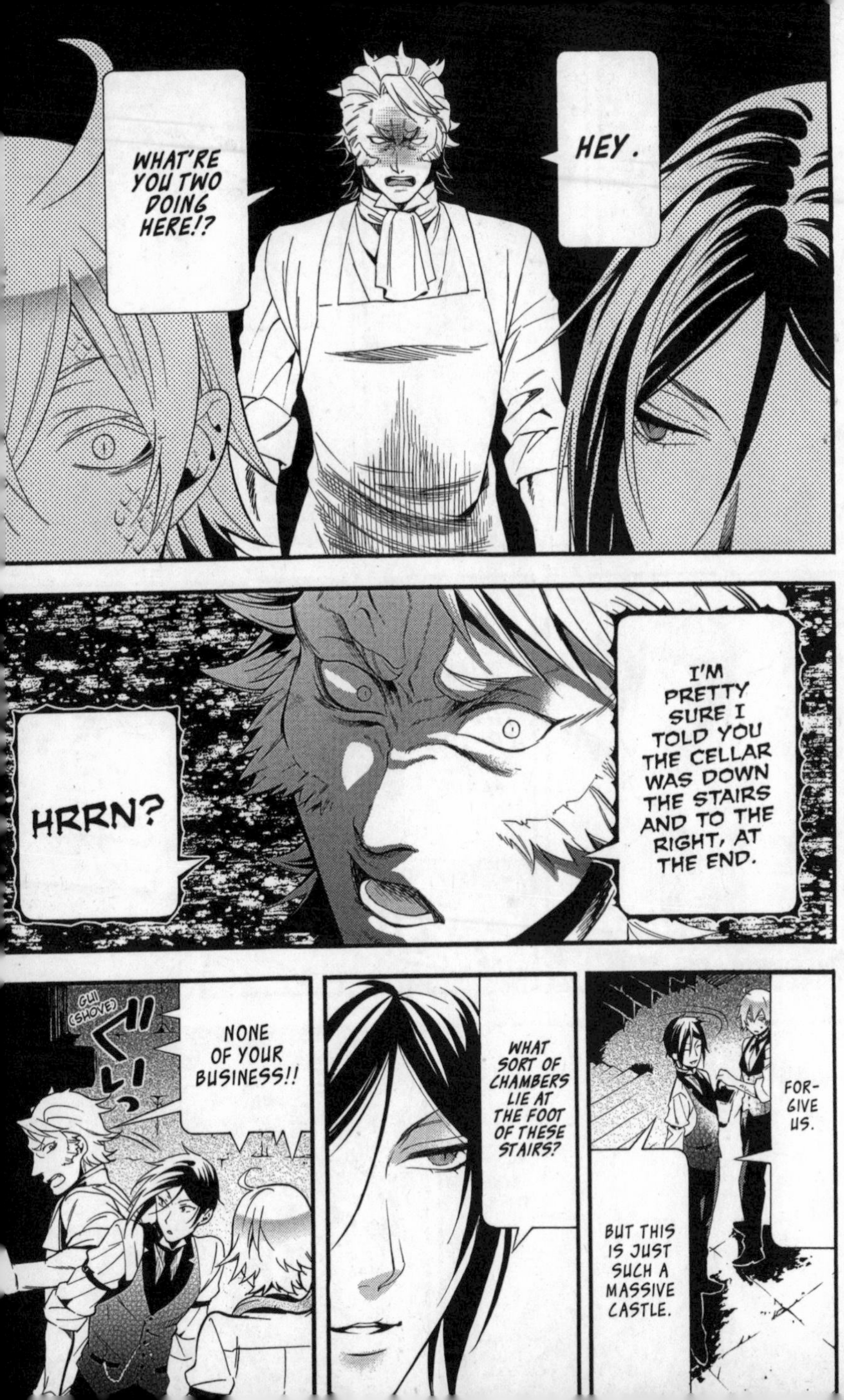
HEY.
WHAT'RE YOU TWO DOING HERE!?
I'M PRETTY SURE I TOLD YOU THE CELLAR WAS DOWN THE STAIRS AND TO THE RIGHT, AT THE END.
HRRN?
FOR-GIVE US.
BUT THIS IS JUST SUCH A MASSIVE CASTLE.
WHAT SORT OF CHAMBERS LIE AT THE FOOT OF THESE STAIRS?
NONE OF YOUR BUSINESS!!
GUI (SHOVE)

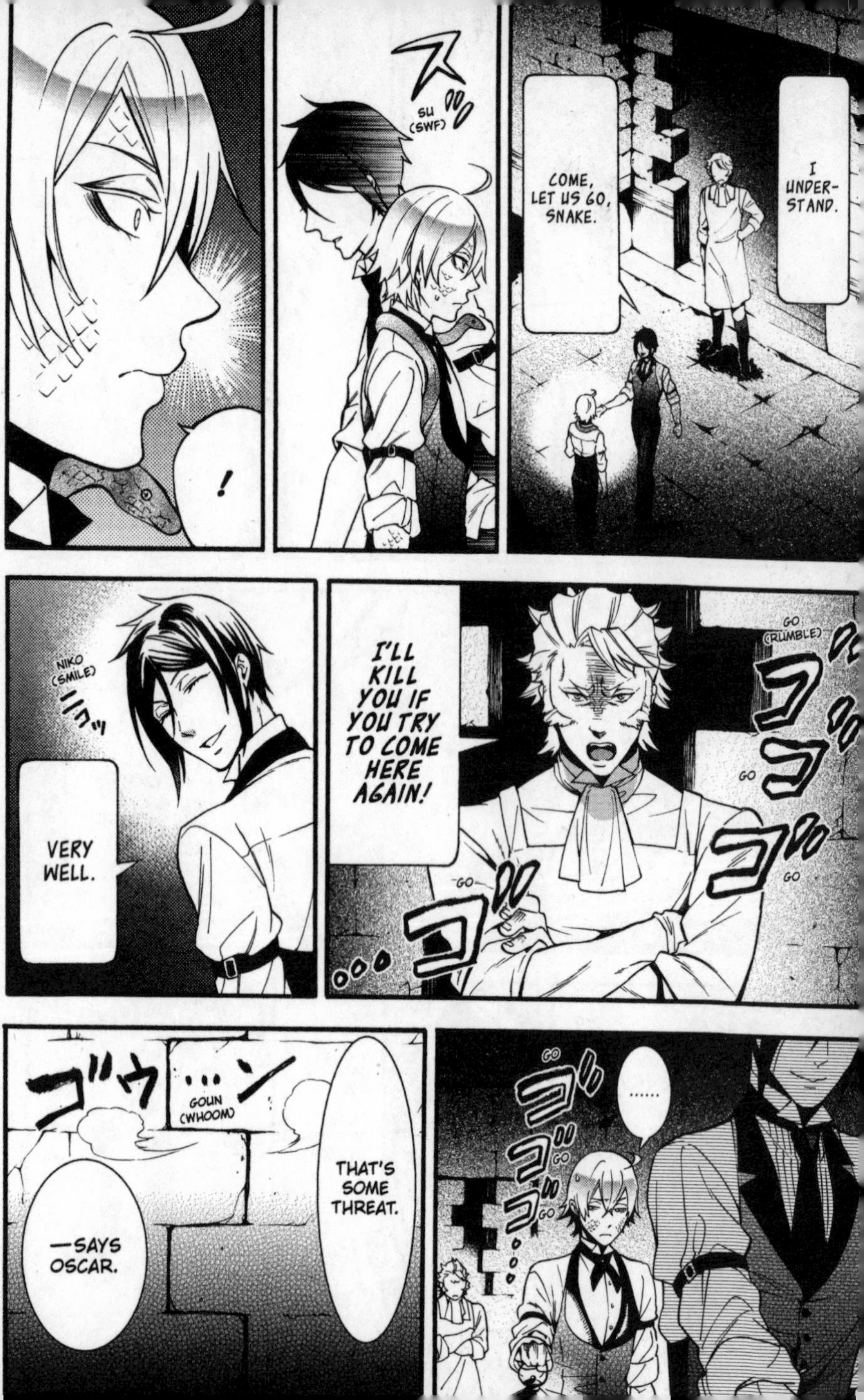
I UNDERSTAND.
COME, LET US GO, SNAKE.
SU (SWF)
!
GO (RUMBLE)
GO
GO
I'LL KILL YOU IF YOU TRY TO COME HERE AGAIN!
GO
NIKO (SMILE)
VERY WELL.
GO
GO
GO
......
THAT'S SOME THREAT.
—SAYS OSCAR.
GOUN (WHOOM)

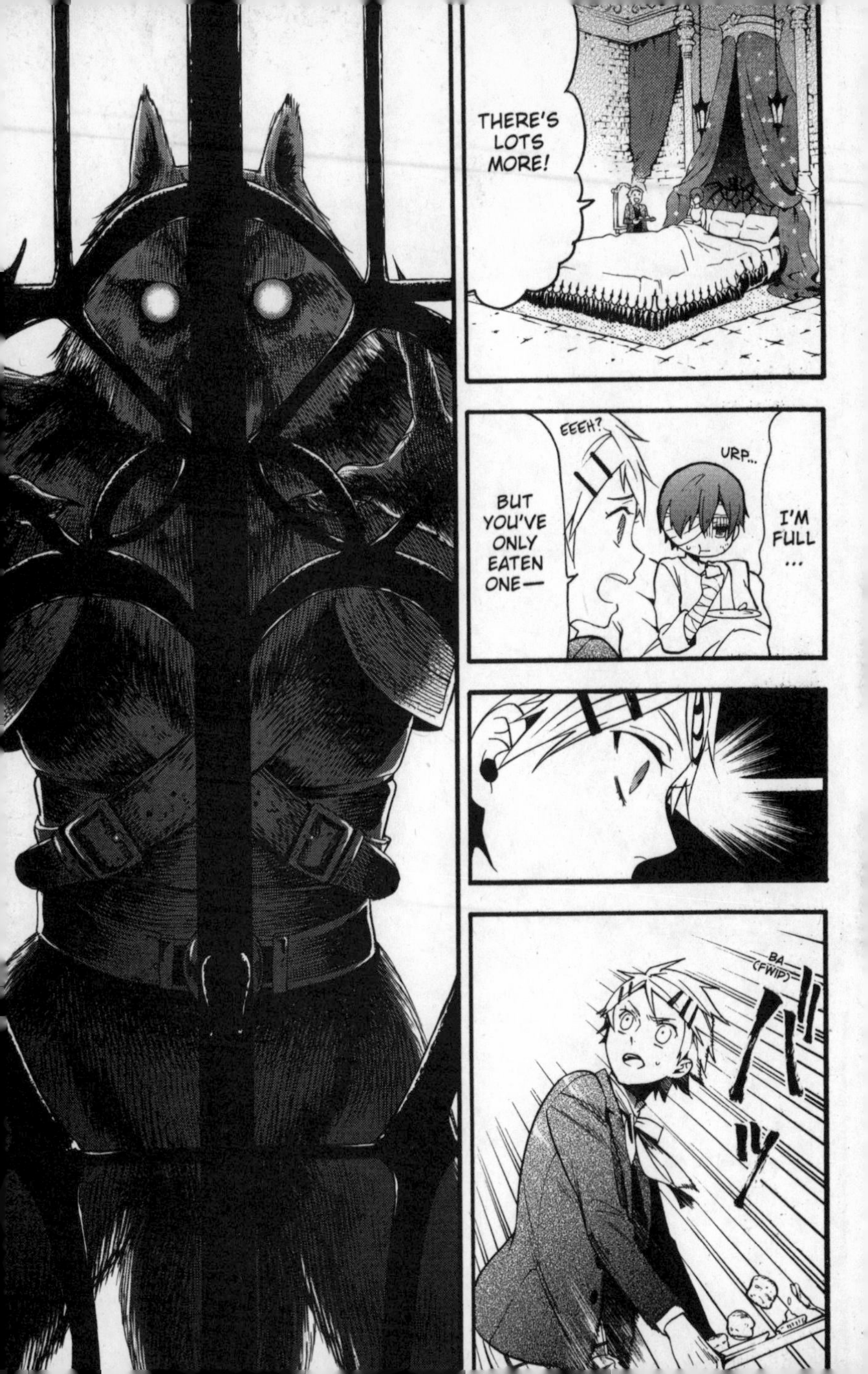
THERE'S LOTS MORE!
URP...
I'M FULL ...
EEEH?
BUT YOU'VE ONLY EATEN ONE—
BA (FWIP)

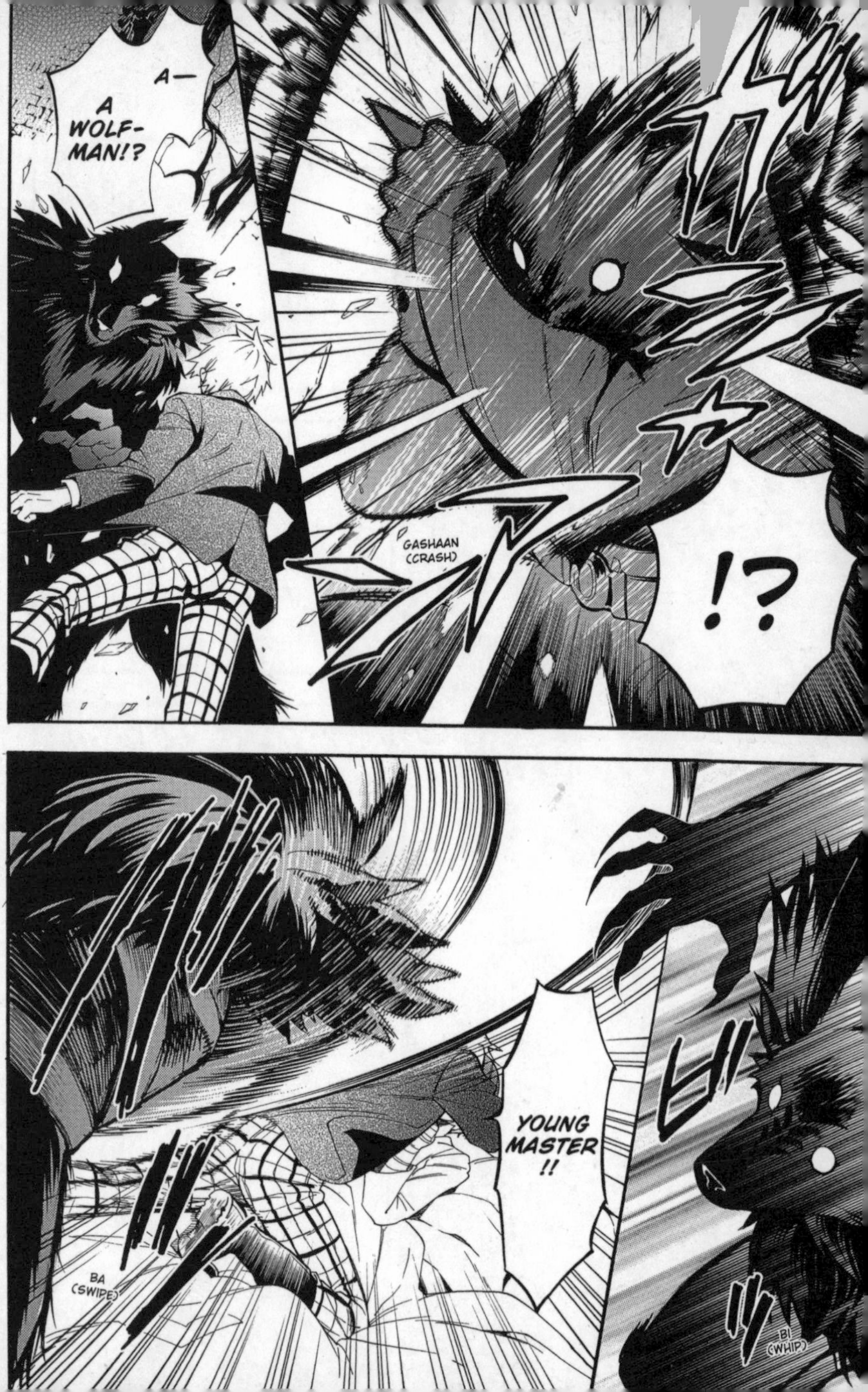
!?
GASHAAN (CRASH)
A—
A WOLF-MAN!?
BI (WHIP)
YOUNG MASTER !!
BA (SWIPE)

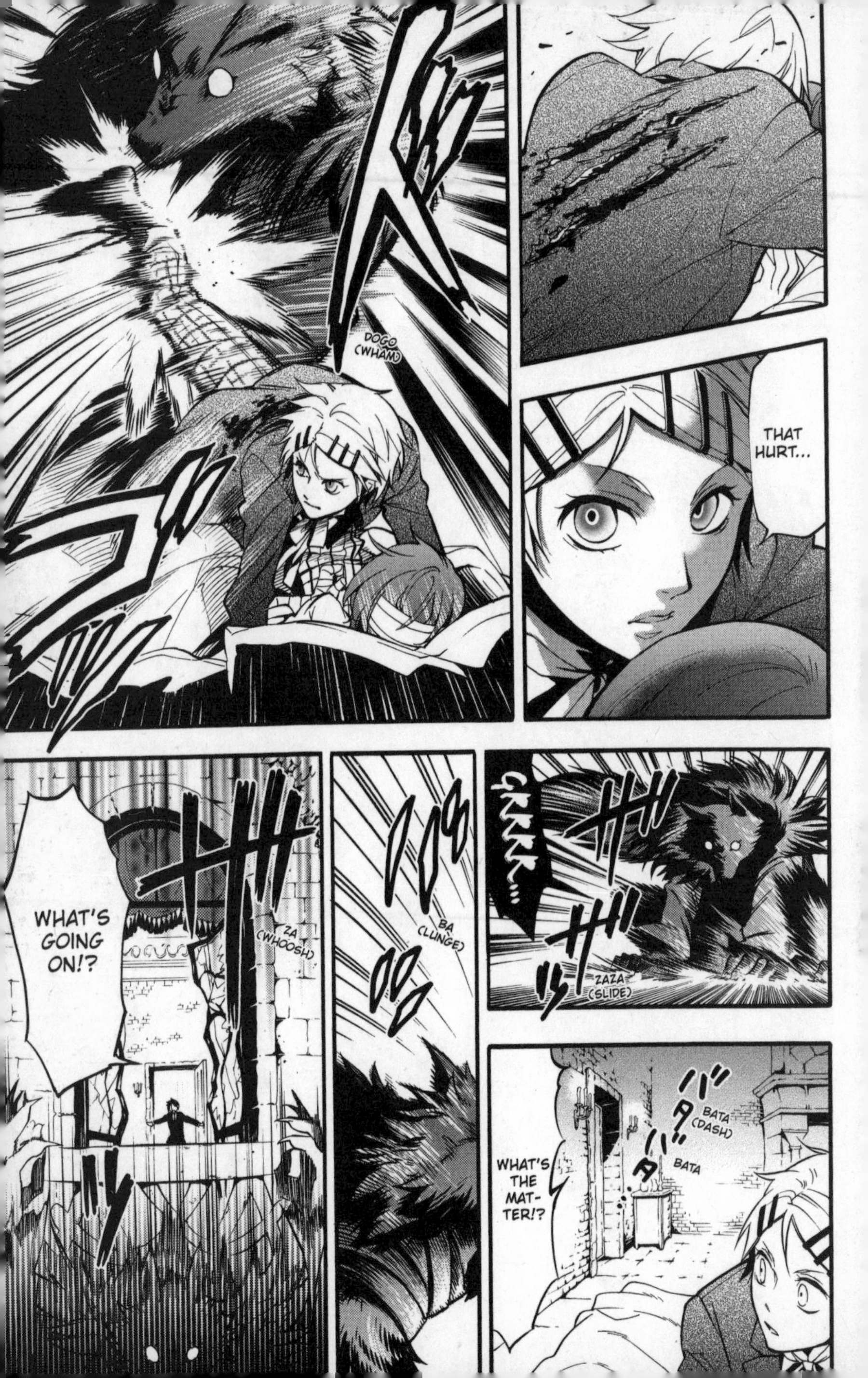
THAT HURT...
DOGO (WHAM)
GRRRR...
ZAZA (SLIDE)
BATA (DASH)
BATA
WHAT'S THE MAT-TER!?
BA (LUNGE)
WHAT'S GOING ON!?
ZA (WHOOSH)

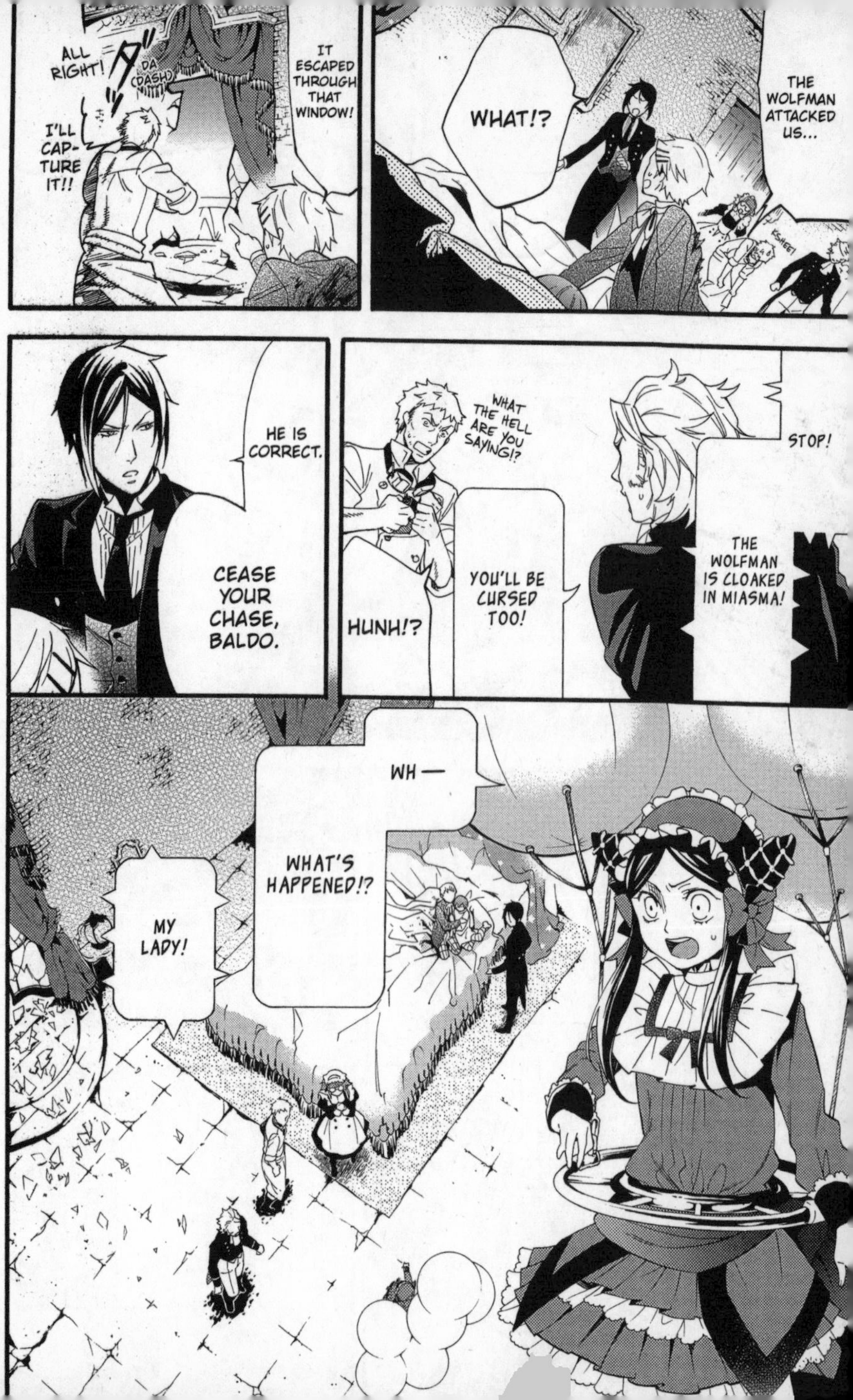
THE WOLFMAN ATTACKED US...
WHAT!?
KSHEE!
IT ESCAPED THROUGH THAT WINDOW!
ALL RIGHT!
DA (DASH)
I'LL CAPTURE IT!!
STOP!
WHAT THE HELL ARE YOU SAYING!?
THE WOLFMAN IS CLOAKED IN MIASMA!
YOU'LL BE CURSED TOO!
HUNH!?
HE IS CORRECT.
CEASE YOUR CHASE, BALDO.
WH—
WHAT'S HAPPENED!?
MY LADY!

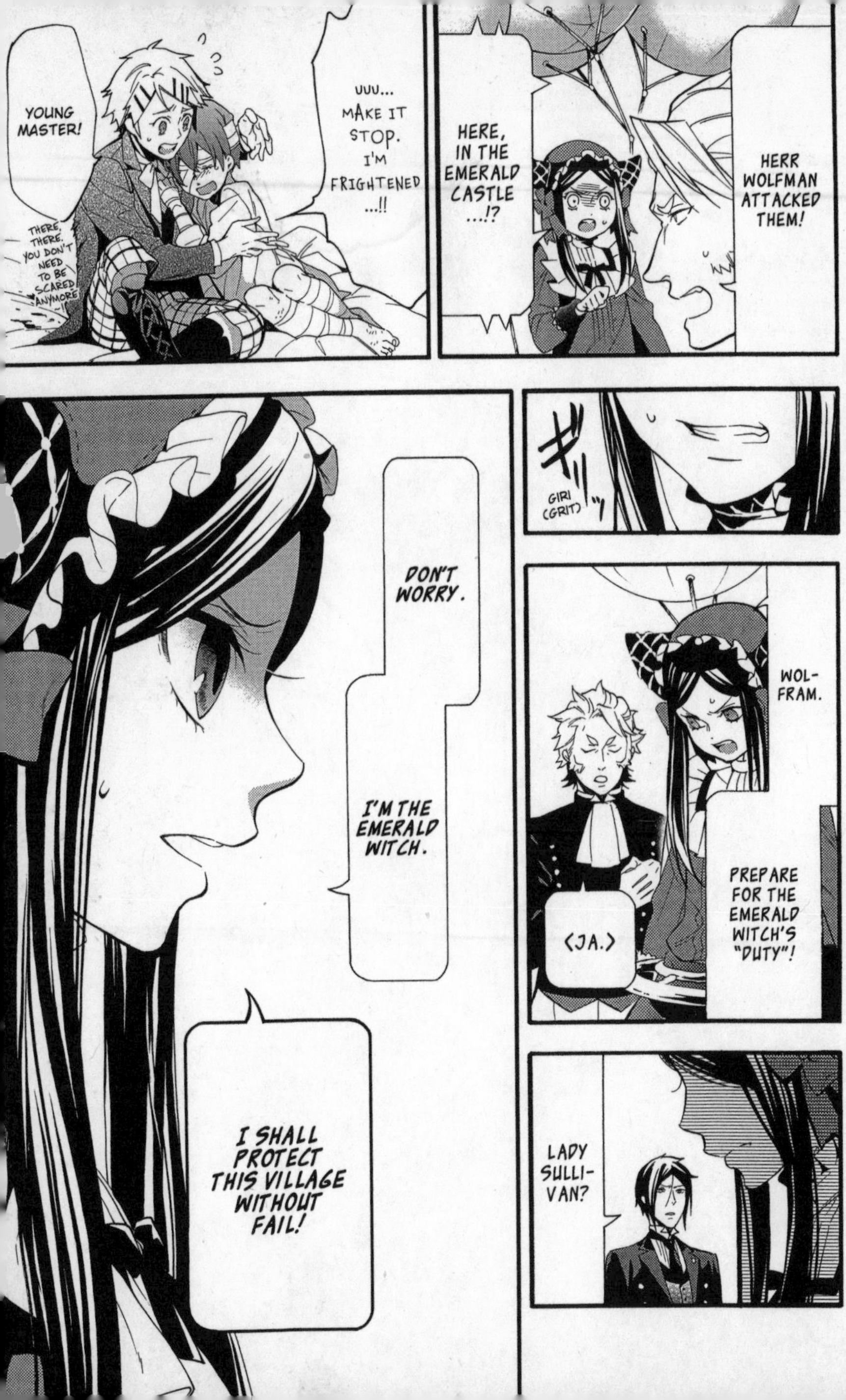
HERR WOLFMAN ATTACKED THEM!
HERE, IN THE EMERALD CASTLE ...!?
UUU... MAKE IT STOP. I'M FRIGHTENED ...!!
YOUNG MASTER!
THERE, THERE. YOU DON'T NEED TO BE SCARED ANYMORE--!!
GIRI (GRIT)
WOL-FRAM.
PREPARE FOR THE EMERALD WITCH'S "DUTY"!
〈JA.〉
LADY SULLI-VAN?
DON'T WORRY.
I'M THE EMERALD WITCH.
I SHALL PROTECT THIS VILLAGE WITHOUT FAIL!

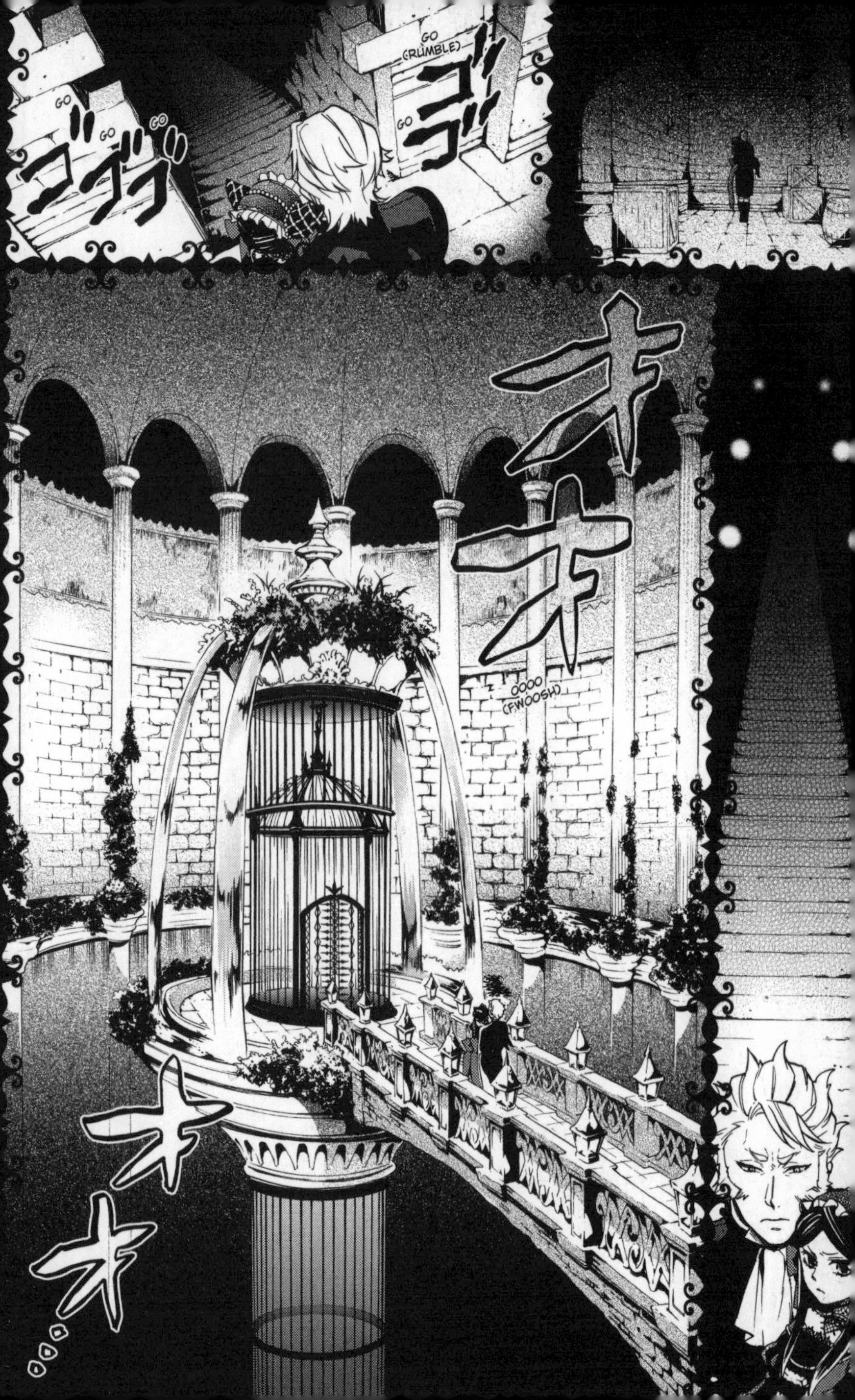
ゴゴ
GO (RUMBLE)
GO
ゴゴゴ
GO GO GO
オオオ
OOOO (FWOOSH)
オオ…

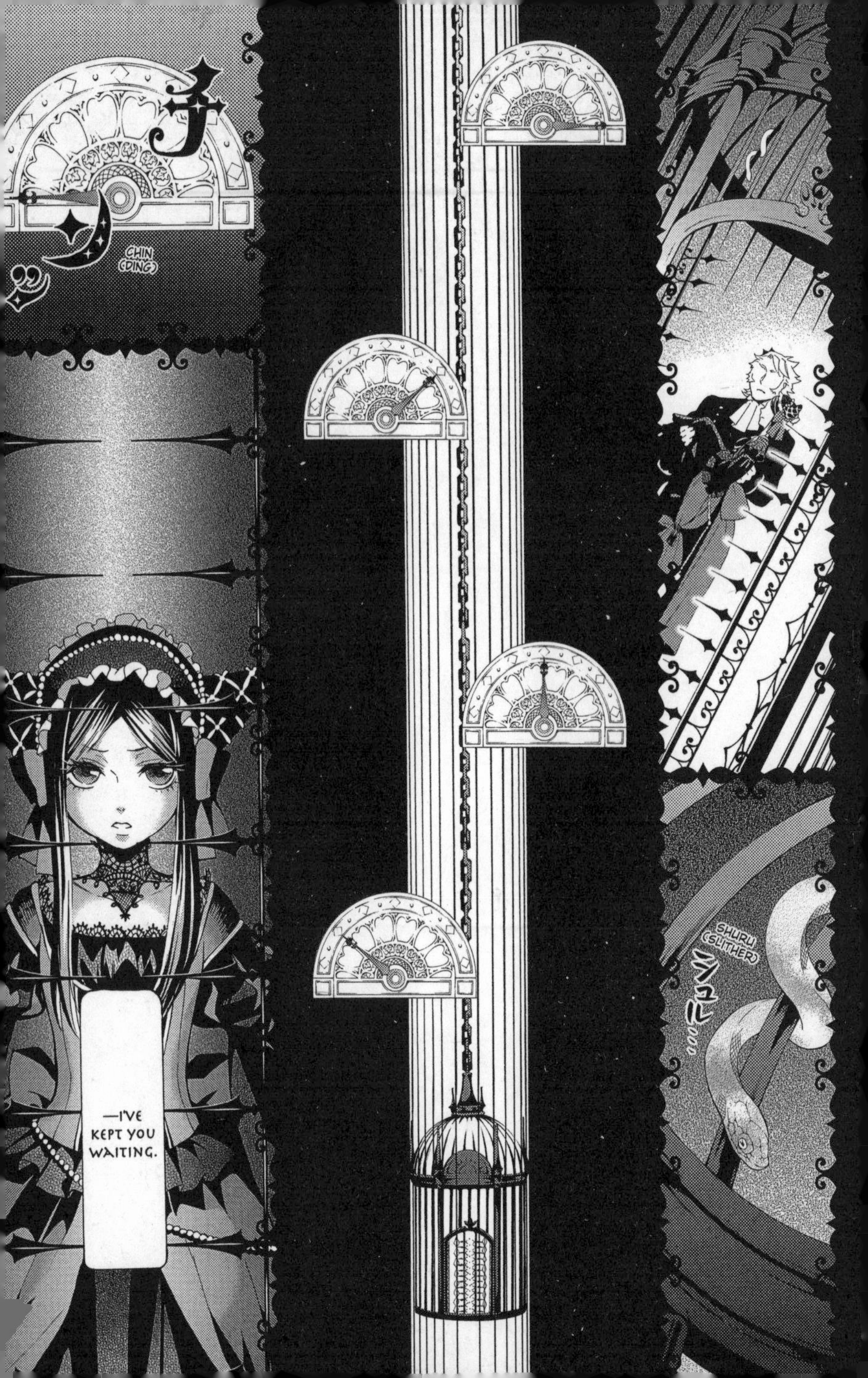
SHURU (SLITHER)
CHIN (DING)
—I'VE KEPT YOU WAITING.

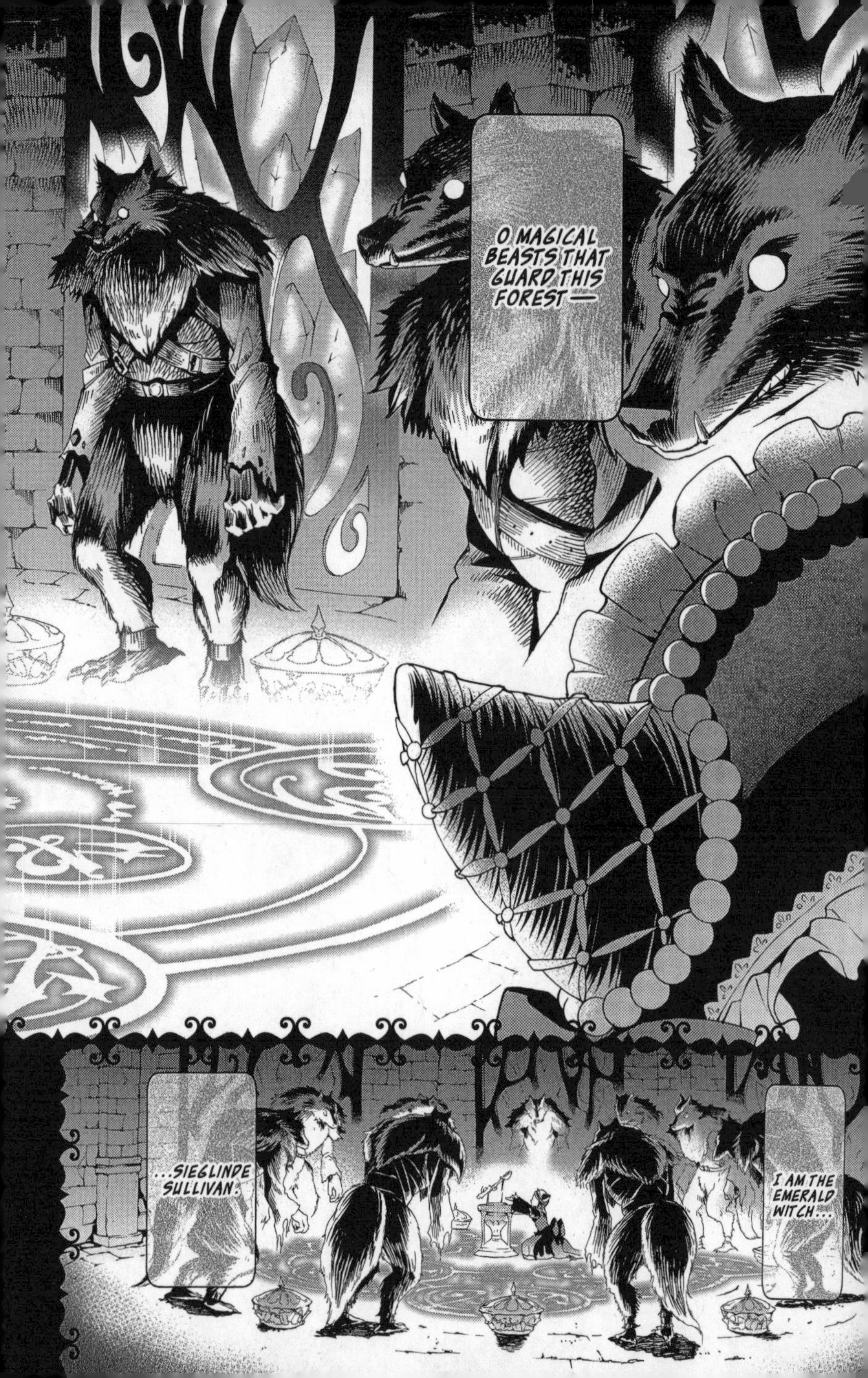
O MAGICAL BEASTS THAT GUARD THIS FOREST —
I AM THE EMERALD WITCH...
...SIEGLINDE SULLIVAN.

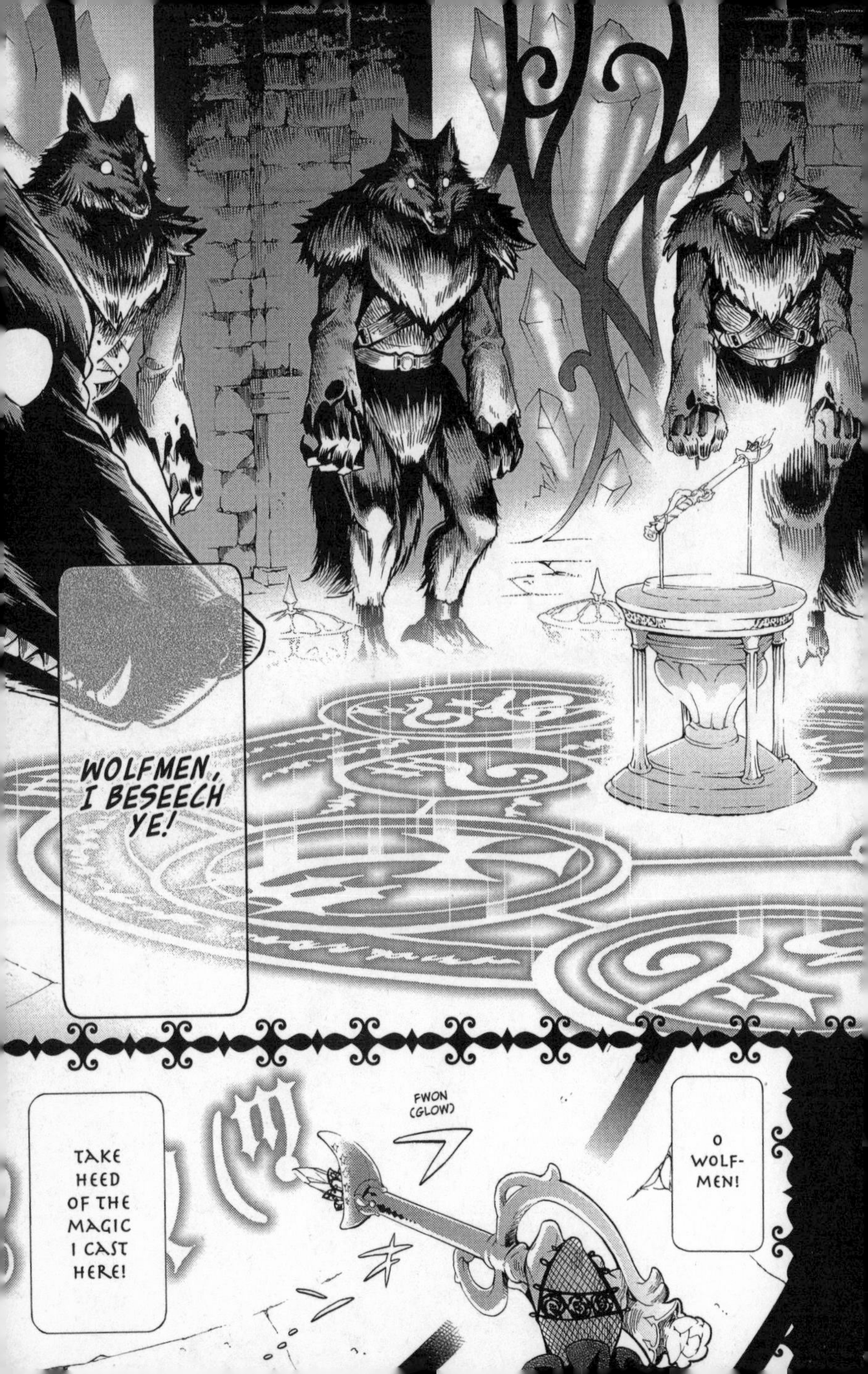
WOLFMEN, I BESEECH YE!
O WOLF-MEN!
FWON (GLOW)
TAKE HEED OF THE MAGIC I CAST HERE!

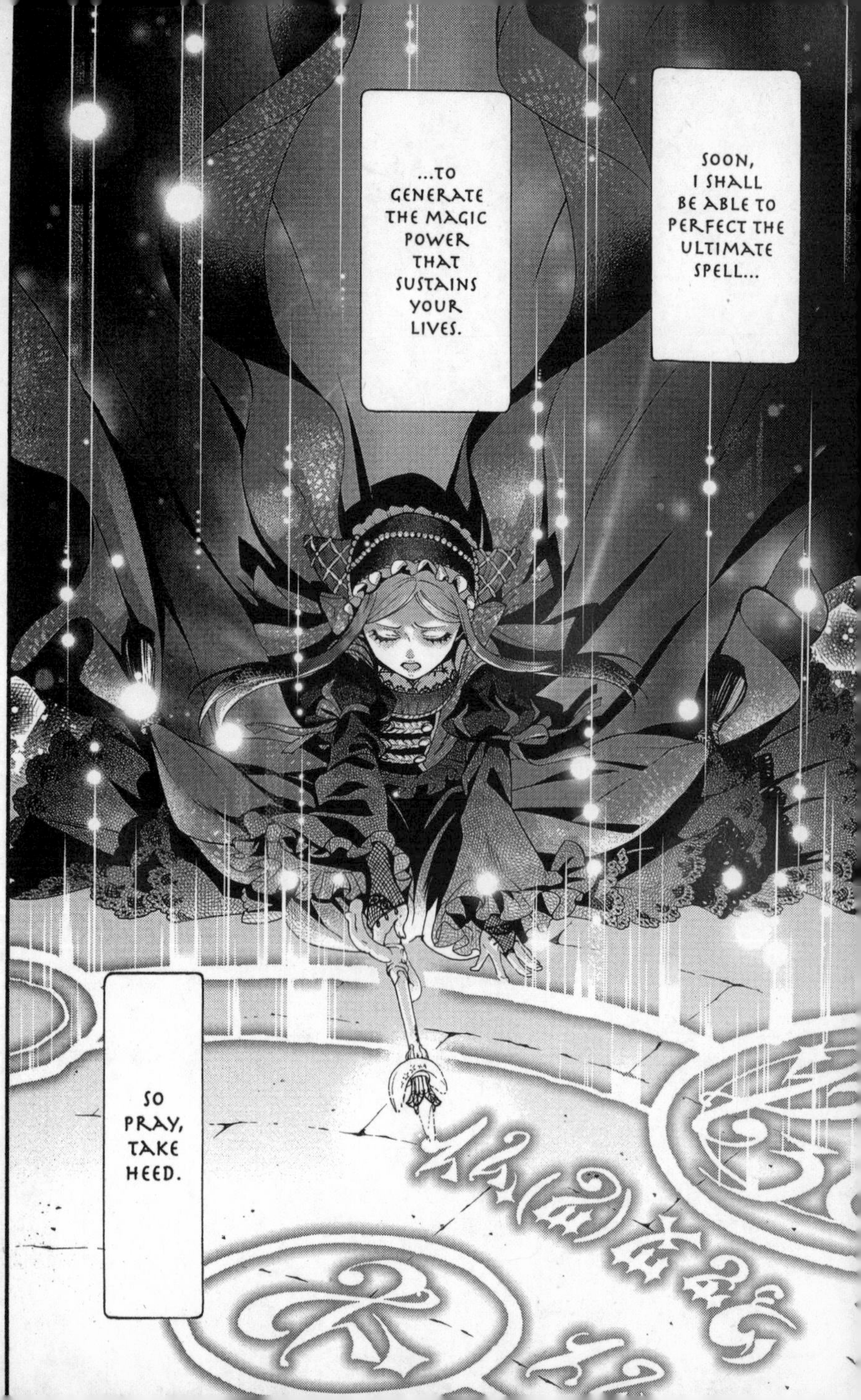
SOON, I SHALL BE ABLE TO PERFECT THE ULTIMATE SPELL...
...TO GENERATE THE MAGIC POWER THAT SUSTAINS YOUR LIVES.
SO PRAY, TAKE HEED.

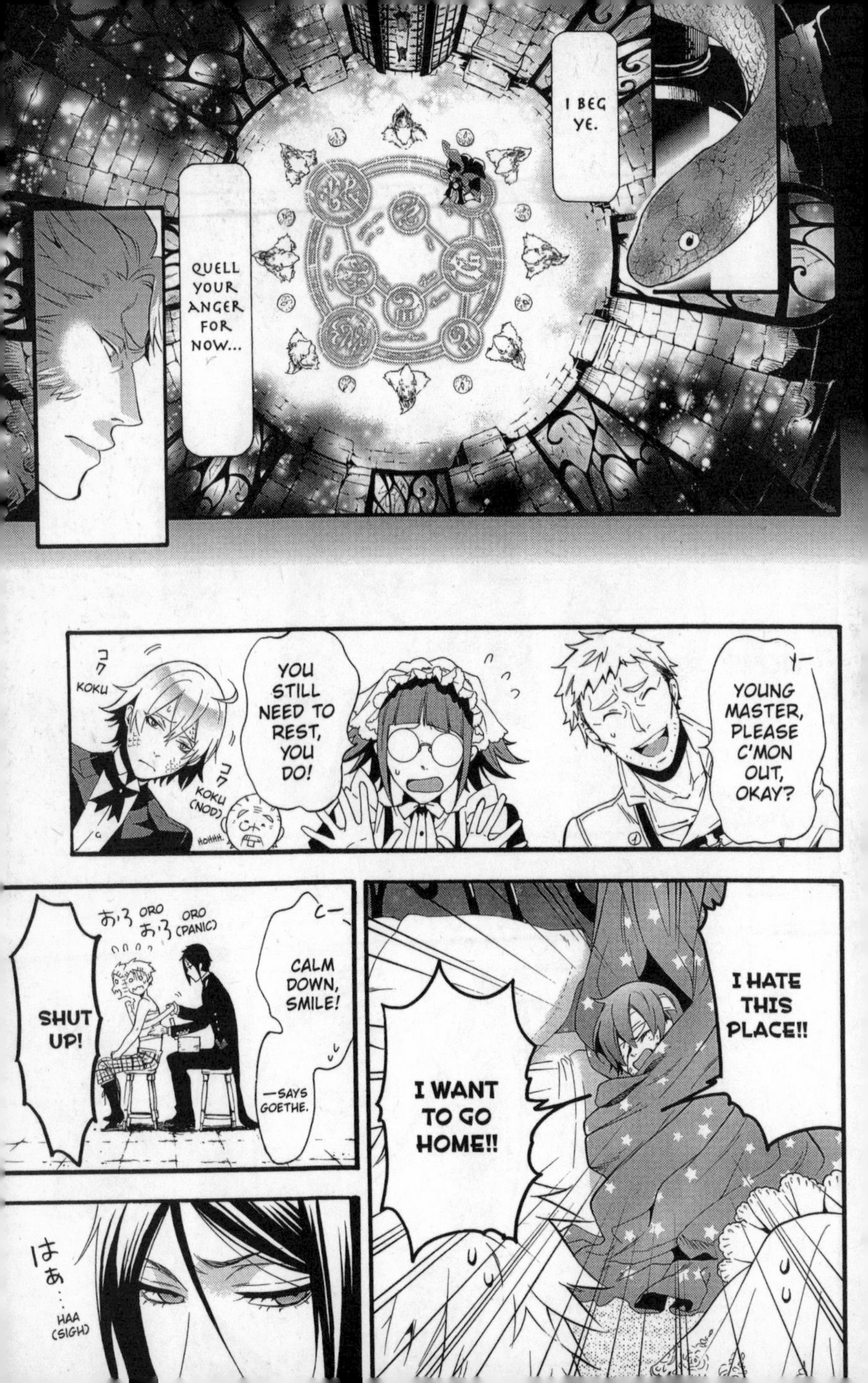

I BEG YE.
QUELL YOUR ANGER FOR NOW...
YOUNG MASTER, PLEASE C'MON OUT, OKAY?
YOU STILL NEED TO REST, YOU DO!
コク KOKU (NOD)
コク KOKU
HOHHH.
I HATE THIS PLACE!!
I WANT TO GO HOME!!
CALM DOWN, SMILE!
—SAYS GOETHE.
おろ ORO おろ ORO (PANIC)
SHUT UP!
はぁ… HAA (SIGH)

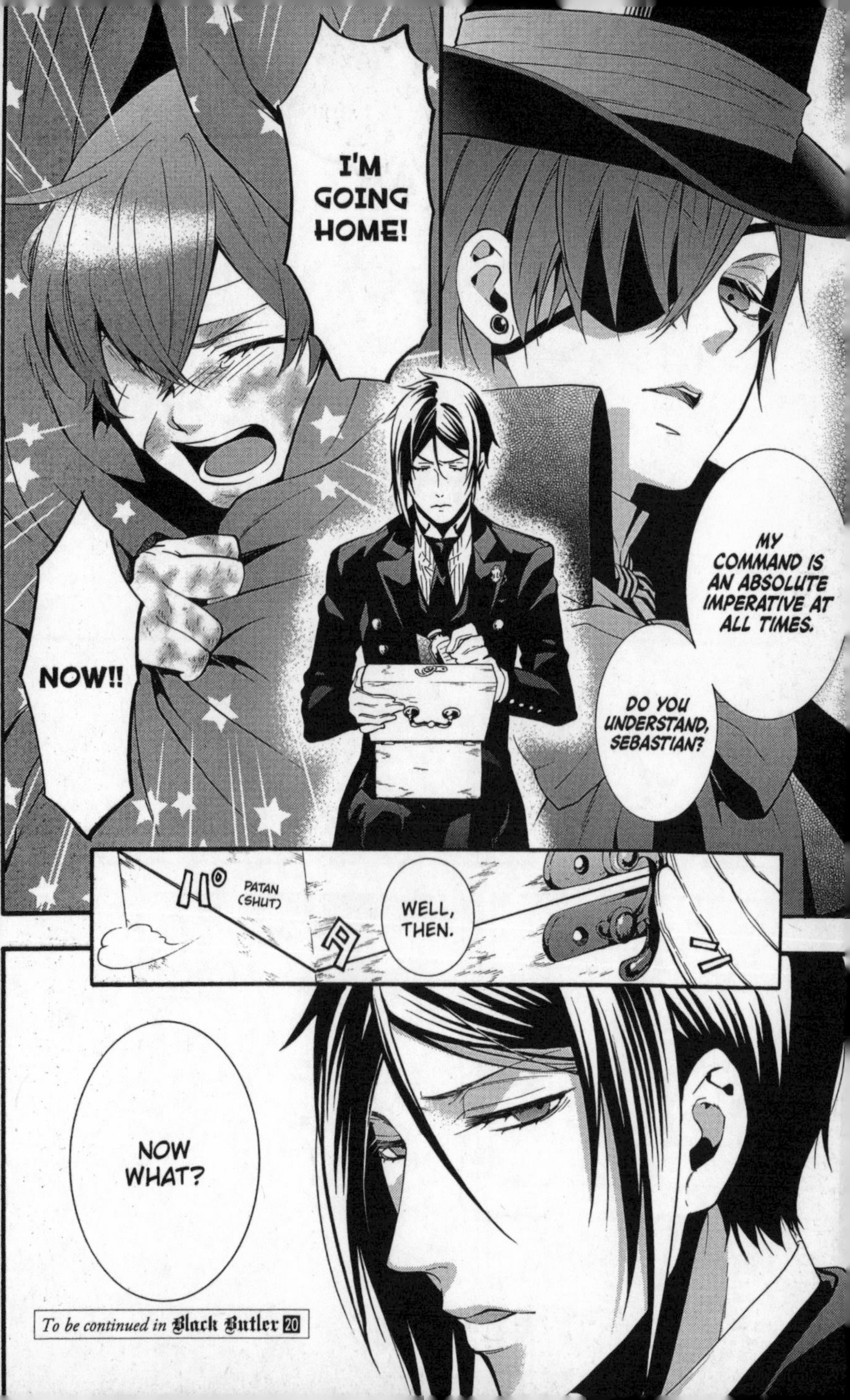
MY COMMAND IS AN ABSOLUTE IMPERATIVE AT ALL TIMES.
DO YOU UNDERSTAND, SEBASTIAN?
I'M GOING HOME!
NOW!!
WELL, THEN.
PATAN (SHUT)
NOW WHAT?
To be continued in **Black Butler** 20

➤ Black Butler ➤

黒執事

✦

Downstairs

Wakana Haduki
7
Saito Torino
Tsuki Sorano
Chiaki Nagaoka
Asakura
*
Takeshi Kuma
*
Yana Toboso

✦

Adviser

Rico Murakami

Special thanks to You!

Translation Notes

Page 6

Wolfsschlucht

The name of the village is German for "wolf's gorge."

Page 8

Herr

The German honorific equivalent of "mister."

Page 9

Ja

Wolfram's oft-used German phrase means "yes."

Page 10

Frau

The German honorific used for a grown woman, often married. *Fräulein* is derived from this honorific and often used for young girls but is sometimes considered disrespectful, especially when used for someone of high social status.

Page 17

Foot binding and lotus feet

A Chinese custom where the feet of young girls were tightly bound with bandages to prevent further growth. The ideal length of a bound foot was three inches, and they were prized as "three inch golden lotuses." The communist government banned foot binding in 1949.

Page 23

Maultaschen

A traditional dish from the southwestern region of Germany, *maultaschen* is similar to Italian ravioli, with pasta enclosing a filling traditionally consisting of minced meat, spinach, bread crumbs, and onions and flavoured with various herbs and spices.

Page 26

Wurst, eisbein, rote grütze

Lady Sullivan is served three different German foods. *Wurst* is German for "sausage." *Eisbein* is a meat dish in which ham hock is stewed with onions, celery, and spices. The dish is often served with sauerkraut, potatoes, and mustard. *Rote grütze* is a jelly-like dessert made of red summer berries. It is served with milk, cream, or custard to balance the sour taste of the fruit acids.

Page 43

Hexenballon

The German word for "witch's balloon."

Page 78

Lady Sullivan's spell

This magic spell is a hybrid of Norse mythology and Hebrew terms. The Nornir are the goddesses of fate in Norse mythology. The three most important goddesses are the sisters Urðr, Verðandi, and Skuld, who represent the past, present, and the future, respectively. The three sister-goddesses live by Urðarbrunnr, or the Well of Urðr, a well that lies right below the world tree, Yggdrasil. The well water has strong purifying properties. Gad is mentioned in the Old Testament as the god of fortune and is also one of the tribes of Israel. Baal was a term originally used by Jews to refer to their god. Sól is the sun goddess in Norse mythology; Máni is her brother and the moon god.

Page 117

Ronnefeldt

A German tea company established in 1823 by Johann Tobias Ronnefeldt.

Page 128

Bacon wrapped around the neck

A Japanese folk remedy recommends wrapping Welsh onions around your neck when you have a cold.

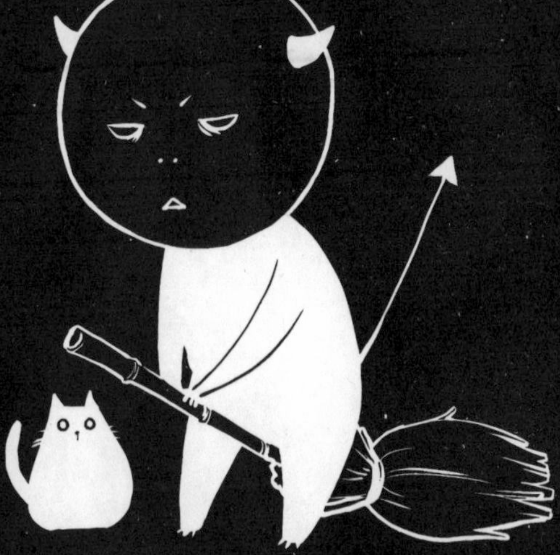

Yana Toboso

AUTHOR'S NOTE

Thanks to everyone, I've been able to make a living as a mangaka for ten years. I'm so very grateful.

I never imagined ***Black Butler*** would be animated into a television series three times. You really never can tell what life will bring.

And so I present Volume 19 with my deepest thanks and gratitude.

WELCOME TO IKEBUKURO, WHERE TOKYO'S WILDEST CHARACTERS GATHER!!

AS THEIR PATHS CROSS, THIS ECCENTRIC CAST WEAVES A TWISTED, CRACKED LOVE STORY...

AVAILABLE NOW!!

Durarara!! © Ryohgo Narita / ASCII MEDIA WORKS © 2009 Akiyo Satorigi / SQUARE ENIX

To become the ultimate weapon, one must devour the souls of 99 humans...

and one witch.

Maka is a scythe meister, working to perfect her demon scythe until it is good enough to become Death's Weapon—the weapon used by Shinigami-sama, the spirit of Death himself. And if that isn't strange enough, her scythe also has the power to change form—into a human-looking boy!

VOLUMES 1-22 IN STORES NOW!

www.yenpress.com

Soul Eater © Atsushi Ohkubo / SQUARE ENIX
Yen Press is an imprint of Hachette Book Group.

BLACK BUTLER ⑲

YANA TOBOSO

Translation: Tomo Kimura • Lettering: Alexis Eckerman

This book is a work of fiction. Names, characters, places, and incidents are the product of the author's imagination or are used fictitiously. Any resemblance to actual events, locales, or persons, living or dead, is coincidental.

KUROSHITSUJI Vol. 19 © 2014 Yana Toboso / SQUARE ENIX CO., LTD. First published in Japan in 2014 by SQUARE ENIX CO., LTD. English translation rights arranged with SQUARE ENIX CO., LTD. and Hachette Book Group through Tuttle-Mori Agency, Inc.

Translation © 2015 by SQUARE ENIX CO., LTD.

All rights reserved. In accordance with the U.S. Copyright Act of 1976, the scanning, uploading, and electronic sharing of any part of this book without the permission of the publisher is unlawful piracy and theft of the author's intellectual property. If you would like to use material from the book (other than for review purposes), prior written permission must be obtained by contacting the publisher at permissions@hbgusa.com. Thank you for your support of the author's rights.

Yen Press
Hachette Book Group
1290 Avenue of the Americas, New York, NY 10104

www.HachetteBookGroup.com
www.YenPress.com

Yen Press is an imprint of Hachette Book Group, Inc. The Yen Press name and logo are trademarks of Hachette Book Group, Inc.

First Yen Press Edition: January 2015

ISBN: 978-0-316-25940-8

10 9 8 7 6 5 4

BVG

Printed in the United States of America